This new standard work on the history of organs built in England between 900 AD and the 1990s takes full advantage of recent research and discoveries. It describes the most significant instruments of each period together with details of their builders, set against a background of changing fashions in music and liturgy. Technical developments are described in an easily understood manner, and links with the continental schools of organ building are made clear for the first time. The illustrations, many of which have not been published before, show significant instruments in their architectural setting. The author's experience in organ building gives the account all the benefits of first-hand experience. Written in an elegant, entertaining and informed manner, the book is a vital and much-needed addition to current organ literature.

THE HISTORY OF
THE ENGLISH ORGAN

THE HISTORY OF
THE ENGLISH ORGAN

STEPHEN BICKNELL

CAMBRIDGE
UNIVERSITY PRESS

Published by the Press Syndicate of the University of Cambridge
The Pitt Building, Trumpington Street, Cambridge CB2 1RP
40 West 20th Street, New York, NY 10011-4211, USA
10 Stamford Road, Oakleigh, Melbourne 3166, Australia

First published 1996

Printed in Great Britain at the University Press, Cambridge

A catalogue record for this book is available from the British Library

Library of Congress cataloguing in publication data
Bicknell, Stephen.
The History of the English Organ / Stephen Bicknell.
p.   cm.
Includes index.
ISBN 0 521 55026 2 (hardback)
1. Organ – History.   2. Organs – Great Britain.   I. Title.
ML578.B53   1996
786.5′1942 – dc20 95-42779   CIP

ISBN 0 521 55026 2 hardback

To

NOEL MANDER

who encouraged me to explore

and to

JOHN PIKE MANDER

who encouraged me to write

Contents

Plates

Preface

The English organ, with its cousins in Ireland, Scotland and the various outposts of colonial influence, is one of the least understood of the various national and local organ-building types. Organ history, much of it the product of twentieth-century commentators and their enthusiasms, is centred round the core schools of northern Europe and France. Rightly so, for these areas have provided the world's organists with the bulk of their repertoire. The organ world allows a lesser, but still significant, acknowledgement of the importance of Italian instruments, whose design, structure and use are quite independent of the rest of the world. The story of the Iberian organ is less well known again, knowledge of its secrets clouded by decline and decay in the nineteenth and twentieth centuries; however, the celebrated batteries of horizontal trumpets that adorn almost every Spanish and Portuguese instrument ensure that at least one splendid aspect of their character is known to every enthusiast.

The English organ has long been seen as the poor relation of these more famous schools. For centuries insular, refined and modest in scope, with an indigenous repertoire that is today poorly understood and still less well performed, it burst into an extravagant and spectacular flowering in the nineteenth century – exactly the period that has been least fashionable in the age that organ histories have been written. In any case, there is no one style or course of development that embraces all English instruments: a Dallam organ of 1630, a Byfield of 1760 and a Lewis of 1890 have very little in common, and the course of experiment and development that links them together is considerably more tortuous than the logical path that links organs of 1600 and organs of 1900 in, say, France or central Germany.

This book attempts to construct the first history of the English organ to tread a critical path between traditionally accepted accounts – some of them undoubtedly apocryphal – and modern understanding of documents and surviving instruments. There have been histories before. Sir John Hawkins's *A General History of the Science and Practice of Music* (London 1776) included the first account of English organs and their builders; his material was rifled and expanded by Charles Burney in his own *A General History of Music* (London 1789). Their sources are unknown, but it seems likely that both relied on a verbal tradition passed down in the community of organists and organ builders; this restricted their account to the 150 years or so up to their own time. In the 1830s articles in *The Christian Remembrancer* added some further biographical details in a series of accounts of notable instruments. The anonymous *A Short Account of Organs Built in England from the Reign of King Charles II to the Present Time* (London 1847), actually written by Sir John Sutton, adds a further layer of personal commentary to the existing tradition.

In the monumental *The Organ* by E. J. Hopkins and E. F. Rimbault (London 1855; revised editions 1870 and 1877) there appeared an account that modified the existing histories in the light of new documentary evidence. Rimbault, who wrote the historical portion of the work, was from the first generation of antiquarian scholars to recognise the need to find and report primary source material. Through his own extensive reading and scholarship he was able to extend the accepted history to a much earlier period, offering a tentative account of the introduction of the organ to the British Isles in the tenth century, describing references to its existence and development in the middle ages, making available early contracts, particularly that of the Anthony Duddyngton organ of 1519 at All Hallows Barking, and attempting to provide more exhaustive catalogues of the work of notable builders. So, where Hawkins and Burney had both named nine instruments by Bernard Smith and Sutton had listed twenty-two, Rimbault manages to cite thirty-eight.

By the end of the nineteenth century the activities of antiquarians had greatly expanded the range of sources. C. W. Pearce, in *Old London City Churches, their Organs, Organists and Musical Associations* (London 1909) and *Notes on English Organs of the Period 1800–1810* (London 1912) combined documentary evidence with transcriptions from an important early nineteenth century manuscript collection of organ specifications, originally compiled by Henry Leffler; more such manuscripts have been found since. Historical accounts of individual instruments appeared in the appropriate music journals from time to time, but in 1921 the new quarterly magazine *The Organ* provided for the first time a dedicated forum for serious scholarly articles. The writer indelibly associated with the early issues is the Revd Andrew Freeman (1876–1947).

Freeman had the energy and opportunity at various times in his life to collect information and secondary source material on an unprecedented scale and with great thoroughness. He also travelled extensively, was an excellent photographer, understood the organ and especially the organ case, and wrote prolifically. The majority of his output was in the form of articles, but he also wrote the well known *English Organ Cases* (London 1921) and *Father Smith* (London 1926). Much of his collected material remains unpublished; there is enough information in his notes and articles to re-write all the accounts of the previous one hundred and fifty years. Sadly he never wrote a general history of the English organ, for which he was better equipped than any of his predecessors. His collected notes and material were inherited by the Revd Bernard Edmonds, who continued to add to them over the years, and are now housed in the British Organ Archive at Birmingham Central Library.

Freeman's material was used extensively by W. L. Sumner in *The Organ* (London

1952), but Sumner was happy to follow the format and principles laid out by Hopkins and Rimbault in their similar work of 1855, simply adding, in a rather haphazard way, a new layer to the now traditional history. The publication of C. Clutton and A. Niland's *The British Organ* (London 1963) brought a further version of events to light. Cecil Clutton (1909–91) was a lively and charismatic man: trenchant, determined and always brief and to the point in prose. Thus in *The British Organ* his history of the organ in Britain is happily condensed into seventy-five pages (Austin Niland's definitive account of organ cases in the same volume occupies twice as much space). Absolute factual accuracy was not Clutton's first purpose: after the second world war he was a supporter of the neo-classical organ, and tended to see little good in late Victorian and Edwardian organs. The history of the English organ was viewed at least in part as a series of lessons on the tonal appointment of new organs.

It was not until the foundation of The British Institute of Organ Studies in 1976 that a new generation of scholars found a voice for their revised critical examination of source material and their application of more thorough archaeological techniques to the study of old instruments. Thanks largely to research since the war, much of it carried out by people who were to become leading members of BIOS, we now know of further important manuscript collections of specifications from the nineteenth century and have access to the workshop records and drawings of a number of important builders; there have also been detailed and accurate technical studies of surviving old instruments. BIOS publications have set an enviable standard for accuracy and presentation. BIOS has been instrumental in setting up the collection of manuscripts, photographs and organ builders' records that forms the basis of the British Organ Archive in Birmingham. This new school of study has produced important monographs by John Rowntree, Nicholas Thistlethwaite, David Wickens and others, and the change in our appreciation and understanding of the organ in Britain has been immense.

Meanwhile the understanding of the English organ in the context of world organ culture has remained rather shallow. In 1956 the Danish organ builder Poul-Gerhard Andersen wrote a brief but balanced account of the English organ in his unmatched *Orgelbogen* (Copenhagen 1956), translated into English as *Organ Building and Design* (London 1969). Peter Williams, who has made the most important and stimulating modern contributions to organ history in the English language, has not really found English instruments to his taste. In *The European Organ* (London 1966) England is excluded, in deference to Clutton and Niland's work, issued a few years before by the same publisher. In *A New History of the Organ* (London 1980) he described the English organ as a subject 'of comparatively minor interest'.

If this account seems hard on more recent writers, I must insist that it is not out of lack of respect for their work or for their importance. Reading Clutton or Williams remains one of the most informative and rewarding experiences in this field. However, in understanding that it is time for English organ history to be given a new platform, it is, in the nature of things, necessary to clear the ground first. If the subject is to progress, then it is for future writers to be equally critical of what they find here.

This is a work of interpretation rather than of primary scholarship. Andrew Freeman showed that it was possible to spend a lifetime collecting material without ever being in a position to publish it all. Today's scholars in the field of organ history work increasingly on matters of detail and on individual builders or instruments: no one of these has drawn up a history which includes all the accumulated background knowledge. As one of the field-workers I have been acutely aware of the lack of a more general history providing pegs on which to hang the myriad details of new research. However, I must state that this work is born out of need and opportunity, rather than from any certainty of being the right person to do it.

I have been particularly concerned with certain areas, which can briefly be summarised. The late mediaeval organ is now much less a matter for conjecture than was the case until recently; careful study of existing sources and the exciting discovery of soundboard fragments allow, for the first time, a clear understanding of some English organs of the sixteenth century. Extensive work on the early seventeenth century has now revealed a good deal about the true position of the Dallam family and has contributed to a new understanding of the instruments associated with the Laudian revival: in particular the pitch relationship between organ and choir has been brought to light. In the period after the Civil War organ building was dominated by Bernard Smith and Renatus Harris, on whom later generations conferred a kind of joint sainthood; I have been concerned to use recent research to reassess their work and their position relative to each other. Most writers have lumped the organs of 1720–1830 together as showing no real development; I wish to suggest that there were successive changes of style and manufacture in this period and that the organs of the Regency builders were in fact a far cry from those built by the successors of Smith and Harris. Changes in English organ building between 1820 and 1870 have been the subject of an excellent recent study by Nicholas Thistlethwaite – *The Making of the Victorian Organ* (Cambridge 1990) – but for the Victorian organ as a whole one is torn between the blazing fame of Henry Willis (a builder much championed by Edwardian writers) and new interest in the work of the more conservative William and Thomas Hill. My view of this period seeks to find new balances between the work of these two firms, and recognises the important contributions of other nineteenth-century builders. In describing the twentieth century I do not accept the view that the organ became decadent and without musical value. Despite the problems caused by war and depression, I recognise the importance of Edwardian builders, of new technology and of the cinema organ. I also hope to have given a reasonably non-partisan account of the classical revival of modern times. Finally, I feel it is important to assess the effect of English organ building on American taste, significant in the work of G. Donald Harrison and many other émigré builders.

As a guiding principle I have tried to be clear about what my sources are, and careful in how they are used. The traditional accounts of organ building between

1660 and 1780, based on Hawkins and Burney, are still valuable material, but in all cases the word 'traditional' in the text should alert the reader to the fact that there is no authenticated source for the information given. I have not attempted to provide opus lists for the builders from 1600 onwards; all such lists that exist are based partly on hearsay and each needs untangling – an extensive task in its own right. Where particular organs are described and stop-lists given, I have tried always to use a contemporary account, preferably a contract. This is especially important, for example, with the organs of Bernard Smith and Renatus Harris, both of whom have suffered incalculable inaccuracies caused by misattribution, and copying of later or faulty texts. I have tried to avoid use of the manuscript collections of stop-lists by Leffler and others; they simply cannot be assumed to be accurate. If a description of an organ is drawn from a non-contemporary source, this is stated. In borrowing from existing writing I have relied on modern scholarship, with what-ever virtues it may claim to have over similar work in the past. For collections of material on the earlier periods I have relied a great deal on Andrew Freeman's pub-lished work and unpublished notes. His own sources were very varied indeed; many of them were themselves published transcriptions of old documents. On a few occa-sions Freeman was happy to adopt the accepted tradition, partly in deference to the stature of previous historians, trustingly assuming that they were as thorough as he was. It is frequently obvious when this is the case and I have tried to be selective.

With a subject so extensive it is necessary to condense the narrative to keep it within the bounds of one volume. Hence, in one major respect, this is an old-fashioned account: the text deals with the most famous builders and assumes that the pattern of their creative work can be illustrated through an examination of their largest and best-known organs. A truly definitive work would explore a wider field of craftsmen and would cite a larger number of more varied instruments. For the same reason phases of innovative development are not always backed by a full dis-cussion of the musical impetus for change. With, for example, the radical trans-formation of the English organ between 1820 and 1860 or the classical revival of 1945–80 it is indeed possible and desirable to indicate the musical background to the changes that took place. It is clear that a similar musical and technical revolu-tion took place between 1660 and 1700, in the wake of the restoration of the monarchy. However, with this and other earlier periods the information available about changes in organ music and playing is incomplete and conclusions would be more speculative. In any case, the organ is unusual in that musical developments often follow technical ones: for example the French romantic school of composition in the nineteenth century is clearly dependent on the innovations in organ building made by Aristide Cavaillé-Coll. Here, in describing the history of the English organ, the musical background has only been described where there is enough source material available to make it abundantly clear that musicians were pressing for change or reform; furthermore, as an organ builder, not a player, I have neces-sarily been cautious in tackling an area of knowledge better understood by the appropriate specialists.

The techniques required to compile material also depend on the period concerned: a perfect organ historian would have the skills of a musician, a craftsman, a palaeographer and an archaeologist, as well as having general interest in antiquarian, ecclesiological and architectural study. As indicated above, I am aware of my own deficiencies in several of these fields. I am happy to acknowledge that this work relies extensively on secondary sources as well as on my own research. I would be grateful to learn of any errors or additional information that might be valuable in preparing any future edition.

I have learnt immeasurably from talking to colleagues in organ building and friends in the organ world. This book has a considerable number of unseen contributors, many of whom have given freely of their time, their advice or of their own research. Some who can be named are as follows: Ian Bell, Andrew Benson-Wilson, Jim Berrow, Julian Bicknell, Marcus Bicknell, Titus Bicknell, Treld Bicknell, John Brennan, Bruce Buchanan, Michael Chapman, Relf Clark, Michel Cocheril, James Collier, Peter Collins, Nicholas Danby, Hilary Davidson, Bill Drake, Timothy Easton, Bernard Edmonds, Audrey Erskine, Kellan Farshea, Donald Findlay, David Frostick, Michael Gillingham, Martin Goetze, Didier Grassin, Dominic Gwynn, Paul Hale, John Harper, Wendy Hinde, Richard Hird, Peter Hopps, Jo Huddlestone, Lynn Hulse, Christopher Kent, James Mackenzie, Geoffrey MacMahon, John Mander, Noel Mander, Betty Matthews, Colin Menzies, Geoffrey Morgan, Richard Morrison, Austin Niland, Herbert Norman, John Norman, Tony Othen, Barbara Owen, Robert Pacey, Nicholas Plumley, Martin Renshaw, John Rowntree, Margaret Sparks, Gerald Sumner, Nicholas Thistlethwaite, Katherine Venning, Mark Venning, Gerard Verloop, Jean-Albert Villard, David Wickens, Peter Williams, the late Ida Willis, Henry Willis IV, John Sinclair Willis and Michael Woodward. I apologise for any omissions. I am also grateful to Sir John Cass's Foundation (whose Bursary awards in two successive years first gave me the taste for research), to friends in the British Institute of Organ Studies, in organ building and elsewhere.

Note on pitch

The following notation is used to indicate pitch:

CC (16′)
C (8′)
c (4′)
c′ (2′: middle C)
c″ (1′)
c‴ (½′)
c⁗ (¼′)

Introduction

The study of any musical instrument depends on some understanding of how it is made. Conveniently, in unveiling a chronological history of the organ, the increasingly complex technical developments of successive periods can be tackled one at a time as and when they appear. Even so, a brief guide to the workings of the organ will be invaluable.

During the development of the organ in the middle ages several sizes of instrument appeared: large organs with a *Blockwerk* (explained below); smaller instruments which were still a permanent fixture (*positive*); organs which were indeed small enough to be carried around (*portative*); and smallest of all, instruments based on ranks of reed pipes (see below), the diminutive *regal*. These categories overlap each other and defy more precise definition. As the organ became more sophisticated so the techniques of making each began to be mixed, expanded and modified; the modern multi-keyboard instrument is an elaboration of the idea of bringing several of these instruments together under the command of one player.

The wind was raised by bellows. At its most primitive an early organ might have had a number of animal-skin bags connected to it; squeezing them successively would give a wind supply of uncertain pressure and constancy. These may have developed through a form like a forge bellows to the diagonal bellows that survives on organs built in England before c1800. Here the addition of wooden ribs, with only the hinges made of leather, makes the bellows stronger and more durable. An organ would have two or more such bellows. One would be lifted by a handle or a rope on a pulley; a weight on the top would make it fall and would provide a reasonably constant pressure. Before it had collapsed completely the next bellows would be lifted. Diagonal bellows might be single-fold or multi-fold. A variation met especially in smaller organs is to use one bellows as a reservoir, with a feeder mounted below it.

Before 1800 the English had developed a horizontal version of the reservoir, and further improved it by providing one set of inverted ribs – the pressure now remained steady regardless of the position of the reservoir top. In the early nineteenth century further steadiness was given by adding small, sprung 'concussion bellows' to the wind trunking. The Victorian builders elaborated on this system. Wind would be raised by feeder bellows as before, though in large organs these

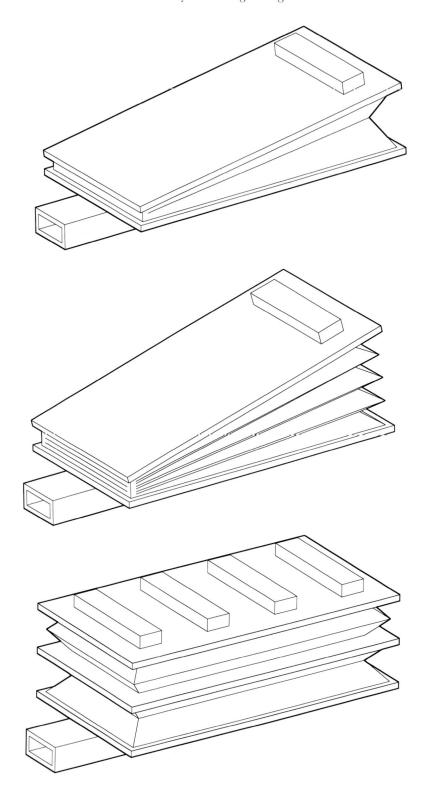

feeders would be operated by a steam engine or other machinery. A main reservoir would collect air at the highest pressure required in the organ. Through a system of trunking, control valves and subsidiary reservoirs the wind could be distributed at different pressures to different parts of the organ.

In the twentieth century feeders were replaced by the electric rotary fan blower, though reservoirs continued in use as before. In some organs the development of more sophisticated control valves allowed reservoirs to be smaller. Since c1960 there has been some use of individual small floating pressure-regulating pans or *Schwimmers*, with a considerable reduction in the number of reservoirs. These regulators are economical to make, but not universally accepted.

From the bellows, wind is trunked to the *soundboard* on which the pipes stand and is admitted to the *pallet box*. Here there is one hinged wooden valve or *pallet* for each note on the keyboard: the linkage between pallet and key is the *key action*. When a key is pressed, the pallet opens and wind is admitted to a channel corresponding to that note. When the key is released a spring under the pallet closes it and raises the key again.

In the early organ, when a channel in the soundboard was supplied with wind, then all the pipes standing on that channel spoke at once – a chorus of voices known as a *Blockwerk*. The developments from this all-or-nothing sound to the modern organ with stops are complex but may be summarised. There are two ways of developing the Blockwerk organ so that it can be played louder or softer. The first is simply to bring a second smaller instrument (a *positive* organ) near to the first, and to turn round and play it when variety is required. If the key action for the second organ is brought under the player's seat and the keyboard placed close to that of the first instrument we have a two-manual organ – in German *Hauptwerk* and *Rückpositiv* (literally: back-positive).

The second method is to elaborate the soundboard so that parts of the blockwerk may be silenced at will. Two significant variants are known in Europe: the slider soundboard, which is found in England, and the rarer spring chest, which is not (though there may once have been examples). The pipes of the Blockwerk chorus are now divided up into several ranks, each consisting of a row of pipes corresponding to the notes on the keyboard. In the slide soundboard each rank stands over a perforated slider moved by a stop-knob near the keys. When the stop is 'on', holes in the slider line up with the holes in the soundboard: when a key is pressed the appropriate pipe from that rank will sound. When the stop is 'off', the slider moves so that the holes no longer line up: the pipes of that rank can no longer sound.

Normally there is one soundboard for each keyboard (or pedalboard) of an organ. In larger or later instruments there may be further divisions into separate soundboards, especially after the invention of non-mechanical key-actions in the nineteenth century.

Other types of soundboard were developed in the nineteenth century and after:

◄ *Plate 1*   The three main types of bellows used in English organs. From top to bottom: single-fold diagonal bellows, multi-fold diagonal bellows and horizontal bellows with inverted folds. The horizontal bellows displaced both types of diagonal bellows from about 1800.

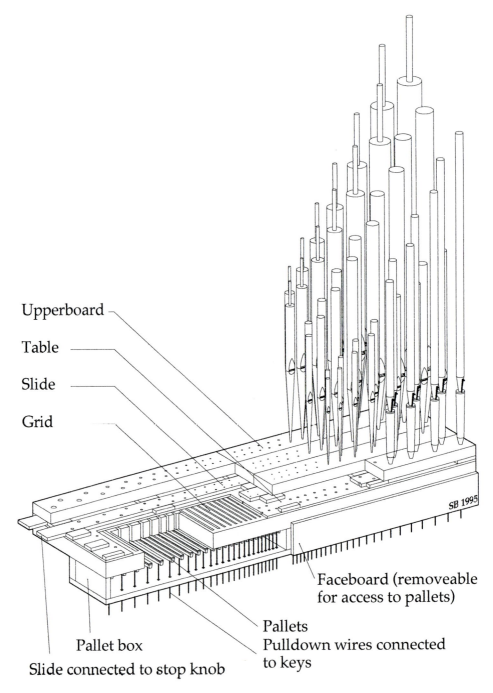

Upperboard

Table

Slide

Grid

SB 1995

Faceboard (removeable
for access to pallets)

Pallets
Pulldown wires connected
to keys

Pallet box

Slide connected to stop knob

Plate 2 View of a slider soundboard partly cut away to show the construction. The example shown has four slides, one for each of the following stops (from back to front): Chimney Flute 8, Principal 4, Fifteenth 2, Cremona 8. The pipes are arranged in the diatonic order characteristic of most English organs: the basses at the ends and the trebles in the middle. Only the pipes of the lowest notes on one side are shown.

the English convention is to describe all those without slides as *chests*. These were usually intended to avoid some of the manufacturing or maintenance problems associated with slider soundboards, or to facilitate the use of a particular novel or patent mechanism (especially once rapid stop changes were required after 1900). Sliderless chests, popular in Germany and America, have never been universal in England, their use being restricted to certain organ builders only in the period from 1885 onwards, or for particular special uses.

The key action provides the link between keyboard and soundboard. At its most simple, the key is pivoted at the tail. From the key a wire or wooden *tracker* rises directly to the pallet. This is known as suspended action. If the spacing of the pallets on the soundboard is wider than the keyboard, then the trackers may need to be splayed. If, as in all but the smallest organs from the late middle ages onwards, the pipes on the soundboard are arranged symmetrically, not in chromatic order, then a *rollerboard* is needed to transfer the movement laterally.

In later organs the key is sometimes pivoted in the middle, with the key action picking up off the tail of the key: a balanced action. From the key tail the movement is transferred via a tracker or sticker to a row of levers or *backfalls* to the soundboard. Again there may be a rollerboard if required. Mechanical key actions of the balanced or suspended types may be made to change direction by introducing further sets of backfalls or *squares* (small bell-cranks). The pedal keys, where provided, operate in a similar way to the manuals. Further developments include *couplers*, making it possible to play two separate departments from one keyboard.

In the middle of the nineteenth century it became possible to harness the power of the wind already in the organ to assist the key action: especially useful in large organs where the key action was becoming increasingly heavy. At first, pneumatic power was used in conjunction with mechanical linkages: the *pneumatic lever* or *Barker Lever*. Replacing the mechanical linkages with small-bore tubing – the message travelling down the tube as a charge of air – gave much greater flexibility in arranging the internal components of the organ. This tubular pneumatic action comes in many different forms, each builder developing his own system. Broadly speaking the various types may be divided into charge pneumatic actions – the earlier, simpler variety – and exhaust pneumatic actions – more complex and arguably more sophisticated.

As a result of much experiment in the late nineteenth century it eventually became possible to replace the pneumatic tubing with an electric cable: by 1900 electro-pneumatic actions (the opening of the pallet still effected by a pneumatic motor) were being attempted on a regular basis. All-electric key action is rare in England, being mostly restricted to very small organs. In the heyday of electro-pneumatic action, from 1920 to 1960, it became usual for almost all the mechanical functions of the organ to be carried out through electrical switchgear, even if the final stages of the movement remained pneumatic. Since 1960 there has been a considerable revival of the use of all-mechanical actions.

The story of stop action – the link between stop-knob at the console and the slide on the soundboard – is similar to that of key action. Mechanical linkages of rods

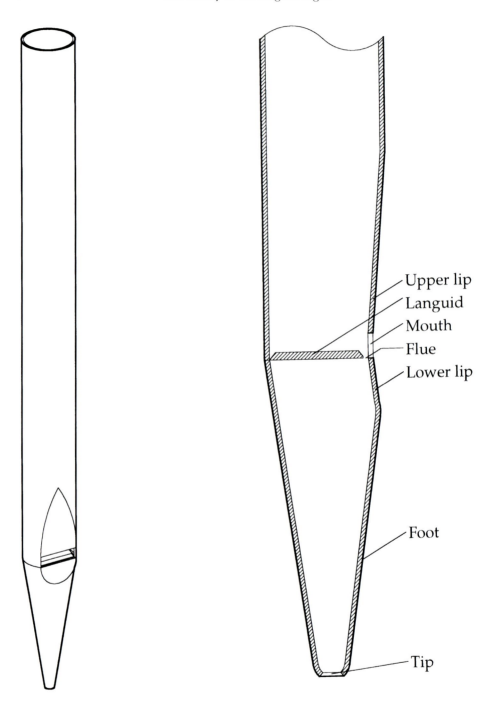

Plate 3   A typical open flue pipe of the Principal family. Left: general view. Right: section through mouth and foot

and levers were superseded in the second half of the nineteenth century by pneumatic machines – at least in large organs. With these came the possibility of harnessing pneumatic power to change the stops quickly, at the press of a pedal or button (*piston*). By 1890 some organs were provided with a limited kind of memory system, allowing the organist to reset the combination of stops brought into play by combination pedals or pistons. The advent of electro-pneumatic mechanisms allowed much more sophisticated systems for stop changing, and all-electric adjustable combinations become a feature during the 1930s, eventually to be transistorised in the 1960s and finally reduced to programmable silicon chips in the 1980s. Again, there is now a movement back to all-mechanical systems.

Keys, pedals, stops all meet under the player's control at the *console*; simple in early organs, but increasingly complex after 1850. With the advent of pneumatic and electro-pneumatic actions it became possible to detach the console from the organ itself (as well as spreading the organ into different and sometimes unlikely parts of the building); the console then became a highly sophisticated piece of apparatus in its own right.

The structure of a fully developed organ includes a case – from the middle ages until 1850 this would be highly decorative and might have had sides, back and roof as well as an ornamental front. The case and its arrangement has some effect on the way the sound is focused and projected into the building. In the nineteenth century casework is in decline: organs are increasingly supported on a wooden building frame, and a case, where provided, may be a façade only. After 1850 it is more and more common for the organ to be more or less exposed, with a screen of front pipes in place of complete casework. The effect on the sound of the instrument is to make it more diffuse, allowing the organ tone to 'fill' the building, rather than having an identified source. Decorative casework then becomes the exclusive preserve of a small group of architects and designers until its revival after 1960.

In English organs from 1712 onwards an important feature is the swell box, completely enclosing one or more soundboards and the pipes that stand on them. The front of the swell box consists of movable shutters connected to a pedal, allowing the organist to make the sound louder or softer.

Finally, the pipes. Some early organs had pipes of copper, but from the middle ages onwards the most common material is an alloy of tin and lead, sometimes with traces of other metals such as bismuth, copper, or in the nineteenth century antimony. An alloy with a high proportion of tin is hard and can be polished, especially useful for front pipes. Pipe metal is cast in sheets, originally on sand but more usually on a stone casting bench. The parts of the pipe are cut out of the sheet, beaten into shape round a former or *mandrel*, and then soldered together. Pipes can also be made out of wood. In the nineteenth century the English pioneered the use of sheet zinc for larger pipes, and in the twentieth century there has been a limited revival of the use of copper.

In the early organ the Blockwerk chorus consisted of cylindrical open metal pipes, each key on the organ playing a number of pipes at different pitches – a chorus. Perhaps related to the early mediaeval practice of sung *organum*, a melody sung in parallel fourths or fifths, perhaps because of an intuitive understanding of the rudiments of harmonics, the Blockwerk chorus might include ranks pitched at the fifth as well as unisons and octaves. As the scale ascended and it became more difficult to make small pipes for the higher-pitched ranks, these might break back to lower pitches duplicating other ranks. The various pipes at different pitches reinforced the natural harmonic structure of the unison: the complex interplay of harmonic corroboration between pipes harmonically related to one another is one of the most characteristic features of organ sound.

Once the development of soundboard mechanisms allowed the Blockwerk to be split up into individual ranks, these would each represent a particular pitch: unison, octave, octave quint, superoctave etc. Remaining high partials might be grouped together as a Mixture stop, each key playing a cluster of small pipes. Each rank is identified by a characteristic name and by the length in feet of the speaking part of the longest pipe in the rank, indicating its pitch. Unison pitch on the modern keyboard, with C as its lowest note, is described as 8' pitch, and this standard is almost universal today, though other pitches were once current and are important to the earlier English organ. Note that a second pipe twice as long as the first will have a frequency half that of the first, sounding exactly an octave lower; thus the use of length to identify pitch is easy to understand at a glance. A simple organ chorus might consist of:

Principal	8'	Unison = first partial
Octave	4'	One octave higher = second partial
Quint	$2^{2}/_{3}'$	One octave and a fifth higher = third partial
Superoctave	2'	Two octaves higher = fourth partial
Mixture	IV	Four pipes per note, various harmonics

The Mixture, following the pattern of the early Blockwerk, will emphasise high harmonics at the low end of the keyboard; as the notes ascend these may break back successively to lower harmonics, duplicating the other pitches. As well as unisons and quints it is also possible to introduce third-sounding ranks or *tierces*, representing the fifth harmonic in the series. Sub-unisons are also common. Other more remote harmonics, especially the seventh and ninth partials, have been explored in the twentieth century.

During the middle ages considerable effort was expended on developing new pipe forms to answer the demand for variety of timbre. Pipes might be made tapered rather than cylindrical. It was found that by stopping the end of a pipe it could be made to sound an octave lower than an open pipe of the same length, with a change in the tone (we now know that the harmonic structure of a single stopped pipe includes only the odd-numbered partials). The use of different alloys or even of wood further varied the possibilities.

To these *flue* pipes, whether open or stopped, were added *reed* pipes, in which a brass tongue vibrating against an opening in a tube (the *shallot*) generates the sound, amplified and controlled by a *resonator*.

The extensive variety of pipe forms thus produced required a vast repertoire of names, some practical, some fanciful. Many are descriptive of a supposed compari-

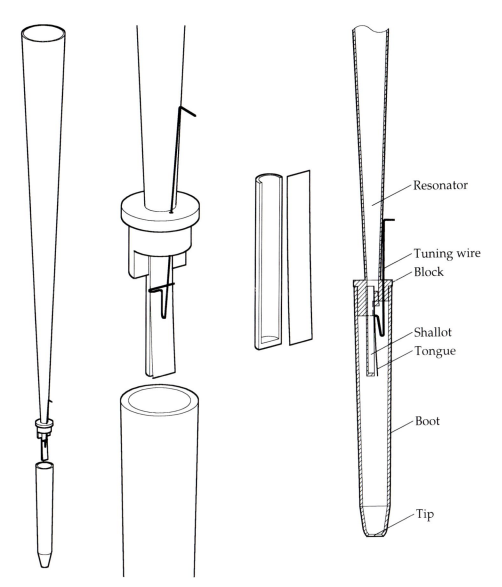

Plate 4   A typical reed pipe of the Trumpet family. Left to right: general view with the boot removed; detail view of block, shallot and tongue; separate views of shallot and tongue removed from block; section through boot, block and base of resonator showing shallot, tongue and tuning wire in position

son to another instrument: thus amongst the flue stops we find *Flute* and *Recorder*; amongst the reeds *Trumpet, Bassoon, Hautboy* and *Cremona* (sc. German Krummhorn), even the *Vox humana*. Other names are descriptive of form – the *Chimney flute* has indeed got a chimney on each pipe; some are evocative (*Tuba mirabilis, Voix célestes*); others esoteric (*Keraulophon, Zauberflöte*). Nomenclature has no recognised limits.

   The precise manufacturing dimensions of the pipes may be varied almost infinitely, and the art of determining details of form, construction and especially diameter of pipes from bass to treble, or from one rank to another, is known as *scaling*. This has always required a degree of appreciation of mathematics, even at a time when literacy itself was not taken for granted.

The organ builder has a free hand in deciding what stops or ranks of pipes to provide in an organ. He may draw up a list of stops or specification that reflects current fashion, the intended use of the organ he is building, and his own artistic intentions.

When the pipes are put into the organ, they are *voiced*: the exact tone and speech of each must be adjusted and balanced with the rest of the organ. The scaling of the pipes will determine certain broad features of the sound – for example the diameters of the pipes, the width of the mouths compared to the diameters, and so on. Pipes of a large relative diameter will give a broader sound and/or greater power; pipes of a smaller diameter will be keener in sound and/or softer. Decisions about wind-pressure, the layout of the pipes in the organ, and the position of the organ in the building will also have a significant impact. The process of voicing allows considerable further leeway in determining the finished sound, as well as adding a final polish to the instrument. As pipe metal is soft and can easily be bent or cut with a knife, adjustments are physically quite easy to make, though requiring great skill of hand, eye and ear. The precise height to which the mouth of a flue pipe is cut in relation to the width is a vital factor – the *cut-up*. The vast repertoire of voicing techniques includes manipulation of the upper and lower lips, the languid and the foot-hole, chamfering the upper lip, nicking the languid and/or lower lip, introducing slots of various dimensions near the top of the pipe, and so on. All these techniques are for flue pipes: reeds have their own extensive battery of voicing methods, much attention being lavished on the shape of the shallot and the exact thickness, hardness and curvature of the brass tongue, as well as on the form, scale and length of the resonator.

As the voicing progresses the pipes will be brought gradually nearer to their final pitch, until they are finely tuned. At its simplest, pipes are flattened by making them longer, sharpened by making them shorter. This may also be achieved on smaller open pipes by hitting them with a brass cone: flaring the end of the pipe sharpens; closing the end of the pipe flattens. Tuning may also be achieved with flaps, caps, cylindrical tuning slides and slots. Stopped pipes are tuned by moving the stopper or by shading the mouth with soft metal *ears*. Reeds are tuned at the tuning spring on the tongue, though the exact length of the resonator is also important in securing the right pitch and tone, and some resonators are equipped with some form of regulation.

In a large organ of several thousand pipes it will be appreciated that the possibilities afforded by the design of the organ and its specification, its layout and construction, and the materials, scaling and voicing of the pipes are almost endless. From this bottomless store of variety and invention arises the fact that no two organs are remotely similar to each other. The organ builder creates a completely individual and new musical instrument at every attempt. Herein lies the enduring fascination of the organ and the special importance of its history.

CHAPTER ONE

EARLY HISTORY
c900–1500

Several antique sources credit the invention of the organ to Ctesibius, an engineer working in Alexandria in the third century BC. Among these is the Roman Vitruvius, writing in the first century AD, who probably used instruments from his own period to give extra detail to his account. At about the same time the organ is described by Hero of Alexandria, who gives details of how the wind was steadied by the weight of water in a cistern. Vitruvius remained a source of information through the middle ages. Representations of antique organs survive in mosaics, coins, terracottas and other objects. A small organ dated 228AD was excavated at Acquincum, near Budapest, in 1931. It is believed that its four ranks of open and stopped pipes were tuned to four different scales or modes of 13 notes each. Its wooden keys operated on metal sliders.

The organ survived in the Byzantine empire, acquiring animal-skin bellows, and returned to northern Europe in the dark ages. A celebrated instrument was that reputedly given by the Emperor Constantine Copronymus to Pepin, King of the Franks, in 757.

How the organ came to be used by the church is not clear, but it is probable that initially, like bells, organs were for making an audible signal, or for providing general clamour on feast days, rather than for playing music in a sense that we would understand today. A large number of early references are connected with Benedictine houses.

Organa in early sources may mean many things apart from organs with pipes: musical instruments in general, performed music itself, even 'works' in the sense of manufactured or crafted objects. Also there may have been a knowledge of the organ on two distinct levels: one purely literary, the notional idea of an instrument with pipes, perhaps connected with a wish to appear cognisant with something that was known to the ancients or of which there were a few very rare examples; the other a practical understanding of real instruments. Where there are definite references to real organs they may even then be clouded by literary hyperbole: at a time when writing was rarer than it is now, the simple idea that an account should be accurate and factual was by no means taken for granted. A degree of licence may have been assumed, even thought desirable, when writing about something rare or splendid.

Plate 5   An illustration of a portative organ from a mid fourteenth-century English lectern Bible. The instrument shown is representative only: keys and pipes are shown, but the purpose of the illustration is iconographic, even though similar small organs certainly existed.

By the end of the tenth century there appear a number of unequivocal and important accounts of organs in English Benedictine abbeys. The fact that there is little definite up to this date does not mean that there were no organs, but with nothing to describe from any earlier period it makes sense to begin with an organ given by St Dunstan (died 988) to Malmesbury Abbey and described by William of Malmesbury in the twelfth century.[1]

> Ideo in multis loco munificus,
> quae tunc in Anglia magni
> miraculi essent,
> decusque et ingenium
> conferentis ostenderent,
> offerre crebro.
> Inter quae signa sono
> et mole praestantia, et organa
> ubi per aereas fistulas
> musicis mensuris elaboratas
> 'Dudum conceptas follis
> vomit anxius auras'
> Ibi hoc distichon
> laminis aereis impressit:
> Organa do sancto praesul
> Dunstanus Aldhelmo,
> Perdat hic aeternum qui
> vult hinc tollere regnum.

> Generous with many things in that place,
> things that at that time in England
> were thought to be great wonders
> and to display the honour and intelligence
> of the donor
> he [was] to donate frequently.
> Among them bells outstanding in tone
> and size, and an organ
> in which, through bronze pipes
> prepared according to musical proportions,
> 'The agitated bellows discharges
> channelled breaths [?]'
> Then he engraved this distich
> on the bronze plates:
> I, Bishop Dunstan, give this organ
> to St. Aldhelm,
> let him lose the kingdom of heaven,
> who wishes to remove it hence.

---

[1] Information on the Saxon organs, the Latin verses and their translation is taken from P. Williams, *The Organ in Western Culture 750–1250* (Cambridge 1993).

Elsewhere William credits St Dunstan with the spread of organs throughout England. A similar account survives in an account dealing with events in 991 at Ramsey Abbey.

> Triginta praeterea
> libras ad fabricandos cupreos
> organorum calamos erogavit
> qui in alveo suo
> super unam cochlearum denso
> ordine foraminibus insidentes
> et diebus festis follium
> spriamento fortiore pulsati
> praedulcem melodiam et
> clangorem longius
> resonantem ediderunt

> Furthermore [Count Ailwin] granted thirty
> pounds for making copper
> pipes for the organ,
> which in their cabin [= on their soundboard?]
> up on one of the spirals [= staircase?] in close-packed
> rows, sitting on their [topboard?] holes
> and on feastdays, set in motion
> by the strong breathing of bellows,
> emitted very sweet melody and
> strong sound
> resonant over some distance.

There is a further reference to Aethelwold making an organ with his own hands at Abingdon in about 980. From there he had moved to Winchester as Bishop, where he was succeeded by Alphege in 984. Between 984 and 994 Alphege carried out an extensive programme of reforming works which included a particularly notable organ. The account of this instrument, a panegyric to Alphege written, in verse, in a prologue to the life of St Swithun by the contemporary Winchester cantor Wulfstan and dated 993–4, is the most remarkable account of an organ anywhere before 1000.

> talia et auxistis hic organa, qualia nusquam
> cernuntur, gemino constabilita solo.
> bisseni supra sociantur in ordine folles,
> inferiusque iacemnt quattuor atque decem.

> flatibus alternis spiracula maxima reddunt.
> quos agitant ualidi septuaginta uiri
> brachi uersantes, multo et sudore madentes
> certaminque suos quique monent socios,
> uiribus ut totis impellant flamina sursum,

et rugiat pleno kapsa referta sinu,
sola quadrigentas, quae sustinet ordine musas,
quas manus organici temperat ingenii:
has aperit clausas, iterumque has claudit apertas,
exigit ut uarii certa Camena soni,

considuntque duo concordi pectore fratres,
et regit alphabetum rector uterque suum,
suntque quaterdenis occulta foramina linguis,
inque suo retinet ordine quaeque decem.
huc aliae currunt, illuc aliaeque recurrunt,

seruantes modulis singula puncta suis,
et feriunt iubilum septem discrimina uocum,
permixto lyrici carmine semitoni,
inque modum tonitrus uox ferrea uerberat aures,
preter ut hunc solum nil capiant sanitum,

concrepat in tantum sonus hinc illincque resultans,
quisque manu patulas claudat ut auriculas,
haudquaquam sufferre ualens propiando rugitum,
quem reddunt uarii concrepitando soni,
musarumque melos auditur ubique per urbem,

et peragrat totam fama uolans patriam.
hoc decus ecclesiae uouit tua cura tonanti,
clauigeri inque sacri struxit honore PETRI.

and you enlarged [endowed?] the organs here, such as are nowhere else
seen, fixed on a double floor [= on two levels?]
Twice six bellows are joined above in a row,
and below lie four and ten.

With alternating breaths [vents?] they render a great amount of air.
Which [bellows] seventy strong men work
moving their arms and dripping with much sweat,
each eagerly encouraging his companions,
to drive the air upward with all strength

and make roar the full chest with its ample curve [or: from the full reservoir?]
which by itself supports the four hundred muses [pipes] in order,
which the hand of the organic skill controls:
it opens the closed and in turn closes the opened,
as the prescribed song [or: chant] of diverse notes requires,

and two brothers of harmonious spirit sit together,
and each, like a ruler, rules his alphabet,
and there are hidden openings in four times ten tongues,
and each holds ten in its own rank [= in due order?]
Hither some tongues run, thither some return,

serving the individual holes in their own places [= the separate holes in the chest
    according to their pitches?]
and the seven separate voices strike up the jubilant song,
mixed additionally with the song of the lyric semitone.
And in the manner of thunder the iron voice beats upon the ears
that they receive no sound beyond only this,

the sound so clamours, echoing here and there,
that everyone closes the opening of his ears with his hand
totally unable to bear the noise when drawing near,
which the various sounds producing in their clamouring.
And the melody of the pipes is heard everywhere in the city,

and flying fame goes through the whole country.
It was your care that consecrated this glory of the church to the Thunderer,
and set it up in honour of the holy keybearer PETER.

What is described here is an organ with two players, each managing his own alphabet (keyboard) of eight sounds – the seven notes of the scale plus the 'lyric semitone' (C, D, E, F, G, A, B♭, B?). Forty tongues (do the keys operate sliders, as in the
Roman organ? does each keyboard have twenty notes?) have holes for ten ranks
each, giving a total of four hundred pipes. The organ is constructed on two levels;
there are twelve bellows on the upper level and fourteen on the lower, worked by
seventy strong men. We can assume that the organ is of the Blockwerk type; there
is no evidence of the appearance of stops until around 1400 on the continent, about
1500 in England. Note the possibility in the opening line that the instrument was
an enlargement of one already existing.

How much of the account can be taken as literal truth will never be known. The
numbers given for bellows, pipes and blowers may be poetic rather than exact,
though the fact that 40 tongues × 10 ranks = 400 pipes suggests that the facts are
accurate; it has also been pointed out that these numbers may have been chosen in
order to add up.

The location of the organ is a problem. Excavation has shown that the Saxon
Winchester Cathedral was not as vast as the building we see today. Was there in fact
space anywhere for seventy blowers, two players and four hundred pipes? – or even,
allowing for poetic exaggeration, a smaller organ? If at the west end of the building – one of many possibilities – the organ could have been at an upper level; in an
unglazed building it might then have spoken as much to the outside world as to
those in the church. The parallel with bells then seems all the more important.
Could the entire organ in fact have been outdoors?

The answers are not known. All the more frustrating is the fact that no further
instrument is described until the twelfth century. In accounting for this we have to
bear several things in mind. First, that England in the eleventh century was threatened by the Danes and then invaded by the Normans; secondly, that once organs
were found in several places then they would be less astonishing and newsworthy;

thirdly, that poetic descriptions of the kind referring to Saxon organs are no longer found and we rely instead on the very patchy survival of early account rolls or occasional chance references. The organs may well have been there, especially in the Benedictine churches, though they were not accepted everywhere. In 1141–2 Ailred, Abbot of the Cistercian Rievaulx Abbey, voiced his dislike of organs in a tone that recurs throughout English organ history:

> Why, I ask, since images and statues are now being rejected, why [are there] in the church so many organa, so many bells? For what, I ask, [is] this fearful bellows-blast, more able to express the crash of thunder than the sweetness of the voice? . . . Meanwhile the people standing, trembling and thunderstruck, wonder at the noise of the bellows, the clashing of bells and the harmony of pipes.[2]

Where organs did appear in England, it is plausible that they may have been related to instruments in mother-churches in Normandy, such as that at the abbey of Fécamp built around 1100.[3] References appear to instruments in the great churches at Ely in 1133,[4] Winchester in 1172,[5] Bury St Edmunds in 1182[6] and Rochester in 1192,[7] but even then the interpretation of the word *organa* is not absolutely certain. Gervase of Canterbury wrote about Canterbury Cathedral soon after a fire in 1174.[8] He describes two floors in the south transept, on the upper of which was an organ. In this position, remote from the enclosed quire and on the more public south side of the church, it may well have been intended for clamour and display, perhaps related to pilgrimages to the shrine of St Augustine and the place of martyrdom of Thomas à Becket. At Winchester Cathedral the Norman north transept has a substantial stone platform above the main arcade of the kind that might have housed an organ.

Through the thirteeth and fourteeth centuries references simply show that organs existed, at first in the great churches (Westminster 1242,[9] Dunfermline 1250,[10] Rochester 1264,[11] Durham 1264,[12] Bisley 1274,[13] Exeter 1286,[14] again with reservations about the use of the word organa), and gradually in buildings of middle rank. Branscombe in Devon had an organ in 1307,[15] Orpington in Kent in 1340.[16]

An account of a late fourteenth-century instrument survives in a nineteenth-century transcription of an account roll from Ely Cathedral; the original is lost. Details are given of expenditure in 1396; it refers to *organis* in the plural. One instrument is meant: in old English usage 'a paire of organs' is a singular object, like 'a pair of scissors', 'a pair of trousers', or, indeed, 'a pair of bellows'.[17]

[2] Ibid., 217   [3] Ibid., 214   [4] A. Freeman MS, 'Notes on Organs', British Organ Archive, note 1308
[5] Williams, *Organ in Western Culture*, 223   [6] Freeman, 'Notes', note 3436
[7] Williams, *Organ in Western Culture*, 224   [8] Ibid., 223
[9] A. Freeman, 'The Organs of the Abbey Church at Westminster', *The Organ*, 2 (1922–3), 130
[10] Freeman, 'Notes', note 1913   [11] P. Hale, *The Organs of Rochester Cathedral* (Rochester 1989), 5
[12] R. Hird and J. Lancelot, *Durham Cathedral Organs* (Durham 1991), 7   [13] Freeman, 'Notes', note 3442
[14] Williams, *Organ in Western Culture*, 225   [15] Freeman, 'Notes', note 1913
[16] A. Freeman MS, 'Small Scrap Book', British Organ Archive, note 53
[17] Ely Cathedral MSS., Cambridge University Library, Add. MS. 2957, f. 46

1 In 20 petr. plumbi empt. pro organis ex parte australi ecclese operand.
   & emendand.   16s 9d
2 In clavis empt. ad idem   1d ob
3 Et in expens. 1 hominis cum 1 equo conduct. labor. usque Ramesseye pro
   diversis Instrumentis ibid quarend. pro eisdem   12d
4 Et in meremio & bord. empt. pro eisdem faciend.   4s
5 Et in cond. 1 hominis pro les belwes faciend. ex conven.   3s 4d
6 Et in expens. alterius hominis labor usque Rameseye alia vice   10d
7 In 4 coreis equin. dealb. empt. pro 4 paribus be belwes ad dict. Organ. habend. 7s 8d
8 In circulis fraxin. empt. pro belwes inde habend. ad idem   4d
9 In visco empt.   8d
10 In wyro empt   12d
11 In 16 paribus de gemewes empt. ad idem   22d
12 In clav. empt. ad idem   14d
13 In stipend. 1 carpentart. conduct. per 8 dies pro fact. conflatoris dictorum
   organorum   2s 8d
14 In clav. empt. ad idem   6d
15 Pro 1 pec. meremii empt pro fistulis vertend   6d
16 In wyr empt. pro fistul. simul ligand   7d
17 In 1 ligamine ferr. empt. ad idem   4d
18 In 12 springs empt. ad idem   3d
19 Et solut. carpentar. pro 1 trabe faciend. supra dict. organorum   6d
20 In 3 hoks & 3 staplis ferr. empt. ad idem   6d
21 In 1 lib visci empt.   1d
22 In 1 lib stanni empt. ad idem   3d
23 In 6 cor. vitul. dealb. empt ad idem   2s 6d
24 In 12 pell. multon   2s 4d
25 In 2 libr. argenti vivi empt.   2s
26 Et in conductione 1 hominis pro dict. organis faciend. & reparand.   40s ad mens
27 Et solut. pro parvis organis reparand. et emend   2s 6d
28 In mensa de operar. ibid. exist. per 13 septimanas simul cum mens. servien.
   sui per idem temp.   8s 10d

The total expenditure of £5 1s 5½d, plus a further 2s 6d for the repair of a smaller
organ, is a significant amount. What is not clear is how much of the organ is new.
Though there is expenditure on lead, if new pipe metal had been cast we would
expect references to coals or faggots for the fire, a melting pot and equipment, a pit
or casting bench and other expenses. As much of the work seems related to the
making of new bellows, it may be that the soundboard and pipes of the organ survived from an earlier instrument. There is indeed no unequivocal reference in the
document to the soundboard or keyboard.

Further details emerge, here grouped roughly by subject.

3 Also for the cost of one man and a horse conveying the workman to Ramsey
   to seek various tools for the same   12d
6 Also for the cost of another workman to Ramsey for another purpose   10d

  5 Also for fetching one man to make the bellows from the Abbey   3s 4d
 13 For the wages of a carpenter brought for 8 days to make the
      conflatorium for the said organ   2s 8d
 26 Also for fetching a man to make and repair the said organs   40s board
 27 Also for wages for the repair and emending of the small organs   2s 6d
 28 For the board of the said workman for a period of 13 weeks together
      with the board of his servant for the same period   8s 10d

Of the various workmen assembled for the operation it is interesting to note that
the source of craft expertise seems to be Ramsey, presumably the Abbey, where we
have already noted the presence of one of the Saxon organs. The conflatorium,
referred to in early texts, is the shaped trunk which collects wind from the bellows
and delivers it to the chest.

  4 Also spent on timber and boards for making them   4s
  7 Spent on 4 white horse hides to provide 4 pairs of bellows for the said organ   7s 8d
  8 Spent on providing hoops of ash for the bellows of the same   4d
  9 Spent on glue   8d
 10 Spent on wire   12d
 11 Spent on 16 pairs of hinges for the same   22d

Deciding which items refer to the making of new bellows is somewhat arbitrary, but
my feeling is that these lines belong together. The ashen hoops and hinges imply a
forge-like bellows with a rounded tail and a hinged top board; the presence of wire
suggests the binding of the nozzle.

  1 Spent on 20 stones of lead for working on and amending the organs from
      the eastern part of the church   16s 9d
 22 Spent on 1 pound of tin for the same   3d
 25 Spent on 2 pounds of quicksilver   2s

If one is right in assuming that there was no wholesale manufacture of new
pipework for this organ, then the remaining possibility is this: the lead was for
bellows-weights, perhaps implying a conversion from unweighted bellows in which
pressure was supplied by the weight of the bellows-treader himself to bellows with
weights in the then new manner. The small quantity of tin would allow for repairs
or a few new pipes, the quicksilver (mercury) is for soldering.

 15 For 1 piece of timber to hold the pipes up   6d
 16 Spent on wire to hold the pipes together   7d
 19 Also paid to the carpenter for making a roof over the said organs   6d

There might not have been a roof before: it is assumed that the earliest organs had
their pipes out in the open, and that the provision of enclosing casework is a mediaeval development. At Exeter Cathedral in 1286–7 money was spent on the enclosing of the organ (in expensis circa organa claudenda . . . 4s[18]); perhaps a similar
operation – the remaking of bellows was again involved.

[18] Williams, *Organ in Western Culture*, 225

18 Spent on 12 springs for the same   3d

The only reasonably certain use for springs is as pallet springs. Given the unpredictability of early drawn brass wire it is likely that springs would have needed replacing frequently. There may well have been only twelve notes in the organ, but this must remain conjecture only.

  2 Spent on nails for the same   1d ob
12 Spent on nails for the same   14d
14 Spent on nails for the same   6d
17 Spent on one iron strap for the same   4d
20 Spent on 3 hooks and 3 staples of iron for the same   6d
21 Spent on 1 pound of glue   1d
22 Spent on 6 white calf hides   2s 6d
24 Spent on 12 sheep skins   2s 4d

The use of ironwork on this scale is interesting. This suggests that the constructional technology of the organ, whether its case or its soundboard, relies on the sort of simple joinery found in early mediaeval furniture – chests and caskets – rather than on the technique used in carved stall canopies or the framing of roof timbers. Nails, clasps, staples and hooks come into their own, as much as the mortise and tenon or wooden pegs. To make any part of the construction wind-tight depends less on accuracy in the joinery than on the liberal use of leather and glue, and it is surely skills here that allow the development of the more sophisticated late mediaeval organs as much as improved techniques in wood.

    Though it is obvious that after a lapse of four hundred years the organ at Ely was no longer an instrument such as that at Winchester, it is barely possible to be specific about how it has changed. The provision of a case, the conversion to weighted bellows, and the presence of springs (perhaps implying some kind of keyboard, rather than key sliders) may be all we can identify at this stage.

    In the fifteenth century organs were to be found not just in cathedrals, abbeys and priories, but in new collegiate churches: Winchester College, founded in 1387, had an organ by 1400;[19] Eton from its foundation in 1440;[20] Oxford had organs at New College, Queen's College, Merton, and Magdalen;[21] Cambridge at King's College at least.[22] Instruments were also appearing in important parish churches. By the end of the fifteenth century the City of London had organs at St Mary at Hill,[23] St Peter Cheap,[24] St Michael Cornhill,[25] St Stephen Walbrook,[26] St Mary Aldermanbury,[27] St Botolph Aldersgate,[28] St Andrew Hubbard[29] and St Martin Orgar.[30] Outside London organs were also appearing in the important parish

---

[19] E. T. Sweeting, 'The Organs of Winchester College Chapel', *The Organ*, 4 (1924–5), 211–20
[20] A. Freeman, 'The Organs of Eton College', *The Organ*, 4 (1924–5), 157
[21] R. Pacey, *The Organs of Oxford* (Oxford 1980)   [22] N. Thistlethwaite, *The Organs of Cambridge* (Cambridge 1983)
[23] Freeman, 'Notes', note 1148   [24] Ibid., notes 436, 2363   [25] Ibid., note 1134
[26] C. W. Pearce, *Old London City Churches, their Organs, Organists and Musical Associations* (London 1909), 54
[27] Freeman, 'Notes', note 2197   [28] Ibid., note 2377   [29] Ibid., notes 2277, 2162   [30] Ibid., note 2392

churches: Bishops Stortford,[31] St Edmund, Salisbury,[32] Andover,[33] Great Yarmouth,[34] Derby,[35] Boston,[36] Coventry[37] and elsewhere.

It may still be too early to talk about any consensus of style, manufacture or function, even if some instruments, such as those in the London parishes, may have resulted from local competition and neighbourly emulation and therefore had local similarities.

We should be aware of some possibilities for the form and technology of these instruments, connecting developments in England to innovations in organ building elsewhere. The Winchester organ would have its natural successor in large and spectacular instruments, grand in size, number of pipes and sheer volume. Was the Ely organ one of these, or of less ambitious scale? One would expect great organs to be remarked on, but only one other more or less remarkable large instrument is described before 1500, at St Albans Abbey c1450:

That young men and maidens, and old people besides should be able to praise the Lord of Heaven, and extol Him in the highest, not indeed with the drum and the dance, but with stringed instruments and the organ and its pipes, and a sound as of sweet voiced cymbals, he [Abbot Wheathampstead] caused to be made an organ than which there was not to be readily found, as was believed, an instrument more beautiful to look upon or more sweet to hear, or more elaborate in workmanship in any monastery throughout the kingdom. As to its cost, in the making and fixing it in position more than fifty pounds was spent.[38]

What can one assume about such an instrument? Whatever one might conjecture about Ely, in the period between Winchester in 994 and St Albans c1450 the keyboard had definitely moved on from the hand-sliders of the ancient organ. Praetorius's *Syntagma musicum* of 1619 describes the organ of Halberstadt Cathedral, built in c1361 and rebuilt 1495.[39] This appears to have had four keyboards: two of fourteen notes each with broad keys operated by the whole hand, one of twelve notes worked perhaps by the knees, and a pedal keyboard of twelve notes for the feet. From around 1400 belongs the gradual reduction in size of the keys, reaching the finger keys of more or less modern width described by Schlick in 1511.[40] The keyboards at Halberstadt allowed the Blockwerk to be played in toto, or just the case principals alone (manuals I and II), the operation of bass pipes (manual III), and pedal pull-downs to part or whole of the rest. This kind of variety of sound is confirmed in the treatise of Henri Arnaut de Zwolle, written in Dijon between 1436 and 1454: the Blockwerk beginning to be divided up into separate sounds; the idea of the Rückpositiv; keyboards spanning up to four octaves; the first appearance of reed pipes; separate keyboards for playing large bass pipes; an early reference to registra or stops; mixtures with tierces as well as unisons and quints.[41] To this armoury of techniques, quickly spreading across Europe, were added

[31] Ibid., notes 1200, 1202   [32] Ibid., note 1265   [33] Ibid., note 1313   [34] Ibid., note 313
[35] Ibid., note 1141   [36] *Musical Times*, 45 (1904), 230   [37] Freeman, 'Notes', note 3474
[38] *Musical Times*, 50 (1909), 634   [39] M. Praetorius, *Syntagma Musicum, II. De Organographia* (Wolfenbüttel 1619)
[40] A. Schlick, *Spiegel der Orgelmacher und Organisten* (Speyer 1511)
[41] Henri Arnaut de Zwolle, MS. treatise, Paris, Bibliothèque Nationale lat. 7295

experiments in pipe forms and the development of variety of timbre between one rank and another; some of these are described by Schlick.

To the middle ages belongs a gradual schism between the organs of northern Europe and those of the south. In the north the Blockwerk-based organ sprouted additional keyboards. In Italy (and southern France), from as early as details survive, a single long-compass keyboard operated several stops of only one rank each – the Blockwerk dismantled and reconstituted in its component parts, instead of surviving residually in a chorus including multi-ranked mixture stops.

The notable St Albans organ may well have shown any one of these developments or, if England was as insular at this time as it was at almost any other, it might still have been an undivided Blockwerk. But, costing upwards of fifty pounds, it was exceptional. Compare this with the cost of other new organs in the fifteenth century:

1428	Lincoln Cathedral	anon. £9-0-0[42]
1442	Lincoln Cathedral	Arnald Organer £3-6-8[43]
1447	Canterbury Cathedral	Nicholas Rawnce £3-6-5½[44]
1474	Southwark	anon. £5-6-8[45]
1475	London St Michael Cornhill	Mighell Glaucets £9-0-0 + old organ[46]
1480	Thame	John Organmaker £3-13-5[47]
1482	Lichfield Cathedral Organ on screen	anon. £26-3-4[48]
	Organ by Jesus Altar	anon. £12-0-0[49]
1484	London St Mary Aldermanbury	anon. £2-4-4[50]
1487	Oxford Magdalen College	Thomas Wotton £13-0-0 part payment only[51]
1489	Oxford Merton College	Thomas Wotton £28-0-0[52]

This range of costs holds good for much of the sixteenth century also, and the indication is of modest-sized instruments. It is true that sometimes the sum mentioned may just be the organ builder's pay or reward, and that costs for materials should be added in. From accounts in the sixteenth century we can be clearer about what is included or not. For example, we can calculate the weight of pipe metal involved from the amount spent on its purchase: from this it is reasonable to guess that most of the English organs that we know are to be identified as positives rather than large

---

[42] *Musical Times*, 39 (1898), 795; (1904), 297
[43] A. Freeman, 'Records of British Organ Builders' (First Series), in *The Dictionary of Organs and Organists* (London 1921), paragraph 10   [44] Freeman 'Records of British Organ Builders' (First Series),11
[45] Freeman, 'Notes', note 2158   [46] Freeman 'Records of British Organ Builders' (First Series),12
[47] Ibid., 13   [48] R. Greening, *The Organs of Lichfield Cathedral* (Lichfield 1974), 5
[49] Freeman, 'Notes', notes 287, 2735, 3487   [50] Ibid., note 2197
[51] Freeman 'Records of British Organ Builders' (First Series),19   [52] Ibid., 19

organs. Sums of £20–£30 represent the cost of such an organ, including all materials. Later evidence will also suggest that the English organ is developing on lines similar to southern Europe – usually a single-long compass keyboard, up to forty-six notes as early as 1500, with stops operating individual ranks and no mixtures; however, certain individual features suggest that this may be a local feature independent of Italian organs, not derivative from them; it may even be a relict of a once widespread practice in smaller organs, becoming dominant in Italy and England but gradually dormant on the continent.

The modest size of the average English organ is obliquely confirmed by evidence of their position. In larger buildings there may have been several instruments. As early as 1307 the Temple Church had two organs.[53] Around 1450 Croyland Abbey had an organ over the main door of the church and a smaller one in the quire.[54] We have already seen that Lichfield had an organ on the screen and one at the Jesus Altar. York had an organ at the altar of the Blessed Virgin Mary in 1457[55] as well as the great organ in the quire mentioned in 1433,[56] and a spare instrument lent to the house of the Minorite Brethren in 1485. Where there is a single instrument it is often associated with a position on the rood loft – quite cramped in many English buildings – or in the quire, or identified with use in a named chapel: the Chapel of St John the Baptist at Lincoln Cathedral in 1428;[57] the Beauchamp Chapel in St Mary, Warwick, c1440;[58] the Lady Chapel at Lesnes Abbey, Erith in 1470.[59]

The suggestion is that the large organ for display, in the tradition of the Saxon organ of Winchester, remains a rarity. That at St Albans some four and a half centuries after Winchester may have been one unusual example; we shall encounter another isolated instance at Exeter in 1513.

The great majority of instruments are positioned carefully near centres of liturgical activity. From later developments there is every reason to believe that these instruments were largely for the accompaniment of singing; their key-compass, pitch, modest scale and individual ranks all assisting to that end. As far as the building, rebuilding and decoration of churches was concerned much depended on the patronage of the great men of the day; their numerous chantry chapels emphasise the importance of lay finance and of the sung mass – whether commemorating the dead or otherwise – and suggest links between the financial support of the church and the reasons why small organs became widespread. The Beauchamp Chapel in Warwick was an example, built with its organ and organ loft in 1440.[60] Lord John Beauchamp endowed a further new chapel in 1475, and provided it with 'vestments and stuff, besides an organ of my own'.[61] John Baude bequeathed money to provide for mass to be sung for him at Woolpit church in Suffolk in 1501, and a further sum

[53] E. J. Hopkins in *The Archaeological Journal*, 45 (1888)   [54] Freeman, 'Notes', notes 290, 291
[55] Freeman 'Records of British Organ Builders' (First Series),11   [56] Freeman, 'Notes', note 507
[57] *Musical Times*, 39 (1898), 795; (1904), 297
[58] E. J. Hopkins and E. F. Rimbault, *The Organ, its History and Construction*, 3rd edn (London 1877), part I, 52
[59] Freeman, 'Notes', note 1974
[60] Hopkins and Rimbault, *The Organ*, Part I, 83   [61] Ibid., Part I, 52

Plate 6   A small organ from a stained glass window in the Beauchamp Chapel, St Mary, Warwick (mid fifteenth century). The chapel, endowed by successive generations of the Beauchamp family, is typical of chantry and other chapels added to churches in the 150 years up to the Reformation, though this example is more richly decorated than most. The chapel had its own organ, standing on a stone gallery over the door. The instrument shown in the window is more than merely iconographic: it has a keyboard which suggests the presence of accidentals; it also has bellows and blower, a symmetrical display of pipes surrounded by decorative casework, and handles to carry it with. In these respects it is probably indicative of the size and appearance of small organs of the period 1450–1550.

to buy an organ.[62] In 1496–7 William Bradway left £10 'to the church of Wetheringsett [also in Suffolk] for a pair of organs to be set in the church, that God's service might be the more solemnly sungen'.[63] What may be the remains of the soundboard of this instrument, or one from a neighbouring church, are described in the next chapter.

[62] Ibid.   [63] Information kindly supplied by Timothy Easton, Esq.

CHAPTER TWO

THE TUDOR ORGAN
1500–1570

From the beginning of the sixteenth century we encounter evidence of a different calibre. Important early contracts and occasional descriptions with hints of technical detail survive. Recently some important organ fragments have surfaced, and these considerably increase our knowledge. Even so, there is considerably less evidence for the English organ than there is for instruments in other countries. Why is this so? First, the majority of English organs were modest in size and therefore conformed to a small group of standard patterns or types. Unlike large organs, where the recipe for the design might be a crucial part of the agreement with the purchaser, the stop-list of a small organ could be taken as read. Thus the only contract surviving from before 1500, that for an organ at York Minster built by Adam of Darlington and dated 24 January 1338, mentions only that the Chapter will find all materials and that the organ builder will be paid 11 marks (£3-13-4).[1] Secondly, English church records are usually restricted to financial transactions only. The survival of contracts is a matter of chance, not the result of good record keeping. Thirdly, the religious upheavals that lasted from 1536 until the end of the Civil War in 1660 wiped out a huge mass of material; although there are parallel situations in other countries, nowhere else does the organ have quite such a rough ride.

After 1500 it becomes clear that organs are by now provided with stops.

to be made wt iij stoppis after the new making
(Westerham, Kent, 1511–12[2])

payd for ij lokks to the same organs, one for the stopps and the othr for the keys
(St Laurence, Reading, 1513[3])

pd for one of the yrons of the stoppys of the organs
(St Peter West Cheap, London, 1521[4])

---

[1] *The Scarborough Mercury* (13 April 1923)
[2] A. Freeman MS, 'Notes on Organs', British Organ Archive, note 1343
[3] C. Kerry, *A History of the Municipal Church of St. Laurence Reading* (Reading 1883)
[4] C. W. Pearce, *Old London City Churches, their Organs, Organists and Musical Associations* (London 1909), 142

for the Draught stoppes and other things pertaining to the organs
(Salisbury Cathedral, 1530[5])

The picture of instruments of this period is further fleshed out by a list of possessions forming the subject of a dispute between Robert Colyns ('wyerseller') and Thomas Broune ('organmaker') in 1514–15:[6]

> Imprimus ii grete organ cacez with carven worke
> Itm. ii cobbordes for to ley in the belowes to the same casez
> Itm. ii smaller casez with carved worke and the song-bordes redy wrought to set in pypes
> Itm. xxviii of fyne tynne in plate redy wrought
> Itm. in ley metal xiiii lb. weight
> Itm. In lede iiii lb. weight
> Itm. a pytt of erthe to melt tyn inn
> Itm. iiiixx [i.e. 4 × 20] pypes of tymber, the most part redy made
> Itm. a stoke and a grete hammer for the same
> Itm. a longe planke for to plane metall uppon
> Itm. an organ case peynted grene, with keys and a song-borde redy made to set in
>   pypes, with a case of white tymber therfor redy made
> Itm. ii planes for to plane metall with, and the irons to the same
> Itm. iiii planes with irons to the same
> Itm. ii crest planes with irons to the same
> Itm. ii hollowe planes
> Itm. v gowges and formes and metall coffyns
> Itm. ii irons for to shave metall bright in square
> Itm. iii mawndrells
> Itm. a grete knyff for to cutt lede with
> Itm. iiii rowndes for to tune pypes with
> Itm. iiii peces for to cast with metall
> Itm. ii swages with branches and byrdes

This description of a busy workshop (or part of it) is of considerable interest. Five organs of various sizes are under construction, with bellows, keys, soundboards and cases mentioned. None of them can be very big. The pipes may be of wood, tin or lead, or lay metal (an amalgam of the two): these are the materials still used today. Much of the equipment relates to the making of pipes. There are few wood-working tools mentioned – perhaps some of the planes; casework may have been made by another craftsman. The hints at decoration – an organ case painted green, the carved swags of branches and birds – suggest a lively interest in the appearance of the instruments. This is a lay workshop: organ building has become a trade able to survive independently of monastic learning or craftsmanship. The name Browne appears a few times in connection with known instruments at Cambridge, Henley and Oxford.[7] It is not clear whether the same builder is involved.

[5] B. Matthews, *The Organs and Organists of Salisbury Cathedral* (Salisbury 1972), 3
[6] Public Record Office, Early Chancery Proceedings 287, nos. 44–5
[7] A. Freeman, 'Records of British Organ Builders' (first series), in *The Dictionary of Organs and Organists* (London 1921), paragraphs 22–3

For the technical detail of the sixteenth-century organ there are five sources. Taken singly each has serious problems of interpretation. Viewed together, a certain amount of corroborative evidence emerges. These sources are:

First, the contract for a new organ at All Hallows Barking, London, built by Anthony Duddyngton and dated 1519. The document was discovered in 1862.[8]

Secondly, the contract for a new organ at Holy Trinity, Coventry, built by John Howe and John Clynmowe, and dated 17 December 1526. This agreement has been known at least in part since 1818.[9]

Thirdly, part of a soundboard found at Wetheringsett in Suffolk in 1977, where it was used as a door in a house, believed to date from c1520.[10]

Fourthly, part of a soundboard from Wingfield in Suffolk, from an organ which seems to have been known to antiquarians at the end of the eighteenth century but which has received little attention in modern times.[11]

To these may be added a fifth instrument, that at Tong in Shropshire, described in very general terms at the end of the eighteenth century and long since lost.[12]

At All Hallows Barking next to the Tower of London three documents survive relating to the building of a new organ in 1519–21. They are an indenture or contract, a receipt, and an incomplete bond and warranty. The receipt and bond give no details of the organ, but are useful in assessing the ability of the scrivener and therefore the trustworthiness of the indenture. The text of the indenture is as follows:

This endenture made the yere of oure Lorde god M1 v c xix and in the monethe of July xxix day: Witnessethe that Antony Duddyngtone Citezem of londone Organ maker hathe made a fulle bargayne condycionally wythe maister William Patensoune Doctour in Diuinte vicair of Alhalowe Barkyng Robert Whytehed and John Churche wardeyns of the same Churche and maisters of the parisshe of Alhalowe Barkyng next the Tower of Londone to make an Instrument: that ys to say a payer of Organs for the foreseid Churche of Dowble Cefaut: that ys to say xxvij playne kayes and the pryncipalle to conteyne the lengthe of v foote so following Wythe Bassys called Diapason to the same conteynyng lengthe of x foot or more: And to be Dowble pryncipalles thorowe out the seid Instrument so that the pyppes wythin for them shalle be as fyne metalle and stuff as the vtter partes that ys to say of pure Tyne wythe as fewe stoppes as may be conuenient: And the seid Antony to have Ernest vj li xiij s iiij d: Also the foreseid Antony askythe v quarters of Archaungelle next folowing to the

[8] The All Hallows Barking indenture is well known from E. J. Hopkins and E. F. Rimbault, *The Organ, its History and Construction*, 3rd edn (London 1877), part I, 56–7. The modern transcriptions (used here) and commentary are in P. R. W. Blewett and H. C. Thompson, *The Duddyngton Manuscripts at All Hallows by the Tower* (London 1977). The manuscripts themselves are: (1) Indenture: All Hallows Muniments Book No. 120(a); (2) Receipt: All Hallows Muniments Book No. 120(b); (3) Bond and Warranty: All Hallows Muniments Book No. 1.
[9] T. Sharp, *The History of Holy Trinity Coventry* (Coventry 1818). The transcription used here is D. Gwynn and M. Goetze, 'A Conveyance of a Pair of Organs, Holy Trinity Church, Coventry 1526', *BIOS Journal*, 9 (1985), 40–1. The contract itself is: Warwickshire County Record Office: DR 801/12/item 12.
[10] I am grateful to T. Easton for bringing this soundboard to my attention. T. Easton and S. Bicknell, 'Two Pre-Reformation Organ Soundboards', *Proceedings of the Suffolk Institute of Archaeology and History*, 34/3 (1995)
[11] F. C. Eglen, 'A Tudor Organ Relic', *Journal of the Incorporated Society of Organ Builders*, 1/3 (1951), 22–3; the sound-board was then lost, and was rediscovered by Dominic Gwynn in 1995.
[12] 'Observator', *The Gentleman's Magazine*, 1789

Fest of Seynt Mighelle the condicione that the foreseid Antony shalle convey the belowes in the loft a Bowff in the seid Quere of Alhalows wythe a pype to the song bourde Also this promysed by the seid Antony that yf the foreseid maister Doctour vicaire Churche Wardeyns maisters of the parisshe be not content nor lyke not the seid Instrument: that than they shalle allowe hym for convayng of the belows xl s for his cost of them And to restore the rest of the Truest agayne to the seid maisters And yf the seid Antony Decesse and depart his naturalle lyf wythin the forseid v quarters that then his wyff or hys executors or his Assignez shalle fully content the foreseid somme of iiij li xiij s iiij d to the seid vicaire and Churche wardeyns and maisters of the parisshe wythout any delay And yf they be content wythe the seid Instrument to pay to the seid Antony fyfty poundes sterling In witnesse wherof the seid parties to theses endentures chaungeably haue set their Sealles. Yoven the day and yere aboueseid.

[signed] Antony duddyngton

In fact the three documents have been drawn up by a very inexpert scrivener and contain considerable errors and inconsistencies. This fact must be carefully considered when trying to extract precise information from them. Furthermore, it must be understood that in drawing up a contract, the terminology used was likely to be familiar only to the organ builder, and not to the other parties involved, least of all the scrivener. If, as seems probable, the organ builder gave a few phrases that might be included in the contract to describe the work he was about to do, there is no particular reason why we should assume that any such phrases that appear are correctly transcribed, are in the right order, have been understood by the scrivener, or are a complete description of the organ. As is the case today, many further details must have been the subject of discussion between the organ builder and his client and would not have appeared in the contract, which inevitably states the situation in brief. It must therefore be borne in mind that the contract is formulaic, not precise.

At Holy Trinity, Coventry the indenture dated 1526 is better written, and in some ways considerably more informative. However, the description of the organ itself again depends on the transcription of formulaic phrases, probably dictated by the organ builder, and not necessarily fully understood or correctly written down.

This Indenture made the xvijth day of December in the xviijth yere of the Reign of King Henry the viijth betwene John Howe & John Clynmowe Citizens & Organmakers of London of the oone partie and Guy Speke William Foster William Killingworth & Ric Sewall the yong Churchwardens of the parissh Church of the Holie Tirinitie in Coventry on the other partie witnesseth that the sayed John & John for thitie pownds sterling to theym well & trulie to be payed have bargeyned & sold and by thes presents bargeyneth and selleth unto the sayed Churchwardens A peir of Organs wt vii Stopps on & besides the Towers of Cases of the pitche of Doble Cffaut wt xxvij pleyn Keyes xix Musicks xlvj Cases of Tynn & xiiij Cases of Wodd wt two Sterrs & the Image of the Trinitie on the Topp of the sayed Organs to be made & sett up here in the sayed parisssh church on this side the Feast of Pentecoste next comyng after the Date of thes presents & to be caried at the costs & charges of the sayed Churchwardeyns towards which charge of Cariage the sayed John & John shall be contributories at the Juggmt & discressions of the masters of the sayed parissh and if it

happen the sayed Organs to be Crosed or Crusshed by any hurte in Cariage to be amended
at the costs & charges of the sayed John & John Also the sayed John & John covenante &
grant by thes presents that the oone of theym at his own proper costs & charges shall come
wt the sayed Organs to the sayed parissh Church there to sett up the sayed Organs well con-
nynglie & werkmanlie as thei owght to be and if it happen the sayed Organs at any tyme on
this side the Feast of Pentecost which shalbe in the yere of our Lorde god mcccccxxxiij to
dekay or be broken for lakk of good or true Werkmanship that than the sayed John & John
or the oone of theym apon a lawfull Warnyng shall at his own costs & charges come hither
to Coventry to amend the sayed defaults as often as such cases shall happen betwene this &
the sayed Feast of Penetcost above expressed provided allway that if the sayed Organs at
any tyme here after be mysused & hurt by negligens that than the sayed John & John or the
oone of theym on comyng hither to amend the same shall have their costs & charges payed
for wt such reasonable Reward for their Labour as shall be thought convenient by the
Juggmt of the masters of the sayed parissh For the which Organs thus Fynysshed & sett up
the sayed Church wardeyns well & trulie shall pay unto the sayed John Howe & John
Clynmowe or to the oone of theym xxxl i st in manner followeng that is to say xl s in hand
the which xl s the sayed John & John do knowlegge theym self wel & trulie to be payed and
viij li parsell of the sayed xxx li to be payed at London at the Feast of the Purificacion of or
Ladie nexyt comyng after the date herof and xx li residue of the sayed xxx li to be payed
when the sayed Organs be sett up immediatlie after the setting up of the same For the which
bargeyn & covenant on the behalf of the sayed John & John well and trulie to be kept &
observed the sayed John Howe & John Clynmowe by thes present bynd theym selfs & either
of theym their heirs & executors unto the sayed Churchwardeyns & to their Successors in
ten pownds sterling by theym & their executors well & trulie to be payed for the non performance of the sayed covenant on their behalf to be observed In Witness wherof the
parties abovesayed unto thes present Indentures enterchangeablie have put their Seales the
day & yere above expressed

[signed with John Howe's rebus]

The fragment from Wetheringsett, Suffolk was discovered by accident in 1977,
having been in use as a door in a house, possibly for over three hundred years. Its
existence was later communicated to Timothy Easton, an artist with a considerable
knowledge of the archaeology of domestic buildings; it was he who recognised that
the oak panel with its complex array of holes was part of an organ soundboard, in
fact the complete grid and table. Dendrochronological tests (dating by measurement of tree rings) shows that the timber was still growing in 1517, and the soundboard therefore made in about 1520.[13]

  The fragment measures 1520mm × 680mm × 45mm and is made of straight-
grained oak carefully trued and finished. On the underside long channels are
routed into the solid timber to form the soundboard grid and on which to bed the
pallets. On the upper surface are over three hundred holes for pipes. Grooves in
the upper and lower surfaces convey wind to remote bass pipes and to the façade.
Preliminary investigation suggests that the organ had forty-six keys. The pipes were

---

[13] Dendrochronological test carried out by the Museum of London Archaeological Services department
    in June 1995

Plate 7   The grid and table of an organ soundboard discovered in 1977 in a house at Wetheringsett in Suffolk, and dated by dendrochronological tests to c1520. The soundboard is constructed from four planks of high-quality oak, probably of Baltic origin. The wind channels are in the form of slots routed directly in the underside of the table. On the upper surface individual holes lead wind to the pipes, via slides and upperboards (not extant). The staggered arrangement of pipe holes indicates the existence of slides. The soundboard is contemporary with the earliest mention of stops in documentary sources.

arranged symmetrically with the largest in the middle and the smaller pipes towards each end, implying the existence of the customary roller-board mechanism between the keys and the pallets. A forty-seventh groove appears to have had a different function, connected either to a toy such as a rotating star, or possibly used as an escape valve to empty the bellows quickly in case of malfunction. That the organ had sliders is evident from the staggered layout of the pipe holes. There appear to have been eight stops, though the holes bored in the table for one stop are centres pricked through for position only and not bored out to their final size, suggesting that one rank of pipes was prepared for but not in fact installed. Other evidence still visible includes: scraps of thin leather or parchment glued into the walls of the grooves and channels, to prevent leakage from one channel to the next through the end grain of the timber; the remains of brass pallet guide pins between the channels on the underside of the table; the existence of a large number of bleed holes bored at an angle into the pipe holes on the upper surface of the table, to draw wind away from pipes tending to 'murmur' because of faulty or unsound pallets.

A highly speculative reconstruction of the stop-list, accounting for the sizes of the tip holes in the table, follows:

Wetheringsett fragment, anon c1520: speculative reconstruction of original stop-list

Slide	Stop	Remarks
1 (front)	? unison (open wood)	Large foot holes suggest wooden pipes
2	Principal	
3	Principal	Nos. 4–33 grooved to façade
4	Octave	
5	Octave	
6	Superoctave	
7	Superoctave	Holes pricked through but pipes never installed
8	Diapason (i.e. suboctave) (open wood ?)	Lowest 19 notes only; large foot holes suggest wooden pipes

Slide 1 may have operated a rank of stopped pipes, wood or metal. However, c1500 would be a very early date for these (stopped pipes are not mentioned by Schlick in 1511) and an open wooden rank is perhaps more likely.

The organ formerly at the collegiate church at Wingfield, Suffolk was seen there in 1799[14] and again towards the end of the nineteenth century by H. P. Raven and M. R. James but apparently disappeared a few years later.[15] The soundboard resurfaced and was described by F. C. Eglen in an article in the Journal of the Incorporated Society of Organ Builders in 1951.[16] It was then lost, but was rediscovered by Dominic Gwynn in 1995.

The soundboard is much smaller than that at Wetheringsett, measuring c1180mm × c330mm; it seems to be made of walnut or chestnut. Again there are channels routed on the underside communicating with the pipe holes above. Two upperboards survive, made of oak and nailed to the soundboard, each with two slides. There appear to have been forty-one notes, again arranged in mitre form with the basses in the middle and the trebles at the extreme ends. One stop is permanently 'on', its pipes grooved alternately to form façades both front and back. This suggests that the organ may have stood on a screen or at any rate have been

[14] Gillingwater MSS, quoted in Davy, 'Church Notes: (Hoxne Hundred)', British Library, Add. MS 19092
[15] H. M. Cautley, *Suffolk Churches and their Treasures* (London 1937)   [16] Eglen, 'A Tudor Organ Relic'

Plate 8   The grid, table and upperboards of an organ from the collegiate church of Wingfield in Suffolk, believed to date from c1500. This instrument, smaller than that at Wetheringsett, appears to have had display pipes front and back. One stop was permanently 'on', the remaining four operated by slides. Here the soundboard proper is made of walnut, only the upperboards being of oak. As at Wetheringsett, the wind channels are routed in the underside of the soundboard. Much of this instrument seems to have survived *in situ* until the beginning of the nineteenth century; the soundboard is now all that remains.

visible from both sides. The 1799 account refers to surviving pipes made of wood, now lost, and a reference from c1855 states that the largest was about five feet long[17].

A tentative reconstruction of the stop-list, accounting for the apparent relative sizes of the tip holes, is:

[17]   E. Kite, *The Churches of Devizes* [sic] (London c1855), 312

Wingfield fragment, anon., undated: speculative reconstruction of original stop-list

1   Principal   Permanently on (no slide)
2   Octave
3   Octave
4   Superoctave
5   Superoctave

Another small instrument standing on a screen was described thus in 1789:[18]

In the parish church of Tong (once Collegiate), in Shropshire, the gallery over the entrance to the choir is yet unremoved, and the organ-case remains, with little more room than was sufficient for the player. This organ, to judge by what is left of it, seems the most ancient of the sort that has come under my observation, which, for the entertainment of your musico-mechanic readers, I shall endeavour to describe. And first the case. It is in the true Gothic, with pinnacles and finials, after the manner of ancient tabernacles, and very like the one just finished and erected in Lichfield Cathedral, only on a smaller scale [the Lichfield Organ was by Samuel Green and was opened in November 1790; the case may already have been finished in 1789 ready for Green to work inside]. Now as to the other parts. The keys are gone but the sounding board remains, and is pierced for one sett of pipes only, seemingly an open diapason, whether of metal or wood could not be determined, there being not a single pipe left; from the apparent positions and distances, I presume they were of metal. I perceived no registers or slides for other stops, and observed the compass to be very short, only to A in alt for the treble part, two short octaves in the lower bass; therefore of more than forty tones in the whole. The bellows are preserved in a lumber room near the vestry, double-winded, without folds, and made with thick hides, like unto a smith's or forge-bellows.

If described correctly, this appears to have been a tiny instrument of one rank only, falling into the portative category. As the keys were missing, it is difficult to confirm the author's guess at key compass, but if he had made a rough count of pipe holes to arrive at his figure of forty notes it at least bears comparison with the other organs described above. Even such a small organ as this had a decorated case, and the confirmation of the use of bellows similar to those used by blacksmiths is interesting.

    Glimpses into the working of these organs are vital, for no further contract or organ fragment survives from before 1600. None of them is large. The Tong organ is tiny, that at Wingfield small, and those at Wetheringsett and Coventry very comparable to each other: Wetheringsett with eight stops (but only seven actually installed), Coventry with seven stops 'on & besides the Towers of Cases' (should 'Cases' read 'Basses' throughout?). The Barking organ, costing £50 against £30 at Coventry, might be larger, but the phrase 'as fewe stoppes as may be conuenient' gives nothing away, even understanding that the word 'few' is not loaded as it would be today, and could equally be read as 'many'. These five organs tend to confirm the supposition that the modest sized portative or positive was the norm.

---

[18] 'Observator', *The Gentleman's Magazine*, 1789

Key compass and pitch: both Coventry and Barking have keyboards starting at CC fa ut (the terminology is that of the Guidonian scale; CC fa ut = C two octaves below middle C). At Coventry 'xxvij pleyn Keyes xix Musiks' (twenty-seven naturals, nineteen accidentals) gives only one possibility for the compass: a remarkable forty-six–note keyboard, fully chromatic from C to a″. Barking also had 'xxvij playne kayes', probably the same compass overall, and Wetheringsett can be shown to have had forty-six notes.

Only Barking gives pipe lengths: 5 foot for the Principal (unison) and 10 foot for the Diapason (an octave lower). Evidence from later centuries will show that we can take these lengths as read: they are indeed the speaking lengths of the pipes, giving a pitch standard quite different from that in use today (a 5′ pipe gives a note roughly equivalent to a modern G or G♯). The Wetheringsett soundboard gives no information on pipe lengths, except that the space allowed for front pipes suggests that the Principal rank started with a pipe of c100mm diameter – about right for a 5′ pipe. The fact that the soundboard is exactly 5 feet long may be a rule of thumb for manufacture, relating the size of the soundboard to the longest pipe to be accommodated: this method is indicated in an early treatise on organ making.[19]

The Wingfield soundboard, with shorter compass and generally much smaller in size, may have been higher in pitch. If of the same pitch standard as the other organs, then a keyboard compass of F–a″ (forty-one notes, or forty if low F♯ or high g♯″ is omitted) is entirely appropriate: the longest pipe, a C played by the F key, would be just under 4′ long (perhaps a tone sharp by modern standards). Another possibility is that this smaller organ (and perhaps Tong also) had a keyboard starting at C, but pipes pitched a fifth higher than Barking. This relationship of organs pitched a fifth apart from each other is described by Schlick and discussed further in chapter 5.

At Wetheringsett we find one stop of basses operating on the lowest nineteen keys of the organ only, the large tip-holes suggesting wooden pipes. This seems to find a parallel in the 'xiiij Cases (Basses?) of Wodd' at Coventry and the 'Bassys called Diapason to the same conteynyng lengthe of x foot or more' at Barking.

At Barking the stops are not specified; the Diapasons are mentioned in particular, and the term 'pryncipalles' seems to be used more generally. At Wetheringsett the layout of the pipe holes suggests strongly that the ranks were arranged in pairs of similar pitch to each other: two Principals, two Octaves, two Superoctaves (one prepared for only). Wingfield is similar. This is surely what is meant at Barking by 'And to be Dowble pryncipalles thorowe out' – two chorus ranks of each pitch. It further suggests that the word Principals is used to cover the entire chorus with the exception of the basses or Diapasons.

The two simple categories of principals and diapasons appear in maintenance records later in the sixteenth century, mostly associated with the Howe family's

[19] P. Barbieri, 'An unknown 15th Century French Manuscript on Organ Building and Tuning', *Organ Yearbook*, 20 (1989), 5–20

operations in London. It is possible that the principals and basses may sometimes
have had separate actions. The clue is in frequent references to springs: 'Item paied
to How for mending of the springs of the basses of the organes and other things xij
d.' St Mary Woolnoth, London 1555[20] (Further springs for the basses were needed
in 1560 and 1563–4, also at St Benet Gracechurch Street, London in 1561–2[21]).
This suggests one of two things; either that in certain organs the bass pipes
(Diapasons) were on an action of their own, separate from the soundboard
(Principals), or that the entire organ was on a spring chest. Though it is possible that
examples of the spring chest existed in England at some time, no evidence of them
has yet appeared. From the evidence of Wetheringsett and Wingfield, both slider
chests, and from the fact that springs are usually referred to in connection with
basses only, I would suggest that the separate action for the bass pipes of the
Diapason is the most likely possibility (related to the trompes found on the continent? – this question is discussed in Chapter 4).

   Two further accounts help to confirm this hypothesis:

Item. Payed for 2 skins of leather for to leather the bellows of the grate woden organs and
leathering the sou boords.
Item. Payed for latten wyre for to make springs for the grate bass and ten principalls.
Item. for sowder to sowder small pipes which were broken   (Westminster Abbey c1558[22])

Itm payde more to the same howe for two skynnes for the bellowes and the sounde borde
and for latten wyer for the spryngs bases & pryncypalls & for sowdryng vj smalle pypes and
for workemanshipp of the bellowes, ij s. viij d.
Itm more to hym for latten wyer for viij grett bases, vj d.
Itm more for lether & glewe for the sounde bourde, ij d.
                                              (St Peter West Cheap, London 1557–8[23])

The leathering of the soundboard is characteristic of some slider chests, particularly if routed out of solid timber as at Wetheringsett and Wingfield. Springs are
needed here for the basses and for principals; just two carefully defined categories.
Again this suggests a main action to a slider soundboard and a separate action for
the basses only.

   All five organs had one manual only. It is, however, just possible that there were
isolated examples of organs with two manuals. The evidence for this appears in
inventories of church contents made during and after the dissolution of the monasteries and is discussed in the next chapter.

   Churches may have kept, in addition to one or more organs, a regal (a portable
organ with a short-resonator reed stop only, or with a reed and a few ranks of high-
pitched flutes); these required frequent attention to tongues and tuning springs as
well as to pallet springs: 'pd to howe for iiij spring for the regalles, xij d.' (St Mary
at Hill, London 1559).[24] The regals varied in size as did larger organs: 'It'm to Howe

---

[20] Freeman, 'Records of British Organ Builders' (First Series), 16
[21] A. Freeman, 'Father Howe, an Old-time Maker of Organs', *Musical Times*, 62 (1921), 633–641
[22] Freeman, 'Records of British Organ Builders' (First Series), 17   [23] Ibid., 17   [24] Ibid., 14

organ maker for makynge sprynges to the doble regalls and for tonges of the ij regalls which is called the pryncypalls in the base regall, iij s.' (St Peter West Cheap, London 1556).[25] Though these references show that English organ builders were acquainted with reed pipes, it is impossible to say whether any appeared as organ stops rather than in the diminutive regal itself.

However widespread small organs were, there is a tantalising glimpse of a larger organ type in an account surviving at Exeter Cathedral and dating from 1513–14. The fact that the document is fortuitously fastened to the fabric accounts for that year, which give a record of everyday income and expenditure, explains its survival. It also suggests why such documents are not more common: large organs would have needed special finance, perhaps depending on the donations of wealthy benefactors, and the accounts would usually have been kept separately, or even disposed of after completion. This instrument cost £164 15s 7¼d, a princely sum compared to the cost of any other organ we have encountered so far:[26]

Computus predicti domini Johannis Maior Clerici Operis hoc anno pro diversis rebus Emptis et expensis factis ut patet per unum quaternum inde factum et super hunc computum ostensum pro novis Organis in pulpito

Expensa	Imprimis in expensis factis ut patet per unum quaternum inde factum et super hunc computum ostensum	
		xlij li iiijs vjd ob q
	Summa	xlij li iiijs vjd ob q
Empcio Stagni	Item Johanni Wyllyams et Johanni Petyr pro sragno ab ipsis emptis ut patet in eodem quaterno	
		xxxiiij li xs vd
	Summa	xxxiiij li xs vd
Ferramenta	Item Johannis Lylbye fabro pro diversis rebus necessariis ab ipso emptis ut patet in eadem quaterno	
		iv li vijd ob
	Summa	iv li vijd ob
Liberacio denariorum	Item ego Johannis Maior Clerici Operis et computus eiusdem deliberavi to Laurencio Playssher per indentur.	
	hoc anno ut patet in eadem	lxxj li
	Summa	lxxj li

Summa omnium expensarum cum solusione denariourum ut patet per predictum quaternum inde factum et super hunc computum ostensum

clj li vxs vijd q

et sic in excessu expensarum huius computis ?vis ?d quos recepi de predictis senescallis super computum et eque hoc anno

---

[25] Ibid., 17   [26] Exeter Cathedral Library MSS., D&C 2704/7

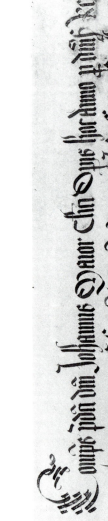

Plate 9 The account roll for the building of a new organ on the pulpitum at Exeter Cathedral by Laurence Playssher in 1513. The organ was unusually large and expensive (£164 15s 7½d). The document itself is a very rare survival, preserved only by the chance of its being attached to the main cathedral fabric accounts. The high quality of the penmanship is indicative of the importance of the project.

Memorandum de x li datis Laurencio Playssher per decretum
        capituli ex rewardo citra hunc computum
        Summa   x li

Memorandum de 1 planks emptis de Johanne Grynewaye et
        resolutis domino de Devonschere   iiij li

Expensa organorum cum regardo   clxiiij li xv s vij d q

The various items are easily explained. The three opening lines state the purpose of the account: to show expenditure on the new organ on the pulpitum. The first item of expenditure, £42 4s 6¾d, refers to another document to which this account is attached, recording the whole year's payments from the fabric chest to the clerk of the fabric. It is not clear which items on this further account are to be included in the £42 4s 6¾d spent on the organ, but a purchase of tin totalling £30 5s 9d can only really be explained as being intended for organ pipes.

The second item is a further purchase of tin costing £34 10s 5d. Then follows a payment to a blacksmith for ironwork at £4 0s 7½d. The organ builder Laurence Playssher is given £71, as agreed in the indenture. (Playssher is known only from this organ and a reference at Glastonbury Abbey: a bond dated 1508 acknowledging a loan to Playssher of £6 13s 4d from the Abbott of Glastonbury, and leaving in pledge in the Abbey 'a peire of Organs not Fully performed', was sold at Sotheby's, London, on 10 May 1984 for £520.) The total expenditure so far is £151 15s 7¼d. Two further items are added: a further reward of £10 to Playssher granted by the Chapter, and £4 spent on timber, bringing the total to £164 15s 7¼d.

Exactly how big was this organ? In the latter part of the sixteenth century the price of tin bought for organ pipes remained relatively stable: 7½d per pound at St Edmund, Salisbury in 1567,[27] and 7¾d per pound at King's College, Cambridge in 1605–6.[28] If we assume that the price was similar in 1513 (although, on account of inflation later in the century, it may have become more expensive) the total expenditure on tin of £64 16s 2d suggests a minimum of about 2000lbs (908kg) weight. Compare this with the nearest estimate we have for the amount of metal needed to build a large organ: at New College, Oxford in 1661 Robert Dallam proposed an organ with twenty-four stops and a façade whose longest pipe was to be 24 feet long. For this he estimated that he required only 1000lbs of tin plus 200lbs of lead for the feet of the inside pipes.[29] On this basis, if the pitch of the Exeter organ was related to the 5′ or 10′ standard of its contemporaries, then its bass pipes would certainly have been 20 feet long. The manufacture of pipework in 1513 may well have been heavier than Dallam's refined French-style pipework of the 1660s, but even so this is a very substantial instrument and, despite lack of detailed information about its

[27] Freeman 'Records of British Organ Builders' (First Series), 33
[28] Hopkins and Rimbault, *The Organ*, part I, 64–7
[29] New College, Oxford MSS., Robert Dallam's scheme and estimate for a new organ, 1661

musical potential, it is the largest organ we know of in the British Isles before the Civil War. The fact that the next known organ with 20-foot basses is also at Exeter Cathedral, built by John Loosemore in 1665 and again standing on the screen, is probably no coincidence.

What was this organ for? Since it is isolated amongst the many records of smaller instruments, it is difficult to say. Was this a late example of a tradition of large organs for display, founded on instruments like that at Winchester five centuries before? Was it an isolated experiment, perhaps at the behest of a wealthy donor, or influenced by a craftsman who had seen great organs abroad? More evidence is needed before such questions can be answered with any degree of certainty.

On the eve of the Reformation we can attempt to summarise the development of the English organ so far. Of organ builders we know little; numerous individuals are mentioned in churchwardens' and fabric accounts, but few names appear more than once, or give us a coherent picture of the structure of the craft. Only John Howe, whom we have met in connection with Holy Trinity, Coventry, will appear again, as the founder of a dynasty whose fortunes we will follow in the next chapter. Of the organs themselves we still know only a little, but enough to show that the English organ had several highly individual features. Among them were:

The appearance of the long forty-six–note keyboard, C–a″, with a fully chromatic bass, at a time when the rest of northern Europe was happy with thirty-eight or forty-one notes for most organs, reserving long compass for the largest instruments only (such as FF–a″ in some organs in the Netherlands).

Though other pitch standards may have existed, we know only of the 5′ pitch played by a C key at Barking, with the Diapason 10′ speaking an octave below. It is this pitch standard which appears in connection with church organs in the early seventeenth century, and its relationship to choral accompaniment will be described in Chapter 5.

A simple chorus of pairs of single-rank stops at unison, octave and superoctave pitch, without mixtures and possibly without quint-sounding ranks, supported by basses (the Diapasons) which may at first have operated on the lowest notes of the keyboard only, and which may sometimes have had an independent mechanism. One row of holes on the Wetheringsett soundboard suggests an occasional open wooden flute (or, less probably, a stopped rank) for contrast.

CHAPTER THREE

THE ENGLISH REFORMATION
1536–1600

The dissolution of the monasteries from 1536 onwards was the political gesture of a monarch who cared to have no rivals in status and supremacy in his own kingdom. It is unlikely that Henry VIII foresaw the eventual effects of the closure of the religious houses on arts and music. It was not just that the church was a wealthy patron commissioning works of every kind; the monastic houses provided economic and intellectual support for training craftsmen, whether from amongst their own members or laymen; they helped maintain continuity from one generation to the next. They may also have provided a network of intellectual communication that encouraged visits from foreign craftsmen. The closure of no less than 800 houses would have affected not just the flow of new work but the whole economic and social base on which the craft of organ building was founded.

An example of the role that monks may have had before the dissolution survives in an account written by Sir Thomas Butler, the last Abbot of Shrewsbury, describing the talents of Sir William Corvehill, a former monk of Much Wenlock Abbey (here the title 'Sir' is equivalent to 'Father' or 'Brother', not an indication of nobility). Corvehill was:[1]

excellently and singularly expert in divers of the seven liberal sciences . . . and few or none of handicraft but that he had a very good insight in them, as the making of organs . . . and no instrument of music being but that he could mend it, and many good gifts the man had, and a very patient man, and full honest in his conversation and living.

There were surely many like him, whether priests or lay craftsman, whose livelihood suffered.

The richness of organ culture before the Reformation is touchingly described in *The Rites of Durham*, a retrospective account supposedly written by a former monk of the Priory at Durham, describing the situation before dissolution in 1539.[2]

Tere was 3 paire of organs belonginge to the said quire for the maintenance of god's seruice and the better selebrating thereof one of the fairest paire of the three did stand

---

[1] A. Freeman, 'Records of British Organ Builders' (First Series), in *The Dictionary of Organs and Organists* (London 1921), paragraph 41   [2] Davies, *The Rites of Durham* (Durham 1672)

41

ouer the quire dore only opened and playd uppon at principall feastes, the pipes beinge all of most fine wood, and workmanshipp uerye faire, partly gilted uppon the inside and the outside of the leaues [doors] and couvers up to the topp with branches and flowers finely gilted with the name of Jesus gilted with gold: there was but 2 paire more of them in all England and of the same makinge, one paire in Yorke and another in Paules [St. Pauls] Also there was a lanterne of wood like unto a pulpitte standinge and adjoininge to the wood organs over the quire dore, where they had wont to singe the nine lessons in the old time on pryncipal dayes, standinge with their faces toward the highe altar. The second paire stood on the north side of the quire beinge neuer playd uppon but when the 4 doctors of the church was read, viz. Augustine Ambrose Gregorye and Jerome beinge a faire paire of large organs called the cryers . . . The third paire was dayly used at ordinary seruice.

There were two further organs: one was in front of the Jesus altar in the nave and was used for the singing of Jesus mass every Friday; the other was in the Galilee chapel at the west end of the building.

Henry VIII's break with Rome was not intended to change the nature of worship: his church was still Catholic. However, his challenge to Rome's leadership could only have been contemplated in an age when reformation was in the air. From the dissolution until the early 1600s radical changes to the life and liturgy of the church follow hard upon each other's heels and, as far as the English organ is concerned, the picture is very confused and ultimately bleak. For the period between 1526 and 1600 no organ contracts have yet come to light; by the fourth quarter of the century it is clear that organs had been removed or destroyed across large parts of the country.

The story of this decline is the story of the English Reformation itself. Henry VIII established the fact that the old ecclesiastical hierarchies could be dismantled, to the undoubted benefit of the royal purse and to the nobility, who acquired much former church property. Under his successor, the young King Edward VI (r1547–53), the radical Protestants at court were able to consolidate the process, further sequestrating church property and introducing an English prayer book making clear the independent Protestant nature of the embryonic Anglican church. Playing of organs was frowned on in advanced circles; the results of this attitude are discussed later.

Following a succession crisis which saw the brief appearance of Lady Jane Grey as a hoped-for Protestant queen, it was the Catholic Mary who took the throne in 1553. Although it was possible that she would maintain the Church of England as

◄ *Plate 10*   The early sixteenth-century organ case at St Stephen, Old Radnor, Powys. The case was restored under the direction of F. H. Sutton and a new organ installed in 1872. The horizontal linenfold panels may be a solecism dating from 1872 but, in the rest of the case, the combination of gothic structure overlaid with early mannerist details is convincing. The pipes in the three towers and two lower flats (the present front pipes date from 1872) would have made up forty-five pipes of a 5′ Principal. The arrangement of the pipes, the size of the case and the rich decoration suggest a more substantial and expensive instrument than that indicated in the Wetheringsett soundboard. It is not clear why such an organ should have found its way to a relatively lonely spot in Wales, although this very isolation may account for its survival.

established by law, she in fact moved slowly but firmly towards a reunion with the Roman church. She married Prince Philip of Spain in July 1554 in Winchester Cathedral; Philip's organist Antonio de Cabezon was brought over for the occasion. By 1557 England and Rome were reconciled, though confiscated property could not by then be returned to the churches and there is no real sign of an upturn in organ building.

The coronation of Elizabeth in January 1559 was performed according to the old Roman rite[3] and at first the Latin services re-introduced under Queen Mary remained in use. However, Puritan thinking had matured and strengthened in exile during Mary's reign and now it found much fuller expression. In new Acts of Supremacy and Uniformity in 1559 the Anglican church was confirmed and consolidated. However it is important to observe what was considered right for the Elizabethan church at large was not necessarily followed to the letter at court; this is revealed later by the special position and practices of the Chapel Royal, which was under royal not episcopal control and reflected the monarch's need for a degree of stylish pomp to be maintained as a political tool – perhaps especially to win the admiration and confidence of foreign ambassadors, many of whom were Catholic. It was the Chapel Royal that was to concentrate the musical talent of the age and, despite the vicissitudes of musical life elsewhere in the country, to allow the flowering of Tallis and Byrd.

Throughout the Reformation music and therefore organs were at the centre of discussions about ritual. Though an anti-organ attitude had existed for some time and there was some dismantling of instruments under Edward VI, it is not until Elizabeth's reign that it prevailed and hardened into a general desire to remove them completely. In 1563 the Canterbury Convocation rejected a move including the silencing of organs by only one vote.[4] After the Queen's excommunication in 1570 there is evidence that, in this second wave of anti-organ feeling, instruments were removed in large numbers.

Temperley[5] observes that only in certain places were the Puritans in the majority; for the innately conservative population at large there was a residual, perhaps nostalgic, affection for Roman ritual and music. The authorities were aware of the general feeling and did their best to deflect it, for example in the Homilies of 1563:[6]

A woman said to her neighbour: Alas, gossip, what shall we do now at church, since all the saints are taken away, since all the goodly sights we were wont to have, are gone, since we cannot hear the like piping, singing, chanting and playing upon organs that we could have before. But (dearly beloved) we ought greatly to rejoice and give thanks, that our churches are delivered out of all those things which displeased God so sore, and filthily defiled his holy house and his place of prayer.

Though it is reasonably clear that many organs were dismantled in the 1550s and again in the fourth quarter of the sixteenth century, evidence to indicate the decline

[3] P. Le Huray, *Music and the Reformation in England 1549–1660* (London 1967), 31   [4] Ibid., 35
[5] N. Temperley; *The Music of the English Parish Church*, 2 vols. (Cambridge 1979), vol. I; 40   [6] Ibid.

in the craft of organ building after the Reformation is varied. Churchwardens' or fabric accounts can give a good idea of when a new organ is built even if no contract survives. If not actually stated as new, the expenditure of sums of money greater than about £8 (St Michael Spurriergate, York, 1536)[7] may be taken to indicate major work. Using Andrew Freeman's collection of notes on early English organ building, which remains the most extensive compilation of material yet attempted, it is possible to show numbers of organs that can be described as new or largely new in the decades 1500–99:

1500–09	3
1510–19	12
1520–29	12
1530–39	15
1540–49	4
1550–59	4
1560–69	4
1570–79	0
1580–89	1
1590–99	5

This period of decline leaves us with very little information about those organs that were built or maintained during the later sixteenth century. After the contracts at Barking and Coventry no further description of an organ, written by someone who understood the instrument, has yet appeared from before the seventeenth century. A comparison with the rest of Europe is interesting: most of the really informative descriptions of European instruments, especially early stop-lists, come from the middle and end of the sixteenth century, notably those dealing with the Niehoffs, the Langheduls, with Scherer, with the Antegnatis, and with the early French organs of Beaune, Alençon, Arras and Gisors. This period of great development overseas is marked by near silence in Britain.

However, the inventories of church contents commissioned at the end of the reign of Henry VIII and by Edward VI in the 1550s provide some useful information.

First, it is possible to get a partial impression of how widespread organs were. Temperley[8] observes that in Kent 16 parishes out of 136 for which inventories survive were recorded as having organs; of these 6 were in the cathedral cities of Canterbury and Rochester. In the East Riding of Yorkshire there were 19 organs out of 207 parishes with inventories; in the city of Exeter 5 out of 21.

Given that the parish churches of England are both very numerous and small in size compared to the churches of the colleges and religious houses, this is a significant number of instruments. Observe also that the 'snapshot' provided by the inventories is not complete: in Kent alone we find evidence of sixteenth-century

---

[7] A. Freeman MS, 'Notes on Organs', British Organ Archive, note 1249
[8] Temperley, *The Music of the English Parish Church*, vol. I, 8

organs at Westerham (1511),[9] St. Andrew Canterbury (1520),[10] Folkestone (1528),[11] Hoo (1533),[12] Smarden (c1547),[13] Hawkhurst (1548)[14] and St Dunstan Canterbury (c1567),[15] in addition to those in the inventories. Before the dissolution the organs in the religious houses would have doubled the total for the county to something like forty locations. This number was probably not to be reached again until the nineteenth century. Even then the inventories themselves may not paint a complete picture: many valuable objects were hidden from the commissioners.

Some of the buildings had more than one organ. If we stay with Kent for the time being: 'ii payer of great organes' at Ashford parish church;[16] 'two payer of organes' at Warehorne.[17] This habit of providing more than one instrument confirms what we know of their use: the account in *The Rites of Durham* associating different organs in Durham Cathedral with different liturgies and festivals is enough on its own to indicate the organ's supporting rather than primary role. The use of two or even several instruments also suggests that each one did not need to be bigger than its specific liturgical function would require; this may have established a pattern of usually small instruments – mostly five foot, sometimes ten foot – that would have been easily accommodated in the small structures of English parish churches and would have had parallel uses in larger buildings.

Where there are two or more organs we may have an indication of relative sizes. 'ij paire of organs one smaller than the other' (St Mary, Bletchingley)[18] is no more informative than 'ij paire of organs the one gretter then the other' (St Mary at Hill, London).[19] However, the words 'great' and 'little' remind us that the bigger an organ the deeper its largest pipes, so that 'a base peare of organes' (Bethersden)[20] is a more substantial instrument. It is possible that the identification of 'great' and 'little' organs might correspond to those with a ten foot Diapason rank and those without, but the inventories do not record this. The 'greytt orggonol of braus in the queyr' recorded at Holy Trinity, Coventry in 1558[21] is probably that built by Howe and Clynmowe described in the last chapter, with seven stops. A specific reference to stops gives a clue to size in another church: 'ij faire payre of organs' each with 'iiij stops' (Fotheringhay Collegiate Church)[22] – possibly both small instruments similar to the five-stop fragment at Wingfield described in Chapter 1. Numbers of pipes are sometimes mentioned – though a count of twenty-six pipes (Farnham, Surrey)[23] or 'j row of xviij organ pyppes' (Calne, Wiltshire)[24] must result from a lay observer counting front pipes and not realising that more were concealed inside the case. But another inventory at Calne from 1532 gives 'Itm v score & xxiij orgens pyppes' (i.e. 123 pipes).[25] If this sum represents an intact playable organ then three stops of 41 notes each (the compass of the Wingfield fragment) is perfectly possible. A later record (churchwardens' accounts for 1588 at St Mary, Nottingham)[26]

---

⁹ Freeman, 'Notes', note 1343   ¹⁰ Ibid., note 2119   ¹¹ Ibid., note 1350   ¹² Ibid., note 1347
¹³ Ibid., note 1344   ¹⁴ Ibid., note 1341   ¹⁵ Ibid., note 1346   ¹⁶ Ibid., notes 1341, 2032
¹⁷ Ibid., note 1343   ¹⁸ Ibid., note 1322   ¹⁹ Ibid., note 1148   ²⁰ Ibid., note 1341   ²¹ Ibid., note 1232
²² Ibid., note 2736n   ²³ Ibid., note 1317   ²⁴ Ibid., note 1930   ²⁵ *The Organ*, 19 (1939–40) 18

gives 'orgayne pypes is in number xij score and xv' (i.e. 255 pipes) – not far from the probable size of the Barking and Coventry organs for which contracts survive.

The inventories sometimes describe the position of the organ, thus providing a further confirmation of its function. At Colne Priory in the choir 'a payer of organes at xxxiij s. iiij d.' and 'a payer of olde organes the pipes of leade broken at x s.'; in the lady chapel 'a lytell payer of very olde portatyves at xx d.'[27] At Hatfield Broad Oak Priory a similar situation: 'a payer of old organys at v s.' in the choir and 'a lytell paire of orgaynes vj s. viij d.' in the lady chapel.[28] At Ottery St Mary there were three organs: 'a paire of organs in the Rood loft praysed at xl s.', 'a new paire of organs in the quere praysed at v li', and 'a paire of organs in our Lady Chapel praysed at x s.'.[29] This is almost a complete list of possible positions for organs in all English churches before the seventeenth century: most often in the choir, on one side unless stated otherwise; sometimes on the rood loft – a cramped position in most parish churches – or on the pulpitum if the building was large; there were also further small instruments in side or chantry chapels. There is barely any evidence of west-end organs (Croyland Abbey c1450?;[30] Beauchamp Chapel in St Mary, Warwick c1440?[31]); this development, associated especially with the seventeenth and eighteenth century organs of the continent, passed England by.

The prices assigned to organs in the inventories must usually represent the scrap value of the pipework: few are shown to be worth more than the five pounds indicated for a new organ at Ottery St Mary mentioned above; most are worth a pound or two. Sometimes an organ is described as having pipes of tin or lead, but not consistently enough or with enough detail to draw any conclusions. Most organs are noted but no value given. Wooden pipes are never mentioned, but as the purpose of the inventories was to list things that could be transformed into hard cash – Edward VI's main quarry was the church silver – these would be of no interest and there is no reason to suppose that they did not exist.

A further characteristic of the inventories is the number of organs that are described as incomplete, broken or decayed; evidence also appears of the first wave of organ removals under Edward VI. Back in Kent again: at Smarden the organ was sold c1548;[32] at St Mary Bredman and St George in Canterbury the organs were sold in about 1553;[33] at Hawkhurst the organ case went in 1548 for two shillings and ninepence;[34] at Erith in 1552 the organ had 'the pips half stollen'[35] and at Hayes at the time of the inventories the organ had recently been sold to provide money for the repair of the church.[36] Apart from showing the collapse of care and regular maintenance, this also hints that it is not just the Crown that is short of money and trying to realise the value of church property, but the churches themselves. The later sixteenth century was a period of drastic inflation, perhaps

[26] Freeman, 'Notes', note 1991   [27] Ibid., notes 1326, 989   [28] Ibid., note 1327
[29] Ibid., notes 1916, 3469
[30] E. J. Hopkins and E. F. Rimbault, *The Organ, its History and Construction*, 3rd edn (London 1877), part I, 82
[31] Ibid., part I, 83   [32] Freeman, 'Notes', note 1344   [33] Ibid., note 1346   [34] Ibid., note 1341
[35] Ibid., note 1342   [36] Ibid., note 1342

CHORI ECCLESIÆ CATHEDRALIS S. PAVLI PROSPECTVS INTERIOR.

Plate 11   Old St Paul's Cathedral, London, drawn by Wenceslaus Hollar for Dugdale's *The History of St Paul's Cathedral in London*, 1658. A late mediaeval organ stands on the north side of the choir. It appears to have front pipes from 10′ long or thereabouts, with the largest pipe in the middle (as in the Wetheringsett and Wingfield soundboards). The case is surmounted with a crocketed gable and there are doors in front to protect the instrument from dust and damage.

fuelled by the economic upheavals of the dissolution and attempts at re-distribution of wealth and property. There can have been very little encouragement to look after organs.

Shortly after the date of the inventories we see the first of several waves of organ removal and destruction. Royal Injunctions to St George's Chapel, Windsor in 1550 show that organ music had ceased, though the organists were still to draw their fees.[37] In 1552 Archbishop Holgate ended the use of organs at York Minster:[38]

we will and command that there be no more playings of the organs, either at the Morning Prayer, the Communion, or the Evening Prayer within this Church of York, but that the said playing do utterly cease and be left the time of Divine Service within the said Church . . . .we think it meet that the Master of the Choristers for the time being who ought to play the same organs in times past who can no more do so, that the said Master of the Choristers do his diligence to his power to serve God in such vocation as he can conveniently and may.

At Worcester Cathedral three organs were taken down in 1550 and 1551 under Bishop Hooper (although once Queen Mary was on the throne the organs in the Choir were put back again).[39] Practice varied from place to place; York, Worcester and others exhibited the harder Puritan line while in more conservative or more isolated parts of the country organs might still be maintained and used. As anti-organ polemic grew in the 1560s, organs disappeared in large numbers, particularly in places like London where Puritan feeling ran high:

St Peter Cheap, London	Sold 1566[40]
St Benet Gracechurch Street, London	Sold 1569[41]
St Clement Danes, Westminster	Sold before 1571[42]
St Matthew Friday Street, London	Sold 1572[43]
St Michael Cornhill, London	2 organs sold 1572[44]
St Mary Magdalen Milk Street, London	Sold 1576[45]
St Helen Bishopsgate, London	Sold 1576[46]
St Mary Aldermanbury, London	Pipes sold 1577[47]
St Christopher le Stocks, London	Sold 1581[48]
St Alphege London Wall, London	Removed from screen 1560, sold 1581[49]
St Dunstan, Stepney	Sold 1585[50]

In Cambridge and East Anglia organs were taken down, even though this was an area with an influential recusant aristocracy (the Dukes of Norfolk):

Long Melford, Suffolk	Taken Down 1560s[51]

---

[37] Le Huray, *Music and the Reformation*, 25   [38] Ibid., 25
[39] C. Beswick, *The Organs of Worcester Cathedral* (Worcester 1967), 5   [40] Freeman, 'Notes', note 2363
[41] A. Freeman, 'Father Howe, an Old-Time Maker of Organs', *Musical Times*, 62 (1921), 633–641
[42] Freeman, 'Father Howe'   [43] Freeman, 'Notes', note 2370   [44] Ibid., note 1148
[45] Freeman, 'Father Howe'   [46] Freeman, 'Notes', note 2001   [47] Ibid., note 2189   [48] Ibid., note 2112
[49] Freeman, 'Father Howe'; Freeman, 'Notes', note 2258   [50] Freeman, 'Notes', note 2725

St Margaret, King's Lynn	Sold 1565[52]
St Nicholas, King's Lynn	Sold 1565[53]
St Edward, Cambridge	Sold 1566[54]
Norwich Cathedral	Taken down 1570[55]
Queens' College, Cambridge	Taken down 1570[56]
Bungay, Suffolk	Taken down 1571[57]
Cratfield, Suffolk	Taken down 1576[58]
Holy Trinity, Cambridge	Sold 1577[59]
Jesus College, Cambridge	Case sold 1582[60]

At Holy Trinity, Coventry, Howe and Clynmowe's 'greytt orggonll of braus' came to a sad end: its bellows were sold in 1570 and its pipes 'weyeng eleven score & thirtene pound at iiij d. halfe farthing the pound' were sold in 1583.[61] At St Lawrence, Reading in 1578 it was agreed that the organs should be sold 'for that they shoude not be forfeited into the hands of the organ takers'.[62]

Modern scholarship suggests that the effects of the Reformation may have been rather patchy. The situation may well have been different in certain conservative parts of the country; we shall see that organ building may have survived in the south-west of England better than anywhere else.

An interesting question remains unanswered. From the evidence discussed in chapter one we can establish the existence of modest-sized organs and we know of one large instrument at Exeter; is there any further evidence from the inventories to suggest the presence of developed, larger organs in England?

There may be a hint of the appearance of two-manual instruments in England, or 'double organs' as they would be called in the seventeenth century. It is generally assumed that the two-manual organ was developed by standing two organs, one large and one small, on the same gallery and running the mechanism for the smaller organ under the organist's seat to a keyboard immediately below that of the larger instrument. In Europe the two organs thus linked were often a large Blockwerk instrument and a smaller Positive with several stops offering variety and colour. Two listings in the inventories indicate the possibility of this arrangement. At Waltham Abbey there was 'a great large payre of organs above, one in the north Quyre, and a lesser payre beneath';[63] at Canterbury Cathedral in 1585 'In the quyre a lytle paire of orgaynes & a great paire above'.[64] These are highly suggestive of double organs, but by no means conclusive. Far better evidence comes from Christ Church, Oxford, the date as early as 1546: 'a pair of organs with a turned chair to the same'.[65] Here the terminology is correct: this is a reference to a Chaire Organ (not to the organist's seat, which would have been a bench or form[66]). In view of this,

[51] Information kindly provided by Timothy Easton   [52] Freeman, 'Notes', note 2016   [53] Ibid., note 2014
[54] Ibid., note 2062   [55] G. Paget, 'The Organs of Norwich Cathedral', The Organ, 14 (1934–5), 67
[56] Freeman, 'Notes', note 931   [57] Information kindly provided by Timothy Easton
[58] Freeman, 'Notes', note 2159   [59] Ibid., note 2263   [60] Ibid., notes 935, 1922
[61] Freeman, 'Records of British Organ Builders' (First Series),15
[62] A. Freeman, 'A Short History of the Organs of the Church of St Lawrence, Reading', The Organ, 1 (1921–2),109
[63] Musical Times, 54 (1913), 791   [64] Freeman, 'Notes', note 1225   [65] Ibid., note 219

and realising that a lay observer would not necessarily perceive the distinction between two organs placed close to each other and a true double organ, it is worth reconsidering mentions of two organs in close proximity to each other. At St Osyth's Priory there was 'a grete peyr & a lyttle pare of organs in the Rodelofte':[67] in the restricted space of a loft it is actually improbable that the two instruments were separate from each other, even if small. The likelihood is that they had a common wind supply at the very least, and possibly some further mechanical link with each other. Descriptions such as that of Westminster Abbey ('ij payre of orgaynes in the quyre'[68]) or Ixworth Priory ('ij payer of old organs one lytell the other great at xx s. . . . at the alter in the Quyer'[69]) could be double organs or separate instruments. Even if separate, to have two organs, one large and the other small, operating in one liturgical space suggests the need for variety of tone or pitch in one location. As we shall see in Chapter 4 the connection of the Canterbury organ with foreign organ builders gives good evidence to suggest that this instrument was advanced, perhaps with two manuals. In 1609 Thomas Dallam was to rebuild the organ in St George's Chapel, Windsor and the agreement is for a 'greate Organ and a Chayre portative';[70] this, with its reminder of the many 'portatives' scattered through the inventories, is probably an excellent witness to how the double organ had developed by the beginning of the seventeenth century. The evidence is that in the sixteenth century the two-manual organ has either already arrived or is in development.

To extrapolate solely from the history of the Reformation in England and from the material in Edward VI's inventories emphasises the gradual decline in organ building. But even in this confused period organ building continued, whatever the pressures for reform of the instrument's use. We can trace the activities of several organ builders.

Some are known only from occasional references. Cuthbert Swynbanke repaired the organ in Chichester Cathedral in 1558.[71] John Tysdale mended the organ in Sheffield Parish Church in 1570 and tried a new or rebuilt organ at Ecclesfield in 1572.[72] Others may have been involved in the removal of organs they had maintained. Nicholas Horganmaker and his family appear in the accounts of St Michael in Bedwardine, Worcester, where the organ was sold in 1548.[73] Betts of Wethersden mended the organ at Boxford in Suffolk in 1541, and in 1548 was paid to remove it.[74] Several other builders appear in isolated references during the sixteenth century, but no definite pattern emerges.

Three groups of organ builders deserve more attention. William Beton or Bytton (there are various spellings of his surname) appears as a freeman of Kings Lynn in 1518 together with his son (1536), also William Beton, and his apprentices James Croxton (1526) and William Bull (1536).[75] Beton built new organs at Ely (undated),

[66] B. B. Edmonds, 'The Chayre Organ: an Episode', *BIOS Journal*, 4 (1980), 22–4
[67] Freeman, 'Notes', note 1323   [68] Ibid., note 1213   [69] Ibid., note 1337
[70] W. L. Sumner, 'The Organs and Organists of St. George's Chapel Windsor', *The Organ*, 45 (1965–6), 146–7
[71] *Musical Times* (1915), 84   [72] Freeman, 'Records of British Organ Builders' (First Series),42
[73] Freeman, 'Notes', note 2757   [74] Freeman, 'Records of British Organ Builders' (First Series), 38

Louth (c1531) and Christ's College, Cambridge (1532).[76] By 1537 he or his son was organ maker to Henry VIII and references to his work for the court exist until 1552, when his name appears next to that of William Treasorer (of whom more in Chapter 4).[77] Henry VIII's extensive work on the establishment and refurbishment of numerous royal residences included the provision and fitting out of their chapels, and by the mid 1520s there was an organ workshop at Bridewell Palace.[78] After the King took over Cardinal Wolsey's seat at Hampton Court in 1529, he set about rebuilding the Chapel in much the form it exists today, adding an 'organ house' in the south-east corner.[79] The Bridewell workshop built a new organ for the chapel in 1538, where it was installed by John Bytton (another son of the elder William?) and his servants.[80]

We have already encountered John Howe in association with the organ he built with John Clynmowe at Holy Trinity, Coventry in 1526. The work of the Howe family covers the period 1485–1570; the considerable extent of surviving references to their work suggests that they were the leading organ builders of their day. They are the first English builders for whom a tentative biography can be assembled, though sadly there are no technical details of the organs concerned. Andrew Freeman was the first to collect material on the Howes[81] and he suggested that there were three generations of builders, represented by John Howe, a younger John Howe and his son Thomas Howe. It is not possible to be certain which references refer to which of the John Howes, but the fact that John Heweson received the freedom of York in the 1540s suggests that from that decade on we are more likely to be dealing with the younger of the two. [82]

The older John Howe was working on the organ at the lady chapel altar in York Minster in 1485[83] and received the freedom of the city in 1489.[84] Further appearances are at St Mary at Hill, London (1500),[85] Eton College (1505–6; a new organ for which he was paid £2),[86] and St Stephen Walbrook, London (1507).[87] Howe was churchwarden at St Stephen Walbrook in 1519.[88]

After a gap of a few years it may be the younger John Howe who was in partnership with John Clynmowe at Coventry in 1526. Clynmowe was churchwarden at St Stephen Walbrook in 1534–5 and built a new organ at Eton College for £4-13-4 in 1531–2, where he was working with 'fratris eiusdem':[89] was John Howe his brother-in-law? John Howe appears on his own at St Mary Magdalen Milk Street, London (1528),[90] and in 1531 he was paid for the 'intronizacione' (voicing

---

[75] Ibid., 26   [76] Ibid.   [77] Ibid.
[78] S. Thurley, *The Royal Palaces of Tudor England* (New Haven and London), 1993
[79] Le Huray, *Music and the Reformation*, 76–7   [80] Thurley, *The Royal Palaces of Tudor England*
[81] Freeman, 'Records of British Organ Builders' (First Series), 14–18; Freeman, 'Father Howe'
[82] Letter from R. C. Hope, *Musical Times*, 30 (1889), 429
[83] Freeman, 'Records of British Organ Builders' (First Series),14
[84] Letter from R. C. Hope, *Musical Times*, 30 (1889), 429
[85] Freeman, 'Records of British Organ Builders' (First Series),14   [86] *The Etonian*, (October 1919)
[87] Freeman, 'Records of British Organ Builders' (First Series),14
[88] A. Freeman, 'A Brief Account of the Organs of the Church of St Stephen's Walbrook', *The Organ*, 1 (1921–2), 161–7   [89] *The Etonian* (October 1919)

or tuning) of the organ in the choir of York Minster, and he returned in 1536 to carry out repairs.[91] In a tuning contract of 1534 at St Andrew Hubbard, London, preserved by the chance of its having been written on a page of the church accounts, he announced himself as a member of the Skinners' Company and revealed that writing did not come easily to him:[92]

Be it kne to all men I Jhon Howe skenser of london haffe promeset ffor the tyrem of xx yere to kepe In tuene the orgens off the parres off Sent tanderos hupberds In estchep an ffor es payne to Rew. xij d. by the yere to be payde the ffurst payement at the ssumsschun off ore lade daye m v honder & xxxiiij. [Be it known to all men I John Howe Skinner of London have promised for the time of 20 years to keep in tune the organs of the Parish of Saint Andrew Hubbard, Eastcheap and for his pain to reward 12d. by the year to be paid the first payment at the Assumption of Our Lady day 1534.]

He is again referred to as a Skinner at St Stephen Walbrook in 1548, where he bought 133lb of unwanted organ pipes.[93] In 1531 the City of London noted:[94]

Forasmuche as this court is credeblye enfromed that the olde name and companye of organ makers ys nowe consumed and dyssolved, wherefore now at the speciall request of John Howe the yonger, organ maker, he ys transposed to the mistery and company of skynners.

The records of the Skinners' Company show that in 1553 his son Thomas was apprenticed to John Hallywell for the standard term of seven years.[95] This may have been an arrangement of convenience, for in 1554–6 he was signing receipts for his father at Westminster Abbey[96] and repairing the organ at St Michael Cornhill, London.[97]

The tuning contract shown above explains why there are so many references to the Howes. By arranging at many churches that he should be paid an annuity for looking after the organs, John Howe ensured that he and his son appear in the account books on a regular basis. As we shall see it also provided an income in later years when John Howe was an old man and the organs themselves had gone.

By including the references to tuning the Howes' work list includes the following:[98]

York Minster	1485, 1531, 1536
St Mary at Hill, London	1500, 1535–79
Eton College, Berkshire	1506–7 and repairs thereafter
Winchester College, Hampshire	1521
Holy Trinity, Coventry	1526
St Mary Magdalen Milk Street, London	1528–70
St Andrew Hubbard, London	1534–71

[90] *Musical Times*, 62 (September 1921) [91] Freeman, 'Records of British Organ Builders' (First Series),14
[92] *Musical Times*, 62 (September 1921) [93] Freeman, 'Records of British Organ Builders' (First Series),14
[94] C. Clutton and A. Niland, *The British Organ* (London 1963), 47 [95] *Musical Times*, 62 (September 1921)
[96] A. Freeman, 'The Organs of the Abbey Church at Westminster', *The Organ*, 2 (1922–3), 130
[97] Freeman, 'Records of British Organ Builders' (First Series), 16
[98] Ibid., 14–18, plus annotations in Freeman's own copy now in the British Organ Archive, Birmingham

St Alphege London Wall, London	1537–71
St Mary Woolnoth, London	1539–71
St Martin in the Fields, Westminster	1542–69
Bletchingley, Surrey	1545–c1552
St Benet Gracechurch Street, London	1548–70
St Michael Cornhill, London	1548–60
St Peter Cornhill, London	1548–9
All Saints, Wandsworth, Surrey	1549–65
St Saviour, Southwark near London	1550–1
St Botolph Aldersgate, London	1550–71
St Dionis Backchurch, London	1551
St Michael le Querne, London	1551–71
St Matthew Friday Street, London	1552–71
St George's Chapel, Windsor, Berkshire	1554–5
St Clement Danes, Westminster	1554–9
St Peter Westcheap, London	1556–71
Westminster Abbey	1553–71
Sheffield, Yorkshire	1560
St Mary Woolchurch Haw, London	1560–71
St Helen Bishopsgate, London	1564
St Mary, Lambeth, Surrey	1567–8
St Mary Aldermanbury, London	1570
St Andrew by the Wardrobe, London	1570–1

The younger John Howe lived 'at the sign of the Organe Pype' in the parish of St Stephen Walbrook, London, where he was churchwarden in 1535–6. His home was bought by the parish in 1551 and he rented it until his death in 1571; his widow stayed there until her death in 1585.[99] He is sometimes referred to as Father Howe or Goodman Howe. Though this may suggest that he was a priest, it is also possible that this appellation was to distinguish him from his son and in later years in appreciation of his age.

The later references confirm Father Howe's decline into poverty as the organs of London fell into disuse and were removed: 'pd to Goodman Howe orgynmaker for his yere fee being a Very poremane xijd' St Alfege London Wall 1565–6;[100] 'paide to father howe of charytie this yere ij s.' St Peter West Cheap, London 1568–9 (he was paid three shillings in 1569–70 and 1570–1);[101] 'Itm. paid to the Organmaker for his ffee ij s. (in consideracon of age)' St Andrew by the Wardrobe 1570–1;[102] 'paid to a poore man that was wont to tune the organs xij d.' St Michael le Querne 1570–1.[103]

Thomas Howe appears to have abandoned organ building early in the reign of Queen Elizabeth, as by April 1561 he was 'servante with doctor Freer Doctor in phisyck'; at this time he was examined by the Lord Mayor of London on suspicion of adhering to the Roman faith. Freer was acquainted with the then Spanish

---

[99] Freeman, 'Records of British Organ Builders' (First Series), annotations in Freeman's own copy now in the British Organ Archive   [100] Freeman, 'Father Howe'   [101] Ibid.   [102] Ibid.   [103] Ibid.

Ambassador, Bishop Aclorys.[104] That organ builders should be recusants is no surprise at all; the English Reformation had all but deprived them of their livelihood and a revival of the old faith would be seen as an obvious way of restoring their position. What is more significant is that the recusant circle in London would inevitably provide links with foreigners. These international Catholic connections would provide the Dallams with their escape to France in the troubled 1640s.

Meanwhile in the south-west of England things were proceeding slightly differently. Away from the heated arguments of Puritan-inclined London it was possible for organ building to proceed in comparative calm.

The Chappingtons of South Molton, Devon are known to have been involved in organ building from 1536 to 1620;[105] there are five members of the family known. Richard Chappington built new organs at St Olave, Exeter and Woodbury in Devon in 1536 and 1539. An unspecified Chapington was at Exeter Cathedral in 1554 (13s 4d was paid to him 'for safe custody of said organs' – perhaps indicating that he had removed and cared for the instrument during the reign of Edward VI), and at Woodbury again in 1560–1. This may have been Hugh Chappington who built new organs at St Edmund, Salisbury in 1567, St Thomas, Salisbury in 1568–9, at St Brannock, Braunton in 1569 and who worked at Sts John and George, Braunton at about the same time. An unspecified Chappington at Winchester College in 1569–70 may also have been Hugh. John Chappington seems to have succeeded Hugh, working at St Thomas, Salisbury (1571–2 and 1579–80); at Ashburton, Devon (1575–6); at Mere, Wiltshire (1580, 1584); at St Edmund, Salisbury (1587–1606); at Richmond Palace (1590–1)[106] at St Margaret Westminster (1596 and major work in 1600–1), at Magdalen College, Oxford (major work in 1597), at the Palaces of Greenwich and Whitehall (1599, with Samuel Chappington, otherwise unknown)[107] and at Winchester College in 1603–4. He died, probably in Winchester, in 1606. From his will we know that he was born in South Molton, lived latterly in Winchester, had an apprentice called William Manfielde (of whom nothing further is known), and was in dispute with his brother Ralph ('My brother Rauphe Chappington shall not have to doe with any goods I haue for he is very troublesome'), though he left the considerable sum of £20 to each of Ralph's two daughters. Ralph cared for the organs at St Thomas, St Edmund and St Martin, Salisbury and Barnstaple, Devon. His will, proved in May 1620, describes him as of Netherbury, Dorset, and indicates money owing to him from Our Lady, Salisbury; St Augustine, Bristol; Wedmore, Somerset; and Bridgewater, Somerset.[108]

No details of any Chappington organs survive, and though the organ case at Tewkesbury Abbey, formerly in Magdalen College, Oxford, was long attributed to

[104] Ibid.

[105] Accounts of the activities of the Chappington family from Freeman, 'Records of British Organ Builders' (First Series), 31–7, unless stated otherwise

[106] Public Record Office, Accounts of the Treasurer to the Chamber, PRO E351/542   [107] Ibid.

[108] Freeman, 'Records of British Organ Builders' (First Series), 36

John Chappington it is now known to be the main case of the Robert Dallam organ of c1632.[109] However, the accounts for the construction of Hugh Chappington's organ at St Edmund, Salisbury survive in full.[110] They give no details of the organ, but the purchase of 214 pounds of lead, tin and bismuth (in a proportion by weight of about 100 : 108 : 4) suggests a small ten-foot instrument. Expenditure on gold and pigments (brasell = red; byse = blue or green; synyper (cinnabar) = red) suggests a lavish scheme of decoration similar to those we know from the seventeenth century. The total cost of this instrument was £37 12s 10d; that at St Thomas cost £35 5s 6d; John Chappington's work at Magdalen College, Oxford in 1597 cost £33 13s 8d; this suggests a degree of uniformity and a possible comparison with the £30 Howe and Clynmowe organ at Coventry in 1526 – seven stops or so. The Chappingtons' influence over the south west of England over a period that includes the troubled late sixteenth century suggests their importance and also indicates that in one part of the country at least organs were able to survive the harsher Puritan strictures.

The organ case at Old Radnor, Powys, Wales may belong to the period 1500–50. I have left it until now because an understanding of the effect of the Reformation on English organ building helps in trying to date it – and this is indeed a vital question. Though it is undoubtedly the oldest English organ case surviving and though it is the only tangible evidence of early instruments (apart from the Suffolk fragments), until it can be dated with reasonable accuracy it has to be treated with a good deal of circumspection (plate 10; p. 42).

It was 'discovered' in the mid nineteenth century by Sir Henry Dryden, who brought it to the notice of Revd F. H. Sutton. Sutton published an illustrated monograph on it in 1868,[111] and supervised its renovation in 1872 (by Rattee & Kett of Cambridge, with a new organ inside by J. W. Walker & Sons.) An old soundboard and any other remains of the original instrument were unfortunately discarded at this time. It has been suggested that the organ is not quite as genuine as Sutton hoped, and therefore it is worth commenting on the question of authenticity.

The late Susi Jeans believed that the organ was introduced to the church in the early nineteenth century, felt that it was unlike early organ cases abroad and therefore suspect, and had perhaps been made up out of bits.[112] Having examined Lady Jeans's research notes carefully,[113] I believe that she started with this opinion more than twenty-five years before her views were published and that she selected all her evidence to fit the theory. In a letter to Lady Jeans the antiquarian W. H. Howes disagreed with her strongly, pointing out that Old Radnor was a collegiate church with unusually rich furnishings without equal in the area. Others have pointed out that

[109] J. Harper, 'The Dallam Organ in Magdalen College Oxford, A new account of the Milton Organ', *BIOS Journal*, 9 (1985), 51–64   [110] Freeman, 'Records of British Organ Builders' (First Series), 33–4
[111] F. H. Sutton, *Some Account of the Mediaeval Organ Case Still Standing at Old Radnor, South Wales* (London 1866)
[112] S. Jeans, 'Old Radnor', *The Organ*, 70 (1991), 118–33
[113] University of Reading, Department of Music, Jeans papers, files 49 and 50

the church was in the gift of the wealthy Mortimer family until 1502, and then in the gift of the King. It is not surprising that the organ is not mentioned until the visit of Jonathan Williams c1832: these were the very early days of antiquarian interest in church furnishings, and even then the great majority of observers would have seen a derelict organ as so much old rubbish. There is no reason at all to doubt that it has been at Old Radnor since before 1800; isolated in an inaccessible part of the country there can have been few major events touching the life of this church since the Civil War. Other early organs are known to have survived until the late eighteenth century or early 1800s, only to be lost thereafter (Wingfield,[114] Tong,[115] Uley,[116] Hesset[117]). It is relatively unlikely that an organ could have been installed here at any time after the dissolution of the college of priests in 1534, particularly as the living then passed to the new foundation of Worcester Cathedral and its days of prosperity were at an end. One would expect that neither the Marian nor Laudian revivals would have burnt with enough strength to warm such a remote spot.

In fact this instrument does bear comparison with continental examples, though the scheme of decoration is uniquely English in its combination of late gothic and early mannerist detail. The bucolic carving and certain infelicitous details of the nineteenth century restoration (the horizontal linen-fold panels are a solecism on Sutton's part) further deceive the eye: underneath this is a perfectly straightforward case. The layout of three pointed towers and two-storied flats is unexceptional; the strong rectangular framing of the upper case is crude but practical. If it lacks the grace of a gothic case like Middelburg, Koorkerk (1480) or an early mannerist one like Metz Cathedral (1537); it makes up for it in sheer enthusiasm. The dimensions of the case suggest a knowledge of harmonic proportion (the lower case is square, the upper case a golden rectangle) and the form and decoration is as rich as it is hybrid in style. In fact the comparison with Metz is a useful one: the organs are of similar size, the carving is lively but not of the very best quality, and in both cases one is very much aware of the timber framing that forms the structure of the whole. Other comparisons might be with Oosthuizen (1530) or Krewerd (1531). No two of these organs are quite the same as each other; hardly surprising in a transitional period in the decorative arts. However, all of them unite to provide a coherent back-gound against which to judge Old Radnor.

The front corresponds to a five-foot stop. In early organs it is quite normal for the layout of the front pipes to be reflected precisely by the mechanism inside, and the division into five groups, each symmetrical and with the tallest pipe in the middle, is complex and elegant. The pipes in the upper flats may have spoken (though later builders would have been more likely to leave them silent dummies),

[114] H. M. Cautley, *Suffolk Churches and their Treasures* (London 1937)
[115] Hopkins and Rimbault, *The Organ*, Part II, 9, 278; *The Gentleman's Magazine* (1789)
[116] Hopkins and Rimbault , (1877), part I, 47
[117] D. MacCulloch, 'Henry Chitting's Suffolk Collections', *in Proceedings of the Suffolk Institute of Archaeology*, 34/2 (1978), part 2, 103–28

perhaps in connection with doubled ranks. If Sutton was right in guessing the number of pipes in each bay – and he may have had some old tip-blocks to hand – then his sketch showing forty-five pipes on the lower level fits the English long compass of forty-six notes or so. Sutton claims to have found evidence of five stops, operated by iron levers at the treble end of the case; this seems wholly plausible. Sutton's additional claim that two holes below the keyboard may correspond to further stops on a second manual is more questionable. Further functions may have included toy stops, a ventil to empty the wind in case of murmurs or ciphers, or even the operation of bass Diapasons and their separate springs. So much evidence about this organ is now irrecoverable that one can offer no more hard facts, particularly on the technical side.

On the question of date, it is difficult to believe that a case with such a complex form and such rich decoration could have housed a soundboard as crude as the Wetheringsett fragment; one is therefore tempted to assume that the instrument was grander than the four organs from the early sixteenth century described in Chapter 2 (Barking, Coventry, Wetheringsett and Wingfield). Does this mean that it is later in date? Or, if we assume that the Wetheringsett organ was purchased for the £10 bequeathed by William Bradway, is Old Radnor equivalent to the £50 organ built by Duddyngton at All Hallows Barking? This is something of a problem: the size, style and richness of the instrument suggest a later date; but how could an organ have arrived at Old Radnor after the Reformation? There is no clear answer.

Other surviving cases formerly attributed to the end of the sixteenth century are now thought to be of considerably later date. This subject has been explored by Michael Gillingham; the remarks here are based on conversations between him and the author. The case now at Tewkesbury Abbey, already mentioned, has been shown to date from c1631; that at Stanford on Avon turns out to be the Chaire case from the same organ, built by Robert Dallam for Magdalen College, Oxford.[118] The Chaire case at Gloucester Cathedral is now also thought to be by Robert Dallam, dating from c1640.[119] The ex-Cambridge cases at Old Bilton, Warwickshire and Framlingham, Suffolk show some similarities in detail to each other; my feeling is that the Framlingham case originally had a tall centre tower like that at Old Bilton, and that some of the carving on the two organs is comparable. In view of the re-dating of other early cases they are unlikely to be earlier than c1630; as both instruments have connections with Thomas Thamar it may well be that they date from 1663 (Old Bilton) and 1674 (Framlingham).[120] The case at Appleby, Cumbria, once in Carlisle Cathedral, is a typical, though crude, Harris-style case of the post-Restoration period, and

[118] Harper, 'The Dallam Organ in Magdalen College Oxford'; J. Harper, 'The Origin of the Historic Organ at Stanford-on-Avon: Connections with Magdalen College Oxford and the Surviving Dallam Case at Tewkesbury Abbey', *Organ Yearbook*, 23 (1992), 37–69

[119] M. Gillingham and others, *Gloucester Cathedral Organ* (Gloucester 1971), 3–5

[120] A. Freeman, 'Records of British Organ Builders', (Second Series), in *Musical Opinion* 1922–5, paragraph 201

attempts to show that it is made from earlier material do not ring true.[121] Thus, with a discussion of Old Radnor the description of the early English organ comes to a natural break. There is no evidence of comparable quality until well into the seventeenth century.

---

[121] M. R. Holmes, 'A Tudor Organ Case at Appleby in Westmorland', *Antiquaries Journal*, 58 (1978)

CHAPTER FOUR

FOREIGN INFLUENCES
BEFORE 1600

We would know more about the early English organ if we could identify its position in the wider organ world. Evidence of contact with other countries would help show what influences might have been at work and perhaps forge links with an important period of development in European organ culture. It is not surprising that several attempts have been made to speculate on links with foreign schools.

There is barely any evidence to hand. Until now all that survived from before 1600 were two relatively uninformative contracts at Barking and Coventry, and the undated Old Radnor case with no mechanism or pipework surviving – plus the various highly enigmatic references in accounts and inventories, with occasional references to stops or springs for the basses. Only in 1993 did the soundboards from Wetheringsett and Wingfield resurface to give detail to the picture.

Despite the lack of information to hand some writers have been keen to reconstruct their idea of an early organ from the slightest and most confusing technical details, and then to link the results with other schools of organ building. The inexpert and poorly written Barking contract has given rise to unfounded explanations from E. J. Hopkins,[1] W. L. Sumner[2] and Cecil Clutton.[3] Subsequent authors, for example Caldwell,[4] have simply added a further layer of conjecture. To say that 'the phrase 'x foot or more' accounts for the acoustical fact, known from the tenth century, that an organ pipe must be slightly more than twice the length of one an octave higher' presupposes accurate detail in the contract and a technical understanding between the organ builder and the scribe who wrote the document: as described in Chapter 2, this is a garbled document and nothing in it can be taken as trustworthy technical evidence. The further claim that parts of the Barking contract 'can be understood as a reference either to a Dutch *Principael (Blockwerk)* or to an Italian *Ripieno*'[5] was never easy to justify, and is now contradicted by the evidence

---

[1] E. J. Hopkins and E. F. Rimbault, *The Organ, its History and Construction* (London 1855; 2nd edn 1870; 3rd edn 1877)

[2] W. L. Sumner, *The Organ, Its Evolution, Principles of Construction and Use* (London 1952; 2nd edn 1955; 3rd edn 1962; 4th edn 1973)   [3] C. Clutton and A. Niland, *The British Organ* (London 1963)

[4] J. Caldwell, 'The Organ in the British Isles until 1600', *Organ Yearbook*, 2 (1971), 7–12

[5] P. Williams, *A New History of the Organ* (London 1980), 132

of Wetheringsett and Wingfield. Caldwell's reconstruction of the stop-list of the Coventry organ[6] is fantasy. All we know is the key compass and that it had seven stops: we cannot expect to reconstruct whole dinosaurs from the fossil remains of one toe. Indeed the stop-lists proposed for the Wetheringsett and Wingfield organs in Chapter 2 are at best highly speculative.

Nor are there many significant clues to outside influence to be gained from terminology. Many of the words associated with the early English organ are peculiar to these instruments. The relationship between Principal (unison) and Diapason (octave lower) is without exact parallel elsewhere. The 'dowble pryncipalls' at Barking echoes the use of the word *double* in early French contracts, but the meaning seems to have been different. The Wetheringsett fragment shows simply that there may have been two separate, similar Principal stops, two ranks at the octave, and two at the superoctave (one prepared for only). In France *double du Principal* might mean a rank an octave higher than the principal, as at St Severin Bordeaux in 1514.[7] The use of *Doppelt Prinzipal* at Antwerp in 1505,[8] meaning a stop with two ranks, is closer to the English usage, but still not exactly the same. Other terms contrast strikingly with their equivalents in other languages: *stops* for shutting off the ranks, rather than *tirants* (Fr.) for pulling them on; the *song-borde* (Thomas Browne 1514) or later *soundboard* instead of *secret* or *sommier* (Fr.) or *Lade* (Ger.). The origin of the word *Chaire* for the Ruckpositif of the English organ is interesting but obscure,[9] but it does have a parallel in certain organ documents written in French: at St Michel, Bordeaux in 1510 the organ included *la cheière de devant*.[10] Another instrument suggestive of parallels with England on account of terminology and pitch is that at St Jean, Valenciennes, built by Charles Waghers of Hazebrouck in 1515.[11] As will be seen below, the suggestion of links between Franco-Flemish organ building and England makes this tentative parallel more striking.

Valenciennes, St Jean: Charles Waghers 1515

Grant Ouvriage	**La Cheyere**
(Blockwerk 10′)	Principal de quoy la grande buse aura 5 piez
	Double (2½′)
	Fluttes
	Triple Octave (1¼′)
	Cymballes

Cecil Clutton makes a speculative link with Europe,[12] but with Italy rather than the North. Noting that Henry VIII introduced Italian craftsmen to this country and that he owned Italian keyboard instruments, he suggests that there may well have

[6] J. Caldwell, 'The Pitch of Early Tudor Organ Music', *Music and Letters*, 51 (1970), 156–63
[7] F. Douglass and M. A. Vente, 'French Organ Registration in the Early 16th Century', *Musical Quarterly*, (1965), 632
[8] M. A. Vente, *Die Brabanter Orgel* (Amsterdam 1963), 32–3
[9] B. B. Edmonds, 'The Chayre Organ, an Episode', *BIOS Journal*, 4 (1980), 19–33
[10] N. Dufourcq, *Livre de l'Orgue Français*, 4 vols. (Paris 1935–), vol. I, 77ff.   [11] Vente, *Die Brabanter Orgel*, 29
[12] Clutton and Niland, *The British Organ*, 51

been Italian influence on English organ building. He wonders whether examples of English organs with wooden pipes (Durham) are connected with, for example, the Italian instrument at the Silbernenkapelle at Innsbruck. Other authors have echoed this view[13] and have additionally been seduced by the single-rank stop-lists of the early seventeenth century into suggesting a link with Italy.[14] For all this there is no hard evidence at all. The appearance of the Suffolk fragments suggests a northern technology, not a southern one, and the indications from the few bits of early case-work that survive show no link with the classic triumphal arch cases of the Italian school. Nor do we know of any Italian organ builders in England, though there are some Flemings. This speculation proved to be all the more unfortunate when, in 1990, the Robert Dallam organ at Lanvellec in Brittany was restored in a supposedly Italianate tonal style by Bartolomeo Formentelli – all in deference to these English authors' expertise.

As will appear below, there is some concrete and important evidence for links with organ building in the Low Countries. Peter Williams has mentioned this possibility, but his method is, perhaps, over-confident:

Over a century ago, E. F. Rimbault claimed that the John Roose, Brother of the Order of Preaching Friars, who 'repaired and restored the organ at the altar of the B.V.M. in the Cathedral Church of the City of York' in 1457, was 'the first English organ builder of whom we have any authentic account'. But Roose was almost certainly not English, for a builder of that family name lived in Utrecht in the sixteenth century, built the organ in the Wasserkirche, Münster in 1572 and even left registrations for it. John Roose may have been an earlier member of that family; he was probably a Dutch Dominican, placing the York organ near the BVM altar in the Dutch manner; and he certainly personifies the Dutch or Flemish influence on the English organ during the late Mediaeval period.[15]

Roose could equally be an English name; there is a place called Roos on Humberside; the Utrecht Roose appears over a century later; in any case when the English builder received the freedom of York in 1463 he appears simply as John Ross;[16] Roose did not place 'the York organ near the BVM altar' – the account shows it may have been there already. In the final sentence of the extract Williams gets from 'may' to 'probably' to 'certainly' in three moves; perhaps one should be more cautious.

Useful hard evidence for connections with the continent has long been available and has awaited careful interpretation. William Treasorer was an immigrant who came to England in about 1540[17] when he was granted the Freedom of York;[18] he lived in the parish of Christ Church Newgate Street, London from 1549. In 1552, in a reference adjacent to one concerning William Beton (see Chapter 2), he is described as regal maker to Edward VI. There may be a connection between the

[13] P. Williams, *The European Organ 1450–1850* (London 1966), 207
[14] Williams, *A New History of the Organ*, 133–4   [15] Ibid., 131   [16] *Musical Times*, 30 (1889), 429
[17] A. Freeman, 'Records of British Organ Builders' (First Series), in *The Dictionary of Organs amd Organists* (London, 1921), 38   [18] *Musical Times*, 30 (1889), 429

two makers. In 1553 he is mentioned as musical instrument maker to Mary and
Philip in a document permitting him to export large quantities of ashes and worn
shoes – a curious early example of making profit out of waste disposal; the licence
was granted in recognition of the fact:[19]

that the said William Treasorer hathe devised and gev[en] unto us a newe instrument
Musicall geving the sound of Flutes and recorders And Lykewise hathe promysed and taken
uppon him at his Laboure Costes and charge to re[pair] and amende before the Feast of
Saincte Michaell thar[changel] next ensuynge the Date hereof owre great Organes
stand[yng] in owre Chappell within our manoure of Greenewich.

Treasorer made a pair of virginals for Queen Mary in 1556.[20] He died in 1584 and
the parish register at Christ Church Newgate Street describes him as organ maker
and servant to Elizabeth I.[21]

Treasorer was joined in 1566 by Jasper Blankard, also an immigrant, who lived
in his house for a time and whose name appears until 1582.[22] Treasorer and
Blankard between them seem to have worked at Canterbury Cathedral between
1573 and 1578. Blankard received a reward of 'xx li. over and besides the bargayne
and agrement made with hym for the amending of the greate orgaynes'.[23] This is
a very large sum of money: the reward alone sufficient to buy a five-stop organ. The
organ Blankard left may be the one described in an inventory of 1585 and mentioned in Chapter 3 as a possible two-manual instrument.

There is also a connection between the Flemish Langhedul family and
England. Michael Langhedul worked at Salisbury Cathedral in 1530, when he
was paid £13 6s 8d, and he returned later in the year to work on the organ in the
Trinity Chapel.[24]

Other foreigners had appeared earlier in English organ building: William
Barbour of Brussels and Lawrence of Nijmegen settled in England in 1436;[25] one
of Henry VIII's organ makers was Michael Mercator of Venlo.[26] Other names are
suggestive: John Showt or Scute at Magdalen College, Oxford in 1529 and 1530[27]
and Edmond Schetz, a court organ builder between 1587 and 1600.[28] Perhaps the
name Lawrence Playssher, encountered as the builder of the large organ at Exeter
described in Chapter 1, is also of foreign origin.

Brussels, Venlo and Nijmegen all indicate modern Belgium and Holland as a
source of influence, confirmed by the knowledge that there was a Blancart at work
in Ghent and that the Langheduls were an influential organ building family from
Ypres. Blancart first; Vente gives the following stop-list for the organ built by Charles
Blancart for the Bavokerk, Ghent in 1569–70:[29]

[19] Freeman, 'Records of British Organ Builders' (First Series), 37   [20] Ibid., 38   [21] Ibid., 37   [22] Ibid.
[23] Ibid., 42   [24] Salisbury Cathedral MSS, Fabric Accounts 132 and 12: 15
[25] Freeman, 'Records of British Organ Builders' (First Series), 10
[26] Freeman, 'Records of British Organ Builders' (First Series), 31; Vente, *Die Brabanter Orgel*, 146
[27] Freeman, 'Records of British Organ Builders' (First Series), 31   [28] Ibid., 43
[29] Vente, *Die Brabanter Orgel*, 121–2

Ghent, Bavokerk: Charles Blancart 1569–70

Hauptwerk					Brustwerk	
Principal:		Andere Register:				
Praestant	8	Gemshorn	2		Quintadena	8
Bordun	8	Sifflöte	1		Hohlpfeife	4
Oktave	4	Kornett			Offenflöte	2
Mixture	IX–X	Trompete	8		Gemshorn	1⅓
Scharff		Schalmei	4		Krummhorn	8
					Regal (treble)	4

Compass C–a″; Manual coupler; Tremulant; Drum; Nightingale
The Hauptwerk pipework divided between two soundboards as shown above

The interpretation of the stop-list and the modern German nomenclature is
Vente's. The division of the Hauptwerk into two sections (perhaps with ventils controlling them) is the precursor of the typical Dutch divisions of Hoofdwerk and
Bovenwerk. Vente also gives a very similar specification (without the Brustwerk) for
the same church, attributing it to Aert de Smet and giving the date 1592–5.[30] This
may have been a new organ in another part of the building, a replacement, or a
rebuild or pitch-change – but see further details of organs at this church below.

If the Blancart connection is suggestive, the story of the Langheduls is more
definitive. They were a substantial family of Flemish organ builders whose work
spans the period 1481–1635. From their home town, Ypres, members of the clan
spread their influence through Flanders, worked extensively in France and also in
Spain. The nature of this influence, shared with other important Flemish builders,
is a vital component in the story of the European organ. The connections of
members of this school with northern France (for example the builder Crespin
Carlier working with Titelouze at Rouen Cathedral) and Spain (the Brebos family
at El Escorial) fundamentally affected the path of organ culture in Western
Europe.[31]

Guillames Langhedul rebuilt the organ at St Bavo, Ghent in 1590. The fact that
we meet a Langhedul following in the footsteps of a Blancart at this church suggests
we are homing in on the right area. The specification was now:[32]

[30] Ibid., 118
[31] H. Klotz, *Über die Orgelkunst der Gotik, der Renaissance und des Barock* (Kassel 1975); F. Peeters and M. A. Vente, *De Orgelkonst in de Nederlanden van de 16de tot de 18de Eeuw* (Antwerp 1971); English translation by P. Williams (Antwerp 1971); Vente, *Die Brabanter Orgel*, especially pp. 124–6; Williams, *The European Organ*, 174–6
[32] Vente, *Die Brabanter Orgel*, 126

Ghent, Bavokerk: Guillames Langhedul 1590

Hauptwerk		Rückpositiv		Récit (played from Hw keys)	
Bordun	16	Quintadena	8	Kornett	IV
Prinzipal	8	Prinzipal	4		
Hohlpfeife	8	Gedeckte Flöte	2		
Oktave	4	Gemshorn	1		
Gedeckte Flöte	4	Mixtur			
Nasat	2⅔	Scharff			
Gedeckte Querflöte	2	Krummhorn	8	**Pedal**	
Sifflöte	1			pulldowns to Hw	
Mixture					
Scharf					
Trompete	8				
Schalmei	4				
Regal	4				

Manual compass C–a″, Kornett c–a″.

Meanwhile in Paris, Jehan Langhedul built this at St Jacques de la Boucherie in 1588:[33]

Paris, St Jacques de la Boucherie: Jehan Langhedul 1588

Jeu d'orgues		Pédales	
Monstre	8	Jeu de pédales	8
Bourdon	8		
Octave	4		
Flûte à neuf trous	4		
Nasard bouché à biberons	2⅔		
Flûte traversine	2		
Flageolet	1		
Fourniture	V		
Cymbale	III		
Trompette	8		
Jeu d'enfants	8		
Petite trompette	4		
Cornet à bouquin IV–VI (from c′)			

Manual compass C, D–c‴; Pedals C,D–B

From this stop list the influence on the later French school is abundantly clear, even if some characteristic details, such as the wide tierce rank, have not yet appeared. The influence of these builders and their school on England is considerably less clear, because there is nothing to compare them with. These exciting stop-lists of instruments built by the most advanced builders may have no relevance to England at all: they are all from the late sixteenth century, by which time English organ

---

[33] Klotz, *Über die Orgelkunst*, 186

building was at a low ebb. As for earlier or smaller organs that might be more comparable, the Reformation was as disruptive to organ building in the Low Countries as it was in England, and there is a real shortage of information on organs built in the mid 1500s. It may well be that, as far as understanding the English organ is concerned, the specification of Waghers's 1515 organ at Valenciennes, given earlier in this chapter, is much more useful to us than the colourful and highly developed stop lists of the later Langhedul instruments.

An interesting technical point is that in 1605 St Jacques de la Boucherie, Paris, was visited by Matthijs Langhedul, who reported:[34]

est de besoign otter toutes les petites souppapes et lesser la grande graveure libre et faire en dessus dudict sommier des registres à lattes, lequel est une chose de longue durée et subject à peu de refection

In other words his relative Jehan had built the organ with a spring chest; Matthijs is proposing to remove the pipe pallets and rebuild the soundboard with slides as this will be more reliable. Later Matthijs was to link up with the expatriate English organist and composer John Bull at Antwerp, building a ten-stop organ of Franco-Flemish type (including Nasard, Tierce, Cornet and Trumpet) for the Cathedral in 1626–7.[35]

Michael Langhedul reappears at Kortrijk after his work in Salisbury, and later worked in Bruges, Veurne, St Winorksbergen, Nieuwpoort, Dunkirk, Ninove and Dendermonde.[36] The family renewed its acquaintance with England after the fall of Ypres in 1580. Jan Langhedul, with others from his home town, settled for a time in Norwich; he was not an organ builder.[37]

While all this makes an interesting hypothesis about the connections between organs in England in the sixteenth century and their foreign counterparts, there are few safe conclusions to be drawn. We know from the later history of Smith, Harris and Snetzler how much English insularity could modify ideas imported from abroad. Treasorer, Blankard and Langhedul may or may not have introduced the latest continental ideas to England; we cannot tell. It would be dangerous to extrapolate backwards from the organs of the early seventeenth century: in the period 1570–1600 English organ building nearly came to a halt, and when it picked up again under the Dallams the traditions may have been fragmented or broken.

Furthermore there was some two-way traffic. Builders from Britain worked overseas. Dufourcq identifies Thomas Alport from Staffordshire at work in Brittany and Guillaume Lesselier (William Leslie) from Scotland – neither known in Britain.[38] Leslie is interesting; he worked at Le Grand Andely in 1611, then at Mortain, Bernay, Mortaigne (= Mortain?), Neville, Veules, Bordeaux (1624) and Rouen (1631–41), and Dufourcq states that he died in early 1642. At Bordeaux he was working with Valeran de Héman, who came from Rouen and was married to Elisabeth Carlier, the daughter of the famous Flemish builder Crespin Carlier.[39]

[34] Peeters and Vente, *De Orgelkonst in de Nederlanden*, 19   [35] Vente, *Die Brabanter Orgel*, 126   [36] Ibid., 124
[37] Vente, *Die Brabanter Orgel*, 125; L. W. Forster, *Janus Gruter's English Years* (London 1967)
[38] Dufourcq, *Livre de l'Orgue Français*, vol. I   [39] Vente, *Die Brabanter Orgel*, 127

This suggests that links with Flemish organ building were operating in both directions. As we shall see in a later chapter there is also a faint possibility that the
descendants of the Howe family ended up building organs in France, their name
usually rendered as Haon, and an equally faint possibility of a connection with the
Dallam family. Further research may show that the Franco-Flemish connection
runs very much deeper than I have wished to suggest here.

The Wetheringsett and Wingfield soundboards are slider soundboards, not
spring chests, and the routed channels show an obvious similarity to the Blockwerk
chest of 1480 surviving at Middelburg Koorkerk, though not so neatly made.
However, there are not so very many ways that a craftsman of c1500 could make a
soundboard and the similarity may mean nothing. If we are right in identifying the
Suffolk fragments with the general type and size of organ represented in the
Barking and Coventry contracts (and in considering it broadly typical of standard,
modest-sized English organs of the period) then we must observe equally that there
is no evidence of the survival of the Blockwerk here: the Wetheringsett and
Wingfield organs had one rank per stop and no mixtures.

The occasional references to springs for basses in early English accounts may well
represent a small-scale version of the trompes familiar from other regions of
Europe, but the Wetheringsett fragment suggests a bass stop with its own slide, operating on the lowest notes of the keyboard with no separate pallets. This may be a
development from organs with a slider chest for most ranks and a kind of bolt-on
chest with its own pallets for the basses only as described in Chapter 2; however, this
is only one of many solutions. Some continental organs also had bass pipes associated with relatively small manual divisions. At Meerhout in 1519 the ruckpositif had
De Perdoenen luydende een decem verre – a Bourdon with about ten pipes only;[40] such an
arrangement may have been connected with the use of the pedals, as at Notre Dame
Antwerp in 1505, where several bass-only manual stops seem to be connected with
a set of pedals *de dutsche maniere*.[41] The appearance of separate towers for a double
Diapason stop at Exeter in 1665 is surely a late survival of what are trompes in all
but name. Here Loosemore may well have copied a feature peculiar to Exeter before
the Civil War: knowing that the Cathedral had an unusually large organ in 1513 it
is even possible that the 20′ basses survived for Loosemore to use again.

One feature of Barking, Coventry and the Wetheringsett fragment is uniquely
English: the unusually long and apparently fully chromatic compass of forty-six
notes from a C key is not found abroad. In 1617 John Bull advised on the building
of a new organ at St Jan, 's Hertogenbosch and recommended keyboards from C
to c‴ with all accidentals included, forty-nine notes. This was too revolutionary and
the plan was not adopted;[42] meanwhile in England key compass reached fifty-one
notes C–d‴ as early as the 1630s.[43]

[40] Ibid., 30   [41] Ibid., 33   [42] Ibid., 176–82
[43] J. Bunker Clark, *Transposition in Seventeenth Century English Organ Accompaniments and the Transposing Organ* (Detroit 1974), 26; R. Greening, *The Organs of Lichfield Cathedral* (Lichfield 1974), 5

This is enough to note that there is some contact of a consistent kind between English organ building and the organs and organ builders of Flanders and Northern France; hardly surprising since the journey across the English Channel was easily as safe and convenient as travel by road within England, and Calais – one of the main ports of embarkation for the area – was in English hands until 1558. What information survives from the modest-sized organs of Barking, Coventry and Wetheringsett is insufficient to speculate from, though there is every possibility that further work will add considerably to our knowledge of this question. Of England's larger organs we know virtually nothing yet, and may never know very much more. This simple fact will always make it difficult to construct theories of any real value. Yet the question of key compass shows that in one respect at least English builders were following a path of their own without continental imitators. In the next chapter, by lifting the curtain on how the English organ was used in choral accompaniment during the early seventeenth century, we may show that the instrument was already evolving in a highly idiosyncratic way.

CHAPTER FIVE

THE LAUDIAN REVIVAL
1590–1642

For musicologists the riches of the Chapel Royal in the age of Tallis and Byrd have seemed a glorious phase in English church music. However, the status of the Chapel Royal is peculiar; by the end of the sixteenth century music in the cathedrals and collegiate churches was at a low ebb and the evidence from the parish churches is that organs and whatever music went with them had gone.

Of the few instruments that may have survived and been put back into use we have a full description of only one. At St Mary Woolnoth an organ that appears to have stood in the church until the Fire of London in 1666 shows every sign of being already very old, though the nineteenth-century manuscript in which it is described attributes it to the seventeenth-century builder Robert Dallam. The manuscript includes a drawing of the organ, taken in turn from 'a rough print' of 1676 (now lost).[1] This shows a curious asymmetrical design with no upper casework; if the drawing is remotely accurate then the organ must surely be very old or archaic. A stop-list is given, seemingly transcribed from an old document, and though this source is unverifiable, one can take the instrument as being an oblique confirmation of some of the assumptions made about the Tudor organ in Chapter 2:

London, St Mary Woolnoth: anon., undated

Organ containeinge five stoppes of 44 pipes each

Item	One Open Diapason	
"	One Stopp Diapason	these in wood
"	One Flute	
"	One Principall*	
"	One Small Principall	these in tynn
	Two Bellows	

* some to stand in sight

---

[1] W. H. Essex, MSS booklet, 'S. Mary Woolnough.–The Organ–by Robert Dallams & Father Smith' (1881), now in the possession of M. Gillingham Esq., to whom I am grateful for this information.

Plate 12   The main case of the organ of c1632 built by Robert Dallam for Magdalen College, Oxford, now in Tewkesbury Abbey, Gloucestershire (photograph c1942). The case has been painted black and the front pipes gilded (probably at the end of the eighteenth century). Despite the seventeenth-century date, the case is clearly in a line of descent from that at Old Radnor. The vestiges of gothic form survive, though here the arrangement of towers and flats is more complex and sophisticated, and the mouldings have taken on a renaissance feel. The carvings in the pipeshades are archaic, using a repertoire of beasts and foliage that stretches back to the romanesque and earlier. The elaborate embossing of the front pipes (taken from two 10′ Open Diapason stops), formed by rubbing the pipe metal in a channelled mould while it is still in sheet form, is of a type peculiar to England. The pipes left unembossed were originally decorated in gold and colours. A few Dallam pipes survive inside the organ, though considerably altered.

Despite this example and a handful of others, disuse and removal seems to be the general rule. In the 1640s the parishioners of St Michael Crooked Lane, London were being pressed to restore the use of the organ by Sir John Lambe on behalf of the High Commission Court; their petition reveals poignantly the circumstances in which the organ had fallen into dereliction:[2]

St. Michael, Crooked-Lane: The reasons why Inhabitants and Parishionrs. are not able to sett up the Organs againe and the time since they were taken downe.

That the organs were never used in the church since Queen Maries dayes and when the roodlofte which was the place where they stood was taken downe they were also sett aside.

That they are soe old rotten and decayed that noe workeman can repaire them, there is only 37 old pipes worth 9d a pound and all the rest not worth anything.

That whereas the inhabitants heretofore have bin marchants, stockfishmongers and men of great estates, now for the most parte they are poore handycrafte tradesmen and not able to maintaine a paire of orgens.

There was never noe land nor any maintenance given in our Parishe for that use as wee understande Sr. John Lambe was informed.

That consideringe that our Ordinary & necessary general collections such as must of necessity be collected as the shipp money, and for the maintenance of the poore and visited houses have been of late more than we are well able to bare wee humbly desire Sr. John Lambe not to put us to this charge but to dismisse the court of this business that wee may be no further troubled.

Their plea encompasses everything we know about the sixteenth century: religious uncertainty, dismantling of church fittings, the ending of patronage for the furnishing of parish churches, and the decline of wealth in a period of savage inflation. Add to this information the fact that stipends for clergy and musicians remained unaltered despite massive rises in the cost of living and the picture is complete.

At the end of Queen Elizabeth's reign efforts were made to restore the prestige of the clergy and to confirm the assumptions of the Elizabethan settlement. Debate between radical Puritans and more traditionalist Anglicans continued; at the accession of James I in 1603 the state of the church was again in question, and there was pressure for further reform (the Millenary petition). A conference was held at Hampton Court in 1604 at which Anglicans and Puritans could air their views; in the event James came down strongly against the Puritans. Richard Bancroft, James's first Archbishop of Canterbury, continued the work of reconstruction, and influential opinion began to turn more in favour of cathedral music. Through the early seventeenth century the high church movement grew, reintroducing relatively elaborate musical performance as part of divine service and encouraging the building of organs. The content of the revival was derived from practices in the Chapel Royal, where high churchmen held sway with the support of the King. There William Laud was Dean from 1626 to 1633, after which he became Archbishop of

---

[2] A. Freeman, 'The Organs of the Church of St Magnus the Martyr London Bridge', *The Organ*, 5, (1925–6), 7

Canterbury. The accelerating revival of high church ritual and furnishings in the 1630s and 1640s bears his name.

For the craft of organ building the change in fortunes was evident, for even if the parish churches remained largely without organs, work for the cathedrals and colleges kept organ builders fully occupied; moreover the instruments built were of unparalleled richness. In this period of opportunity one organ builder rose quickly to pre-eminence and founded a dynasty of craftsmen whose distant great-grand-apprentices are still at work today: Thomas Dallam.

The family is named after the hamlet of Dallam in Lancashire, now part of Warrington. Thomas was born at nearby Flixton in 1575.[3] There is evidence to show that the Dallams (and later their in-laws, the Harrises) were recusant Catholics,[4] and several suggestions that the family was of noble lineage.[5] Nothing is known of how Thomas Dallam learnt the craft of organ building, but in 1599 he springs to our notice as the hero of a notable adventure.[6]

Here is a great and curious present going to the great Turk which no doubt wilbe much talked of, and be very scandalous among other nations specially the Germans.

The present, sent by Queen Elizabeth to Sultan Mehmet III (but paid for by the Levant Company), was a combined clock and organ; the organ was operated either by a barrel mechanism set in operation by the clock, or from its own keyboard. It also sported an array of complex automata and mechanical toys, described in Dallam's own words later.

Dallam, sent to Constantinople with the organ, wrote a remarkable diary of his journey,[7] and it is from this that we know he was the maker. We learn a good deal about Dallam: fluent in prose, modest, sharp-witted and good-humoured, he is on several occasions able to turn difficult situations to his own account and still has time to entertain his fellow travellers on a pair of virginals bought specially for the trip. Any such journey would have been eventful four hundred years ago; Dallam's is no exception. He weathers 'a marvalus greate storme' in the Channel, encounters a squadron of seven pirate ships, is unexpectedly interrogated by the King of Algiers, enjoys the hospitable ceremonies traditional in Greece at Easter, narrowly escapes arrest in Rhodes and marvels at the remains of Troy before he finally arrives at his destination. His ability to describe the various wonders he meets is quite remarkable: in a thunderstorm he sees lightning 'lyke a verrie hote iron taken out of a smythe's forge, sometimes in liknes of a roninge worme, another time lyke a horsshow, and agine lyke a lege and a foute'. When the organ is unpacked it proves to be damaged and mildewed, and Dallam and his assistants spend ten days on

---

[3] G. Sumner, 'The Origins of the Dallams in Lancashire', *BIOS Journal*, 8 (1984), 51–7

[4] B. B. Edmonds, 'The Dallam Family', *BIOS Journal*, 3 (1979),137–9; Sumner , 'The Origins of the Dallams in Lancashire'; S. Bicknell, letter to the editor, *BIOS Journal*, 9 (1985), 102–3

[5] M. H. Sefton, G. Sumner, letters to the editor, *BIOS Journal*, 8 (1984), 128–9

[6] Queen Elizabeth's State Papers, letter dated 31.1.1598/9, quoted in S. Mayes, *An Organ for the Sultan* (London 1956), 19   [7] British Museum, Add. MS 17480

repairs before moving it to the Seraglio and re-erecting it. Dallam describes the ceremony at which the organ is presented to the Sultan; at the appointed hour the clockwork sets the instrument going:

All being quiett, and no noyes at all, the presente began to salute the Grand Sinyor; for when I left it I did alow a quarter of an hour for his coming thether. Firste the clocke strouke 22; than The chime of 16 bels went of, and played a songe of 4 partes. That beinge done, tow personagis which stood upon to corners of the seconde storie, houldinge tow silver trumpetes in there handes, did lift them to their heades, and sounded a tantarra. Than the muzicke went of, and the orgon played a song of 5 partes twyse over. In the tope of the orgon, being 16 foute hie, did stande a holly bushe full of blacke birds and thrushis, which at the end of the musick did singe and shake their wynges. Divers other motions thare was which the Grand Sinyor wondered at.

Seeing the keyboard move as the organ sounded, the Sultan asked if any man present could play it. Sure enough, the nervous Dallam was ushered into his presence, and 'stoude thar playinge suche thinge as I coulde'.

Dallam's diary leaves us completely in the dark about the organ itself or about his work as its builder; we would know nothing more if it was not for the fact that a contemporary description of what is clearly the same instrument (or at least a proposal for it) surfaced in 1860.[8] Though the account of the movements set off by the clock is different from Dallam's description of the finished instrument, this document notes that it is to cost £550 (the large price accounted for by the unusual complexity of the mechanism and elaborate decoration in silver and gold) and gives us the earliest surviving specification of an English organ (spelling and punctuation probably of 1860).

There shall be placed in the lower part of the instrument three several strong, forcible and artificial bellows, with a very strong, sufficient motion of wheels and pinions, very well wrought, and sufficient to drive and move the bellows at all times from time to time, for the space of six hours together, whensoever the wheels and pinions shall be applied to such purpose; and that there shall be contained within the said instrument a board called a sound-board, with certain instruments or engines called his barrels and keys, and five [sic] whole stops of pipes, viz. one open principal, unison recorder, octavo principal, and a flute, besides a shaking stop, a drum and a nightingale.

Presumably the stops may be interpreted as two unisons (principal, recorder) and two octaves (octavo principal, flute), though the flute may possibly have been at unison pitch also. The 'shaking stop' is a tremulant, the nightingale is a small organ pipe mounted upside down in a bowl of water, where it would twitter convincingly.

In the years immediately after his return to England Thomas Dallam took on the most prestigious organ building projects in the country. It is natural to suppose that the success of the organ for the Sultan and Dallam's personal triumph considerably enhanced his reputation, but one is left asking how his connection was established so quickly in the early years of his career, especially after a period in which organ building had been in serious decline.

---

[8] *Illustrated London News* (20 October 1860); the original is now lost.

In 1605–6 Dallam built a new organ for King's College, Cambridge, for which complete accounts survive.[9] The cost of the instrument was about £370: even allowing for the cost of living having doubled in the period 1550–1600 this is organ building on a scale we have only encountered before at Exeter in 1513. We do not know the specification of the organ, but the accounts give us other information.

The organ had Great and Chaire cases, decorated with the King's arms, the arms of King's College and Eton College and other embellishments. The carvings and the front pipes of both cases were extensively decorated with colours and gold, some of the pipes also being embossed in moulds. This elaborate decoration of front pipes is uniquely English, neither the extent of the painting nor the richness of the embossing being found anywhere else. Something of the effect obtained can be gauged in the surviving material at Stanford-on-Avon (Robert Dallam c1632 for Magdalen College, Oxford).

A plan made by John Smythson between 1605 and 1615 shows that the organ at King's was in the centre of the third bay from the east end of the chapel, not on the screen, and would therefore have needed only one front, facing west.[10] Evidence from the accounts suggests that the main case standing on the screen today is not that of 1605–6 as has often been stated: the main case of the Dallam instrument, made by the joiners Chapman and Hartop, had a 'middle tower', 'round towars' and 'finishing or square towars'. If this is taken at face value then there are five towers – a design quite different from that which we see today, and perhaps more comparable to that at Tewkesbury Abbey, built by Robert Dallam c1632.

There are hardly any clues about the instrument itself, beyond the purchase of 16 cwt (815 kg) of tin, 6 cwt (305 kg) of lead and 22 lbs (10 kg) of bismuth for the metal pipes, wainscot (i.e. oak) for the wooden pipes, ebony and boxwood for the keys and flannel cloth to lay underneath them, 'brasse for the shaking stoppe' (presumably a spring for Dallam's version of the *tremblant doux* or tremulant), miscellaneous materials – wire, leather, glue – typical of organ building then and now, as well as, of course, large quantities of timber for both organ and case.

More significant is that the organ was too large to be built in a workshop and transported; it was built entirely on site. Dallam and his men stayed in Cambridge from 22 June 1605 to 7 August 1606, a total of fifty-eight weeks: there was expenditure on lodgings, hire of bedding, washing, and food. Four hundredweight (204 kg) of tools were transported from London. Benches were made on site, preparations were made for the casting of pipe metal (on fustian cloth covered with chalk), and even mandrels turned from poplar on which to form the pipes. When finished, the larger pipes were laid on mats in the vestry. Dallam and his men (we do not know how many) received wages of 30s per week to be divided between them, rather than constructing the organ to a contract price.

Back in London, Dallam worked at Westminster Abbey with George Pendleton

[9] E. J. Hopkins and E. F. Rimbault, *The Organ, its History and Construction*, 3rd edn (London 1877), part I, 64–7
[10] Royal Institute of British Architects: d'Ewes Coke Collection

in 1606–7[11] and succeeded the Chappingtons in the care of organs in the royal palaces in or before 1607.[12] He was retained by Robert Cecil, Earl of Salisbury for the care of his musical instruments from 1607;[13] Cecil had been Queen Elizabeth's Secretary of State and this connection may have been a fruitful outcome of the Turkish adventure. There followed a new organ for Norwich Cathedral in 1608–9; again the accounts for the building of this instrument survive.[14] The organ seems slightly smaller than that at King's, costing £340-4-7 (this sum probably includes the organ, its case, and the loft on which it stands). Again it was built on site: the toolkit, this time weighing 500lbs (227 kg), made another journey out of London together with Dallam and his man. Again the wages were 30s per week, and again the work took him just over a year to complete. Arriving in early June 1608, Dallam was casting metal in July, and in August the Chaire case was ready for gilding. The main case followed, and was ready for gilding in April the following year. One page of the accounts is missing, but there are still payments for 1244 lbs (565 kg) of tin, 204 lbs (93 kg) of lead and 18 lbs (8 kg) of bismuth, again suggesting a slightly smaller organ than King's. Unfortunately there are even fewer clues as to the organ's appearance or specification than in the Cambridge accounts.

Dallam's next major work, immediately following his return from Norwich, was the extensive reworking of the organs at St George's Chapel, Windsor in 1609–10.[15] Here it is the agreement which survives. The main organ 'Consistinge of a greate Organ and a Chayre portative' is to be enlarged, incorporating pipes from the organ then in the choir. In the Chaire Organ he is to add the 'Open octave in the forpart of the organ now in the quier' and the wooden recorder from the same source; in the Great Organ he is to add the 'open principal stop of five foote pipe' from the Choir Organ 'And also to place in the backe of the saide greate Organ one open stop of tynne pipes of tenne foote pipe called an open diapason the same to be newlie made and cast'. From the enlargements to casework needed it seems that the Great Organ did not have a 10′ open stop until Dallam's rebuild. The keys of the Great and Chaire Organs are described separately, and the soundboard of the Chaire is to be altered 'to such a convenient length and breadth as maye need but one paire of stickers': it is possible that the key action for the Chaire Organ did not run under the player's seat and that he was obliged to turn round to play it.

Robert Cecil employed Dallam again during the construction of his magnificent new house at Hatfield in 1611, 'setting up and perfecting the great wind instrument', for which he received £53.[16] This exceptional organ is worthy of further attention because of its astronomical cost and because the organ case surviving at

[11] *Musical Times*, 48 (1907), 370
[12] Public Record Office: Accounts of the Treasurer to the Chamber, PRO E351/543 f.178r
[13] Salisbury Family Papers and supplements 2; 2nd supplement FP 1/55, Bills 14, and subsequent entries
[14] B. Matthews, 'Thomas Dallam at Norwich Cathedral', *BIOS Journal*, 10 (1986), 102–11
[15] W. L. Sumner, 'The Organs and Organists of St. George's Chapel, Windsor', *The Organ*, 45 (1965–6), 145–56
[16] Salisbury Family Papers and supplements 4/117a; accounts 160/1

Plate 13   The organ in Hatfield House, the mansion built by Robert Cecil, Earl of Salisbury, in the second decade of the seventeenth century (photograph c1910). The organ, installed in 1611, is ascribed to one John Haan (from the Netherlands or Germany), but Thomas Dallam was involved in its erection and subsequent maintenance. The case is of some opulence, and compares interestingly with the Compenius organ of c1609 in Frederiksborg Castle, Denmark. The case now houses a later organ.

Hatfield House today appears to be from this instrument. But the builder is not necessarily Dallam himself: in 1609 the family papers refer to 'Haan a dutchman',[17] who provides a portative organ for £35 and the 'great wind instrument' for the huge sum of £1,084-6-8.[18] Such expense is almost completely inexplicable; not until the nineteenth century do we regularly find organs worth thousands of pounds rather than mere hundreds. Yet the organ case that survives is small, similar in size and form to that at Nettlecombe Court in Somerset, for an instrument built by John Loosemore in 1665 for only £100.[19] The design and decorative detail are hardly comparable to anything that survives on the continent today (except perhaps for the Compenius organ at Frederiksborg Castle, Denmark), and Haan is a name otherwise unknown. Even the fact that the organ was 'garnished with silver' does not fully account for its cost. One possibility – an unsubstantiated guess only – is that Cecil obtained for himself an automatic clockwork organ, having been suitably impressed by that sent to the Sultan. One of the decorative artists at work at Hatfield House was Rowland Buckett, who had travelled to Constantinople with Dallam.[20] Could Haan have been the engineer and Dallam the organ builder, collaborating here on a second such instrument? Is the surviving case essentially that of an English organ?

Dallam's next major instrument, built at Worcester Cathedral in 1613, is central to our understanding of the English organ. It is the first large instrument of which details survive, confirmed in two separate sources. Its association with the composer Thomas Tomkins adds further important authentic information. The Worcester organ is indeed the basis for our understanding of how the English organ was used and how to solve the riddle of its pitch. Habington's *Survey of Worcestershire* describes its outward appearance:[21]

At the west and highest ascent into the quire is mounted alofte a most fair and excellent organ adorned with imperiall crowns, red roses, including the white flowredeluses, pomgrenades, being all Royall badges. Towards the topp are towe stars, with the one, W. Parry, Episcopus; with the other, A. Lake, Decanus; and written aboute the Organ, By the meditation and mediation of Thomas Tomkins, Organist heere unto the Righte Reverend Bishop and venerable Deane, who gaue theise munificent guiftes and invited their fryndes by the industry of the said Thomas Tomkins.

The final account for the organ in the Cathedral library gives technical detail.[22]

ANNO DOM 1613

All the materialls and workmanship of the new double organs in the Cathedrall Church of Worcester to Thomas Dallam organ maker came to	211 00 0
The Case and Joyners' worke about the loft to Robert Kettle	64 14 8
The floore and loft in Carpenters' work about	13 00 0
The guilding and painting to William Peacy	77 8 0

[17] Ibid., accounts 160/1   [18] Ibid., accounts 9/5   [19] Hopkins and Rimbault, *The Organ*, part I, 63
[20] E. Croft Murray, *Decorative Painting in England 1537–1837*, 2 vols. (London 1962), 1970
[21] C. Beswick, *The Organs of Worcester Cathedral* (Worcester 1967), 5–6   [22] Ibid., 6

The particulars of the great organ

Two open diapasons of metall CC fa ut a pipe 10 foot long
Two principals of metall
Two Smal principals or 15ths of metal
One twelfth of metal
One recorder of mettal, a stopt pipe

In the Chaire Organ

One principal of mettal
One diapason of wood
One flute of wood
One Small principal of fifteenth of mettal
One two and twentieth of mettal

[inserted in a later hand:] July 2nd 1666, Add in ye new organ An open Diapason
of wood leaveing out nine of ye Bases.

For painting the Escutchions about the loft to Jo: David of Worcester

11 00 00
381 2 8

From these few details we can see that organ pitch is described as 'CC fa ut a pipe
10 foot long' for the Diapason (therefore five foot for the Principal). But the question
as to which of these is nominally the unison rank of the organ has now shifted
somewhat. The Small Principals, sounding an octave above the Principals, are
referred to also as 'fifteenths', i.e. two octaves from the Diapasons. The quint-
sounding Twelfth is also counted from the Diapason, as is the Two-and-twentieth
in the Chaire Organ. Note also the unequivocal appearance of Flute and
Recorder in metal and wood respectively, both presumably sounding five-foot pitch.
   We have already noted in Chapter 2 that a pipe five foot long played by a C key
sounds a note far removed from modern C. A letter from Thomas Tomkins's
brother Nathaniel to John Sayer, dated May 1665, gives a further description of
Dallam's Worcester organ and its pitch:[23]

The great Organ wch was built at Worcr consisted of 2 open diapasons of pure and massy
mettall double F fa ut (of the quire pitch & according to Guido Aretines scale (or as some
term it double C fa ut according to ye keys & musiks) an open pipe of ten foot long. ye diameter 7 inches & an half. (at St. Pauls Lond. ye diameter was 8 inches).

Tomkins goes on to confirm the specification given above, states that the Chaire
Organ Flute was indeed unison with the Principal, says that the Two-and-twentieth
was also called 'squeelers', and adds that Thomas Dallam built an organ with the
same stops at St John's College, Oxford shortly after.
   A further and initially confusing piece of evidence concerning pitch appears in
a copy of Thomas Tomkins's *Musica Deo Sacra* of 1668:[24]

---

[23]   Oxford, Bodleian Library, Add. C 304a, fol.141
[24]   T. Tomkins, *Musica Deo Sacra* (Worcester 1668), amongst the errata of the copy formerly at St Michael's College
    Tenbury

[f] sit tonus fistulae apertae longitudine duorum pedum et semissis; sive 30 digitorum geo-
metricorum.

(f is the tone of a pipe of two feet and a half; or 30 inches in length)

There are two related pitch standards in use here.[25] The organ keyboard ('keys and
musiks') starts at C, but this is in fact the same note as Choir pitch F. The organ is
thus a transposing instrument, exactly as the modern clarinet or French horn, and
organ accompaniments of choral works at this period show the appropriate transposition at work. The five-foot principal of the organ is regarded as the unison stop,
its range of about four octaves from F (keyboard C) being exactly that covered by
the human voice. The accompanist can use registration based on the principal (or
flute), with its octave (the small principal or fifteenth) and superoctave (the two-and-
twentieth); or the accompaniment can double the voices an octave lower by adding
the diapasons. It is quite possible that free use was made of the two manuals to vary
the emphasis of texture and pitch in the accompaniment. Note finally that the
Choir pitch remains rather sharp by modern standards, and the note F sung by the
Choir (the organist's C) would sound somewhere between modern G and G♯.

Even if the practicalities of this arrangement seem complex, it is clear that transposition was taken for granted, at least as far as church organs were concerned.
Domestic organs may well have been at untransposed pitch: evidence is scarce. The
arrangement of certain two-manual harpsichords, such as those by Ruckers with
the two manuals pitched a fourth apart, is a further indication of the once widespread use of transposition, and a similar argument has been made in other fields,
for example in the cornett parts of Monteverdi's Vespers of 1610.[26] Sixteenth-
century organs on the continent were sometimes in C pitch or F pitch, and various
types are described by Schlick.[27] The English transposing organ may be a late survival of a type once much more common.

The indication of a close link between the constructional details of the organ and
its use in choral accompaniment is perhaps much more important than the more
academic question of pitch. By understanding that the five-foot principal of the
early English organ has an exact parallel with the range of the human voice, by
observing the close relationship between the organs built during the Laudian revival
and the nature of choral liturgy, and by casting our minds back to the few details of
English organs from earlier periods, we may reasonably be led to the conclusion
that the entire development of the instrument in the British Isles is linked to its role

---

[25] The evidence for the relationship between organ pitch and choir pitch in seventeenth-century England has been
assembled slowly over a number of years. Some examples are: J. Steele, 'English Organs and Organ Music from
1500 to 1650' (Ph.D. dissertation, University of Cambridge 1958) P. Le Huray, *Music and the Reformation in England
1549–1660* (London 1967); J. Bunker Clark, *Transposition in Seventeenth Century English Organ Accompaniments and the
Transposing Organ* (Detroit 1974). Three short articles giving the same information from slightly different points
of view are: D. Gwynn, 'Organ Pitch in Seventeenth Century England', *BIOS Journal*, 9 (1985), 65; S. Bicknell,
'The Transposing Organ', *BIOS Journal*, 9 (1985), 79; (P. Le Huray, 'Organ Pitch and Organ Accompaniments
in Elizabethan and Jacobean Church Music', *BIOS Journal*, 16 (1992), 8.
[26] A. Parrott, 'Transposition in Monteverdi's Vespers of 1610: an "aberration" defended', *Early Music*, 12 (1984),
490–516   [27] A. Schlick, *Spiegel der Orgelmacher und Organisten* (Speyer 1511)

in accompanying a choir or being used in dialogue with singers. Though the solo use of the organ is by no means precluded, an assumption of its intimate connection with singing and liturgy is as much a key to understanding the instrument as it is with, say, the Italian organ. The position of the organ as a complement to the choir, rather than as a principal or solo instrument, may also help explain why English organs remained small compared to some of their continental cousins. Despite the abandonment of the transposing system at the end of the seventeenth century, the position of the English organ as an accessory in choral music remains influential at every period to the present day.

Thomas Dallam's work continued with an organ for Eton College Chapel in 1613–14, of which the stop-list was:[28]

Eton College Chapel: Thomas Dallam 1613–14

1   a diapason of Tynn fyve foote longe stopped
2   a principall of Tynn, a open stop fyve foote longe
3   a fflute unison to the principall fyve foote long of Tynn
4   an octavo to the principall of Tynne
5   a ffyftenth of Tynne

Note that in the absence of a ten-foot Open Diapason the Fifteenth (no. 5) is probably two octaves above the Principal, where at Worcester it was one octave above. The instrument cost £117-1-6.

Thomas Dallam's other known major works are as follows: in 1616 he built a new double (i.e. two-manual) organ for the chapel at the Palace of Holyroodhouse, Edinburgh for £300 (probably exclusive of decoration). This was in conjunction with a complete refitting of the chapel by Inigo Jones. In 1620 a new organ was built at Wells Cathedral for £398-1-5 (including decoration),[29] another for All Saints, Wakefield,[30] and in 1621–22 an instrument for Durham Cathedral.[31] At Bristol in 1629 Thomas Dallam built 'the greate Double Organ and Chaire Organ' for £258-2-7 (here exclusive of decoration?), and a further £5 was 'given unto him his sonne and his servants for their most honest paines and their Charges from London to Bristoll and back againe'.[32] The son is probably Robert; we do not hear of Thomas again by name, and he may have died at about this time.

The next Dallam organ of which details survive, that at Magdalen College, Oxford built in c1631, is currently attributed to Robert.[33] Though no contract exists, nor accounts for its construction, the instrument itself survives in part. The larger Great Organ section of the double case is now at Tewkesbury Abbey, Gloucestershire, resplendent with its original front pipes and a handful of inside

---

[28] *Etoniana*, October 1919
[29] R. Bowers, L. S. Colchester and A. Crossland, *The Organs and Organists of Wells Cathedral* (Wells 1979), 3
[30] A. Freeman, 'The Organs of Exeter Cathedral', *The Organ*, 6 (1926–7), 90
[31] R. Hird and J. Lancelot, *Durham Cathedral Organs* (Durham 1991), 10
[32] A. Freeman, 'The Organs of Bristol Cathedral', *The Organ*, 2 (1922–3), 65–73
[33] J. Harper, 'The Dallam Organ in Magdalen College Oxford', *BIOS Journal* 9, (1985), 51–64

Plate 14   The chaire case of the organ of c1632 built by Robert Dallam for Magdalen College, Oxford, now in St Nicholas, Stanford-on-Avon, Northamptonshire. In its original home, on the north side of the Magdalen chapel, it would have stood in front of the case now at Tewkesbury at floor level (a 'double organ'). Moved to Standford-on-Avon at the beginning of the eighteenth century, it was raised on a new base section and provided with a screen of dummy wooden pipes to hide the player. The front pipes, part of a 5′ Principal stop, retain their original embossing and polychrome decoration. The Dallam soundboard survives, though altered. The organ has not been playable in modern times, and the façade is all that remains of the Dallam pipework.

pipes. The smaller case of the Chaire Organ, with what appears to be a Dallam soundboard, is at Stanford-on-Avon, Northamptonshire,[34] where it was rebuilt in the eighteenth century as a one-manual instrument. It is now derelict; it retains the original front pipes but is empty inside. At Tewkesbury the case has been painted black and the front pipes (many of them embossed) are now gilded; at Stanford the

[34] J. Harper, 'The Origin of the Historic Organ at Stanford-on-Avon: Connections with Magdalen College Oxford and the surviving Dallam Case at Tewkesbury Abbey', *Organ Yearbook*, 23 (1992), 37–69

oak case retains signs of paint and some pipes are magnificently decorated with gold and colours, the embossed pipes are left in natural polished tin. At the first sight of these fragments one is immediately aware of being in the presence of craftsmanship of the richest possible quality.

For the specification of this organ we are indebted to Renatus Harris, who recorded the stops in 1686 as part of his proposal for rebuilding it. He found:[35]

Oxford, Magdalen College Chapel: attributed to Robert Dallam c1631. Stop-list recorded by Renatus Harris in 1686

On the Great Organ:
two Diapasons
two Principals
two Fifteenths
two Two-and-twentieths

On the Chaire Organ:
one Stopped Diapason
two Principals
one Recorder
one Fifteenth

Harris confirms that the Recorder was at unison pitch. In an agreement with Harris dated 1690[36] it is stated that the pitch of the organ is 'Gamut in Dsolre'. This indicates the transposing arrangement: when the organ key Gamut (G) is played, the sound that emerges in Choir pitch is Dsolre (D). Harris's connection with the organ was first made in 1672; according to a note in the college registers he stated that it was originally made by his grandfather. The details of the Dallam/Harris family tree are not entirely certain, but the weight of evidence is that Harris's father Thomas had married Robert Dallam's daughter, and therefore that Robert, not Thomas, was the original builder.[37]

From the surviving material it is possible to gain important insights into Dallam's style. At Magdalen the organ stood on the north side of the chapel, built partly into an 'organ house' made specially to receive it.[38] It had one front only, and the presence of two Open Diapasons on the Great (parts of both survive at Tewkesbury) is not to be explained by the organ standing on a screen with both front and back façades. The surviving pipes are beautifully made. The rich tin metal is hard enough to have survived for three hundred years, but must have been extremely ductile to have withstood the amount of working required to form the extremely elaborate decorative embosses. These were probably formed by pressing the metal into a channelled wooden mould; such moulds appear in the accounts for the

[35] Hopkins and Rimbault, *The Organ*, part I, 122   [36] Ibid., part I, 122
[37] M. Cocheril, 'The Dallams in Brittany', *BIOS Journal*, 6 (1982), 63–77; B. Matthews, 'The Dallams and the Harrises', *BIOS Journal*, 8 (1984), 58–68; S. Bicknell: letter to the editor, *BIOS Journal*, 9, 102–3
[38] Harper, 'The Dallam Organ of Magdalen College Oxford'

Thomas Dallam organ at King's, Cambridge. The mouths of the front pipes are formed by scoring and pressing, not by soldering in separate leaves as practised on larger display pipes in France; they are made in several different decorative shapes. Inside pipes are made in the same way as front pipes, with tin feet and bodies (contrasting with lead feet and tin bodies for inside pipes in France, or hammered lead inside pipes in parts of northern Europe) and scored bayleaf pattern mouths for even the smallest surviving pipes. The soundboard at Stanford-on-Avon is conventional in construction, the grid of bars and channels being made up as a frame, rather than being routed out of solid material as at Wetheringsett. There are fifty-three channels, though Harris records a compass of fifty notes at the time of his rebuild in 1690. The original compass may have been fifty-one notes, C–d‴, as seems to have been provided by Robert Dallam at Lichfield Cathedral in 1640.[39] The order of the pipes on the soundboard follows the arrangement of the front pipes in the case.

The overall appearance of the cases, with towers linked by single-storey flats, is reminiscent of some renaissance cases in France. The detail is mannerist, and both the extent and quality of carved decoration is especially rich. The actual subject matter of the carving is both distinctive and archaic: though the animals climbing up the pipe shades of the larger towers include elements derived from contemporary patterns and have something of the feeling of strap-work, they also echo a noble lineage of mythical beasts that harks back to the romanesque and even to the carving in Norwegian stave churches. The finished result is a surprising combination of new craftsmanship and old iconography, in some ways very conservative for its date.

As far as the sound of the organ is concerned we must be cautious. The pipes at Tewkesbury have been radically revoiced. Those at Stanford are more original, despite various changes of pitch and position, but are so few in number as to make firm conclusions impossible. Of those pipes that survive there is nothing exceptional about scale or construction, apart perhaps from the fact that there is no trace of the large foot-holes and ultra-narrow flues that have been used in the twentieth century to create 'baroque' effects, and to observe the mouths are not cut up as high as might be the case in the Netherlands at the same time. At Tewkesbury there is evidence that the duplicate ranks were made to slightly different scales, but this does not necessarily indicate a desire for them to sound different from each other so much as to avoid the fault of 'sympathy': two pipes of identical pitch, scale and treatment are likely to put each other off speech. The feeling amongst organ builders who have examined the pipes, notably Martin Goetze and Dominic Gwynn, inclines towards a gentle sound, warm but possibly quite sibilant, on a wind pressure of between 50mm and 60mm.[40] The absence of mixture or reed stops or of developed choruses of flutes leaves the organ with only those ranks and pitches that sound most

[39] R. Greening, *The Organs of Lichfield Cathedral* (Lichfield 1974), 5
[40] G. Gwynn, 'Voicing Developments in the 18th Century English Organ', *The Organbuilder*, 4 (1986), 24–8

'vocal', and would have emphasised an overall impression of rich, restrained tone rather than power or brilliance.

The tonal character of these organs is obliquely confirmed by *A relation of a Short Survey of Twenty-six Counties* , a diary of travels around England made by *A Captain, a Lieutenant and an Ancient* in 1634, and by the Lieutenant (named Hammond) on his own in 1635.[41] At Hereford they heard 'a most sweet organ, and voyces of all parts, tenor, counter tenor, treble and base'; at Durham they were 'wrapt with the sweet sound and richnesse of a fayre organ'; at Winchester Hammond found that 'The Organs in this Church are not exceeding faire, nor rich, but sweet & tunable, and sweetly played on, by one of the rarest organists that this land affords' (Thomas Holmes). Interestingly, at Exeter the party found 'a delicate, rich and lofty organ which has more additions than any other, as faire pipes of an extraordinary length and of the bigness of a man's thigh, which with their viols and other sweet instruments, the tunable voices and the rare organist together make a melodious and heavenly harmony, able to ravish the hearer's ears'. The Exeter organ's unusually large pipes may well have survived from the Playssher organ of 1513, and were an unusual feature of this instrument until the nineteenth century. Thomas Dallam was in Exeter in the 1620s, but we do not know what work he did there.[42]

At York Minster the party of tourists 'saw and heard a faire, large, high organ, newly built, richly gilt, carv'd and painted'. It had been completed only that year. Robert Dallam 'citizen and blacksmith of London' contracted to build the instrument on 21 March 1632/3.[43]

York Minster: Robert Dallam 1632–4. Stop-list as given in contract

. . . The names and number of the stoppes or setts of pipes for the said great organ, to be new made; every stopp containeinge fiftie one pipes; the said great organ containing eight stoppes.

Imprimis two open diapasons of tynn, to stand in sight, many of them		
to be chased [embossed]	lxxx	li
Item one diapason stopp of wood	x	li
Item two principals of tynn	xxiiij	li
Itm one twelft to the diapason	viij	li
Itm one small principall of tynn	vi	li
Itm one recorder unison to the said principall	vi	li
Itm one two and twentieth	v	li
Itm the great sound-board with conveyances, windchestes, carryages and		
conduites of lead	xl	li
Itm the rowler board, carriages and keyes	xx	li

---

[41] British Library, Lansdowne MSS 213, ff. 317–48
[42] B. Matthews, *The Organs and Organists of Exeter Cathedral* (Exeter 1974), 2
[43] York Minster, Fabric Roll E1/135.

Plate 15   A painting of the interior of York Minster, showing the choir seen from the east (John Harwood, 1827). The organ on the screen stands in the case presumably made for the Robert Dallam organ of 1634 and eventually destroyed in a fire in 1829. The organ originally stood on the north side of the choir, being moved to the screen only in 1688.

The names and number of stoppes of pipes for the chaire organ, every
  stopp containeinge fifty one pipes, the said chaire organ containeinge
  five stoppes.

Imprimis one diapason of wood	x	li
Itm one principal of tynn, to stand in sight, many of them to be chased	xii	li
Itm one flute of wood	viij	li
Itm one small principall of tynn	v	li
Itm one recorder of tynn, unison to the voice	viij	li
Itm the sound bord, windchest, drawinge stoppes, conveyances, and conduits	xxx	li
Itm the rowler board, carriages, and keys	x	li
Itm the three bellowes with winde trunks, and iron workes and other things thereto	x	li
Sume total	cclxxxxvii	li

The Great Organ Recorder and Chaire Flute should be understood as unison (i.e.
5′) stops. The Chaire Recorder, 'unison to the voice' may be at 5′ pitch also, though
it is just possible that it was an isolated stop tuned to Choir pitch. Dallam's contract
mentions neither case nor building frame, and separate accounts show that Dallam
was paid £307 and work about the organ came to a further £302-7-9.[44] These
accounts indicate that the construction of the organ took exactly a year, as at
Cambridge and Norwich.

Two smaller organs in Cambridge followed. For that in Jesus College, built in
1634–5, Dallam received £200, plus £12 'pro Peds. etc.'[45] This latter reference is
highly enigmatic; it is possible to take it as a reference to pedal keys, in which case
they are the first and for a long time the only set recorded in the British Isles. At St
John's College in 1635–6 Dallam built an organ for £185 with the following stops
of forty-nine pipes each:[46]

Cambridge, St John's College Chapel: Robert Dallam 1635–6

one diapason most part to stand in sight
one Principall of Tynne
one Recorder of Wood
one small Principall of Tynne
one two and twentieth of Tynne

We know of two further cathedral organs by Robert Dallam. That at Lichfield, built
in 1639–40, cost £315. Here Dallam was to build the case and decorate it, and he
also took the old organ in part exchange. The specification was to be:[47]

[44] M. Sayer, 'Robert Dallam's Organ in York Minster, 1634', *BIOS Journal*, 1 (1977), 60–68
[45] A. Freeman, 'Records of British Organ Builders' (First Series), in *The Dictionary of Organs and Organists* (London 1921), 55   [46] N. J. Thistlethwaite, *The Organs of Cambridge* (Oxford 1983), 84
[47] Lichfield Cathedral MSS, P1

Lichfield Cathedral: Robert Dallam 1639–40

[Great Organ]
2 open diapasons of Tynn
two principalls of Tynn
one twelfe of Tynn
one smal principall
& one two & twentie

& for the Chayre organ
one principall of Tynn chased
one Stopped diapason of wood
one flute of wood to singe to
one smal principall of . . .
& one 22tie

& that evrie one of the said stopps shall have and containe 51 pipes a piece.

Again the presence of the 'flute of wood to singe to' suggests the possibility of one rank tuned to Choir pitch, not Organ pitch.

The last major project undertaken by Robert Dallam before the Civil War was the building of a new organ for Gloucester Cathedral. No description survives, but we know that it was built in consultation with Thomas Tomkins, the organist at Worcester, who approved it in 1641.[48] The beautiful Chaire case surviving today is now assumed to be from the Dallam organ. The design is slightly more advanced than at Magdalen ten years earlier, especially in the elegant curve of the flats. The joinery is of similar impeccable quality. The lone large centre pipe in a tower of its own is an interesting feature. The 5′ bottom note would have stood in one of the side towers; from the fact that some English music requires a low AA (which in chamber organs was provided by omitting C♯ and using the spare key to sound AA) we can guess that this pipe sounded AA at organ pitch (D in choir pitch).

From this extensive list of activity and further instances of repairs and tunings up and down the country it is clear how much Thomas and Robert Dallam commanded the craft in the British Isles. However, they were not completely alone. John Burward worked at Dulwich College in 1618–20, adding 'a dyapason stop' in 1619, and the following year 'mending ye bellowes & tuning ye orgaine & making ye Conveighaunce for ye starrs turning'. He also worked at Westminster Abbey (c1625), built a new organ for Belvoir Castle, Rutland, carried out repairs at St Edmund, Salisbury in 1633–4, moved the organ at Salisbury Cathedral and added a Chaire Organ in 1635, and rebuilt the organ at Winchester College in 1637–8. One further specification survives, of an organ built by him for Sir Thomas Middleton of Chirk Castle in Denbighshire in 1631. The agreement states a price of £150, describes a case with five towers and four flats and promises to place . . .[49]

---

[48] M. Gillingham, R. Downes, H. and J. Norman and B. Frith: *Gloucester Cathedral Organ* (Gloucester 1971), 1
[49] Freeman, 'Records of British Organ Builders' (First Series), 51, plus annotations in Freeman's own copy now in the British Organ Archive, Birmingham.

Plate 16   The double case of the organ in Gloucester Cathedral. The small chaire case was probably built
by Robert Dallam in 1641. A new organ and main case were built by Dallam's son-in-law Thomas Harris
in 1663–6 after the loss of the original instrument in the Civil War. Harris's main case and a quantity of
seventeenth-century pipework survive, the latter much altered. The organ originally stood on the north side of
the choir and was moved to its present position on the screen in 1718. Dallam's chaire case is finely detailed
and exquisitely made, though still somewhat archaic in style. The largest pipe in the side towers is 5′ C (organ
pitch), equivalent to F (choir pitch). The large centre pipe may have played AA in organ pitch (D choir pitch).
The cases were restored in 1970–1.

Chirk Castle, Denbighshire: John Burward 1631

. . . within the case of the foresaid Organ two settes of keyes and two sound boordes and tenne stoppes all of good metall pipes namelie to the upper sett of keyes to be fitted,

one stopt diapason
one open diapason from gamut upwards
one principall for the fore front paynted and guilded workmanlike
and inwardlie a Recorder
a small principall
a fifteenth
and a two and twentieth:

for the lower sett of keyes three more of metall
one diapason
a principall
and a small principall,

and that the said Organ shall have three bellowes with two sound boordes, conveyaunces, Conduittes, Ironworke and all other thinges fitting for such an Organ well and workman-like wrought and performed . . .

Here the sequence of pitches on the Great Organ is interesting: the presence in turn of Diapason, Principal, Small Principal, Fifteenth, and Twenty-second suggests that the last rank is indeed four octaves higher than the first. Or is this an instance where the Small Principal is small in scale, not small meaning an octave higher?

Other builders are known by name; some, such as William Hathaway,[50] Samuel and John Loosemore (active in Devon and possibly connected with the Chappington family),[51] and John and Robert Hayward of Bath,[52] will reappear later. However, Burward's Chirk Castle organ and the various instruments by the Dallams are the only sources for stop-lists. Of the instruments themselves, the Chaire case at Gloucester and the scattered remains of the Magdalen College, Oxford organ are all that has survived to this day, apart from a handful of chamber organs that can be discussed separately. This poor rate of survival is due to the looming Civil War and Commonwealth of 1642–60.

As the political situation deteriorated it must have become clear to the Dallams that their position as organ builders, as Catholics and as members of the court circle, was no longer tenable under Parliamentary rule. They left for Brittany; we will follow their activities in France in the next chapter. The English builder William Deacons, who settled in Utrecht and built an organ at Goes in 1641–4, may also have been an exile.[53]

[50] A. Freeman, 'The Organs and Organists of St. Martin's in the Fields, London', *The Organ*, 1 (1921–2), 1–19
[51] Freeman, 'Records of British Organ Builders' (First Series), 58–61
[52] Freeman, 'Records of British Organ Builders' (First Series), 57–8, plus annotations in Freeman's own copy now in the British Organ Archive, Birmingham.
[53] F. Peeters and M. A. Vente; *De Orgelkonst in de Nederlanden van de 16de tot de 18de Eeuw* (Antwerp 1971); English translation by P. Williams (Antwerp 1971), 144

In 1644 came the Lords and Commons Ordnance:

for the speedy demolishing of all organs, images and all matters of superstitious monuments
in all Cathedrals, and Collegiate or Parish-Churches and Chapels, throughout the kingdom
of England and the Dominion of Wales, the better to accomplish the blessed reformation
so happily begun and to remove offences and things illegal in the worship of God.

Organs either fell into disuse, or were hurriedly (and probably inexpertly) taken
down, or were enthusiastically destroyed by Parliamentary troops on their progress
through the country. At Salisbury Cathedral, in 1643, the Dean and Chapter anticipated dangers to come and 'deemed it prudent, in order to save the organ from
destruction and in the hope of better times, to have it taken down and the material safely preserved'.[54] At Rochester in 1642 Parliamentary troops began to break
up the furnishings in the choir; they threatened to return and tackle the organ next,
but it was quickly dismantled before any damage could be done.[55] At Durham in
1641 Scottish soldiers began to vandalise the organ before being stopped by one of
their leaders. The Cathedral staff moved in and removed the pipes at night to
prevent any further damage being done.[56] Other instruments did not escape. At
Exeter:[57]

they brake down the organs, and taking two or three hundred pipes with them in a most
scorneful and contemptuous manner, went up and downe the streets piping with them; and
meeting with some of the Choristers of the Church, whose surplices they had stolne before,
and imployed them to base servill offices, scoffingly told them 'Boyes, we have spoyled your
trade, you must go and sing hot pudding pyes'.

[54] B. Matthews, *The Organs and Organists of Salisbury Cathedral* (Salisbury 1972), 5
[55] P. Hale, *The Organs of Rochester Cathedral* (Rochester 1989), 6
[56] Hird and Lancelot, *Durham Cathedral Organs*, 10
[57] Mercurius Rusticus, *the Country's Complaint recounting the Sad Events of this Unparalleld Warr* (London 1647)

CHAPTER SIX

———

INTERLUDE – THE DALLAMS IN FRANCE 1642–1700

At the start of the Civil War, with Charles I's court removed from London to Oxford and the Puritan element in Parliament on the ascendant, Robert Dallam left England with his mother, his wife, and six children, for Morlaix in Brittany. Evidence assembled from various quarters suggests that the children were Thomas (later known as Thomas Dallam Sieur de la Tour or Thomas de la Tour Dallam), Katherine, Ralph, George, Mary and Cécile.[1] The flight from England must have been unpleasant; the arrival in France was tragic, for Cécile died in 1642, followed by her mother in 1643. It is also assumed that the party included, or was shortly joined by, one Thomas Harrisson. Harrisson, the son of Lancelot Harrisson, a mercer from Egton in Yorkshire, had been apprenticed to Thomas Dallam in 1627;[2] he married Robert Dallam's daughter Katherine, possibly during the family's exile in France. A Francis Harrison had worked at York Minster during the construction of Dallam's organ in 1633–4[3] and may be linked.

   Some explanation of this account of the family tree is needed as it contradicts earlier versions. For the names of Robert's children and the connection between the Dallams and the Harrissons evidence is incomplete, but the facts seem to be as follows. Thomas Dallam de la Tour was the eldest son, and is referred to as such in records relating to the building of the organ at St Jean-du-Doigt in 1652. The entry for Cécile's death in Morlaix in 1642 states that she was an infant, so we assume that she was the youngest. Ralph and George are known as organ builders in their own right in England after the Civil War; a letter of introduction from one Philip Timber recommending Robert Dallam to the authorities at New College, Oxford in 1661 states:[4]

---

[1] Information on the activities of the Dallam family in France has been collected by various authors, especially: G. Servières, *La Décoration Artistique des Buffets d'Orgues*, Paris and Brussels 1928; N. Dufourcq, *Livre de l'Orgue Français*, 4 vols. (Paris 1935–); H. Stubington, 'The Dallams in Brittany', *The Organ*, 19 (1939–40) and 42 (1962–3). The account given here is based on the research of, and on conversations with, Michel Cocheril. See M. Cocheril, 'The Dallams in Brittany', *BIOS Journal*, 6 (1982), 63–77.
[2] Guildhall Library, London, MS 2882–1, Blacksmith's Court Minute Book 1625–33
[3] M. Sayer, 'Robert Dallam's Organ in York Minster 1634', *BIOS Journal*, 1 (1977), 60–8
[4] A. Freeman, 'The Organs of New College Oxford', *The Organ*, 9 (1929–30), 149–56

Plate 17 The organ in Quimper Cathedral, Brittany, built by Robert Dallam in 1643–8. Dallam's case, here housing an organ larger than any he had built in England, is still mannerist in feeling, and very old-fashioned compared to the latest French designs. The illusion of receding perspective is a favourite conceit of seventeenth-century English design, perhaps related to stage-set design or even, it has been suggested, to the symbolism of freemasonry.

he is at this time imployed in the making of Windsor organ, but he hath two sonnes very excellent in the same faculty whom he can leave to finish that worke that he may waite upon you whensoever you shall be pleased to send for him.

One suggestion has been that the two sons are Thomas and Toussaint Dallam, but in fact Thomas de la Tour was still at work in France at this time, and Toussaint is his son, not Robert's. Ralph and George are the only two who fit this section of the puzzle. That they are indeed Thomas's younger brothers and the sons of Robert is confirmed by Ralph Dallam's will, which names his brothers and sisters: Thomas, Katherine, George and Mary.[5] Of Mary we know nothing, except that she appears as a witness to a christening in St-Pol-de-Léon in 1658. That Katherine married Thomas Harrisson is known from the registers recording the births of five children during their stay in Brittany. Another child, Réné (later Anglicised as Renatus) was born c1652, but we do not know where.[6] This relationship is obliquely confirmed in a letter concerning Thomas Harris(son)'s proposals of 1665 at Worcester Cathedral in which it is stated that he was 'Old Dallow's servant and married his daughter'.[7] Old Dallow here refers to Robert Dallam, recently deceased, to distinguish him from the younger Dallams, Ralph and George. Even though we know that Thomas Harrisson was originally apprenticed to Thomas Dallam in 1627 (see above), as the latter died soon afterwards the greater part of Harrisson's eight year apprenticeship would have been served under Robert.

It was not long before the Dallams found employment in their new home. In 1643 Robert Dallam was engaged to build three new organs for Quimper Cathedral at a cost of 5,300 livres – the biggest contract of his life.

Questions immediately spring to mind. Through what influence did Dallam secure profitable work for himself and his family immediately on his arrival in France? Once he had started work, how did he learn to build organs in the French style, radically different from that to which he was accustomed? The answers to these questions are vital, for the influence the family had on its return to England in the 1660s, laden with new French recipes, affects the entire future of English organ building.

Contacts with the English Catholics in exile explain much. Robert Dallam arrived at Morlaix with a letter of recommendation written in Latin by Richard Smith, the English Bishop of Chalcedony.[8] This is our source for the presence of his wife, mother and children; it also refers to Dallam's ancient and noble family, and to the entire family's adherence to the Catholic faith.

The choice of Brittany is interesting. Sharing a common Celtic past with Cornwall, it had close connections with the south-west of England. The journey across the English Channel was probably easier than the respective road journeys to Paris or London. Brittany was indeed isolated from the rest of France, and had

---

[5] B. Matthews, 'The Dallams and the Harrises', *BIOS Journal*, 8 (1984), 61. Matthews is under the misapprehension, shared with earlier writers, that Ralph and George are the sons of Thomas not of Robert.
[6] Cocheril, 'The Dallams in Brittany'   [7] Oxford, Bodleian Library, Tanner MSS 45, f. 19
[8] Archives Départementales Finistère 150 G 149

allied itself with Henry V of England during his campaigns to establish his claim to the French throne, only later submitting to direct rule from Paris. English organ builders had worked in Brittany before: John Bourne had worked at Quimper in 1610 and built an organ at Roscoff in 1613; Thomas Alport appeared briefly in the 1640s,[9] and there is a long-standing tradition that the magnificent case at St Brieuc is of English manufacture. Furthermore, the lonely and wind-swept peninsula of Finistère had begun to enjoy a period of relative prosperity, and the opportunities for organ building were good.

The last organ builder to work in the area before the Dallams arrived was Pierre Tribolé. His surviving case at Lannion suggests a lively awareness of the latest styles and probably contact with Paris. When the Dallams arrived they built in a much more old-fashioned manner. Robert Dallam's contract for a large one manual organ at the Priory of Lesneven, dated 16 August 1654, gives a stop-list that departs radically from everything that Dallam had done before.[10]

Lesneven Priory: Robert Dallam 1654–5

le 1er qui fera parement de 8 pieds d'etain	8
le 2me un cornet de 5 tuyaux sur touches	V
le 3me un bourdon de 4 pieds, unisson du parement	8
le 4me un prestant de 4 pieds ouverts	4
le 5me une flûte de 2 pieds bouché, unison du prestant	4
le 6me un nazard	$2^{2}/_{3}$
le 7me une doublette	2
le 8me une quart de nazard	2
le 9me une tierce du quart	$1^{3}/_{5}$
le 10me une petite quinte, octave du nazard	$1^{1}/_{3}$
le 11me un flageolett	1
le 12me une fourniture de 3 tuyaux sur touches	III
le 13me une symballe de 2 tuyaux sur touches	II
le 14me une trompette	8
le 15me une voix humaine coupée	8
le 16me un bigearre	?
le 17me un petit cromorne	8

Le tout au grand clavier, tant en haut qu'en bas avec 3 soufflets de 4 pieds et demi de long et 2 pieds de large chacun.

First, the 8′ pitch of the first stop ('parement', normally called Montre in French, denoting the pipes on show in the case) indicates that the 10′ and 5′ standards of the English transposing organ have been forgotten for the time being. Secondly, the chorus of principals (known in France as the Plein Jeu) includes not just octave (Prestant 4′) and superoctave (Doublette 2′), but also mixtures: the Fourniture with three pipes per note, and the high-pitched 'Symballe' (normally Cymbale) with two.

[9] Dufourcq, *Livre de l'Orgue Français*, vol. I
[10] Transcribed from contract in Archives Départementales Finistère by M. Cocheril

In addition a sequence of stopped flutes and wide-scale open stops made up a Cornet décomposé. The Bourdon 8′ and Flûte 4′ were stopped (the lengths given in the contract are actual lengths, not nominal speaking lengths), and we know from surviving Dallam stops in Brittany that these were metal ranks, sometimes fitted with chimneys or made as characteristic French flûtes à biberon in the shape of a baby's bottle. They were not wooden stops as might have been the case in England. The Nazard 2⅔′ (fifth sounding), Quarte de nazard 2′ (superoctave), Tierce 1⅗′ (third sounding), Petit quinte 1⅓′ (sometimes called Larigot; an octave above the Nazard), and Flageolett 1′ (one octave higher than the quarte) were all broad-scale open ranks (except, perhaps, for stopped basses in the Nazard). They provided a wide range of variety and colour, including the jeu de tierce. The reeds, Trompette, Voix Humaine and Cromorne gave a further range of sounds completely unknown in England. There is also a Cornet: a compound stop of five ranks operating on the treble keys only and usually conveyed by tubes to a block standing above the soundboard, sounding 8′, 4′, 2⅔′, 2′ and 1⅗′ pitches with no breaks. Added to the Trompette (and perhaps the Bourdon to fill out the tone and cover irregularities in the reed stop) it was used for the Grand Jeu.

Though the registrations indicated here are given the names familiar from later periods, there is no doubt that their use is taken for granted in a specification of this type. The narrow channels in a seventeenth-century soundboard would hardly have provided enough wind for seventeen stops to be played at once: their subdivision into characteristic groups of four or five stops is a matter of necessity as well as a means of categorising different varieties of colour. Finally, there is the Bigearre; unique to the Dallam organs of Brittany. This stop is a complete mystery: in this specification, where the stops seem to be mentioned in the order they appear on the soundboard, it stands amongst the reeds. In another contract it is shown as having two ranks, playing from the treble keys only, and is listed among the high-pitched fluework. M. Cocheril has suggested that the Bigearre may have been a Piffaro or undulating stop;[11] my feeling is that a Sesquialtera (2⅔′ + 1⅗′) is more likely. The name Bigearre (also Bijarre, Bisare) is of uncertain meaning, and may be of Breton derivation: could it be an imitation of a local instrument? Despite there being no hard evidence as to what it was, it certainly adds another exotic colour to the recipe.

The Lesneven organ, exhibiting on one very fully developed manual characteristics that are common to all the Breton organs by the Dallams and their followers, is characteristic of French organ building in the early seventeenth century, though it is by no means as up to date as the latest Parisian examples. The most illuminating fact to bear in mind is that this style is derived in a direct and clear line of evolution from the very school of Flemish builders with whom links were postulated in Chapter 4. The forerunners of the Lesneven organ were being built by the Langheduls and Carliers in Flanders and Normandy only two generations before. Does Dallam's French style mark a renewal of links with this school, after a period of independent activity?

---

[11] Cocheril, 'The Dallams in Brittany'

Plate 18   The organ at Lanvellec in Brittany, built by Robert Dallam in 1653 for the nearby village of Plestin-les-Grèves, moved here in 1860, and recently returned to working order by Bartolomeo Formentelli. For a small parish church Dallam has provided a simplified flat version of his favoured perspective front, revealing a structure directly descended from the gothic and by now very much out of date. The organ inside the case seems typical of provincial French practice in the first half of the seventeenth century, and owes almost nothing to Dallam's English background. A near-identical organ was built by Dallam in the same year for St Jean du Doigt, Brittany and survived until it was destroyed by fire in 1955.

Before attempting to answer this question, we need to remark further on the archaic nature of the Dallam organs in France. Some of the larger instruments are built in cases with a characteristic design imitating a colonnade viewed in receding perspective, notably those at Quimper Cathedral (Robert Dallam 1643–8), St Pol-de-Léon (Robert Dallam and Thomas Dallam de la Tour 1658–60), and St Thegonnec (Jacques Mascard 1670, in imitation of the Dallams). This is a mannerist device on a grand scale, rather démodé in a country where classicism was in the ascendant. There is something theatrical about the use of such a bold *trompe-l'œil* device: since in court circles in London it was Inigo Jones who had a hand both in theatre design and architecture, and who had refitted the Chapel Royal at the Palace of Holyroodhouse, Edinburgh, where Thomas Dallam built an organ in 1616, it is tempting to suggest Jones as the inspiration behind this design, which also appears in several English organs. Amongst the smaller organs, that at Roscoff, built by Thomas Harrisson in 1649–50, is eccentric and bucolic, with three outsize pipes displayed as peculiar one-pipe round towers; its design may owe something to a previous instrument. Something similar survives in a much-altered organ at nearby Lampaul-Guimiliau; Harrisson may have been involved here too. At St Jean-du-Doigt and Plestin-les-Grèves, Robert Dallam built twin organs in 1652 and 1653; the former was burnt in 1955, the latter survives at Lanvellec. These two cases are an extraordinary throwback to the gothic. Their flat fronts, channelled stiles, and simplistic carving are about a hundred years out of date; their construction, similar to that of a half-timbered house and complete with overhanging jetties with drop-finials decorating the ends of the upper posts, is no less archaic (the overhang itself is common enough, but the arrangement of posts and rails behind the skin of decorative carving and mouldings is truly mediaeval in spirit).

When hunting for links between these instruments and other work in France, the appearance of an instrument of the same type at St Lizier in the foothills of the Pyrenees (Ariège) is something of a shock. However, its similarities in design, construction and appearance to the Dallam organ now at Lanvellec are so striking as to lead one on a path of conjecture that begins to suggest answers to the questions surrounding the Dallams' experience in France.[12]

Searching for a likely builder for the anonymous and undated St Lizier organ, and perhaps with an ear open for rumours of English influence, one is immediately attracted by the name and reputation of Jean Haon. According to Dufourcq he was English.[13] He worked at Bordeaux Cathedral in 1656, where in 1624 the Scotsman William Leslie had collaborated with Valeran de Héman, the son-in-law of the illustrious Crespin Carlier. Haon's organ at Moissac, built in 1677, though larger than that at St Lizier, exhibits many related features in its case design, and again presents a curiously archaic character, as though born many years out of its time. Did Haon build St Lizier? Or did one of the Dallams travel to the far south west of France?

[12] Comparison between Lanvellec and St Lizier based on author's examination of both instruments.
[13] Dufourcq, *Livre de l'Orgue Français*, vol. III, part 2, 16

Plate 19   The organ in the cathedral of St Lizier, Ariège, France. The maker of this instrument has not been identified; it is thought to date from c1650 and has now been restored. The appearance of this instrument strongly suggests a link of some kind with the Dallam family, even though it stands at the opposite end of France from the seat of their activities in the Finistère region of Brittany. The remote possibility of a connection between the Dallams and the Haon family is discussed in the text.

In examining the latter question, it is worth knowing that of the three sons of Robert Dallam, only one is recorded as an organ builder in Brittany; this is Thomas, later known as Thomas Dallam, Sieur de la Tour (indicating aspirations to minor nobility). Of Ralph and George we hear nothing until they reappear in England in the 1660s: were they working elsewhere in France?

It will be appreciated immediately that in trying to track down the sources of influence on the Dallams' French period, the links given here are becoming increasingly tenuous and speculative. In pushing the theory one step further one is stretching credibility to the limit, but the possibilities that open up are too intriguing – and entertaining – to be ignored. M. Cocheril first mentioned to me the possibility that the name Haon is in fact a French corruption of the English Howe, and went on to wonder whether members of the Howe family (also recusant Catholics, it will be remembered) had escaped to Europe around 1570 and had been employed in organ building in Flanders or France over the next two or three generations. Is this in fact an indication that the Dallams were able to pick up expertise and perhaps staff from a circle of English organ builders already working in exile? Is the presence of John Bourne and Thomas Alport in Brittany a further suggestion of well-established links between England and parts of France? Cocheril has found one marriage certificate in Brittany between a member of the Dallam family and a Haon, but both individuals are otherwise unknown to us. One French author has even suggested that the iconography of the decoration on Robert Dallam's organs shows that he was a freemason, perhaps with specific links to the exiled English court at Fontainebleau. Until further evidence emerges to prove or disprove the links, we can only ponder and speculate on the idea that the Dallams' work in Brittany picks up a long standing connection between organ builders in England and north-western Europe.

Whatever the truth of the matter, the work of the Dallams was prolific. Robert Dallam built the organs at Quimper, St Jean-du-Doigt, Plestin-les-Grèves and Lesneven already mentioned, and collaborated with his son Thomas Dallam de la Tour on the instrument for the Cathedral at St Pol-de-Léon, where the spectacular receding perspective case survives.

Invited to advise at Roscoff, Robert recommended his son-in-law Thomas Harrisson, who built the organ in 1649–50. The extensive accounts for this instrument exist, though there is no original specification.[14] They reveal a method of working no different from Thomas Dallam at King's College, Cambridge and Norwich Cathedral. The organ is built entirely on site from materials paid for directly by the church. In this unusually complete record it is possible to follow the construction of the instrument step by step. After the contract had been signed, Harrisson and others made expeditions to buy materials and choose timber. A room was rented for use as a workshop. The building of the organ proceeded on an ad hoc basis, further expeditions being made to procure unusual items: saffron to yellow the keys, and special crimson cloth to lay underneath them. The pipes of the montre were the last to be made, probably scaled to fit the openings in the case. Last minute alterations were made to stop the weights of the clock in the tower behind the organ from hitting the bellows as they descend. Harrisson also built organs at Brelévenez (1654–6) and Notre-Dame du Mûr, Morlaix (1656–61).[15] He was

[14] Ibid., vol. I   [15] Cocheril, 'The Dallams in Brittany'

Plate 20 The organ at Guimiliau, Brittany, built by Thomas Dallam de la Tour c1677 and now restored (this photograph 1937). Thomas Dallam, working on his own after the return of his father and brothers to England in 1660, has moved away from the designs favoured by Robert Dallam, preferring something more obviously French, though still archaic. The prow shape of the centre towers is characteristic of Thomas Dallam's cases.

wealthy enough to buy property, and his estate at Nec'hoat can still be seen from the motorway viaduct that crosses the estuary just north of Morlaix.

With the restoration of the monarchy in 1660 Robert Dallam and his sons Ralph and George return to England, where we will follow them in the next chapter. Thomas Harrisson followed in 1661.

Thomas Dallam de la Tour remained to carry on a career fertile in every sense. He lived until the 1720s, married four times, and had twenty children that we know by name. Among them Toussaint and Marc-Antoine are known as organ builders, the latter (Mark Anthony Dallam) in England: his case at Whitchurch, Shropshire (1715) survives, and he died in York in 1730.[16] Thomas Dallam de la Tour was also a landowner (hence the somewhat pretentious title); his house at Plougastel-Daoulas is still standing. He built new organs at Daoulas (1667–9), Locronan (1671–2), Ergué-Gaberic (1680), Sizun (1683–4), Pleyben (1688–92), Brest, St Sauveur (1694–6), Landernau, St Houardon (1690-4), Rumengol (undated), Morlaix, St Melaine (undated), Ploujean (undated), Guimiliau (undated) and Guipavas (undated). The organ at Daoulas Abbey was highly regarded.[17]

Daoulas Abbey: Thomas Dallam de la Tour 1667–9

Compass C–c′′′, 49 notes

Grand orgue		Positif	
Montre (low 5 stopped)	16	Montre	8
Montre	8	Bourdon	8
Bourdon	8	Prestant	4
Prestant	4	Nasard	2⅔
Bourdon	4	Doublette	2
Nasard	2⅔	Tierce	1⅗
Doublette	2	Fourniture	III
Quarte	2	Cymbale	II
Tierce	1⅗	Cromorne	8
Larigot	1⅓		
Flageolet	1		
Bigearre	II		
Fourniture	IV		
Cymbale	III		
Trompette	8		
Voix Humaine	8		
Clairon	4		
Cornet	V		

The stop-list is still somewhat provincial: the Bourdon 4, Flageolet 1 and Bigearre distinguish it from the latest Parisian developments, for example the work of the

---

[16] B. Matthews, 'The Dallams and the Harrises', 61; B.B. Edmonds, 'Yorkshire Organ Builders, The Earlier Years', *BIOS Journal*, 9 (1985), 42–50   [17] Cocheril, 'The Dallams in Brittany'

facteur du Roi, Thierry, who was beginning to move on to something a little more sophisticated.

Of the Dallam oeuvre in Brittany more material survives than in the whole of Britain, though mostly in the form of spectacular polychrome cases and handfuls of battered pipework. However, several Dallam organs have been restored. Those at Lanvellec, Ploujean and Ergué-Gaberic are regarded by most English visitors as reflecting the taste and style of their restorers more than that of the Dallams, but that at Guimiliau, an instrument with a very chequered history recently reconstructed by Guillémin, is reputed to be far more sensitively handled. Its rescue from the very brink of collapse (the gallery was, until the recent work, an alarmingly rickety structure) is a matter for some celebration. On account of the French style of stop-lists and pipework, the sound of these organs certainly owes more to the French tradition than to the Dallams' English background, and it would be unwise to draw any firm conclusions, particularly from the instruments built by Thomas Dallam de la Tour after his father had left for home. However, at Lanvellec (1653) one striking feature may give a clue to Robert Dallam's taste in voicing.[18]

Lanvellec: Robert Dallam 1653

Compass C–c''', 49 notes

Bourdon	8
Prestant	4
Nazard	$2\frac{2}{3}$
Doublette	2
Tierce	$1\frac{3}{5}$
Larigot	$1\frac{1}{3}$
Flageolet	1
Fourniture	III
Cymbale	II
Cromorne	8
Voix Humaine	8

Some pipework in this organ may in fact be by Thomas Dallam de la Tour, dating from an early repair or rebuild, but the façade, made of pipes from the Prestant 4 is original. These are remarkable for their very low mouths: at the bottom note the upper lip is gently arched, cut up to about one fifth of the mouth width in the centre and reducing to one sixth at the sides. This would certainly suggest a desire for a gentle, rather sweet tone, even though the hard, thin tin metal and the complete absence of any nicking on the languid would suggest a degree of bright sibilance. As restored by Bartolomeo Formentelli the organ does not have a reputation for sweetness of tone, nor does the treatment described here quite match with the surviving material at Stanford-on-Avon. More evidence is needed before making any definite judgement.

[18] Author's examination

At first sight this interlude in France may appear to be just that: an extended summer holiday abroad for a well-to-do family business, a temporary exile across the English Channel. However, much though one may enjoy the more romantic aspects of this episode, it is important to note that the experience of organ building in France permeates the deepest strata of the English craft, and the traces of French influence survive in the English organ right up to the early nineteenth century.

CHAPTER SEVEN

THE RESTORATION
1660–1680

With the Dallams and Thomas Harrisson making haste to return home, we can pick up the story in England. From 1660 on the resources of surviving documentation and indeed extant whole or part instruments are extensive. From here on only selected and well-authenticated instruments appear as examples.

There had been limited activity in England during the Commonwealth. A chamber organ bearing the name Christianus Smith and dated 1643 is now in the possession of N. P. Mander Ltd. The Robert Dallam organ at Magdalen College, Oxford remained in place until 1654. Later it was taken by Oliver Cromwell to Hampton Court Palace, re-erected for his pleasure and, according to tradition, played on by John Milton.[1] Also in Oxford, John Hayward repaired the organ in the Music School in 1657;[2] his relative Robert sold land in Bath in 1653.[3] John (who seems to be the older of the two) is presumably the Hayward active in the west country and Coventry in the 1630s and 40s.[4] John Loosemore, like his father Samuel, had been working in Devon before the Civil War.[5] He is often stated to be the maker of a positive organ at Blair Atholl Castle, Perthshire, dated 1650. In fact this instrument is dated 1630 and is unlikely to be of English manufacture.[6] However, in 1655 he made a pair of virginals now in the Victoria and Albert Museum.[7] In Cambridge Thomas Thamar was establishing an important connection; he was at work at Christ's College in 1658.[8] He also had a son in the choir at Trinity College[9] and took premises formerly occupied by Lancelot Pease.[10]

At the restoration of the monarchy in 1660 the demand for organ builders must have been considerable: the organs of the cathedrals and colleges had all been

---

[1] C. Clutton and A. Niland, *The British Organ* (London 1963), 5

[2] A. Freeman, 'Records of British Organ Builders' (Second Series), in *Musical Opinion* 1922–5, paragraph 151; Freeman's annotation in his own copy now in the British Organ Archive, Birmingham

[3] A. Freeman, 'The Organs of Bath Abbey', *The Organ*, 6 (1926–7), 194

[4] Freeman, 'Records of British Organ Builders' (Second Series), paragraph 151, plus Freeman's annotations in his own copy.   [5] B. B. Edmonds, 'John Loosemore', *BIOS Journal*, 5 (1981), 23–32

[6] Author's examination   [7] Edmonds, 'John Loosemore'

[8] R. Willis and J. W. Clark, *The Architectural History of the University of Cambridge*, 3 vols. (Cambridge 1886), vol. II, 205–14; *Christ's College Magazine*, 1893–4.

[9] G. F. Cobb, *A Brief History of the Organ in the Chapel of Trinity College Cambridge* (Cambridge 1895; 2nd edn (ed. A. Gray) 1913).   [10] J. Mainstone, 'Young Mr. Newton and the Overblown Pipe', *BIOS Journal*, 16 (1992), 44–9

Plate 21   A coloured draught of an organ case, formerly in the archives of New College, Oxford, now lost. This is thought to be the drawing that accompanied Robert Dallam's proposal of 1662 for a large new organ in the French style. The design is unusual in that it consists entirely of towers without intervening flats, and though this instrument was never built, the proposal is indicative of the means available to an organ builder to sell a scheme to a prospective client.

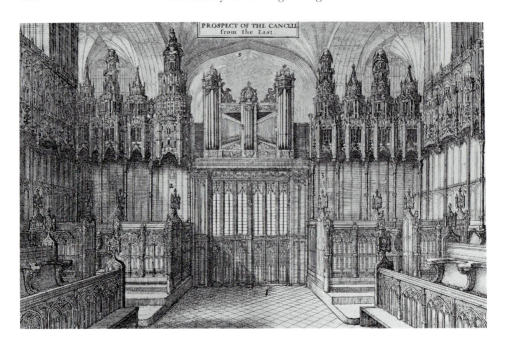

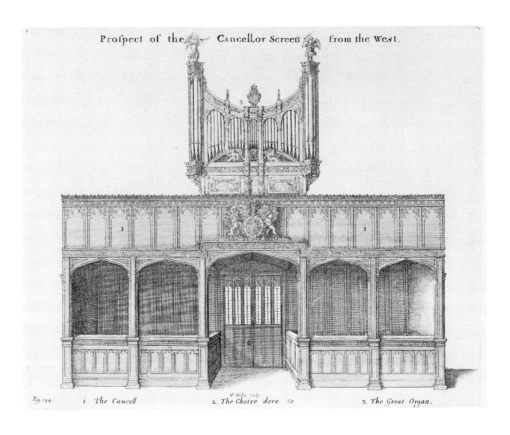

Pag. 144.   1. The Cancell.   2. The Choire dore.   3. The Great Organ.

◄ *Plate 22*   Two views of the organ in St George's Chapel, Windsor engraved for Elias Ashmole's *The Institution, Laws and Ceremonies . . . of the Garter* of 1672. The views appear to show (1) the chaire case, facing east, with the main case omitted, and (2) the west face of the main case. This probably represents the state of the organs as left by Robert Dallam in 1660–2, although the cases may have survived from before the Civil War. The main case follows the favourite Dallam receding perspective plan; the chaire case is comparable to that at Lanvellec, Brittany (built by Dallam in 1653), though here the end towers are pointed rather than flat.

dismantled or destroyed and there was plenty of work. At first old instruments that had survived were brought out of storage and hurriedly repaired, or small organs were installed for temporary use. However, within a very short time the major craftsmen can be identified by name and the building of important new organs recommenced.

The Dallams were at once in the vanguard. On 22 October 1660 Robert Dallam contracted to build a new organ at St George's Chapel, Windsor for £600.[11] He was assisted by Ralph and George. With this important royal connection established, the Dallams must have felt that their future was secure. The building or repairing of organs at Hampton Court Palace, Whitehall Palace, and St. James's Palace at this time all bear the name of John Hingeston, the 'keeper, tuner, and repairer of his Majesty's organs, virginalls and other instruments';[12] Hingeston was a musician and therefore the agent for the works covered by this office, not the executant. Given that the Dallams had secured the contract for the Windsor organ and were generally returning to their pre-Commonwealth sphere, it is reasonable to suppose that they were amongst those engaged by Hingeston to do the work. By the end of 1661 George Dallam had signed a contract for a new double (two-manual) organ at Durham Cathedral, to cost £550.[13] He may have set up a small organ which appeared at the same time. Meanwhile Thomas Harrisson appeared at Salisbury in March 1660–1, where he was to settle.[14] He signed his name Thomas Harriss; one possible reason for the shortened form is that one of the signatories to the warrant to execute Charles I was named Thomas Harrisson: this association would be an uncomfortable one, and Harris(s) he remained from then on.

However much the Dallams and their in-laws might have hoped to restore the influential connection the family enjoyed twenty years before, there were by now several rivals on the scene.

At Exeter John Loosemore was both organ builder and the cathedral's Clerk of Works. In February 1662–3 he was buying tin in Cornwall for a new organ. In October 1663 he visited Salisbury 'to see the Organ there, the better to informe himself to make the new Organ of this Church', and by early 1665 his instrument was finished, standing on the screen in a spectacular case that survives today.[15] Of its astonishing bass pipes we shall hear more later.

---

[11] Freeman, 'Records of British Organ Builders' (Second Series), paragraph 202 (where Freeman assumes the organ to have been by Ralph Dallam, as no Christian name is given; that the contract was with Robert is shown by Philip Timber's letter, to which note 36 refers).   [12] Ibid., paragraph 221
[13] R. Hird and J. Lancelot, *Durham Cathedral Organs* (Durham 1991), 11
[14] Salisbury, Cathedral Library, receipt signed by Thomas Harriss[on] dated 10 March 1660–1.
[15] B. Matthews, *The Organs and Organists of Exeter Cathedral* (Exeter 1973)

In Cambridge Thomas Thamar was busy, and his influence soon extended to the building of new organs at Winchester Cathedral (1665–70)[16] and Peterborough Cathedral (1661–3 and 1680).[17] The Cambridge connection is not his alone; Lancelot Pease was active there (King's College, 1661)[18] and in Norwich (1661)[19], and also built new organs for Canterbury Cathedral (from 1662)[20] and Chester Cathedral (1665, with John Frye).[21]

In the west, Robert Hayward resurfaced, building a new organ at Wimborne Minster (1664).[22] His influence was challenged by the appearance of Robert Taunton, who received the freedom of Bristol in 1662,[23] and built a Chaire Organ for the cathedral,[24] followed in the same year by a contract for a new instrument for Wells Cathedral.[25] In the same part of the country William Hathaway reappeared (he was last heard of at St Martin-in-the-Fields, Westminster, in 1637–8),[26] and started work on a new chaire organ for Worcester Cathedral in 1663.[27]

In the north some new work was in the hands of Edward Darby; to him are attributed organs at Southwell Minster (1662–3)[28] and Lincoln Cathedral (1661–3).[29] At Southwell the name Preston also appears, and a reference to Darby's 'brother' suggests that Preston may in fact have been his brother-in-law.[30] Two Prestons are known: Roger, who built a new organ at St Mary, Gateshead in 1672,[31] and William, who built a new organ at Ripon Minster in 1677.[32] At Ely in 1689, William Preston claimed to be 'lately an Apprentice to Mr. Dallam'.[33] Edward Darby, like the Dallams, was a Catholic.[34] Darby and the Prestons may well represent a splinter group emerging from the Dallam workshop.[35]

The organs themselves departed only gradually from the insular type universal twenty years earlier. Robert Dallam made a brave effort to introduce something new in the French manner. During the construction of the Windsor organ, a friend, Philip Timber, wrote recommending him to the authorities at New College,

[16] B. Matthews, *The Organs and Organists of Winchester Cathedral* (Winchester 1970)
[17] W. A. Roberts, 'Peterborough Cathedral and its Organs', *The Organ*, 10 (1930–1), 1
[18] Willis and Clark, *The Architectural History of the University of Cambridge*, vol. I, 519
[19] G. Paget, 'The Organs of Norwich Cathedral', *The Organ*, 14 (1934–5), 67
[20] Freeman, 'Records of British Organ Builders' (Second Series), paragraph 209
[21] A. Freeman, 'The Organs of Chester Cathedral', *The Organ*, 13 (1933–4), 129–39
[22] Freeman, 'Records of British Organ Builders' (Second Series), paragraph 151
[23] J. Latimer, *Annals of Bristol in the Seventeenth Century* (Bristol 1900)
[24] J. Speller, 'Bristol Organs in 1710', *The Organ*, 57 (1978–9), 85–9; Freeman, 'Records of British Organ Builders' (Second Series), paragraph 206
[25] R. Bowers, L. S. Colchester and A. Crossland, *The Organs and Organists of Wells Cathedral* (Wells 1974)
[26] A. Freeman, 'The Organs and Organists of St. Martin's in the Fields, London', *The Organ*, 1 (1921–2), 1–19
[27] C. Beswick, *The Organs of Worcester Cathedral* (Worcester 1973)
[28] W. L. Sumner, 'The Organs of Southwell Cathedral', *The Organ*, 51 (1972–3), 89–98
[29] R. Pacey, 'Alexander Buckingham and the Renaissance Organ at Lincoln Cathedral', *Organ Yearbook*, 23 (1992), 163–89   [30] Sumner, 'The Organs of Southwell Cathedral'
[31] A. Shedden, 'The Organ in the Parish Church of St. Mary Gateshead', *The Organ*, 50 (1971–2), 167
[32] *Musical Times* (1902), 318
[33] S. Bicknell, 'Mr Preston his judgt of the work it self', *BIOS Reporter*, 8 (1984), 1, 7–9
[34] *Lincs. & Notts. Architectural and Archaeological Society Proceedings*, 1889
[35] A more detailed account of organ building activity immediately after the Restoration appears in S. Bicknell, 'English Organ-Building 1642–1685', *BIOS Journal* 5, (1981), 5–22. However, this earlier account is faulty in that it does not take account of transposition and its implications.

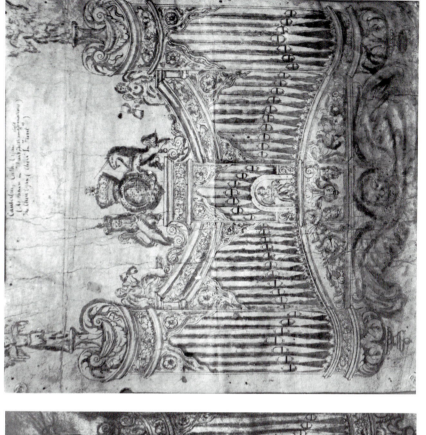

Plate 23 Designs for a new organ submitted by Lancelot Pease to Canterbury Cathedral in 1662. The drawings, by George Woodroffe, were brought to light in the 1930s and are now lost. The general arrangement of the two cases – main case and chaire case – is Pease's, and compares with surviving work in Dublin and Cambridge.

Oxford.[36] Dallam came up with a proposal and case design (see p. 105) of startling originality – at least by English standards.[37]

Oxford, New College Chapel: Robert Dallam's proposal of 1662

1. The fore frunte of the organe the bigeste pipe – 24 fote longe fitting for the place and for the decorment of the churce
2. The nixte stop – in the organe 16 fote longe a 8 above him
3. The nixte stop – 12 fute long a 8 above the 16 fote
4. The bordane 8 fute long a 8 from the other above him
5. The recorder – 4 fote long a 8 to the burdane above him
6. The Simbale in 2 stopes rininge through in 5s
7. The furnitor 3 stopes goin throu in 8s
8. The prinsepale 6 fote longe
9. The small princepal
10. The 2 and 20
11. The Siflet 1 fut longe
12. The 5 to the recorder
13. The nasone stop
14. The flut de alman
15. The Sagbot
16. The Cleron

I oblise My self to performe and maek all thes stopes conformabel to the churce and agmentacion of good musick and give contentment to them that hiris it.

1. The Chere organe the for frunte of it 8 fote longe
2. The burdone 6 fote long stoped
3. The recorder stop
4. The antheme stop in vide
5. The prinsepal
6. The smal prinsepal
7. The 2 and 20
8. The flute

the number of the pipes 12 hudreth

Thes stopes – 16 in the grit organe and 8 in the chaire organe wher upon I vld bind and oblisz to put in – 24 stops in the 2 organes and byde the triele of all the organists in England and organ makers.

The pipes will take to the makeing of them 1000li of Tinne, each pound 0. 1s. 2d. which cometh to 58li. 6s. 8d.

Item for the Socketts to the bottome of the pipes, Lead 200li. weight at 2d. the pound 1li. 13s. 4d.

---

[36] A. Freeman, 'The Organs at New College Oxford', *The Organ*, 9 (1929–30), 149–56
[37] For a copy of this document and this transcription of it I am indebted to Paul Hale Esq.

Item timber for the Sound-bord, bellowes, the antheme Stopp and diurse other parts of the Organ within it.

Item the workmanshipp which will aske a yeare and a halfe for 4 psons continually in hande wth it.

Item Leather and Glew, Ironworke for the Bellows which must be 5, in round to gird and fasten the whole body and frame of the organ to the wall.

Item Bevers for 4 men each man 2d a day for 300 days in ye yeare leavinge out holydayes & soe for a yeare & an halfe it will amount unto 13li .6s. 8d. or thereabout.

Itm charcole for sodering and Billets or faggotts for melting and running ye metall.

There is some considerable confusion here. This appears to be a hybrid Anglo-French organ, and a big one to boot; but what has happened to the key compass? Some stops are marked as 24′, 12′ or 6′, characteristic of an organ with F as the lowest note (presumably at the French pitch, about a tone lower than the old English choir pitch). Mingled amongst them are some 16′, 8′ and 4′ stops, from a C-compass organ. This inconsistent use of pitch lengths makes interpretation difficult. The reeds and mixtures of the French organ are there, but of the mutations only the Nazard is apparent. The 'antheme stop' is a mystery: 'in vide' has no obvious interpretation. As with some pre-Commonwealth organs it might be a stop at another pitch: at choir pitch if the organ is transposing, at old organ pitch if it is not. Curiously the whole scheme is vaguely reminiscent of certain French organs of the earlier seventeenth century and, incidentally, of the lists of stops given in Marin Mersenne's *Harmonie Universelle*.[38] Is the similarity between this stop-list and that proposed by the Scotsman Guillaume Lesselier (William Leslie) at St Godard, Rouen in 1632 coincidental, or a further indication of the sources of the Dallams' French experience (p. 112)?[39]

On 10 March 1661/2 Dallam appeared before the fellows of New College with a further proposal.[40]

Some discourse was then had with one Mr. Dalham an Organ Maker concerning a new fair organ to be made for our College Chapel. The Stops of the intended Organ were shewn unto myself, and the 13 Seniors, set down in a paper and named there by the Organist of Christ Church who would have had them half a note lower than Ch. Ch. Organ: but Mr. Dalham supposed that a quarter of a note would be sufficient. He shewed unto us several sorts or fashions of Organ Cases: he conceived that to be fittest which was open in the midst, & might let in more light from the Western Window into our Chapel . . . About 2 years after, viz. March 16. 1663[/4], the Company having been told that in several other New Organs in other Churches they had more stops than our Organ in New College, I was desired to consider, and advise with the Seniors whether it would not be fitt to add some extraordinary stops, as the Trumpet Stop, the Cornet Stop, & some others. I enquired

[38] M. Mersenne, *L' Harmonie Universelle* (Paris 1635 (Latin) and 1636 (French)).
[39] N. Dufourcq, *Livre de L'Orgue Français*, 3 vols. (Paris 1935–), vol. I, 110
[40] New College Oxford, archives, Warden Sewell's nineteenth-century transcription of the *Onus & Exoneratio Bursariorum, 1664–9.*

Rouen, St Godard: proposal by William Leslie 1632

Grand orgue		Positif	
Monstre	8	Monstre	8
Bourdon	8	Prestant	4
Prestant	4	Doublette	2
Doublette	2	Quinte flute	1⅓
Fourniture	IV	Cromehorne	8
Cimballes	III		
Fleuste	4	**Pédale**	
Quinte fleuste	2⅔	Bourdon	8
Petit fluste	2	Fluste	4
Petite quinte	1⅓	Trompette	8
Sifflet	1		
Cornet	V		
Trompette	8		
Clairon	4		
Régalles	8		
('pour servir du voix humaine')			

of Mr. Dalham what the aforesaid additional Stops would cost. – He told me about £69 viz.

The Trumpet Stop 30-0-0
The Cornet 25-0-0
A Quart 7-0-0
A small Nazien 4-0-0
A Two & Twentieth 3-0-0

The allowance of which stops, with the rate or price therof was agreed unto by the Seniors; And so the whole sum of money that Mr. Dalham was to receive was £419-0-0. Item in a gratuity to Mr. D's Son who made all the pipes 20s – in toto £420-0-0.

The same account states that Dallam actually received £443-12-7 in the end, and that the gallery and case were built by an Oxford joiner William Harris, on Dallam's recommendation, for a further £222-12-0. For the organ case Harris used Flemish oak: by the seventeenth century English oak was already in short supply and imported timber was the rule for high-quality joinery. Painting and gilding of the pipes, organ case and loft cost an additional £120. A separate account of the meeting in March 1661/2 observes that the case made 'to open in the midst' was the same as at Windsor. It was a receding perspective case such as survives in Brittany and at King's College, Cambridge. The organ built by Thomas Harris at Worcester in 1666 was also a copy of Windsor.[41]

Note that Dallam's attempt to build an organ bristling with new ideas at New College was not successful: we know from a later list of faults to be repaired that the

[41] Beswick, *The Organs of Worcester Cathedral*, 8

organ finally built had fifteen stops only.[42] It was the fellows of the college who, hearing that other organs were bigger and might contain the Trumpet and Cornet, went to Dallam and asked him for prices for these additions. From this alone we know that someone somewhere had introduced stops after the new manner by the beginning of 1664.

Original specifications survive for several of the organs built immediately after the Restoration, but all are conservative. George Dallam's organ at Durham Cathedral was finished at Christmas 1662 but, apart from a Fourniture, the scheme shows no hint of new influences, French or otherwise. Surviving organ books at Durham suggest that this was a transposing organ after the old pattern.[43] At Wells Cathedral, Robert Taunton of Bristol signed a contract to build a new double organ on 3 July 1662;[44] it was to be in the old style. A fortnight later, on 17 July, Lancelot Pease signed a contract for a fairly large new organ at Canterbury Cathedral. He was to be paid £600, plus £50 gratuity if judged successful, the price to include the case and its painting and gilding. Pease seems to have been aware of the possibilities of a wider range of mutations.[45]

Canterbury Cathedral: proposal by Lancelot Pease 1662

Great Organ
one diapason of mettall
one diapason stopt of wood
two principals of mettall
two fifteenthes of mettall
a small and great twelft of mettall
two two and twentieths of mettall
a flute of mettall
a recorder of wood
a tierce of mettall

Chaire Organ
two stopt diapasons of wood
one principall of mettall in the front
one fifteenth of wood
one flute of wood

No pitch or key compass is given. The 'small and great twelft' are presumably an octave apart from each other; together with the innovation of the tierce they would offer a range of off-unison ranks similar to the French Cornet décomposé.

Thomas Thamar's contract for a new organ at Winchester Cathedral, dated 27

---

[42] New College, Oxford, archives, *An Account of wt is wanting in the Organ, & wt is to be mended taken by the Organist* [William King] *the 10th June 1672*
[43] J. Bunker Clark, *Transposition in Seventeenth Century English Organ Accompaniments and the Transposing Organ* (Detroit 1974), 155; Hird and Lancelot, *Durham Cathedral Organs*
[44] Colchester, Bowers and Crossland, *The Organs and Organists of Wells Cathedral*
[45] Freeman, 'Records of British Organ Builders' (Second Series), paragraph 209

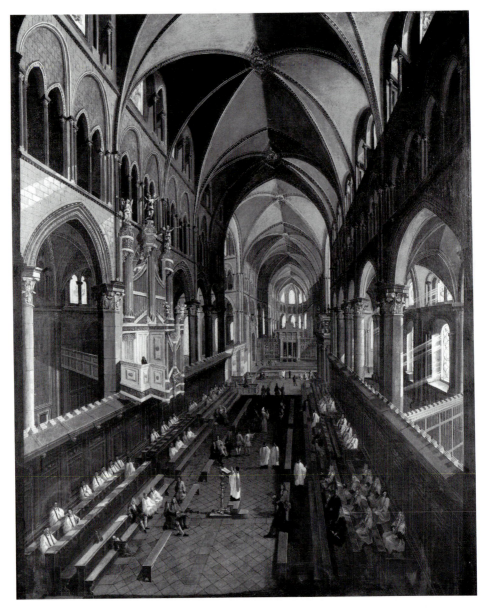

Plate 24 An early eighteenth-century painting of the choir of Canterbury Cathedral, showing the Pease case as actually built, on the north side of the choir, standing on its own gallery. The organ was altered in 1683, 1713 and 1753; instrument and case were removed in 1784.

July 1665, gives another conservative stop-list: as at Durham, only a solitary furniture breaks the traditional pattern.[46] In this contract the pitch is to be 'Gamut in D sol re', indicating the transposing system. However the longest pipe of the open

[46] Matthews, *The Organs and Organists of Winchester Cathedral*

diapason is to be thirteen feet long. This suggests a low C♯ key actually playing AA, sounding choir pitch D.

On 5 July 1666 Thomas Harris, still living in Salisbury, signed a contract for a new organ at Worcester Cathedral. The stoplist was a deliberate copy of that of the pre-Commonwealth instrument, proven by the fact that the account for Thomas Dallam's organ of 1613 was given a marginal note on 2 July 1666, next to the stops of the Chaire Organ: 'Add in the new organ. An open Diapason of wood leaving out nine of the Bases'. The only other change made was in leaving space for another stop on the Great Organ.[47]

Only Loosemore's organ at Exeter, completed in 1665, contained something distinctly out of the ordinary. The organ stood on the screen. The main case had fronts on both east and west sides, with the Chaire case and keyboards on the east. Standing at the north and south ends of the screen, symmetrically disposed in two towers, were a number (fourteen?) of unusually large pipes. This Double Diapason descended to a low note provided by a pipe with a speaking length of 20' 6" standing on a foot four feet high (total length including foot 7.467m), with a diameter of 1' 3" (380mm).[48] This is not the first indication we have had that the Exeter organ was of remarkable size. These basses (there is no evidence of a treble continuation of the stop) are strongly reminiscent of the trompes found on the continent as much as two centuries before, and their treatment is reminiscent of basses in the Tudor organ (but for being an octave lower in pitch than those at All Hallows Barking and in the Wetheringsett fragment). Could the pipes themselves, or at least the desire to make them, have survived since the Playssher organ of 1513?

Immediately after the completion of the Exeter organ Loosemore agreed to build an organ for Sir George Trevelyan at Nettlecombe Court, Somerset. The case and some pipes survive. The stops were to be:[49]

Nettlecombe Court: John Loosemore 1665

One Diapason	[wood]
One Flute	[wood]
One Recorder	[wood]
One Fifteenth	[wood]
One Principall	[metal]
One Flagilett	[metal]
One Trumpett	[metal]
One Shaking Stopp	

From this we know that at least one builder outside the Dallam circle had learned how to make a reed stop.

Though these instruments seem for the most part unadventurous, change was on

[47] Beswick, *The Organs of Worcester Cathedral*

[48] E. J. Hopkins and E. F. Rimbault, *The Organ, its History and Construction*, 3rd edn (London 1877), part I, 63

[49] Sir J. Sutton, *A Short Account of Organs Built in England from the Reign of King Charles the Second to the Present Time* (London 1847), preface

Plate 25   The organ built by John Loosemore on the pulpitum of Exeter Cathedral in 1662–5. This photograph, taken before 1877, shows the organ from the east before alterations. The case, though idiosyncratic in form, is still basically gothic in structure, its stout framing similar to that of a half-timbered house. Visible against the piers of the crossing are the large bass pipes of the famous Double Diapason: the longest had a speaking length of twenty feet. These bass pipes, or at least the idea of making them, may have survived from the large Playssher organ of 1513, and they were indeed mediaeval *trompes* in all but name. They were originally housed in their own twin cases; these were removed when the pipes were laid horizontally in 1825. As the pipes then started to collapse they were soon restored to their former position, but without the casework. All the remaining Loosemore pipework was melted down in 1877.

the way. The reasons why the older English style died out, to be replaced by something new, are many and complex.

Before considering the new style introduced by Renatus Harris and Bernard Smith, a question arises. Why were the great majority of England's cathedral and collegiate organs rebuilt or replaced in the late seventeenth century? Surviving old organs were swept away, and of those built new after the Restoration many were to be the subject of further major work soon after:

Durham Cathedral	G. Dallam 1661–2	Replaced B. Smith 1684–6[50]
Canterbury Cathedral	L. Pease 1662–3	Rebuilt B. Smith 1684[51]
Gloucester Cathedral	T. Harris 1663–6	Rebuilt B. Smith 1687[52]
Norwich Cathedral	Dallam 1664	Rebuilt R. Harris 1689–90[53]
Winchester Cathedral	T. Thamar 1665–6	Rebuilt R. Harris 1693–4[54]

The reasons for this further wave of activity are as follows. First, the fashion for new organs built under the continental influence of Renatus Harris and Bernard Smith rendered the simple tonal schemes of the old English organ out of date. Secondly, there was a general change in standards of pitch. The subject is immensely complex, but it seems possible that the old high choir pitch and a consort pitch one tone lower were gradually superseded by two new pitches, a church pitch and consort pitch, both flatter than before. The Harrises seem to have used a still flatter pitch than Smith, perhaps a French standard: at St Botolph's Aldgate, thought to contain material by Thomas Harris c1676, the bottom note of the Great Principal is marked 'aux ton de Fransz'.[55] Thirdly, the transposing system had fallen out of favour, and by the 1680s we know for certain that new organs were being built with the keys playing the same notes as sung by the choir. The evidence for these changes is scanty, but at Magdalen College, Oxford in 1686 Renatus Harris proposed to rebuild the Robert Dallam organ taking into account these various points.[56] The specification was to be altered, removing the doubled ranks and adding mixtures

[50] Hird and Lancelot, *Durham Cathedral Organs*, 11–16
[51] A. Freeman and J. Rowntree, *Father Smith* (Oxford 1976), 27, 125–9
[52] Freeman and Rowntree, *Father Smith*, 31
[53] Freeman, 'Records of British Organ Builders' (Second Series), paragraph 224
[54] Matthews, *The Organs and Organists of Winchester Cathedral*, 6
[55] D. Gwynn, 'Organ Pitch in Seventeenth Century England', *BIOS Journal*, 9 (1985), 65–78; C. Padgham, *The Organ of St. Botolph's Church Aldgate, London, E.C.3* (London 1975); Information on the Aldgate organ kindly provided by John Mander   [56] Hopkins and Rimbault, *The Organ*, part I, 122–4

Plate 26 A painting by James Cave (1801) showing the choir of Winchester Cathedral with the organ standing on the north side, in the arch of the tower crossing. The case is that provided by Thomas Thamar for his new organ of 1665–70. The main case is notable for having four towers, a plan later to be a favourite of the immigrant organ builder Bernard Smith; in style it appears to bridge the gap between Dallam's mannerism and the more formal classicism of the later seventeenth century. A wall of panelling has been erected on both sides of the choir, probably in order to improve the acoustics. Thamar's organ was altered in 1693 and had been replaced by 1799; the case was removed in 1824.

and mutations; the pitch was to be lowered by a semitone; a laconic reference to the organ 'being now Gamut in D Sol Re' and the provision of new keys suggests that the transposing system was to be abandoned (confirmed by markings on the surviving pipes at Stanford-on-Avon[57]). This last change is expressed more clearly in a bill of 1714 at New College, Oxford, where Harris was paid £35 for altering the pitch 'from Gamut De Sol-re to Gamut proper'.[58] From now on English church organs usually have keyboards that start at GG. A 'long octave' bass would include every note except GG♯, a 'short octave' bass would appear to start at BB, but the apparent BB key would play GG, and the C♯ key would play AA, every other key behaving normally. There are occasional forays down to FF or even CC. The upper limit is c‴ or d‴ in the seventeenth century, rising to e‴ and then f‴ in the eighteenth.

Why the transposing system was abandoned is unclear. It will be noticed that after the Commonwealth organs began to be built again not just in the cathedrals and collegiate churches but in wealthier parish churches as well, where the use of the organ was to develop in the accompaniment of metrical psalms sung by the congregation and in solo organ voluntaries. Here, at least, the choral tradition would have been of no importance, and the new pitch and key compass would be quite satisfactory. We do not know if the spread of the non-transposing organ in churches is due to the influence of the Harrises or Smith, or to a wider range of circumstances.

There were, therefore, changes of style in the late seventeenth century. It should also be understood that, even if organ building in 1660 had picked up where it had left off in the 1640s, there would have been an interruption in the normal pattern of training and turnover of craftsmen. Those builders who worked immediately after the Restoration may have been middle-aged, and many of them would have had no apprentices during the Commonwealth.

Robert Dallam died at Oxford on 31 May 1665 and was buried in the cloisters at New College.[59] Ralph and George Dallam seem never to have fully recovered after this, most of the major contracts going elsewhere. Perhaps they depended on their father's skill and experience. Ralph died in 1672, while building organs for Greenwich Parish Church[60] and Christ's Hospital School, London.[61] These instruments were finished by his partner, James White, otherwise known as a harpsichord maker. George Dallam lived until 1685,[62] but does not seem to have built any new organs after Ralph's death.

Lancelot Pease left for Ireland around 1666,[63] perhaps as a result of the outbreak

---

[57] Author's examination and information kindly provided by D. Gwynn
[58] Freeman, 'The Organs at New College Oxford', 149–56
[59] B. B. Edmonds, 'The Dallam Family', *BIOS Journal*, 3 (1979), 137–9; G. Sumner, 'The Origins of the Dallams in Lancashire', *BIOS Journal*, 8 (1984), 51–7
[60] Freeman, 'Records of British Organ Builders' (Second Series), paragraph 202–3
[61] N. M. Plumley, *The Christ's Hospital Papers I, The Organs and Music Masters* (Christ's Hospital 1981), 17
[62] Freeman, 'The Organs and Organists of St. Martins in the Fields, London', 1–19
[63] *Musical Opinion*, 40 (August 1917), 659

Plate 27   The organ in King's College, Cambridge. Long attributed to Thomas Dallam and associated with his work of 1605–6, this double case probably owes more to extensive work in the 1670s and 80s. The 1606 organ seems to have had a main case with five towers, perhaps similar to that now at Tewkesbury, and was, for a time at least, situated behind the altar at the east end of the building. The present chaire case is almost certainly that provided by Lancelot Pease in 1660–1, and the main case may have reached its present form during work by Thomas Thamar in 1678 or Renatus Harris in 1688. The west front was probably added by Harris in 1710. The main case again follows the receding perspective plan favoured by Robert Dallam, and the composition reflects the conservative style of post-Restoration refurbishments.

of bubonic plague in England in 1665. In Dublin, with the English in the ascendant and the city entering a period of growth, he found plenty of work to do. Edward Darby died at Lincoln in 1670,[64] John Loosemore at Exeter in 1681.[65] Thomas Harris died around 1685, having been referred to as 'my poore aged father' by his son Renatus in 1683.[66] By this time the Prestons, Taunton, the Haywards and Thomas Thamar have all disappeared. Though some of these builders had successors (Pease had a son, John;[67] Loosemore handed his business over to his son-in-law John Shearme[68]), their deaths seem to mark the end of the old school. The only surviving representative is Renatus Harris, but he was soon to be challenged from a new quarter with the arrival from Holland of Bernard Smith.

[64] *Lincs. and Notts. Architectural & Archaeological Society Proceedings*, 1889   [65] Edmonds, 'John Loosemore'
[66] Durham Cathedral Archives, Misc. Charters 5990*h
[67] Freeman, 'Records of British Organ Builders' (Second Series), paragraph 210
[68] Edmonds, 'John Loosemore'

CHAPTER EIGHT

THE GLORIOUS REVOLUTION
1660–1715

The Dallams and Harrises must have had high hopes for their position in Restoration society. Before the Civil War the Dallams had had influence at Court; Robert Dallam described himself as organist to the Queen, presumably Henrietta Maria, Charles I's French wife.[1] At his return in 1660, Charles II, who had been living in France, encouraged French influence on English art and music. The Dallams recovered their position, and even if the death of Robert Dallam left his sons unable to fulfil the family's expectations, the growing reputation of Thomas Harris (and, from the 1670s, his son Renatus) suggested a route for their in-laws to gain influence. As well as the new organs at Gloucester Cathedral (1663–5)[2] and Worcester Cathedral (1666–7)[3] Thomas Harris worked at Winchester College (1664)[4] and presumably at Salisbury where he had settled: he built a small new organ there in 1668–9 in part settlement of a debt to the Dean and Chapter.[5] Renatus was at Magdalen College, Oxford in 1672,[6] and amongst the new organs in the first half of his career were those at All Hallows Barking, London (1675–7),[7] St Nicholas, Newcastle (now the Cathedral, c1676)[8] and Chichester Cathedral (1677–8)[9] (these built with his father), and St Lawrence Jewry, London (1684–5),[10] Bristol Cathedral (1685),[11] and Hereford Cathedral (1686)[12] (built on his own account). We know that Renatus was friendly with members of Charles II's court (engaging the Queen's organist to demonstrate his instrument at the Temple

---

[1] Letter from Robert Dallam to the Chapter of Quimper Cathedral, quoted in Le Men, *Monographie de la Cathédrale de Quimper* (Paris 1877)

[2] M. Gillingham, R. Downes, H. and J. Norman and B. Frith, *Gloucester Cathedral Organ* (Gloucester 1971), 4–9

[3] C. Beswick, *The Organs of Worcester Cathedral* (Worcester 1973), 8–10

[4] E. T. Sweeting, 'The Organs of Winchester College Chapel', *The Organ*, 4 (1924–5), 211–20

[5] Salisbury Cathedral Muniments, articles of agreement between Thomas Harris and the Chapter dated 29 December 1668

[6] A. Freeman, 'The Organs in the Abbey Church at Tewkesbury', *The Organ*, 3 (1923–4), 151–2

[7] Hatton, *A New View of London*, 2 vols. (London 1708)

[8] Traditional; no contemporary documentation has yet been found for this instrument.

[9] N. M. Plumley, *The Organs and Organists of Chichester Cathedral* (Chichester 1986)

[10] C. W. Pearce, *Old London City Churches, their Organs, Organists and Musical Associations* (London 1909), 48–9

[11] C. Kent, 'The Harris Organ of Bristol Cathedral, some recent investigations', *Organ Yearbook*, 22 (1991), 69–96

[12] W. Shaw, *The Organists and Organs of Hereford Cathedral* (Hereford 1976), 28–9

[13] E. J. Hopkins and E. F. Rimbault, *The Organ, its History and Construction*, 3rd edn (London 1877), part I,104n.

Church),[13] and during the short reign of the Catholic James II, the satisfaction of royal preferment fell to him; for the considerable sum of £1,100 he built an instrument for the Queen's Catholic chapel in Whitehall in 1686–8.[14] His hopes may well have run high, but in fact events often turned against him. One soon becomes aware of a remarkable degree of bitterness on Harris's part, especially concerning his rival, Bernard Smith.

The Dallams and Harrises were backing the wrong horse. English society was changing: the Civil War was precipitated by the aggressive attitude of the King and Court in the running of the country. The issues raised by the deposition of the King and his execution in 1649 and by the great experiment of the Protectorate had not been fully settled at the Restoration. The political settlement was not to occur until the flight of James II and Parliament's invitation to the Dutch Prince William of Orange to take the throne in 1688 – the events of the Glorious Revolution. In the meantime, for those who were still apprehensive about the monarchy and its many Roman Catholic connections, the rise of French taste in art and music may have been distasteful.

For the intellectual and trading classes it was Protestant northern Europe that was the source of inspiration in design, social organisation, and commerce. Germans and Dutch were busily employed in England; whether draining the fens (Vermuyden) or managing the embryonic chemical industry (Boyle's associate Hancwitz). Wren, Webb and their contemporaries looked to the Netherlands for practical ways of introducing classicism to domestic architecture. The challenging thinking of European philosophers and scientists was an inspiration to the men who founded the Royal Society; it found expression in the work of Boyle and Newton. The institutions of mercantile activity in the City of London were established on models familiar in Protestant northern Europe. The fact that, in the mid seventeenth century, England was at war with the Netherlands was not so much an indication of enmity as of envy. It was in this atmosphere that the organ builder Baerent Smitt arrived in England and established his claim to fame.

Bernard Smith (as he is known in England) has been the subject of more speculation than any other English builder, some of it of a vivid nature. He was called Father Smith in his own lifetime, perhaps to distinguish him from his nephews Christian and Gerard.[15] This title has conferred on him a general paternity for every development in English organ building since, and over succeeding generations he has acquired a reputation verging on sainthood. Organs attributed to Father Smith are as common – and as unreliable – as beds slept in by Queen Elizabeth. To say anything definite about him is to occupy much trodden and by now very muddy ground.

It has sometimes been claimed that he was English or from an English family;[16]

[14] Ed. J. Y. Akerman, *Moneys Received and Paid for Secret Services of Charles II and James II*, Publ. Camden Society, Old Series vol. LII, London 1851   [15] A. Freeman, *Father Smith* (London 1926), 9

[16] Freeman, *Father Smith*, 1–2; C. Clutton and A. Niland, *The British Organ* (London 1963), 69–70

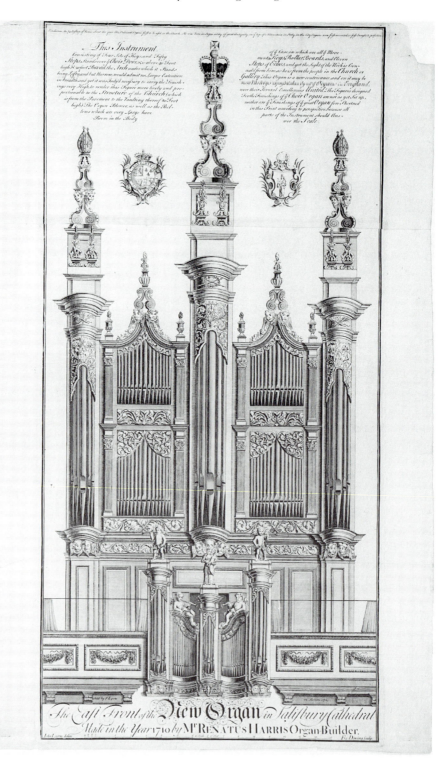

◄ *Plate 28*   An engraving of the organ built by Renatus Harris for Salisbury Cathedral in 1710. This, the largest organ in Britain at the time, with four manual keyboards and fifty stops, was Harris's *chef d'œuvre*. The case is an unusually grand example of the new classicism that flourished under Christopher Wren and the craftsmen who worked on the rebuilding of London, and the final traces of the old gothic tradition have now gone. The upper part of the organ no longer overhangs the sides, and the confident carved decoration of foliage, cherubs and trophies marks this as a truly contemporary design.

there is no firm evidence for this, and one cannot help feeling that, if true, this would have been known to the historians Burney and Hawkins. Amongst contemporaries, Anthony Wood said that he was a Dutchman and Roger North said that he was German.[17] There is a tradition that Smith trained with Christian Förner of Wettin, near Halle in Germany,[18] who wrote a theoretical work on the organ.[19] W. L. Sumner claimed to have found Smith's birthplace in Goslar in the Harz mountains, but if he had any evidence it has not yet been traced.[20]

Certain hard facts about his background have now emerged. Captain James Lane first spotted the possibility that Baerent Smitt of Hoorn in the Netherlands was in fact also Bernard Smith of London. G. A. C de Graaf pursued the theory; James Boeringer published it in 1975.[21] John Rowntree confirmed it in 1978.[22] Smith arrived in Hoorn from Bremen in 1657, where he became organist of the Oosterkerk. In 1662–3 he built a new organ for the Grote Kerk at Edam.

Edam, Grote Kerk: Bernard Smith 1662–3

Hoofdwerk		Positijf	
Prestant	8	Gedacht	8
Holpijp	8	Quintadeen	8
Octaef	4	Prestant	4
Quint	2⅔	Holpijp	4
Mixtuir		Naestquint	2⅔
		Super octaef	2
		Cimbel	II
		Sesquialtera	[1⅗?]
		Sufflet	[1 ?]
		Cromhoorn	8

In 1665–7 he built a small organ for a church in Amsterdam. In 1667 he was in London, tuning at Westminster Abbey, and this is the earliest certain appearance in England.[23]

[17] A. Wood, *The Life and Times of Mr. Anthony à Wood* (Oxford 1730); R. North (ed. E. F. Rimbault), *Memoirs of Musick* (London 1846), 56   [18] Freeman, *Father Smith*, 2

[19] C. Förner, *Vollkommener Bericht, wie eine Orgel aus wahrem Grunde der Natur in allen ihren Stücken nach Anweisung der mathematischen Wissenschaften soll gemacht, probiert und gebraucht werden, und wie man Glocken nach dem Monochordo mensurieren und giessen soll* (Berlin 1684)   [20] A. Freeman and J. Rowntree, *Father Smith* (Oxford 1976), 106

[21] J. Boeringer, 'Bernard Smith (c1630–1708), A Tentative New Chronology for the Early Years', *Organ Yearbook*, 6 (1975), 4–16

[22] J. Rowntree, 'Bernard Smith (c1629–1708) Organist and Organbuilder, His Origins', *BIOS Journal*, 2 (1978), 10–20   [23] Freeman and Rowntree, *Father Smith*, 108

Plate 29   The organ in St Clement Danes, London, attributed to Bernard Smith (undated) (photograph c1890).
The four-tower scheme was a favourite of Smith's (though the 1665 Thamar case at Winchester shows that the
design was not originated by him). This is a rare view of an unaltered example in its original position. The case
was widened towards the end of the nineteenth century and destroyed by bombs in 1941.

Hawkins and Burney believed that Smith had arrived in London immediately after the Restoration, and attributed to him the construction of an organ for the Chapel Royal, Whitehall.[24] John Hingeston was paid £900 for supplying a new organ in 1662–3, and the traditional account is that it was actually built by Smith.[25] In fact Smith was engaged at Edam at this time, and on the organ at Amsterdam until 1667. England was at war with the Netherlands in 1664–7 and it is unlikely that he came to England until 1667; this is the version of events now accepted. He built a new Chaire organ at Rochester Cathedral in 1668, made a new organ for the Sheldonian Theatre, Oxford in 1670–1, and repaired the organ at the Chapel Royal, Whitehall in 1671, importing tools for the purpose. This repair may be the origin of the story that he built the organ in the first place. Smith did build a new organ for the Banqueting House Chapel in Whitehall in 1699, and this has caused further confusion.[26] In 1673 he built an organ for the King's Private Chapel at Windsor, and in 1675–6 organs for St Margaret Westminster and St Mary the Virgin, Oxford.[27] From this it will be seen that within a few years of arriving he had worked in cathedrals, royal chapels, and a university town. In 1681 he was appointed the King's Organ Maker.[28] He became a member of a club founded by Richard Bentley, the Master of Trinity College, Cambridge. Its other members included some of the most famous mathematicians and intellectuals of the day: John Evelyn, John Locke, Isaac Newton and Christopher Wren.[29] His success was obvious and must have been a cause of considerable chagrin to Thomas and Renatus Harris.

Smith may well have been encouraged to come to England by the opportunities caused by the Great Fire of London in 1666. The Rebuilding Act of 1667 allowed those who were not Freemen of London to work in the city for seven years, or until the work of reconstruction was finished.[30] This would have given Smith access to contracts that would have been denied him at any other time. It may also have encouraged Thomas Harris to move to London from Salisbury.

From the ashes of the fire rose a new London, in which both Smith and the Harrises were active. The premise given here is that the Harrises' Catholicism was a significant impediment to their progress, especially amongst the mercantile classes who funded and organised the rebuilding of London and were much involved in the rapid growth of other English towns and cities. In case this should be doubted, consider for a moment an inscription placed on the Monument that marks the point where the Great Fire of London started. It appeared by the order of the Court of Aldermen in 1681, was removed under James II in 1685, put up again at the accession of William III in 1689, and finally removed in 1830, shortly after the Act of Catholic Emancipation:[31]

This pillar was set up in perpetual remembrance of that most dreadful burning of this

[24] J. Boeringer, 'Bernard Smith (c1630–1708)', 4–16   [25] Freeman, *Father Smith*, 13   [26] Ibid., 38–9
[27] Rowntree, 'Bernard Smith (c1629–1708)', 10–20   [28] Freeman, *Father Smith*, 3
[29] Clutton and Niland, *The British Organ*, 75   [30] E. de Maré, *Wren's London* (London 1975), 84   [31] Ibid., 120

Protestant city, begun and carried on by the treachery and malice of the Popish faction in the year of our Lord 1665, in order for carrying on their horrid plot for extirpating the Protestant and old English liberty, and introducing Popery and slavery.

Bernard Smith and Renatus Harris were not contemporaries. Harris was born in 1652, and was only about fifteen when Smith arrived in London. Smith was born in about 1629. As a young man Harris would have seen Smith win the very contracts that would once have been the preserve of the Dallam school. In 1683 he was to write to the dean of Durham, knowing that the Cathedral had previously had an organ built by George Dallam and were now considering its replacement, and having heard from his father:[32]

that he was in great probality [sic] of haveing the honour to serve your Worship and the Chapter about making a new organ for your Cathedral, but latly I understand you have been dissuaded from him and importun'd to imploy another who doubtless is a very good artist, But understanding . . . that no a greement yet is made which hath occasioned me to implore yor favour in my poore aged ffathers behalfe being assur'd he would manifest his thanks by his performance, who I know would be prov'd as well as glad of the advantage to crowne his experience and labour in making his last masterpiece in so ancient and noble a Cathedral . . .

The Harris scheme included mutations, mixtures and a Cornet, but no reeds except 'one natural Vox humain wch stop when play'd on in the Bases will a peare like a mans natural voice and in the middle and upper parts like Women and boys singing in number'. However, by the time this letter was written an agreement had already been signed with Smith.[33]

The organs of Smith and Harris were built in different styles, reflecting their respective background and training. Judging the tonal qualities of their instruments is very difficult, for though considerable numbers of pipes survive in various places, only a handful are in original condition. There are still surprisingly few authentic stop-lists from this period. A knowledge of organ building and particularly of how easy it is to make radical changes in voicing and regulation serves only to encourage further caution.

A useful start can be made by describing the one occasion on which the work of the two builders was compared side by side: two instruments, one by Smith and one by Harris, were erected in the Temple Church, London. The celebrated 'Battle of the Organs' which followed was one of the odder episodes in the history of English organ building.[34]

Smith claimed that he had been awarded the contract in 1682. Whether as a

[32] Durham Cathedral Archives, Misc. Charters 5990*h
[33] R. Hird and J. Lancelot, *Durham Cathedral Organs* (Durham 1991), 12
[34] The account of 'the Battle of the Organs' at the Temple Church is taken largely from: Hopkins and Rimbault, *The Organ*, part I, 104–10; E. Macrory, *Notes on the Temple Organ*, 3rd edn (London 1911); Freeman, *Father Smith*, 24; The depositions made by Smith and Harris before Lord Jeffries, Lord High Chancellor, and the Honorable Societies of the Temple, now in the posesion of M. Gillingham Esq. and printed in *BIOS Journal*, 2 (1978), 21–4; S. Jeans, 'Renatus Harris Organ Maker his Challenge to Mr. Bernard Smith Organ Maker', *The Organ*, 61 (1982), 129–30

result of pressure from supporters of Harris we do not know, but in February 1682–3 the Benchers of the Temple proposed that Smith and Harris should build an organ each, and that they would purchase the instrument that showed 'the greatest number of excellencies'. The organs were duly finished in 1684, and the controversy over which was the better exercised members of the Temple and, no doubt, numbers of amused spectators, for the best part of three years. Smith engaged John Blow and Henry Purcell to demonstrate his instrument, Harris employed the Queen's organist Giovanni Battista Draghi. Harris challenged Smith to make certain reed stops, presumably thinking he was playing a trump card, but Smith responded successfully. According to the composer Roseingrave, Harris's followers are supposed to have sabotaged Smith's organ on the night before the trial of the reed stops by cutting the bellows.[35] Harris claimed that several of his pipes had been 'cut and spoiled' and that after this he had had to employ a watchman day and night for three years at five shillings a week. Smith introduced an octave with fourteen notes instead of the usual twelve (explained further below), demonstrating his intellectual appreciation of the problems of temperament. The members of the Inner Temple and the Middle Temple fell into dispute amongst themselves, and according to tradition it was eventually Judge Jeffries who made a casting vote in favour of Smith's organ. In truth Smith won by four votes. Harris simply would not take no for an answer, and with very poor grace made a further attempt to challenge Smith, accusing him at the same time of 'Scandalous aspersions'.[36] In June 1688 Smith finally made a contract with the Temple for the organ, for which he received £1,000.

London, The Temple Church: Bernard Smith's contract of 1688

THE SCHEDULE

GREAT ORGAN

1	Prestand	61 pipes	12 foote tone
2	Holflute of wood and mettle	61	12
3	Principall of mettle	61	06
4	Quinta of mettle	61	04
5	Super octavo	61	03
6	Cornett of mettle [IV ranks from c#]	112	02
7	Sesquialtera of mettle [III ranks]	183	03
8	Gedackt of wainescott	61	06
9	Mixture of mettle [III–IV ranks]	226	03
10	Trumpett of mettle	61	12
		948	

CHAIR ORGAN

11	Gedackt wainescott	61	12

---

[35] Sir J. Sutton, *A Short Account of Organs Built in England from the Reign of Charles the Second to the Present Time* (London 1847), 25   [36] Jeans, 'Renatus Harris Organ Maker'

12	Hohlflute of mettle	61	06
13	A Sadt of mettle	61	06
14	Spitts flute of mettle	61	03
15	A Violl and Violin	61	12
16	Voice humaine of mettle	61	12
		366	

ECCHOS

17	Gedackt of wood	61	06
18	Sup. Octavo of mettle	61	03
19	Gedackt of wood [from c']	29	[12]
20	Flute of mettle [from c']	29	[06]
21	Cornett of mettle [III ranks from c']	87	
22	Sesquialtera [III ranks FF–b?]	105	
23	Trumpett [from c']	29	[12]
		401	

Some explanation of this scheme is needed. It is England's first known example of a three-manual organ. The Chaire Organ was inside the main case on the same soundboard as the Great.[37] The Echo may have been behind the music desk as at the Banqueting House Chapel, Whitehall in 1699,[38] and possibly also elsewhere.[39] Smith seems to have conceived this department as a hybrid between the northern European Brustwerk and the French Récit. Some stops were of full compass, but most operated only from c' up, and the whole section would have been very compact. If there were no doors in front of the soundboard for the organist to open, then the department would certainly have been distant sounding and the name Echo seems appropriate.

The stop names are unfamiliar. The Principal chorus on the Great is easy enough to follow, and it includes not just the Mixture, but also a Sesquialtera, a compound stop including a tierce rank. The Cornets are similar in intent to those found in France, though perhaps more likely to be used as solo stops. There are no independent tierce ranks. The Stopped Diapasons, Flutes and Recorders of English practice are replaced by Gedackts and Holflutes, the northern European equivalents. As the Chaire Organ does not have a case of its own, it needs no front pipes, hence the Sadt (a tapered rank of Gemshorn type) replaces the usual principal, with a matching Spitzflöte at the octave. The Violl and Violin is a descriptive name for a Cremona or Krummhorn: the resemblance in tone between this stop and stringed instruments is remarked on by Talbot (see below).

The large number of pipes per stop is explained by Smith's introduction of 'quarter tones' from G upwards. The customary twelve notes of the octave cannot be tuned perfectly: some compromise of intonation has to be made: the temperament. In the mean-tone temperament customary in the seventeenth century the notes E♭ and G♯ formed a howling dissonance – the 'Wolf' – and only music in certain keys could be played. In order to try and resolve these problems Smith

[37] Macrory, *Notes on the Temple Organ*   [38] Freeman, *Father Smith*, 38   [39] Sutton, *A Short Account*, 20

added extra keys so that D♯ and E♭, G♯ and A♭ could be played as different notes. The two extra notes in each octave were played from split accidentals, the back part of the key being higher than the front. The key compass at the Temple was FF,GG,AA–c''', with quarter-tones sixty-one notes in all, requiring an extra 150 pipes or so for the whole organ. A similar system had been used by the Saxon builder Gottfried Fritzsche in Hamburg in the previous generation.[40] Smith seems to have made quarter-tones only twice, once at the Temple and again in the organ for Durham Cathedral.[41] Of the competing Temple organ built by Harris we know nothing, except that he is traditionally supposed to have used parts of it in instruments for Christchurch Cathedral, Dublin (where he won the contract from Smith who appeared unable to deliver soon enough) and St Andrew Holborn, London.[42]

The Benchers of the Middle Temple had made their decision in favour of Smith as early as June 1685, and their memorandum gives us the only contemporary assessment of the merits of the two organs. They found:

the Organ in the said Church made by Bernard Smith to bee in their Judgments, both for sweetnes and fulnes of Sound (besides the extraordinary Stopps, quarter Notes, and other Rarityes therein) beyond comparison preferable before the other of the said Organs made by – Harris, and that the same is more ornamentall and substantiall, and bothe for Depthe of Sound and Strengthe fitter for the use of the said Church; And therefore upon account of the Excellency and Perfection of the said Organ made by Smith, and for that hee was the Workeman first treated with and employed by the Treasurors of both Societyes for the providing his Organ; and for that the Organ made by the said Harris is discernably too low and too weak for the said Church, their Marppes. see not any Cause of further Delay or need of any reference to Musicians or others to determine the difference; But doe for their parts unanimously make Choise of the said Organ made by Smith . . .

That Harris's organs may have been milder in tone than those of Smith as well as lower in pitch – 'discernably too low and too weak' – can only be confirmed circumstantially. Having built a new organ at St Lawrence Jewry, London in 1684–5 (where he was chosen in preference to Smith), he returned in 1710 'To new Voice all the old worke and make it boulder and to raise the Cornett four foote above the Sound Board',[43] suggesting that the instrument was soft at first. Otherwise we have to rely on the judgement of later writers. Sir John Sutton, writing in the middle of the nineteenth century, was probably a good judge of any old material still left by then; he writes of the particular quality of Smith's wooden stops (particularly in chamber organs – but here Sutton may be attributing instruments to Smith that may not actually have been by him), and remarks that 'The Chorus is also very fine and very brilliant . . . In Schmidt's Organs every note tells, and the bass is very firm and speaks decidedly; not one note is stronger than another throughout the

[40] P. Williams, *The European Organ 1450–1850* (London 1966), 105
[41] Hird and Lancelot, *Durham Cathedral Organs*
[42] A. Freeman, 'Records of British Organ Builders' (Second Series), in *Musical Opinion* 1922–5, paragraph 204
[43] A. Freeman, 'The Organs of the Church of St. Lawrence Jewry', *The Organ*, 4 (1924–5), 65–76

instrument . . .'[44] Sutton also criticises Smith organs for their spongy touch. Of Harris Sutton says 'His Diapasons are both sweet and rich, and his chorus is vivacious and ringing, even more so than Schmidt's, and his reed stops, though far inferior to those made at present, are also superior to his.'[45]

Far too little pipework remains to confirm these opinions, and though the traditional view of the relative qualities of the two builders' organs generally supports Sutton's statements, any further remarks about tone quality should be treated with extreme caution. More obvious is the subtle difference in stop-lists between Smith and Harris, reflecting their respective training; an understanding of the northern European influence on the one and the inherited French influence on the other may go some way to explaining some of the musical effects they had in mind. We have already seen the kind of instrument Smith built at the Temple. Authentic stop-lists of Renatus Harris organs are rare, but in 1696 he built an organ at St Bride's Fleet Street, London, of comparable size and scope. The version of the stop-list given here is from the original contract (the much bowdlerised version given in the manuscript of Leffler indicates effectively how untrustworthy later sources can be).[46]

London, St Bride Fleet Street: Renatus Harris 1696

Great Organ (middle set of keys)

open Diapason of fine metall in front
Stop'd Diapason all mettall except ye first octave
principall of mettall
Cornett of 5 ranks all mettall
Great Twelfth of mettall
Cart of mettall
Fifteenth of mettall
Tierce of mettall
Sesquialter stop of 5 ranks mettall
furniture of 3 ranks mettall
Trumpett stopp mettall

Chair Organ (lowest set of keys)

Stoped diapason all mettall except the first octave
Principal of mettall
Flute of mettall
Stop'd twefth of mettall
Fifteenth of mettall
Tierce of mettall
Vox Humane stopp

[44] Sutton, *A Short Account*, 28–9   [45] Ibid., 58
[46] A. Freeman, 'The Organ of St. Bride Fleet Street', *The Organ*, 7 (1927–8), 1–9

Echo Organ (top set of keys)

Tribles to the open diapason
    ”   ”   Stop'd diapason
    ”   ”   Principall or Flute
    ”   ”   Great Twelfth
    ”   ”   Cart or Fifteenth
    ”   ”   Tierce
    ”   ”   Trumpet

The compass was GG,AA,C,D–c''' (50 notes) for the Great and Chair, c'–c''' (25 notes) for the Echo.

Smith's Temple organ showed traces of Dutch ancestry in its nomenclature, its variety of flutes, the inclusion of tapered ranks (which he seems never to have repeated in England), the appearance of a Sesquialtera (including the tierce) along-side a mixture (consisting of unisons and quints only?), and the provision of a third manual department on which at least some stops were of full compass in the manner of a *Brustwerk*. Harris's organ at St Bride's shows French influence more clearly, though one should remember that Harris was only eight years old when his father returned to England, and much of what he knew of French style may have been picked up second hand. But here, at least, are the characteristic mutations: independent quint and tierce ranks on all three manuals. On the Chaire Organ the Twelfth is stopped – a true Nazard; on the Great Organ both Fifteenth and Cart (Quarte de Nazard) appear. The short compass Echo organ is reminiscent of a French Récit.

Despite the unrelated backgrounds of the two builders and the various differences noted, in other ways these organs are surprisingly comparable. Smith has already adopted the Cornet, the second manual has no mixture and, whatever it may be derived from, his third manual department is clearly most useful as an Echo to the others, rather than as a self-supporting ensemble in its own right: these features seem, on the surface, more French than Dutch. Harris, in turn, has included the Sesquialtera on the Great Organ: a mixture including a tierce rank that is surely derived from Dutch rather than French practice. Both builders seem to have adopted the practice of making pipework of plain metal (containing between 5 per cent and 20 per cent tin, the remainder lead), reserving metal with a high tin content for occasional front pipes only. Both builders seem to have made rather more wooden pipes than their respective continental backgrounds would suggest, and this may have been inherited in both cases from earlier English tradition. At the Temple Church the front pipes of Smith's organ had a characteristic decorated mouth (half round at the top with an embossed dot over the apex) characteristic of earlier English organs;[47] one of his favourite case designs, with four towers and three flats, was used by Thomas Thamar at Winchester Cathedral in

---

[47] Macrory, *Notes on the Temple Organ*

1665–6.[48] Smith's later instruments, where the nomenclature is anglicised, seem less foreign than the Temple organ, and one has a sense of a new English style developing quite quickly.

Aspects of this style may have been of local origin. In Harris's case one can easily see that his family background in English organ building would be as much of an influence on him as any traits imported from France. Smith, too, may have picked up elements from the English tradition. We know next to nothing about the organisation of an organ-builder's workshop at this time, except that we now hear no more of organs built on site. However, we know that Smith had an organ workshop in Whitehall, on account of his position as organ builder to the King.[49] In view of the large amount of work carried out during Smith's lifetime this workshop must have employed some staff beyond his nephews, Christian and Gerard, and his son-in-law Christopher Shrider. There may well have been English craftsmen amongst them, trained under the old school.

If the Temple was an important stepping stone for Smith, then St Paul's Cathedral, London was his triumph (p. 137). The contract was signed in December 1694, and the organ was built in 1695–7. For Wren's monumental building, Smith had in mind the kind of depth of tone produced by 16′ basses, but in deference to local taste, these were to be included on a long-compass Great Organ descending to CC, rather than by providing an independent Pedal section in the north European manner. It is traditionally held that Wren's strictures over the size of the case prevented the diapasons being carried below FF, and may have forced the omission of some stops.[50]

Smith's achievement at St Paul's unleashed a wave of bitterness from Harris. The following broadside is written in terminology and manner that makes it almost certain that he was the author:[51]

QUERIES ABOUT ST. PAUL'S ORGAN

[. . .] Whether the difficulty this Organ-builder finds in making Pipes to speak whose bodies are but 16 Foot long, does not prove how much harder it would have been for him, to have made pipes of 22 Foot speak, as those at Exeter; or 32 Foot as several Organs beyond the Sea? And whether he has reason to complain of want of height, or room in the case for higher and larger Pipes, since those of a common size have put him to a Non-plus? And whether he has not the greater reason because he gave the Dimensions of the Case himself?

Whether the Double Bases of the Diapasons in St. Paul's Organ speak quick, bold, and strong, with a firm, plump, and spreading Tone, or on the contrary, slow, soft, and only

[48] Watercolour by James Cave of the Choir of Winchester Cathedral, c1801, in the possession of the Dean and Chapter   [49] Freeman and Rowntree, *Father Smith*, 195   [50] Freeman, *Father Smith*, 34–5
[51] Original in British Library; quoted in Hopkins and Rimbault, *The Organ*, part I, 114–15.

Plate 31 A painting of c1830 showing the choir of St Paul's Cathedral, London, with Bernard Smith's organ of 1695–7 on the screen. The case, designed by Christopher Wren, is unusual, not least in containing an organ with pipes down to CC (16′ speaking length). The composition is typical of an architect's design: a relatively flat composition which frames the pipes, rather than one in which the pipes themselves direct the structure and provide three dimensional interest. It is thought that the tabernacles on the two towers may have been added to conceal the tops of the long pipes. The case was originally fitted with sash windows to keep out dust; in

buzzing, when touch'd singly? And whether they may not more properly be called Mutes than speaking Pipes?

Whether the Organ be not too soft for the Quire now 'tis inclosed? And if so, what will it be when laid open to the Cupola, and body of the Church? And what further Addition of Strength and Lowdness will it require to display its Harmony quite through the large Conclave of the Building, and answer the service of the Quire, which is the noblest for Eccho and Sound, and consequently of the greatest advantage to an Instrument, of any in Europe?

[. . .]

Whether there been't Organs in the City lowder, sweeter, and of more variety than St. Paul's (which cost not one third of the Price) and particularly, whether Smith at the Temple has not out-done Smith of St. Paul's? And whether St. Andrew's Undershaft [R. Harris 1696[52]] has not outdone them both?

London, St Paul's Cathedral: Bernard Smith 1695–7

Great	Chayre	Echo
Open Diapason	Quinta Dena Diapason	Diapason
Open Diapason	Stop Diapason	Principal
Stop Diapason	Principall	Nason
Hol fleut	Hol fleut	Fifteenth
Principal	Great Twelfth	Cornet
Great Twelfth	Fifteenth	Trumpet
Fifteenth	Cimball	
Small Twelfth	Voice Humaine	
Cornet	Crum horne	
Mixture		
Sesquialtera		
Trumpet		

Great Organ CC,DD–c′′′ (60 notes, some stops to FF only?)
Chayre FF,GG,AA–c′′′ (54 notes)
Echo c–c′′′ (37 notes)

It is impossible to tell whether any of these criticisms were justified. The complaint about the low notes not speaking properly may be a deliberate misinterpretation of the non-appearance of the bottom notes from CC to FF. That the organ was rather soft may well be possible: the instrument was fitted with sash windows to protect it from dust (initially in consideration of building work still in progress in the dome?) and even when open they must have reduced the openings in the case front by a significant amount. In any case, the cavernous interior of even a part-completed St Paul's would have made any normal organ sound puny compared to its neighbours standing in small City churches.

However, there is evidence of Harris behaving in an objectionable or litigious manner on other occasions. The rumour of sabotage at the Temple has already been mentioned. The difference in tone between the depositions of the two builders

[52] Freeman, 'Records of British Organ Builders' (Second Series), paragraph 224

in the Temple controversy is remarkable: Smith is humble and courteous, Harris is
self-satisfied and grasping.[53] In 1697 there was a disagreement at Christ's Hospital
School, London and it was reported that Harris had 'by some meanes or other
made the said organ useless, upon account of some money remaining due unto
him'.[54] In 1703 he was the deponent in a law suit against a joiner over alleged failings in the making of the case for the ex-Temple organ at St Andrew Holborn.[55] In
1704 the Churchwardens of St Clement Eastcheap, London called in 'Mr. Smith
the Organ maker to shew him the Cheat Mr. Harris putt into the Organ in order
to putt the Organ out of order'.[56]

It is also interesting to record Harris's antics in the wake of Smith's introduction
of the fourteen-note octave with quarter-tones at the Temple Church and Durham
Cathedral. As far as Harris was concerned, dividing up the octave in different ways
was simply a means of venting his spleen in the rivalry with Smith:[57]

Whereas the Division of half a note (upon an organ) into 50 Gradual and distinguishable
parts has been declar'd by Mr. Smith, as also by the Generality of Masters, to be impracticable: All Organists, Masters, and Artists of the Faculty, are, together, with the said Mr.
Smith, invited to Mr. Harris's house in Wine-Office Court, Fleetstreet, on Easter Monday
next (at Two of the Clocke in the Afternoon), to hear and see the same demonstrated.

Harris later returned to this theme, again viewing the division of the octave as a test
of his skill, rather than finding in it the appropriate musical potential.[58]

It has been look'd upon as impracticable, by the ablest Judges in Musick, to divide a Note
into twelve distinct Parts. The Proposer having asserted, that he would undertake to divide
a Note into an hundred Parts, clearly distinguishable by a Musical Ear, did accordingly, in
a full Assembly of Musical-Gentlemen, Masters of the Faculty, and other Artists, on
Tuesday in Whitsun-Week, 1700, perform this Operation on an Organ then standing in his
Work-house, now in St. Andrew's Church in Holborn, to their full and entire satisfaction; . . .

The first sentence suggests that Harris did not actually understand the intellectual
basis of the argument over temperament. Others, like Smith, found the question of
sub-dividing the octave a matter for scientific interest and practical exploration, not
simply as a boastful tour-de-force.

Smith worked extensively in the City of London, at Oxford and Cambridge, and
in the cathedrals of Rochester, Canterbury, Oxford, Durham, Gloucester, St
David's, Chester, Lincoln and York, as well as in the royal connection and in parish
churches up and down the country.[59] Despite any political or religious impediment
Harris was not in fact short of work. His City of London connection was as exten-

[53] The depositions made by Smith and Harris before Lord Jeffries, Lord High Chancellor, and the Honorable
Societies of the Temple, now in the possesion of M. Gillingham Esq. and printed in *BIOS Journal*, 2 (1978), 21–4
[54] N. M. Plumley, *The Christ's Hospital Papers, I, The Organs and Music Masters* (Christ's Hospital 1981), 20
[55] B. Matthews, 'The Organ of St Andrew's Holborn', *BIOS Journal*, 13 (1989), 67–73
[56] Freeman, 'Records of British Organ Builders' (Second Series), paragraph 224
[57] *The Post Boy*, 12 and 30 April 1698
[58] Renatus Harris's Proposal for a west end organ at St Paul's Cathedral, sole copy in the library of St. Paul's
Cathedral.   [59] Freeman and Rowntree, *Father Smith*

sive as Smith's, he was also at work in Oxford and Cambridge, and he and his father between them built new organs for the cathedrals at Worcester, Gloucester, Chichester, Bristol, Hereford, Norwich, Winchester, Dublin (St Patrick and Christ Church), Cork and Salisbury.[60] Smith died in 1708; Harris outlived him by a further sixteen years, and at Salisbury Cathedral in 1710 he built a four-manual organ which clearly outstripped St Paul's in size and ambition (see plate 28, p. 124).[61]

Salisbury Cathedral: Renatus Harris 1710
Compass: Great and Choir GG,AA,C,D–c''' (50 notes); Echo c'–c''' (25 notes)

Great Organ	**Second Great**
Open diapason	(entirely borrowed from Great Organ)
Open diapason	Open diapason
Stopped diapason	Stopped diapason
Principal	Principal
Flute	Flute
Twelfth	Twelfth
Fifteenth	Fifteenth
Tierce	Tierce
Larigot	Larigot
Sesquialtera IV	Sesquialtera IV
Cornet (from c') V	
Trumpet	Trumpet
Cromhorn	Cromhorn
Vox humana	Vox humana
Clarion	Clarion
spare stop	spare stop

Choir	**Echo**
Open diapason (from G)	Open diapason
Stopped diapason	Stopped diapason
Principal	Principal
Flute	Flute
Twelfth	Twelfth
Fifteenth	Fifteenth
Bassoon	Tierce
spare stop	Larigot
	Trumpet
	Vox Humana
	Cromhorn

Drum pedal tuned to C (consisting of two pipes slightly out of tune with each other, producing a 'rolling' effect)

---

[60] Freeman, 'Records of British Organ Builders' (Second Series), paragraph 224
[61] Stoplist noted by Henry Leffler in the early nineteenth century, presumably from an earlier source, quoted in C. W. Pearce, *Notes on English Organs* (London 1910)

◀ *Plate 32*   An engraving of the interior of Norwich Cathedral showing the organ on the screen as rebuilt by
Harris in 1689. Though not to be taken as an accurate depiction of the instrument, the presence of what
appear to be pipes in the lower half of the organ suggests one possible position for the Smith or Harris echo
organs, and the multi-fold diagonal bellows are comparable to French practice (the single-fold diagonal bellows
in the Smith-influenced organ at Adlington Hall are more like German or Dutch examples). The seventeenth-
century case survived until the nineteenth century when it was altered and gothicised; most of what remained
was then destroyed in a fire in the 1930s.

The borrowing of the stops of one manual to be played on another was a stroke of
characteristic Harris ingenuity. This 'communication', as Harris termed it, was
achieved by building a soundboard with two sets of pallets, one for each of the two
keyboards. The stop to be borrowed had two slides and could receive wind from
one set of pallets or the other or both at once. Under each pipe there was a pair of
non-return valves in the upperboard to prevent the keys of one manual from
playing the stops drawn on the other. A contemporary engraving describes how:[62]

The Organ Blower, as well as the Bellows which are very Large, have Room in the Body of
the Case, in which are all the Movements, Keys, Rollar Boards, and Eleven Stops of Echos,
and yet the Sight of the Work is Conceal'd from him, as he is from the people in the Church
or Gallery. This Organ is a new contrivance, and on it may be more Varietys express'd, than
by all the Organs in England, were their Several Excellencies United.

The console and keyboards of this organ must have presented an impressive sight
at the time: not only the four rows of keys, but also fifty stop-knobs. Harris's claim
to have provided more 'varietys' than anywhere else is of interest: the word is a
favourite of his, and looking at the Salisbury specification one realises that his
variety is essentially French in inspiration. The broad categories of chorus, flutes,
mutations and reeds are repeated on the manual divisions, with certain stops being
repeated on every manual. This is not the variety of the northern European organ
which, as Smith showed at the Temple and elsewhere, could ring the changes of
stop-names and pipe construction, including Gedackts, Hohflötes, Spitzflötes,
Gemshorns, Blockflötes and the Quintadena. The provision of the two near-identical Great Organs borrowed from the same set of pipes gives away Harris's thinking: there is a small group of colours that are proper to his tonal scheme, and their
variety is multiplied by having them available from several different places at once,
allowing echoes, dialogues and solos. Indeed, in this search for colourful effects, it
is of all things the Plein Jeu which has dwindled: the Sesquialtera, probably including a tierce, has taken over from the Fournitures and Cymbales of the Dallams'
Breton organs. Ultimately this instrument is an oddity, providing resources more
extensive than any organist would have used at the time. From Harris's scheme for
St Paul's we know that he had ambitions as far as large organs were concerned, but
did he really know what such instruments might be for?

Out of the rivalry between Smith and Harris there emerges a feeling that Harris
was the better craftsman. Hawkins first observed this, saying of Smith that 'the

[62] J. Lyons and F. Dewing, engraving, *The East Front of the New Organ in Salisbury Cathedral . . .* (1710).

organs made by him, though in respect of workmanship they are far short of those of Harris, and even of Dallans, are justly admired; and, for the fineness of their tone, have never yet been equalled'.[63] Burney lambasted him for this opinion,[64] but there may be truth in it. Surviving Smith pipes are roughly made with blunt tools; those of Harris considerably finer and smarter. Smith's casework is good, sometimes exceptionally so, but Harris cases often have an extra richness, with richly carved entablatures, decorated friezes and carving just one degree better than the instruments of his rival. Sutton deplored the spongy key action of Smith's organs, but remarked on the excellence of Harris's reeds.[65]

Beyond this it is very difficult to make an assessment of the two builders' work as so little survives. There is enough Smith pipework left to make preliminary judgements about his principal scaling, which seems to be the same for all ranks in the organ – a so-called 'straight-line' chorus. This alone would account for the supposed brilliance of his organs, with the individual ranks of the upperwork and Mixtures being almost as powerful as the Open Diapason, restrained only by being set further back in the organ.[66] As yet there is not enough data to balance this with a comment about Harris's scaling, but some casual observations may help. From Smith's Dutch experience we would expect to find pipes blown fully with mouths cut up to a height of perhaps two-sevenths or more of the width; this voicing technique is visible on the unaltered front pipes of the organ Smith built in 1673 for the King's private chapel at Windsor, now at Walton-on-Thames, Surrey.[67] In Harris organs, a characteristic feature visible from the outside is that the upper lips of the pipes are often slightly arched. This might encourage a tendency to flutiness, particularly if, as rumoured above, Harris was inclined to voice his fluework mildly. Of authenticated Smith or Harris reeds there is nothing left (some pipes left over from Harris's last organ at St Dionis Backchurch, London, 1722–4 may be by Renatus's son John and are of eighteenth-century type[68]) and it is not possible to trace the influence of either French or Dutch reed construction and voicing. Of soundboards, action and winding systems nothing coherent survives.

Some additional clues are contained in a manuscript now in the library of Christ Church, Oxford.[69] It is an attempt to compile a treatise on organs and organ building; it dates from between 1695 and 1701; the author is believed to be James Talbot of Trinity College, Cambridge.[70] The manuscript is in the form of successive drafts of material, rather confused and much annotated, and relying quite substantially on Mersenne's *Harmonie Universelle* of 1635 (Latin) and 1636 (French). There is also original material from which it is clear that Talbot tried to compile information

[63] Sir J. Hawkins, *A General History of the Science and Practice of Music*, 5 vols. (London 1776)
[64] C. Burney, *A General History of Music* (London 1789)   [65] Sutton, *A Short Account*, 27, 58
[66] N. J. Thistlethwaite, 'Organo Pneumatico, The Construction and Design of Bernard Smith's Organ for the University Church, Cambridge, 1698', *BIOS Journal*, 2 (1978), 31–62; author's examination of the organ at Nayland, Essex, pipework ex Canterbury Cathedral c1684
[67] M. Goetze, *Walton on Thames, Remains of the 1673 Father Smith Organ*, Harley Foundation Technical Report 1992
[68] In storage at the workshops of N. P. Mander Ltd   [69] Christ Church, Oxford, Mus MS 1187
[70] P. F. Williams, 'The First English Organ Treatise', *The Organ*, 44 (1964–5), 16–32

from organs he knew, and that he had some kind of contact with both Smith and Harris. The treatise gives some details of pipe construction and scaling, and it still awaits full study and commentary.

Amongst intriguing material that sheds light on the work of contemporary builders are details of stops of different kinds, some of them rare, or even unknown from other sources. Thus Talbot describes a 32' 'Double double open Diapason, made of fine Block Tin, or Stuff (which is a mixture of Tin & Lead). This is more for show than Sound?' He includes the 'Quintadene', the 'Bassoon or Double Curtel, an Unison to the Double Diapason and consequently proper to the organ of 16' Tone', the 'Spiss-Flute . . . going off Taper from the Mouth', various rare mutation stops such as Tierces at $3\frac{1}{5}$' and $6\frac{2}{5}$' pitch, and 'Mr. Smith's Voice Humaine of Wood', which appears to be what would now be called a Rankett. Talbot also attempts to describe various kinds of mixture, with their compositions and breaks, and it is interesting that he seems to have gleaned information on the Fourniture and Cymbale as well as the Sesquialtera. Talbot's Fournitures seem to include the tierce rank, but he is evidently rather confused by mixtures in general. However he does note that 'in these Stops . . . the 3rds and 5ths must not be so loud as the others'. He also describes the Cornet: 'The Pipes of this Stop are all made of coarse [i.e. plain] Mettal, and have their Bodies very wide to make the sound bold, though all (viz. the third and fifth ranks) are not equally loud.' These notes about the relative strengths of mutation ranks is interesting, and a later comment makes it seem as though this clue came from Harris. Against a list of mutation stops borrowed from Mersenne, Talbot writes:

The following stops are either 3rds or 5ths to some of those already mentioned, from which they differ both as to their Diamater and their Mettal, which must be coarse. because the Sound and Harmony (as Mr. Harris observes) is of a Leaden Tone, which as it gives more Variety, so by this means the 3rds and 5ths are not so hard upon the Ear, and are more easily covered by the Loudness of the Chorus Stops (viz. the open Stops above mention'd. . . . Mr. Smith makes no difference.

This is a rare confirmation of the different scaling and voicing techniques of the two builders. It can be assumed that Smith, in the north European manner, made his open ranks to more or less the same scale and power, regardless of pitch: the 'straight line' chorus. Harris, with his search for 'variety', followed the French practice of distinguishing the mutations by their material, scale and voicing, for the reasons eloquently explained in Talbot's notes.

Here the attempt to discover the tonal qualities of the late seventeenth-century organ would end were it not for the existence of the remarkable instrument at Adlington Hall in Cheshire. Surviving in near original condition and restored by N. P. Mander Ltd in 1958–9 and 1975, it is England's most precious early instrument.[71]

---

[71] J. P. Mander, 'Some Notes on the Organ in Adlington Hall', *BIOS Journal*, 10 (1986), 62–75

Plate 33   The anonymous organ in Adlington Hall, Cheshire, seemingly built to celebrate a family marriage in 1693. This instrument became unplayable before 1800, and survived without alteration until its restoration in 1959. It is the sole surviving testament to the sound of a seventeenth-century English organ, retaining almost all of its original pipework and mechanism. The case is an agglomeration, possibly containing parts from another organ. The two manual divisions, Great and Choir, are on one soundboard in the main case, and the display pipes above the keyboard are dummies. This is one of very few English organs to survive with polished tin front pipes.

Adlington Hall, Cheshire: anon. c1693

Compass: GG,AA,C,D–d‴
Stop-names from the original labels, except for the Trumpet and Vox Humana, where they are missing

Great Organ (upper keyboard)		**Chaire Organ** (lower keyboard)	
Opn diapason	8	St diopason ch	8
St diopason	8	(borrowed from Great)	
Principall	4	St flute ch	4
Gt twelfth	$2\frac{2}{3}$	Bassoon ch	8
Fifteenth	2		
Bl flute bas	2		
Bl flute trib	2		
Ters	$1\frac{3}{5}$		
Sm twelfth	$1\frac{1}{3}$		
2 & twenty	1		
Trumpet	8		
Vox humana	8		

The $1\frac{1}{3}$ breaks back to $2\frac{2}{3}$ at f″
The 1 breaks back to $1\frac{1}{3}$ at c″
A set of toe-pedals of French type, compass GG,AA,C,D–c′ (pulling down the lowest notes of the Great Organ) was provided, but owing to an error in manufacture may never have been completed or used.

The organ is anonymous and undated, but John Mander has made a very good case for it having been installed to celebrate a marriage in 1693.[72] The organ contains some older material, but in style all the pipework is of a piece and the inclusion of various second-hand pipes is probably an indication of economy rather than a clue to the existence of an earlier organ. The instrument shows many signs of rather haphazard construction, even of poor workmanship, and in some ways it may not be altogether typical of its period: this much is confirmed by the slightly quirky specification, which has led some commentators to date it to the period immediately after the Restoration in 1660.[73] In fact its contents show that it cannot have been built before the arrival of Bernard Smith in 1667, and much about it, especially the case, confirms the supposed later date of 1693.

The instrument is a hybrid of styles. The pipe markings are more like those of Smith than Harris, and so is the nomenclature (Block flute not Cart, Small twelfth not Larigot). The reed stops, which survive with original shallots and tongues, have wooden blocks (a link with northern Europe?), but fitted into metal boots. The voicing, on a wind pressure of 79mm with mouths cut up quite high by English standards, is bold and suggests a Dutch heritage. The use of 'communication' to make the Stopped Diapason available on both manuals is a Harris trick. The provision of

---

[72] Mander, 'Some Notes on the Organ in Adlington Hall'   [73] Clutton and Niland, *The British Organ*, 64–6

separate mutations on the Great is Harris-like. The curious pedalboard is of French type. The case has a number of Harris-like features. The very flat pitch (A = 407 Hz) may correspond to French consort pitch. The key action – suspended to the Great Organ and with backfalls to the Choir – is a further surprising combination of two styles of manufacture.

It would be dangerous to try and solve the enigma of this organ's authorship, but the confident attribution to Bernard Smith made at the time of its restoration in the 1950s needs some modification. If the organ is indeed as late as 1693, then there are several other organ builders who might be considered candidates.

Smith appears to have been in dispute with his nephews Christian and Gerard, possibly from 1690, when a 'Petition of Christian Smith against Bernard Smith, organist' is listed in the records of the Lord Chamberlain's Office.[74] Bernard Smith's will, dated 1699, leaves the brothers only a shilling each, and the business effectively passed to Christopher Shrider.[75] Christian and Gerard may not have been with their uncle for all his time in England; in 1703 Bernard stated that he had known Christian for only about twenty years.[76]

Gerard built a new Great Organ at Ely Cathedral in 1691 inside a case specifically made 'after the moddell of that at Christ Church Hospitall, sett up by Mr. Harris'.[77] Later (1725) Gerard Smith and his son (also Gerard) built an organ for St George Hanover Square as a copy of the Harris organ at St Dionis Backchurch, London, in a case copied from the Harris at St Giles Cripplegate, London.[78] Could it be that either Gerard or Christian worked with Harris? Might an association with Harris explain the rift in the Smith family?

Christian and Gerard Smith seem not to have been above criticism. Gerard's rebuilding of the Chaire Organ at Ely in 1689 was not entirely satisfactory and the organ builder William Preston was called in to report.[79] Christian Smith's Bermondsey organ led to a lawsuit in which Jeremiah Clarke and Renatus Harris were called in as experts.[80] If half the things claimed in a deposition made by Harris were true, then the organ was a very bad one indeed. In the Gerard Smith organ at Sedgefield, County Durham, the case (again in the style of Harris) and surviving pipework are roughly made.[81] When the itinerant organ builder A. Buckingham visited in 1824 he found 'The metal pipes is very soft and poor quality mostly on the whole lead. The wood pipes is very bad materials one third of the wood is sap in consequence of which they are rotten and full of worm-holes.'[82]

[74] Freeman, *Father Smith*, 8   [75] Ibid., 7
[76] B. Matthews, 'Christian Smith and the Organ of St. Mary Magdalen Bermondsey', *BIOS Journal*, 11 (1987), 65
[77] Freeman, 'Records of British Organ Builders' (Second Series), paragraph 241
[78] R. Platt, 'Plagiarism or Emulation, the Gerard Smith Contract for St. George's Church, Hanover Square', *BIOS Journal*, 17 (1993), 32–46
[79] S. Bicknell, 'Mr Preston his judgt of the work it self', *BIOS Reporter*, 8 (1984), 1, 7
[80] Matthews, 'Christian Smith and the Organ of St. Mary Magdalen Bermondsey', 62
[81] Conversation with the organ builder Dominic Gwynn
[82] L. S. Barnard, 'Buckingham's Travels', part III, *The Organ*, 51 (1971–2), 99–110

The evidence of the Adlington Hall organ suggests very strongly that someone was working in a style that combined elements from both the Smith and Harris traditions, and whose workmanship was on occasion somewhat less than perfect. On the basis of the evidence above I would suggest that an attribution to Christian or Gerard Smith is possible, but for the time being the case remains unsolved.

The age of Smith and Harris is still a very long way from our own. Though they have been seen by Victorian and modern writers as the founders of modern English organ building, we should remember that they belonged to a generation before the music of Bach and Handel or the organs of Müller or the Silbermanns. It is not until the eighteenth century that we begin to get a coherent idea of what the English organ sounded like.

CHAPTER NINE

THE GEORGIAN ORGAN I
1700–1765

At the accession of William of Orange and Queen Mary in 1688 an age of social and religious conflict drew to a close. Rational thought now guided the nation, contributing to intellectual life, political stability and trading prosperity.

Under Queen Anne (r1702–14) a ground swell of high church feeling arose largely in response to fears that the growth of dissent and irreligion was putting the Church of England under threat. After the general election of 1710 returned a House of Commons with a large Tory majority, several measures designed to strengthen the Church became law. Among them was an act (1711) to build fifty new churches in London, Westminster and the suburbs, to restore Westminster Abbey, to complete the Royal Hospital at Greenwich and to pay arrears on Christopher Wren's salary as surveyor to St Paul's.[1]

Renatus Harris seized the opportunity to suggest a grand project that could be paid for out of taxes: a new west-end organ for St Paul's. Characteristically he was still trying to outdo the *magnum opus* of his rival Smith, even though the latter had died in 1708.[2]

A
PROPOSAL
(by *RENATUS HARRIS*, ORGAN-Builder)

For the Erecting of an ORGAN *in* St. Paul's
Cathedral, over the West Door, *at the*
Entrance into the Body of that Church

[...]

This ORGAN shall contain a double double Diapason, the Profundity of which will comprehend the utmost Notes of Sound. In this Stop shall be Pipes forty Foot long, and above two Foot Diameter; which will render this Organ vastly superior in Worth and Value to the other Diapason Organs; and that the rest of the Work may bear a due Proportion, it shall consist of six entire Sets of Keys for the Hands, besides Pedals for the Feet.

---

[1] J. Summerson, *Georgian London*, Revised edn (London 1988), 57   [2] Sole copy in St Paul's Cathedral Library

Plate 34   The organ in St Mary Rotherhithe, London, built by John Byfield II in 1764–5. This is a typical town church organ with three manuals; it survives today as one of the best examples of the appearance and sound of the English eighteenth century organ. The case is of mahogany imported from the West Indies, a timber soon to dominate English furniture, and this fact indicates that by the middle of the eighteenth century the design and manufacture of organ cases had moved from the field of architecture into that of cabinet making. The carving contains many rococo elements, relatively uncommon in English decorative design.

The first Set to be wholly appropriated for a grand *Chorus*, intended to be the most strong and firm that ever yet has been made.

The second and third Sets to answer all Sorts and Varieties of Stops, and to represent all Musical Instruments.

The fourth to express the Eccho's

The fifth to be a Chair or small Organ, yet to contain more Pipes, and a greater Number of Stops, than the biggest Organ in *England* has at present.

The sixth to be adapted for the emitting of Sounds to express Passion by swelling any Note, as if inspir'd by Human Breath; which is the greatest Improvement an Organ is capable of, except it had Articulation. On this Set of Keys, the Notes will be loud or soft, by swelling on a long Note or Shake, at the Organist's Pleasure. Sounds will come surprizing and harmoniously, as from the Clouds, or distant Parts, pass, and return again, as quick or slow as Fancy can suggest; and be in Tune in all Degrees of Loudness & Softness.

By means of the Pedals, the Organist may carry on three fugues at once, and be able to do as much as if he had four Hands, for the Feet would act upon the Pedal-Keys, when the Hands were employ'd above, and the Sound would be proportionably strong; which, in the grand *Chorus* in so vast a Church, ought to be as strong and bold as possible; and therefore Pedals are us'd in all the great Organs beyond the Seas.

IF at the Charge of the Publick, such an Organ were built in the Place propos'd, which is the most proper to give this Design its full and desir'd Advantage, such an Instrument, containing more Beauties and Variety than all the most celebrated Organs, as it would be by far the compleatest in its Kind, so it would be suitable to the Grandeur of so stately a Fabrick.

SIR,

THE inclos'd Proposal *takes its Rise from the* Organ *I set up in* Salisbury *Cathedral in 1710, which was begun some Years since for a Church in* London, *as a Master-piece of great Value, to have been paid for by Subscription, and was made capable of emitting Sounds to express Passion, by Swelling any Note, as if inspired by Human Breath. But the Place where it is now fix'd, not being proper for that Performance, which requires the Situation to be against a Wall, for the Sound to strike but one way, it loses that Advantage; and yet being prepar'd for that Intent, there may be more Varieties express'd thereon, than by all the* Organs *in* England, *were their several Excellencies united. You are desir'd to observe, that the propos'd* Organ *for St.* Paul's, *is intended to be plac'd at a great Distance from the Choir, and not to interfere with the present* Organ *in the Performance of the Service, being chiefly consider'd in its Situation for the benefit of Swelling the Notes, and study'd to be in all Respects made the most artful, costly, and magnificent Piece of* Organ-Work *that ever has hitherto been invented. The Use of it will be for the Reception of the Queen on all publick Occasions of Thanksgiving for the good Effects of Peace or War, upon all State-Days, St.* Cecilia's-Day, *the Entertainment of Foreigners of Quality and Artists, and on all Times of greatest Concourse, &c. And by the Advice and Assistance of Sir* Christopher Wren, *the external Figure and Ornaments may be contriv'd so proportionable to the Order of the Building, as to be a Decoration to that part of the Edifice, and no obstruction to any of the rest. This instrument will be of such Reputation to the Kingdom, as will far surmount the Expence of it, which will be easy whenever her Majesty and the Parliament shall farther think fit to enlarge their Bounty to St.* Paul's *Church, by appointing a Sum out of the same Revenue which built it, or any other way, as they in their great Wisdom shall judge proper for the Ornament and Grandeur of the State-Church of that City which is the chief of her Majesty's extensive Dominions.*

Several Cities, Corporations, and Gentlemen, have wrote to their Representatives, to vote and use their Interest for promoting this Design. Sir Christopher Wren *approves it, and I have promis'd him, Dr.* Battle,

Sub-Dean of her Majesty's Chappel-Royal, Mr. Crofts, and Mr. Weldon, the Queen's Organists, and others, a Specimen, as Mr. Philip Hart had five Years since, of swelling of the Note, before I reap any Benefit, or that the Work begins, which shall be as soon as the Parliament determines to put this Proposal in Practice . . .

The pamphlet is undated, but must be from c1712: it was mentioned in the *Spectator* for 3 December that year.[3] Knowing that the Jordans had announced their Swell on 8 February that year (see below) one is tempted to suppose that Harris was trying to lay claim to an idea which he may have considered but never put into practice.

Whether because of or in spite of Renatus Harris's self-promotion and tendency to wild claims, it was indeed the Harris school which was to succeed to the major spoils of the eighteenth century.

Smith died in 1708. The general hagiography of Father Smith in the three centuries since he lived has led to a tendency to ascribe to him many organs that he may never have built. This has particularly obscured the importance of Smith's nephews Christian and Gerard, of John Knopple and Charles Quarles. It is not clear how Christian and Gerard Smith divided work between them, or indeed how they related to Knopple. The fact that two cases by Christian Smith (Tiverton 1696, Bermondsey 1699) and one associated with Knopple (Hackney, undated) share the same unusual frieze of foliated coving on the tower caps suggests at least the same case-maker, and possibly therefore a degree of communication or a shared workshop. Knopple may have made the Hackney organ, mentioned above.[4] He also worked at Canterbury Cathedral in 1713,[5] and he is referred to as organ maker at St James Garlickhythe, London where the organ (still largely surviving) appears to have been put up in 1718–19. The Garlickhythe case is a four-tower case typical of Father Smith, and this has led most people to assume that Knopple erected a second-hand Smith organ; we know that there were organs left in Smith's workshop that were sold after his death.[6] However, the pipework at Garlickhythe is not identical with Smith's work[7] and Knopple deserves more credit. The story is similar with Charles Quarles, a Cambridge builder who seems to have inherited the sphere of influence of Thomas Thamar. Though he was organist of Trinity College, Cambridge, it is quite clear that he was an organ builder in his own right with his own staff.[8] On the strength of nineteenth-century hopes that more surviving Smith organs might be found, and on the basis of some similarity between surviving pipes and Smith's work, the organs at Pembroke, Christ's and Emmanuel Colleges in Cambridge were all ascribed to Smith, though Quarles is the only builder mentioned in the records. In fact the old pipework is merely similar to Smith's, not identical, and the cases are quite independent in style. The case is not proven.

Against this flurry of work of the second rank carried out in the wake of Smith's

[3] W. L. Sumner, *The Organ, Its Evolution, Principles of Construction and Use*, 4th edn (London 1973),151
[4] B. B. Edmonds, 'A Lost Organ Case', *BIOS Journal*, 3 (1979), 135–7
[5] A. Freeman, *Father Smith*, (London 1926), 27   [6] A. Freeman and J. Rowntree, *Father Smith* (Oxford 1976), 105
[7] N. J. Thistlethwaite, 'Organo Pneumatico, The Construction and Design of Bernard Smith's Organ for the University Church, Cambridge, 1698', *BIOS Journal*, 2 (1978), 31–62
[8] B. B. Edmonds, 'Charles Quarles, Some Notes', *BIOS Journal*, 16 (1992), 104–11

death, Christopher Shrider stands out as the flag bearer of the Smith school. He is claimed to have been born in Leopoldsberg (near Wettin?) in Germany;[9] if true, this would cement the theoretical link between Bernard Smith and the Wettin organ builder Christian Förner. On Bernard Smith's death in 1708 he was instructed to finish the incomplete organ at Trinity College, Cambridge. He seems then to have succeeded to Smith's business, later becoming organ maker to George II. He is traditionally spoken of as Smith's foreman and son-in-law, though in 1708 he married Helen Jennings – possibly a second marriage.[10]

The anonymous author of articles in the *Christian Remembrancer* for 1833–6 has some informed observations to make:

Although bred and brought up under Schmidt, his organs are of quite an opposite cast to his master's. His *Diapasons* are distinguished by being voiced stronger in the treble than *Schmidt's*, and partaking somewhat of the quality of the *Principal*. Upon examination, *Schmidt's* diapasons appear to have very few *nicks* on the languid, which is the cause of that fine *round* quality of tone that characterises his diapasons; on the contrary, *Schrider's* diapasons have more nicks, and consequently, are more *reedy*.[11]

The author is right in observing the appearance of more regular nicking very early in the eighteenth century, characteristic of several builders at this date (there is already some nicking on the pipes at Adlington Hall), but wrong in his assessment of its effect. A large body of pipework attributed to Shrider survives in the organ at Finedon, Northamptonshire. The claim for Shrider's authorship may be nineteenth-century; however, as the exceptionally well proportioned case is clearly related to the Smith at Trinity College, Cambridge (reputedly finished by Shrider after Smith's death) it is quite clear that it is from a builder with close Smith connections – Shrider is indeed the most likely possibility. The pipes are by no means unaltered; in rebuilding the organ with new soundboards (arranged at 90 degrees to the case front) Holdich seems to have raised the cut-ups of bass pipes throughout the organ and there are certain distinctively mid-Victorian qualities about its present sound. The pipes of the Great chorus are all of similar scale[12] and very comparable throughout to Smith's work at Great St Mary's, Cambridge,[13] but interestingly the mouths of all except the front pipes are narrower than the usual ¼ of the width. This, and the increased nicking would make the tone softer and rounder; if Shrider wished to maintain power he would have had to have blown the pipes harder, and this might account for the apparent keenness noted in the *Christian Remembrancer*. We should also note from the evidence of Walton-on-Thames that Smith voiced with pipe mouths cut up to ²⁄₇ or even ⅓ of the width, giving a quite different effect from the cut-ups of ¼ or lower so characteristic of the eighteenth century.[14] If Smith himself occasionally used moderately high cut-ups, as might be demanded by the

⁹ Sumner, *The Organ*, 167
¹⁰ A. Freeman, 'Records of British Organ Builders' (Second Series), in *Musical Opinion* 1922–5, paragraph 225
¹¹ *The Christian Remembrancer* (1833), 498–9; reprinted in *BIOS Reporter*, 8 (1983), 2, 8–9
¹² Author's examination   ¹³ Thistlethwaite, 'Organo Pneumatico'
¹⁴ M. Goetze, *Walton on Thames, Remains of the 1673 Father Smith Organ*, Harley Foundation Technical Report, 1992

Plate 35   The organ in the parish church at Finedon, Northamptonshire, attributed to Bernard Smith's son-in-law Christopher Shrider and built in 1717. The case and much of Shrider's pipework survives, though revoiced by Holdich in the nineteenth century. The case is derived from that made for the last of Smith's organs, at Trinity College, Cambridge. The combination of traditional three-towered casework with strong 'architectural' features is unusually successful, and the carving is in the rich tradition established during the lifetime of Christopher Wren. The pierced screen above the site of the old console may be an indication of the original position of the Echo Organ. The decorated front pipes (mostly red and brown on a ground of gold leaf) are original and are a late example: plain gilding is the normal eighteenth-century treatment.

cavernous spaces of St Paul's Cathedral (an organ that the author of the articles in the *Christian Remembrancer* knew and used as a benchmark for his appreciation of Smith), then it would further account for the impression of roundness of tone. However, the evidence of Finedon, with its narrow mouths, low cut ups and its finely made pipework – much more impressive than the rough and bumpy pipes of Smith – is that Shrider ushers in an era of greater delicacy and refinement. These are surely key elements in the English organ in the eighteenth century.

Shrider died in 1751. At Westminster Abbey he had worked with the younger Abraham Jordan, and it is traditionally suggested that Shrider also helped the Jordans with the organ of St Magnus the Martyr London Bridge in 1712.[15] The nature of the association is not clear, but through it the Jordans are the only certain link between Father Smith and the main stream of eighteenth-century English organ building. In Shrider's lifetime the most innovative and dynamic work was being done by the descendants of Renatus Harris, with whom the Jordans were later to form an alliance.

The organ built in 1712 at St Magnus the Martyr London Bridge by the Abraham Jordans, father and son, introduced for the first time the delights of the Swell Organ to English ears, whatever Harris may have claimed to have tried at Salisbury.

Whereas Messrs. Abraham Jordan, senior and junior, have, with their own hands, joynery excepted, made and erected a very large organ in St. Magnus' Church, at the foot of London Bridge, consisting of four sets of keys, one of which is adapted to the art of emitting sounds by swelling the notes, *which never was in any organ before*; this instrument will be publicly opened on Sunday next, the performance by Mr. John Robinson. The above-said Abraham Jordan gives notice to all masters and performers, that he will attend, every day next week at the said church, to accommodate all those gentlemen who shall have a curiosity to hear it.[16]

It is not known what form this first Swell box took; the earliest surviving examples consist of a wooden box over the pipes with a sliding sash front operated by a pedal which returns under gravity to the closed position when released – the 'nag's head' Swell. The Jordans tried to patent the invention in February 1713, perhaps as a result of the sudden counter-claim from Renatus Harris in the St Paul's proposal, but failed.[17]

The younger Jordan claimed other technical innovations:

An organ made by Jordan, being the first of its kind, the contrivance of which is such that the master when he plays sits with his face to the audience, and, the keys being but three foot high, sees the whole company, and would be very useful in churches. This organ has but one set of keys, but is so contrived that the trumpet base, and trumpet treble, the sesquialtera and cornet stops, are put off and on by the feet, singly or altogether, at the

---

[15] Freeman, 'Records of British Organ Builders' (Second Series), paragraph 225
[16] *The Spectator* (8 February 1712)
[17] Freeman, 'Records of British Organ Builders' (Second Series), paragraph 246

Plate 36   The organ in St Magnus the Martyr, London, built by Abraham Jordan senior and junior in 1712 (photograph c1910). This instrument introduced the Swell Organ to the English public with immediate and lasting success. The Swell was included in addition to the usual Great, Choir and Echo Organs, and hence there were four manual keyboards. The case is plain in design, though large and richly decorated. The section of pipes above the main cornice may originally have concealed the Swell. Only the case now survives.

master's discretion, and as quick as thought without taking the hands off the keys. The said Mr. Jordan invites all masters, gentlemen, and ladies, to come and hear this performance at the workhouse against St. George's Church, Southwark, and will give his attendance from 2 till 4 o'clock all next week, Ash Wednesday only excepted.

N.B. – This organ was play'd on and approv'd by several masters, in publick, the latter end of November, and is fit for any small church or chappel.[18]

The Jordan family came from Maidstone, where they were originally distillers.[19] Through their business it is supposed that they had connections with Spain and Portugal. As simple swell devices and pedals (or knee-levers) for changing the stops are a feature of Iberian organs at about the same time it is possible that their ideas were not as original as they claimed. The description of a reversed console is clear enough; this is not a bureau organ;[20] no instrument so small could have had a Trumpet stop. The pedal silencing the upperwork is what is latterly known as a 'shifting movement'; claims that these existed before this date are surely spurious and Jordan deserves to be credited with its introduction to this country.

The shifting movement appears in several forms, of which two are common. In the first the stops affected by the pedal stand on a grid of their own, connected to the main part of the soundboard via a single slide linked to the pedal. When the pedal is depressed, any stop on the supplementary grid is silenced, if on, and brought back into use again when the pedal is released. This system can be found in the 1790 John Donaldson organ now in the Holywell Music Room, Oxford.[21] In the second form each stop affected has a second slide connected to the pedal, in addition to the one operated by the stop-knob; the effect is identical; this version can be found in Lulworth Castle Chapel, Dorset, in the organ installed in 1785 by Richard Seede.[22] The first system is found in Iberian organs, may be the earlier version, and hints again at the Jordans' awareness of developments elsewhere. In England the shifting movement is almost exclusively restricted to one-manual organs (or organs consisting of Great and Swell only), in order to simulate the resources offered by two (or three) full-compass keyboards; indeed in the Donaldson organ already mentioned the stops not affected by the shifting movement are all labelled 'Choir', though there is no Choir keyboard.

The reversed console is not found in Spain or Portugal, but had been attempted in Austria, for example by J. C. Egedacher at Salzburg Cathedral in 1703–6.[23] There are no other known eighteenth-century examples in England except that at Lulworth Castle Chapel.

---

[18] *The London Journal* (7 February 1729–30)
[19] Gilbert, *Antiquities of Maidstone*; quoted in E. J. Hopkins and E. F. Rimbault, *The Organ, its History and Construction*, 3rd edn (London 1877), part I, 140
[20] Freeman, 'Records of British Organ Builders' (Second Series), paragraph 246
[21] S. Bicknell, 'The Donaldson Organ in the Holywell Music Room, Oxford', *BIOS Journal*, 11 (1987), 32–49
[22] D. Wright, 'The Organ of St. Mary's Chapel Lulworth Castle – A Symposium Part I – An Introduction to the Restoration', *BIOS Journal*, 11 (1987), 6–31; W. Drake, 'Lulworth Castle Chapel Organ, (1) The Reconstruction of the organ'. *BIOS Journal*, 16 (1992), 60–6; J. Rowntree, 'Lulworth Castle Chapel Organ, (2) Some Reflections', *BIOS Journal*, 16 (1992), 67–9   [23] P. Williams, *The European Organ 1450–1850* (London 1966), 87

The Restoration and the Great Fire of London had given organ building a tremendous boost; work was needed in all England's cathedrals and collegiate churches, in many rebuilt churches in London, and increasingly in wealthier town churches up and down the kingdom. After all this activity there seems to have been a slowing down between 1710 and about 1725. This may be partly due to a lull in high-church refurbishing schemes before the return of the Tories in 1710, overlapping with the economic depression caused by heavy expenditure and high taxes during the War of Spanish Succession (1702–13). There was considerable anxiety about the state of the National Debt, and this was one of the factors leading to the South Sea Bubble crisis in 1721. For Shrider we have seen that there was only one known major contract between 1710 and 1726. The same is true for Renatus Harris. After the building of his magnum opus at Salisbury Cathedral in 1710, we only know for certain of one new organ (St James, Bristol 1718–19[24]) between then and St Dionis Backchurch, London, completed in 1724.[25] According to Hawkins, Harris moved to Bristol towards the end of his life; perhaps to move closer to organ building opportunities in what had become England's second biggest city;[26] we should also consider the possibility that the Salisbury Cathedral organ put him in financial difficulties.

Thomas Swarbrick also moved out of London. He is traditionally supposed to have been German (hence the occasional spelling Schwarbrook), but the name is common around Preston in Lancashire.[27] He was apprenticed to Renatus Harris; his elder brother Henry made several cases for Harris organs.[28] By 1706 he was working on his own, rebuilding the Dallam organ at St Alphege Greenwich.[29] Again there is a gap before his next known works, all in the West Midlands, which confirms that the rich vein of work in the capital seems, for the time being, to have been worked out. His masterpiece at St Michael, Coventry (1733) had Harp, Lute and Dulcimer stops with strings,[30] presumably an organ–harpsichord arrangement on a grand scale.

Two organs from the 1720s confirm the success of the Harris school, and announce some important themes of the Georgian age. The first is Renatus Harris's last organ, built for St Dionis Backchurch, London, in 1722–4 (see p. 158).[31]

This seems to have been an influential instrument. Approved by a board of experts that included Croft and Handel,[32] it set a new model for organs in wealthy parish churches.[33] The remains of French influence survive in the mutations on the Great, but otherwise the most prominent feature is the proliferation and variety of the reeds. These were 'exactly to imitate the natural tone or sound of those several

---

[24] Freeman, 'Records of British Organ Builders' (Second Series), paragraph 224

[25] C. Clutton, 'The Organ in the Livery Hall of the Worshipful Company of Merchant Taylors', *The Organ*, 46 (1966–7), 98   [26] Sir J. Hawkins, *A General History of the Science and Practice of Music* (London 1776)

[27] B. Matthews, ' The Organ of St. Andrew's Holborn', *BIOS Journal*, 13 (1989), 67–71   [28] Ibid.

[29] Freeman, 'Records of British Organ Builders' (Second Series), paragraph 245

[30] Hopkins and Rimbault, *The Organ*, part I, 139

[31] Clutton, 'The Organ in the Livery Hall of the Worshipful Company of Merchant Taylors'

[32] W. L. Sumner, 'George Frederick Handel and the Organ', *The Organ*, 39 (1959–60), 44

[33] R. Platt, 'Plagiarism or Emulation, the Gerard Smith Organ Contract for St. George's Church, Hanover Square', *BIOS Journal*, 17 (1993), 32–47

London, St Dionis Backchurch: Renatus Harris 1722–4

Compass GG,AA,C,D,E–d‴ (51 notes)?, Echo g–d‴ (32 notes)

Great Organ	**Choir Organ** ('the undersett of keys')
Open Diapason	Open Diapason (from c′, bass from Great)
Stoped Diapason	Stoped Diapason
Prinsipal	Prinsipal
Great Twelfth	Flute
Fifteenth	Fifteenth
Tirce	Bassoon
Larigo	French Horne (from c′)
Sesquialtera IV	Cremona (from Great)
Trumpet	Clarion (from Great)
Cremona	
Clarion	**Ecchoes and Swellings** ('the thired sett of keys')
Cornet V (from c′)	Open Diapason
	Stop Diapason
	Prinsipal Full Bodied
	Cornet III
	Trumpett
	Cremona
	Vox Humana

instruments and the humane voice'. Harris also intended to provide 'fullness of body smoothness and justness of the tone'.

These themes were quickly adopted by Harris's successors. Renatus's son John seems to have been much involved in the construction of the St Dionis Backchurch organ. After his father's death in 1724 he made an organ large and original enough to secure his reputation. At St Mary Redcliffe, Bristol in 1726, in partnership with the elder John Byfield, he provided an instrument almost as grand as his father had built at Salisbury Cathedral.[34]

The stop-list on page 160 is taken from Harris and Byfield's own description of the instrument, published in 1728. They add:

N.B. – There are Pedals to the lower Octave of this great Organ, notwithstanding the touch as good as need be desired; and there is an Invention, by which drawing only a Stop, makes it almost as loud again as it was before (or play in a double manner) tho' there are no new Pipes added to the organ, or any keys put down by it.

The octave of pedals is an early example. At St Paul's Cathedral in 1720 Shrider was paid:[35]

For adding 6 large Trumpet Pipes down to 16 ft Tone to be used with a pedal or without	£36
For the Pedal & Its movements	£20

---

[34] Advertisement preserved at St Mary Redcliffe, Bristol
[35] C. Clutton and A. Niland, *The British Organ* (London 1963), 82

Plate 37 The organ in St Dionis Backchurch, London (photograph c1870). This was the last organ to be built by Renatus Harris (here in collaboration with his son John); it was completed in 1724. The oak case is a smaller version of that made by Harris for Salisbury Cathedral in 1710. The organ was influential; features of its design were copied in other instruments and similar cases were made by several builders, confirming the success of the Harris school in dominating English organ building in the first half of the eighteenth century. The church was demolished in the late nineteenth century; some revoiced pipework is incorporated in the organ in the hall of the Company of Merchant Taylors in the City of London.

Bristol, St Mary Redcliffe: John Harris and John Byfield 1726

Great Organ CC–d''' (63 notes)	Chair or Choir Organ GG–d''' (56 notes)	Ecchoes (made to swell or express Passion) G–d''' (44 notes)
Open Diapason	Stop'd Diapason	Open Diapason
Open Diapason	Principal	Stop'd Diapason
Stop'd Diapason	Flute Almain	Principal
Principal	Flute	Flute
Twelfth (GG)	Sexquialtera III	Cornet
Fifteenth (GG)	Bassoon	Trumpet
Tierce (GG)		Hautboy
Sexquialtera V		Vox Humane
Trumpet		Cromhorn
Clarion		
Cornet V		

The botched pedal board at Adlington Hall shows that there were still earlier appearances and we have seen that Renatus Harris thought he knew perfectly well what pedals were for: so that the organist could 'carry on three fugues at once' (St Paul's scheme). Whether pedals existed or not in pre-Restoration organs remains an open question.

Harris and Byfield also make it plain that the instrument that they are trying to outdo is, again, that at St Paul's Cathedral, pointing out that the St Paul's organ had neither low CC♯ nor DD♯, nor the top notes c♯''' and d'''. The wish to surpass Smith's work is in exactly the same vein as Renatus Harris's professional battles with his rival and the wild scheme for St Paul's. However, the organ itself is surely descended from St Dionis Backchurch, with some significant changes of emphasis. Gone are the borrowings – 'communication' appears in organs from now on as an economy measure rather than as a means of securing variety (to use Renatus Harris's favourite word). As at Backchurch, and in contrast to St Bride Fleet Street or Salisbury Cathedral, the Twelfth, Tierce and Larigot appear only on the Great. The variety offered by series of mutations spread over more than one manual has gone; Renatus may have been the last of his family to have known what the possibilities of a Cornet décomposé really were; from now on there are only occasional appearances of the Larigot (seemingly just to fill out the number of stops) and the Cart (Quarte de Nazard) has disappeared.

➤ *Plate 38* The organ in St Mary Redcliffe, Bristol, built by John Harris and John Byfield I in 1726. Harris and Byfield took the opportunity presented by this commission to build an unusually large and splendid organ with Great and Choir keyboards extending to CC. The case was designed by John Strahan: the general form and the use of composite capitals as pipeshades to the towers was copied in other west-country cases. The case was removed in the nineteenth century and any old pipework disappeared when a new organ was built in 1911.

The East Prospect of the Stone Gallerie & Magnificent Organ of S.ʳ Mary Redcliff Bristol being 53 feet high from the Ground to the top of the Crown pinacle The great Cafe about 20 feet Square Contains One great & Lefser Organ the Mufical part perform'd by Mefsieurs Harris & Byfield.

One can also surmise that with the gradual acceptance of tierces in English mixtures, the potential value of a separate tierce rank as *optional* colour in the chorus was not apparent.

In place of mutations and borrowing, a considerable effort and expenditure has been lavished on providing the long compass. The extra notes below GG were extremely costly, both as large pipes in themselves and needing larger soundboards and more commodious casework, and the aim is surely grandeur of effect. The extension of the nine-stop Swell to G – an octave below the normal compass in most of the organs of the day – gave a department of considerable expressive potential, and would equally have demanded space and materials on an ambitious scale. Increased grandeur must also have been the intention behind the 'Invention'. This is usually assumed to have been an octave coupler; the fact that the octave coupler appears for certain in the work of John Smith of Bristol as early as 1824 (St James, Bristol, rebuild of the Renatus Harris organ)[36] suggests strongly that the source of his inspiration was close at hand. Finally the provision of two Open Diapasons in a parish church was not so that there could be one facing east and one facing west as in a cathedral, nor was one necessarily more powerful than the other. Where such an arrangement survives from the eighteenth century (as in the Richard Seede organ of c1785 at Lulworth Castle Chapel, Dorset) one can immediately appreciate the subtle but distinctive effect of two Open Diapasons of similar power and treatment. The effect is, in a sense, stereophonic – the impression of greater breadth and expansiveness, albeit with very little increase in power.

Where variety is retained in the organs of St Dionis Backchurch or St Mary Redcliffe, it is imitative variety. This can be seen in the expressive Echo divisions, with their colourful reeds, and the provision of every kind of woodwind and brass sound that the English organ builder could then produce, from the Flute Almain to the Bassoon, French Horn and Hautboy.

Imitation in the eighteenth century was not the slavish copying of orchestral colour found in a later age: it is part of a noble lineage of invention and colour that has spurred organ builders of all ages. In England it also provided the background for the habits of organists. The emerging Voluntary style of the eighteenth century shows the imitative colours in their full variety; there is also plenty of evidence to show that competent organists drew on a wide variety of secular sources: Walsh's arrangements of works by Corelli and others are an indication of more widespread habits. Though effects such as 'Diapasons' or a solo on the Cornet were *sui generis*, the sounds of the English organ were partly related to the character of contemporary instrumental playing.

Harris and Byfield were operating from London at the time of their great work in Bristol, and it was there that Richard Bridge made a further essay in the grand manner. Fifty new churches had proved to be over ambitious: the coal tax only provided enough money for twelve. However, in Christ Church Spitalfields London

---

[36] N. J. Thistlethwaite, *The Making of the Victorian Organ* (Cambridge 1990), 457–8

there rose the flagship of the scheme and the masterpiece of its architect, Nicholas Hawksmoor. The Bridge organ of 1735[37] was no less impressive, only matched in number of ranks by Harris's instrument at Salisbury (see plate 39, p. 165).[38]

London, Christ Church Spitalfields: Richard Bridge 1735

Great Organ	**Choir Organ**	**Swell Organ**
GG–d''' (56 notes)	GG–d''' (56 notes)	g–d''' (32 notes)
Open Diapason	Stopped Diapason	Open Diapason
Open Diapason*	Principal	Stopped Diapason
Stopped Diapason	Flute	Principal
Principal	Fifteenth	Flute
Principal	Mixture III	Cornet III
Twelfth	Cremona	Trumpet
Fifteenth	Vox Humana	Hautboy
Tierce	French Horn (d)	Clarion
Larigot	Hautboy (d)	
Sesquialtera IV		
Fourniture III		
Trumpet		
Trumpet		
Bassoon		
Clarion		
Cornet V		

Drum pedal, two pipes

*consisting of two ranks below G, Stopped Diapason and Principal. This arrangement, known as a 'helper' bass, is often met in the eighteenth century, sometimes in chamber organs. The stopped rank provides the unison tone; the principal, softly voiced, fills in the missing harmonics. At their best helpers are a surprisingly effective replacement for open pipes of the correct length.

Here the Swell is more modest, extending to g only, and the fancy reeds are on the Great and Choir. The range of imitative colour is increased by the appearance here of the French Horn, a stop found on larger eighteenth-century organs only; no example survives. When the author of the articles in the *Christian Remembrancer* visited the organ a century after it was built, the French Horn was the only reed still giving a good account of itself;[39] this suggests that it may have been capped and was thus protected from dust and dirt. The doubling of ranks is carried much further here than at Bristol; the Great Opens, Principals and Trumpets are a foretaste of much less digestible wholesale duplication in the early nineteenth century.

---

[37] R. Russell, 'The Organs of Christ Church Spitalfields', *The Organ*, 19 (1939–40), 113–17

[38] No original specification of the Spitalfields organ has yet been found; the stoplist given here is based on the accounts of Henry Leffler (c1800), the *Christian Remembrancer* (see note below) and the author's examination of the instrument.   [39] *The Christian Remembrancer* (1833–6); reprinted in *BIOS Reporter*, 12 (1988), 4, 10–11

It is difficult to know exactly what a Bridge organ may have sounded like. Those who knew the Spitalfields organ before it finally fell silent in the 1950s reported a faded grandeur, in part attributable to some fairly gutsy Victorian additions, but still based on a little altered eighteenth-century foundation (the instrument appears never to have been completely dismantled, despite the various overhauls and restorations). The nicking on the languids of the open fluework is by now firm and regular, and this would have made the tone both warmer and less articulate.[40] The Twelfth on the Great Organ – the only surviving mutation rank – is of a larger scale than the other members of the chorus.[41] This, one assumes, is derived from the Harris tradition (Bridge is traditionally supposed to have been trained by Renatus Harris) and a distant memory of the French Cornet décomposé. These features encourage one to think of Bridge's work as being rather suave and sophisticated: very much the urbanity one would expect of a citizen of Georgian London. One assumes that the reeds would have been the glory of this organ, and there is enough material surviving at Spitalfields to hope that the English version of the Grand Jeu might one day be heard again.

Bridge's name alone is attached to the Spitalfields organ, but from internal evidence there appears to have been more than one pipe maker involved. Though some notes are marked in an alphabet that derives from the Dallams and Harrises, other pipes carry letters in secretary hand, characteristic of organs by Smith and his school.[42] It seems possible that this organ was built by a partnership; knowing that at this period John Harris, Jordan, Byfield and Bridge were allied in various ways, the appearance of Smith-like marks at Spitalfields points a finger at the presence of Jordan.

The nature of partnerships and successions in the mid eighteenth century is extremely complex, not least because much of it relies on hearsay. In brief, the builders involved and the relationships traditionally ascribed to them are:

> Christopher Shrider, son-in-law of Bernard Smith
> Abraham Jordan (I)
> Abraham Jordan (II), his son
> John Harris, son of Renatus Harris
> Richard Bridge, trained by Renatus or John Harris
> John Byfield (I), son-in-law of Renatus (or John?) Harris
> John Byfield (II), son of John Byfield (I)

Further members of this chain (Gerard Smith's son, also Gerard; Christopher Shrider's son, also Christopher; John Byfield (III), Samuel Green, Wilcox, Knight) can be ignored for the time being.

It is traditionally claimed that Shrider worked with the Jordans at St Magnus the Martyr London Bridge in 1712; and that the younger Jordan helped Shrider at Westminster Abbey in 1727. John Harris and John Byfield were certainly working together at St Mary Redcliffe, Bristol in 1726. At Great Yarmouth in 1732 the

---

[40] Author's examination   [41] Information kindly provided by Dominic Gwynn   [42] Author's examination

Plate 39 The organ in Christ Church Spitalfields, London, built by Richard Bridge in 1735. The church, by Hawksmoor, was the showpiece of the scheme to build new churches with money raised from the coal tax of 1711. The organ was one of the largest in the country. The case, apparently made of walnut, provides an elegant counterpoint to Hawksmoor's baroque masterpiece. It is the largest of several built between 1730 and 1760 with three towers divided by flats serpentine in plan. The additional upper cornice over the flats was probably added when the organ was rebuilt in the 1850s to mask an enlarged Swell division.

contract was signed by Jordan, the local press gives Jordan and Harris, and tradition ascribes the organ to Jordan, Harris and Bridge.[43] Various other partnerships appear later in the century. According to Hawkins the situation was this:

In consequence of the many new churches that were erected at the commencement of the eighteenth century an equal number of organs was required, which induced many persons who were totally unskilled in the art and mystery of voicing organ pipes to become builders. To prevent, therefore, the sad consequences which must naturally have followed, a coalition was formed between the three eminent artists of the day, Byfield, Jordan and Bridge, who undertook to build organs at a very moderate charge, and to apply their united talents to each; the result of which was a fair, though moderate, compensation to themselves, and superior instruments to our churches. The organ in Yarmouth Parish Church, Norfolk, 1733, and in St. George's Chapel in the same town, were made in this way.[44]

Yet in 1734 Bridge was repairing the organ at St Giles Cripplegate, London, having snaffled the contract from under Jordan's nose.[45] What was actually going on?

These temporary associations are very difficult to follow; note that in the case of Great Yarmouth we have already seen four different versions of the story. In practice one particular confusion has arisen: despite Hawkins's assertion there is only one certain instance of Richard Bridge acting in partnership with others, (repairing the organ at Exeter Cathedral with Jordan in 1742[46]). Whatever practical arrangements may have been going on behind the scenes, in no new organ did Bridge acknowledge partnership with anyone else. Hawkins's assessment is probably partly correct; under pressure it was convenient for builders to pool resources when they could, but the partnerships that evolved probably only related to one contract at a time, rather than representing a common workshop and a long-term commitment. These were arrangements of convenience, and the fact that they come and go is not necessarily an indication of bad feeling or broken promises.

In 1741 Jordan and Harris quoted for a new instrument at St Helen Bishopsgate, London (p. 167).[47]

Here is the eighteenth-century English church organ reduced to its bare essentials. Tierce mixture and solo Cornet compressed into one divided stop; the bass of the Choir organ entirely derived from the Great; the Swell a minimal 116 pipes. Yet all the colours that the age required are there. Jordan and Harris explain:

Tis to be observed that this organ contains 855 valuable speaking pipes besides the advantage of 71 more that speak by communication. Here are no mixtures or supplemental stops of small pipes which serve for little else than to make the appearance of a number of pipes which will be subject to be out of tune upon the least variation of the wind of the Bellows and are of little value and strength to an Organ.

[43] B. B. Edmonds, 'Notes and Queries', *BIOS Reporter*, 3 (1979), 1, 10   [44] Hawkins, *A General History*
[45] Freeman, 'Records of British Organ Builders' (Second Series), paragraph 247
[46] B. B. Edmonds, 'Notes and Queries', 1, 10
[47] Freeman, 'Records of British Organ Builders' (Second Series), paragraph 247

London, St Helen Bishopsgate: unexecuted proposal by Abraham Jordan the younger and John Harris, 1741

On the Great Organ the compass is from GG to E in alt being 54 keys, &c

An open diapason	54 speaking
Stopt do	54 do
Principal	54 do
Great twelfth	54 do
Fifteenth	54 do
Bass sesquialtera of four ranks	104
Cornet of four ranks	112
Trumpet	54
	540

On the Chair or Choir Organ

Open diapazon	21 pipes
by communication	33 otherwise
Stop'd diapazon	29 pipes
by communication, &	25 otherwise
Principal	21
by communication, &	33 otherwise
Flute	54
Vox Humane	54
	199

Eccho's and swelling on ye third sett of keys

Open diapazon	29
Stop'd do	29
Trumpet	29
Hautboy	29
	116

– conveniently forgetting to mention that they have omitted most of the big pipes as well, and offering to set the organ up for £350 after it has been heard and approved.

The slightly larger organ that actually appeared in the church in 1744 was supplied by Thomas Griffin, later Gresham Professor of Music (1762–91). He has been disparagingly referred to as a Barber; in fact he was a member of the Barber Surgeons' Company, which is quite a different matter. In just the same way as Father Howe had been a member of the Skinners' Company and Thomas Dallam of the Blacksmiths', so Griffin used membership of a City livery company as a means of carrying on trade in London, not as an indication of his profession. His name is associated with organs sold under a leasing agreement – he would provide the organ and organist in return for an annuity, having presumably himself provided capital for the building of the instrument. At St Helen's he offered an organ worth £500 in return for £250 down and £25 per annum for life, engaging to play it himself or provide a substitute.[48] It seems likely that Griffin actually obtained organs from John Harris, Jordan, Byfield or Bridge; two of them (St Helen Bishopsgate, London (1744), already referred to, and St Margaret Pattens, London (1749)) stand in distinctive cases with ogee-shaped flats, similar to Christ Church Spitalfields and other organs attributed to these builders. At Bishopsgate, though Jordan and Harris lost the contract, they may have ended up building the organ anyway, under Griffin's name.

At about this time some of the organs supplied by Griffin exhibited a still more compressed version of the typical parish church scheme: the resources of the three manual instrument available from only two keyboards. This was achieved by having both Choir and Swell stops on one soundboard, operated by the lower of the two keyboards. The small short-compass Swell was probably raised above the soundboard and fed by conveyances from the slides below; such an arrangement survives in organs from later in the century. Henry Leffler, recording organs early in the nineteenth century, attributed three such instruments in the City of London to Griffin: St Mildred Bread Street (1744), St Margaret Pattens (1749), and St Michael Bassishaw (1762). At Bread Street some of the Choir organ was further borrowed from the Great by 'communication', suggesting that all three departments were fed from one large soundboard.[49] Could these instruments have been a further development attributable to the inventive Jordans?

We have already seen a willingness from several builders to make technical innovations: long compass, borrowing, swells, shifting movements, reversed consoles, octave couplers. In the same category it is also worth noting the sequel to Smith's quarter-tones. In 1768 an organ was built for the Foundling Hospital, London by Thomas Parker (traditionally believed to be an apprentice of Bridge); it replaced an unsuccessful organ built by Justinian Morse in 1750 and paid for by Handel. Parker's instrument had six levers at the console, two for each of the three manuals, each with three positions. One gave C♯ and E♭ at rest, C♯ and D♯ when moved to the left, D♭ and E♭ when moved to the right. The other gave G♯ and B♭, A♭ and B♭, G♯ and A♯ in the three respective positions. There were therefore sixteen notes per octave, and the system probably required three slides per stop: an operation considerably more complex, space-consuming and expensive than the expedient discovered in other countries: that of moving away from meantone temperament towards a well-tempered tuning system, with no extra pipes or mechanism.[50] An anonymous chamber organ built to a similar system survives, though unrestored.

Until the long derelict Spitalfields organ is restored, the major significant survival from the organs built by the successors of Harris is that at St Mary Rotherhithe (a

---

[48] C. W. Pearce, *Old London City Churches, their Organs, Organists and Musical Associations* (London 1909), 88

[49] Pearce, *Old London City Churches*, 220; Ibid., 116; A. Freeman, 'The Organs of the Church of St. Lawrence Jewry', *The Organ*, 4 (1924–5), 65–76

[50] A. Freeman, 'The Organs at the Foundling Hospital', *The Organ*, 3 (1923–4), 1–19

Thames-side village now part of south-east London). Built by John Byfield (II) in 1764–5, the specification was recorded by Henry Leffler in the early nineteenth century (see plate 34, p. 149).[51]

London, St Mary Rotherhithe: John Byfield II 1764–5

Great Organ		Choir Organ		Swell	
GG,AA,C,D–e'''		GG,AA,C,D–e'''		g–e'''	
Open Diaps	54	Stop Diaps	54	Open Diap	34
Stop Diaps	54	Principal	54	Stop Diap	34
Principal	54	Flute	54	Principal	34
Nason	54	Fifteenth	54	Cornet 3 rank	102
Twelfth	54	Vox Hume	54	Trumpet	34
Fifteenth	54		270	Hautboy	34
SesqA 4 ranks	216				274 (sic)
Cornet to C 5 ranks	145				270
Trumpet	54				793
Clarion	54				1335
	793				

It is now thought that this is the original scheme. However, the organ has been altered more than once, particularly a rebuild to C compass by Gray & Davison in 1881, together with enlargement of the Swell and the addition of Pedals, a pedal Bourdon 16, and couplers with new keys and modifications to the console and wind system. The organ was restored in 1959 by N. P. Mander Ltd in consultation with Cecil Clutton; more recently the tierce rank has been restored to the Great Sesquialtera by Martin Goetze and Dominic Gwynn.

Despite these changes, this organ gives a highly atmospheric impression of an organ of the period, not least because of its setting in a relatively undisturbed contemporary church. One should be wary, however, of describing it as completely authentic.

The scaling of the principals, all of plain metal (only the stopped flutes are wood), remains very close to Smith or Shrider:[52] the Twelfth is of the same scale as the rest of the chorus. Notably, however, the principals on the Swell and Choir are one note smaller than those on the Great. The Great Trumpet (the present Clarion is a second-hand stop installed by Mander) retains original shallots and tongues and was cherished by Clutton as his ideal of reed tone.[53] In the context of a small town church and a generally mild organ it is certainly a triumph, but Clutton's attempt to copy it in a larger building (a pipe from Rotherhithe was experimentally offered in to the new Positive section at St Paul's Cathedral during the rebuild in the early 1970s) must have revealed even to him that it was typically English in its

---

[51] A. Niland, *The Organ at St. Mary's, Rotherhithe* (Oxford 1983)
[52] Author's examination; Niland, *The Organ at St. Mary's, Rotherhithe*
[53] Clutton and Niland, *The British Organ*, 83

moderation and understatement. To say that it is 'quite as good as any Continental reeds of the period' is fine, provided one understands that it is half the power of the best French Trompettes. Clutton also describes the Diapason 'as midway tonally between Renatus Harris and Bernard Smith'; until we can be certain that any dia-pasons by either of these builders remain in a tolerably original state, this statement needs to be treated with caution.

These various qualifications do not compromise the organ or the value of seeing and playing it; here the atmosphere of the English eighteenth-century organ and its context are excellently preserved. Nor should the comments about the reeds be taken to imply a problem with quality; Byfield's reed voicing was renowned; the trumpet and clarion he added to the Renatus Harris organ at St Sepulchre Holborn, London were regarded by the composer William Russell and the organ builder James Davis as the finest in England[54] and Byfield's famous reeds were emu-lated in the nineteenth century by Gray & Davison.[55]

The Rotherhithe organ is a standard town church instrument: three manuals with scope not just for the accompaniment of metrical psalms, but with almost all the variety needed for the execution of the now popular voluntaries. Only the rare French Horn is missing: Trumpet, Vox Humana and Hautboy represented the imi-tative reed family. The Great Organ is small enough for the use of a *tutti* including all the stops (except perhaps the Cornet) to be perfectly possible: wind supply and soundboard grooves would have been adequate to the task. This 'full organ' is taken for granted in the eighteenth-century voluntary. Even if this English instrument of the eighteenth century appears in some ways to be a distant cousin of French organs of the same period, the codes of registration are rather different. The English Cornet is used as a solo stop only; the Grand Jeu has disappeared; the Trumpets may be used with the chorus, which includes a narrow-scaled tierce; the separate mutations have disappeared.

The Rotherhithe organ stands in a case of pale mahogany with gilded details and very fine Rococo carving of a type relatively uncommon in England. The front pipes, with generous overlength in the single-storey flats (rather like a French organ of the period) are also gilt. Gilded fronts are peculiarly English and common to almost all eighteenth-century instruments; after Renatus Harris there are no more tin fronts, plain metal being almost the only pipe metal ever encountered.

We have seen already that Jordan did not make the case for the organ at St Magnus the Martyr London Bridge, and that Renatus Harris habitually subcon-tracted the construction of casework: this was probably the normal custom for organ builders of the day, and at Rotherhithe it is plain to see that there are spe-cialist craftsmen at work. Interestingly, the case is not as deep as the organ, enclos-ing only the Great, with painted pine panelling returning to the wall. This is not unusual (the same is true of the organ at St James Garlickhythe, London), though

[54] *The Christian Remembrancer* (1833–6), reprinted in *BIOS Reporter*, 10 (1986), 1, 13
[55] Thistlethwaite, *The Making of the Victorian Organ*, 290

it is particularly conspicuous here; it is possible that the case was made for a smaller instrument and altered before installation at Rotherhithe. If this is indeed what happened, then the flamboyant carving might suggest a connection with a client of opulent taste.

The layout of the organ follows a pattern standard to most builders at this time. The Choir Organ stands behind the Great, with a passage board dividing the two; the original short-compass Swell stood over the Choir Organ. The layout in the larger Spitalfields organ is identical. The bellows must have been inside the base of the instrument, as now. The console is *en fenêtre* and the keys balanced; on all three manuals the pallets would have been directly under the reed stops.

In this instrument we can see the level of maturity that the Georgian organ had reached. Secure in purpose, the stop-lists of English organs remain much the same from 1730 to 1830. The type was as suitable for parish worship, standing on the west gallery of a town church, as it was for the accompaniment of a cathedral choir, from the choir screen. But the instrument continued to develop. If we can see how far Byfield's Rotherhithe organ is from the typical works of Bernard Smith and Renatus Harris, then we must also understand that the organs from the later eighteenth century by Snetzler, the Englands and Green are different again, even if the specifications are deceptively similar.

CHAPTER TEN

THE GEORGIAN ORGAN II
1740–1800

By the middle of the eighteenth century the organ had become firmly re-established. Since the Commonwealth, organs had been re-introduced to wealthier parish churches. Though the instrument was perhaps not quite as widespread as it had been before the Reformation, where organs were put up they were uniformly of a good size.

The standard English organ had three manuals, following the pattern we have seen at St Mary Rotherhithe. The Great Organ included chorus, Cornet and reeds. The second manual, now called Choir Organ and often standing behind the Great (though sometimes, especially in cathedrals and collegiate churches where it was used for choral accompaniment, still in a separate case), had a small chorus (an open diapason or mixture appeared only in the largest instruments) and a solo reed such as a Cremona, Bassoon or Vox Humana. The short-compass Swell (usually commencing at g) was based around Open and Stopped Diapasons, Principal, Cornet, Trumpet and Hautboy; though some Echo organs may have been behind the music desk in the Brustwerk position, the small Swell division normally occupied a space in the upper case, above the Choir in a three-manual organ. Principals and reeds were made largely of plain metal. Stopped Diapasons and Flutes were of wood or had wooden basses and metal chimney flute trebles. Front pipes were gilded: Shrider's organ at Finedon (1717) has a very late example of decorated front pipes. Though there may have been suspended key actions in the seventeenth century, the action to the Great Organ at Adlington is the only surviving example: backfall actions are now the rule. It seems that Bernard Smith sometimes arranged the planting of the pipes on the soundboards to follow the arrangement of the front pipes in the case;[1] by now soundboards were normally arranged diatonically, with the basses at each end and the trebles in the middle, except in very small organs where the pipes might be arranged chromatically. Wind would be raised by two or more diagonal bellows, but only the merest handful of such systems survives.

---

[1] N. J. Thistlethwaite, 'Organo Pneumatico, The Construction and design of Bernard Smith's Organ for the University Church, Cambridge, 1698', *BIOS Journal*, 2 (1978), 44–6; Letter from J. P. Mander, *BIOS Journal*, 3 (1979) 142–3; E. J. Hopkins and E.F. Rimbault, *The Organ: its History and Construction*, 3rd edn (London 1877), part II, 43

Plate 40   The west end of the nave of Westminster Abbey arranged for the Handel Commemoration Festival
of 1784. This spectacular event confirmed the English taste for Handelian oratorio, and established a new
interest in music making on a large scale. The organ was that built by Samuel Green for Canterbury
Cathedral, erected temporarily in the Abbey for the occasion. The keyboards were detached some distance in
front of the organ, in order to bring the player near to the conductor, and acted on a harpsichord as well as
on the organ. The case is one of Green's excursions into the gothic taste, anticipating the full gothic revival of
the early nineteenth century.

Only where space or finance were restricted was the standard three-manual scheme reduced to two manuals or even one, but the provision of shifting movements or a couple of stops in a swell box could enhance the versatility of even the smallest scheme.

The functions of such an instrument in a parish church were different from those required of the same instrument standing in a cathedral. The former was used for the accompaniment of the congregation singing metrical psalms and for the performances of solo voluntaries; in a cathedral the organ accompanied the choir in sung services, but was not intended to fill the building with sound. Hence a cathedral instrument could follow exactly the same three-manual scheme and be voiced with no greater power than its parish church counterpart.

England had become a nation with a large bourgeoisie that enjoyed artistic performances of every kind. Music making spread rapidly beyond the confines of the court and wealthy patronage into the public domain, particularly in London, by now one of the largest cities in the world. This was a market that was hungry for new developments and new personalities; it proved a magnet to foreigners such as Handel and J. C. Bach. It is no surprise at all to find a continental organ builder making a substantial impact in England in the 1750s.

John Snetzler was born in Schaffhausen, Switzerland in 1710. Recent work by Alan Barnes and Martin Renshaw suggests that he was trained by his cousin, the organ builder Johann Konrad Speisegger.[2] Burney, who knew Snetzler personally, stated that he worked at Passau Cathedral with Johann Ignatz Egedacher, and on Christian Müller's famous organ in the Bavokerk, Haarlem, under construction 1735–8.[3] Though no evidence has been found to support Burney's claim, it seems unlikely that he would even have heard of the work of Egedacher unless the story was founded in truth. The supposed connection with Müller is also plausible, though unverifiable. Snetzler's earliest surviving instruments, a chamber organ at Yale University, USA[4] and one presently at Ripon, Yorkshire,[5] are dated 1742; it is assumed that he arrived in London around 1740. He was acquainted with the immigrant harpsichord makers Shudi and Kirckman.[6] He may have been involved in harpsichord making: he often adopted a key compass rising to f''' in the treble, typical of harpsichords; another early instrument is a claviorganum of 1745 in which a Snetzler organ is combined with a harpsichord by Kirckman.[7]

Barnes and Renshaw point out that Snetzler seems at first to have built small organs (including chamber organs in the shape of a desk or bureau, a speciality of his), and a few instruments for Lutheran and Moravian churches. He was already introducing tone colours new to England; to the Moravians at Fulneck, Yorkshire, he proposed a Solicional, sounding 'like a Violoncello' in one scheme and a Viola di Gamba in another.[8] These narrow-scaled stops, faintly imitative of string tone,

[2] A. Barnes and M. Renshaw, *The Life and Work of John Snetzler* (Aldershot 1994), 2
[3] Barnes and Renshaw, *The Life and Work of John Snetzler*, 3   [4] Belle Skinner Collection, Yale University
[5] Barnes and Renshaw, *The Life and Work of John Snetzler*, 58–60   [6] Ibid., 7–8   [7] Ibid., 66–7
[8] Ibid., 69–70

Plate 41   The organ in St Margaret, King's Lynn, Norfolk, built by John Snetzler in 1754 with the encouragement of the organist and music historian Charles Burney. This photograph, taken in 1873, shows the instrument in its original position on a gallery at the west end of the chancel, and illustrates how a mediaeval church was rearranged and furnished in the classical taste. Snetzler's larger cases, perhaps designed in collaboration with his brother Leonard, were usually of mahogany. The use of cabinet maker's techniques is now firmly established, both in the quality of the joinery and in the design of mouldings and carved details.

were amongst many widely used in southern Germany, Austria and Switzerland in the early eighteenth century.

In 1752 Charles Burney became organist of St Margaret, King's Lynn, Norfolk. He immediately set about providing the church with a new organ (see plate 41, p. 175). John Byfield hoped the church would buy the second-hand Harris instrument from Christ Church Cathedral, Dublin, incorporating parts of Harris's ill-fated Temple organ. In fact, probably acting on Burney's advice, the church contracted with Snetzler for a new instrument;[9] this established his reputation. No reliable specification exists, but we know that the organ had the usual three manual departments and several novelties. The compass was GG,AA–e''', fifty-seven notes. The Swell descended to f, below which the keys acted on basses derived from the Choir Organ. Swell and Choir both had a Dulciana, a narrow-scaled stop of soft, faintly stringy tone and outward-tapering construction, at 8′ pitch. The Swell had a German Flute, a stopped rank of 4′ pitch, but made of pipes of triple length overblowing to the second harmonic. The Great organ had a Bourdon 16 from C; this was England's first true manual double.[10]

Authentic records of Snetzler's larger church organs are rare. An engraving gives the specification of one of the best known, that for the parish church at Halifax, Yorkshire, built in 1763–6.[11]

Halifax Parish Church: John Snetzler 1763–6

Compass: Great and Choir GG,AA–e'''?; Swell g–e'''?

Great Organ
Open Diapason
Open Diapason
Stopt Diapason
Principal
Twelfth
Fifteenth
Furniture
Sesquialtera
Trumpet
Bass Clarion GG,AA–c′
Cornet [c#′–e'''?]

Choir Organ
Open Diapason
Stopt Diapason
Principal
Flute
Fifteenth
Cremona [c#′ – e'''?]
Bassoon GG, AA – c′
Vox Humana

Swell Organ 'down to G in the Tenor'
Open Diapason
Stopt Diapason
Principal
Cornet [III?]
Trumpet
Hautboy

---

9 C. Burney, *A General History of Music*, London 1789
10 Barnes and Renshaw, *The Life and Work of John Snetzler*, 82–6; details of stop-list from the ms. of Henry Leffler, compiled c1800–20, quoted in C. W. Pearce, *Notes on English Organs of the Period 1800–1810* (London 1912)
11 Barnes and Renshaw, *The Life and Work of John Snetzler*, 135–9

The following text appears within the engraving:

The Names of the Stops

GREAT ORGAN.

CHOIR ORGAN.

SWELL.

HALIFAX ORGAN.

Plate 42 The organ for Halifax parish church, Yorkshire, built by John Snetzler in 1765–6. The case is similar to that at King's Lynn, following a favourite design that Snetzler used on several occasions. This engraving, showing the organ to scale, with technical details and appropriate rococo embellishments (including the figure of Handel holding a copy of 'I know that my redeemer liveth' from *Messiah*), celebrates the confident introduction of contemporary taste in the provinces.

It will be seen that, despite his experience on the continent and a handful of innovations at King's Lynn, Snetzler's organs followed the established pattern of his English contemporaries. Only the Dulciana, in a revised cylindrical form, took immediate root on these shores, together with the occasional provision of toe-pedals pulling down the lowest keys of the Great Organ. Otherwise his success came partly from excelling at the kind of organ that already appealed to English taste. Snetzler adopted wooden pipes after the English pattern, gilded plain metal case pipes, shifting movements and the swell box. His stop-lists largely followed existing precedent, including two manual organs where the second keyboard controlled a combined Choir and Swell, as introduced by Griffin and described in Chapter 9.

During the earlier eighteenth century the English builders, as far as one can tell from surviving material by Shrider, Bridge and Byfield, had begun to move towards a slightly warmer and less brilliant tone than that attributed to Bernard Smith, perhaps presaged by Renatus Harris's 'fullness of body smoothness and justness of the tone' at St Dionis Backchurch in 1722–4.[12] This stopped short of being either delicate or refined, as it was sometimes to become later in the century, but it must have left many English organs sounding considerably milder than their continental counterparts.

Enough Snetzler material survives in tolerably original condition to make it clear that he brought with him a vigorous new injection of central European brilliance and sharpness. This was abundantly apparent to Sir John Sutton, who wrote in 1847:[13]

His instruments are remarkable for the purity of their tone, and the extreme brilliancy of their Chorus Stops, which in this respect surpassed any thing that had been heard before in this country, and which have never since been equalled. His reed stops were also much better than those built before his time. His Organs though they are more brilliant than their predecessors, fall short of that fulness of tone which characterized those of Schmidt, Harris, Schreider, &c. &c. but they are nevertheless most charming instruments.

Snetzler's chorus consists of ranks all made to the same scale and voiced at the same power. His choice of scale favours brilliancy, especially in the small pipes of the upperwork and mixtures. The speech of the individual pipes is significantly slower than that of earlier generations, and this encourages brightness (as well as facilitating the development of the new string-toned stops). Any tendency of the pipes to spit or scream is controlled by the consistent use of firm, slanted nicking on the languids of the pipes – a hallmark of Snetzler material. The characteristic Snetzler brilliance can be heard in several organs which retain their original mixtures, such as those at St Andrew by the Wardrobe, London and Hillington, Norfolk. The power of the tierce rank, not at all of the 'Leaden Tone' that Talbot attributes to Renatus Harris, gives an intense reedy tang to the chorus. The musical effects of

[12] C. Clutton, 'The Organ in the Livery Hall of the Worshipful Company of Merchant Taylors in the City of London', *The Organ*, 46 (1966–7), 98
[13] Sir J. Sutton, *A Short Account of Organs Built in England* (London 1847), 73

this method are further discussed in Chapter 12, where an examination of the history of the chamber organ gives an opportunity to examine the nature of a chorus, including a bold tierce rank, in its smallest and simplest form. Of Snetzler's reeds there are no real survivors. Note that in the Halifax specification the Great Organ Clarion operates in the bass only, suggesting that in the tutti the Cornet may have been intended to boost the treble while the Clarion gave brilliance in the bass: the usual convention was to regard the Cornet as a solo stop only. The short-compass Clarion bass appears in early nineteenth-century descriptions of other Snetzler organs.

Snetzler did not build organs in the City of London; presumably he was excluded by the remains of the Guild system. Nor did he succeed notably in the cathedrals and colleges, though he did build his largest organ in 1767–9 for Beverley Minster.[14] He was busy in parish churches throughout England, and with chamber organs of various sizes for private houses he excelled. Many of these survive.

Snetzler established himself in the face of competition from London builders whom we have met already, principally the second John Byfield and Richard Bridge. When Bridge ceased working in the late 1750s, his business seems to have been taken over by George England, who is traditionally supposed to have been his son-in-law. George retired in turn in 1766, handing over to his brother John, who later went into partnership with Hugh Russell. John's son, George Pike England, was born c1765 and took over from his father c1790, extending the Dallam–Harris–Bridge line into the early nineteenth century.[15] The success of the Englands was founded on work in the parish churches of London and its rapidly growing suburbs, but also covered the smarter townships of southern England and a few excursions into the midlands and north. This was an urban connection; like Snetzler, the Englands were not especially favoured with cathedral or collegiate work (where, it must be admitted, the musical tradition was in decline). G. P. England worked only at Chichester Cathedral in 1806[16] and started on a rebuild at Durham Cathedral in 1814, shortly before his death.[17]

Organs by the Englands were much admired by contemporaries and following generations alike. The anonymous author of articles in the *Christian Remembrancer* in 1833–6 likened George England's work to that of Father Smith, remarking that his instruments 'have always been remarkable for brightness and brilliancy in the chorus; or, to use the technical phrase of organ-builders, "they have plenty of devil in them" '.[18]

As with Snetzler, work by the Englands survives in some quantity, enough to give a very reasonable impression of the family's work and to observe some innovations

---

[14] Barnes and Renshaw, *The Life and Work of John Snetzler*, 154–6
[15] B. B. Edmonds, 'Notes and Queries', *BIOS Reporter*, 3 (1979), 1, 10; D. C. Wickens, 'The G. P. England Organ at Blandford Forum', *BIOS Journal*, 16 (1992), 70–93
[16] N. M. Plumley, *The Organs of Chichester Cathedral* (Chichester 1986)
[17] R. Hird and J. Lancelot, *Durham Cathedral Organs* (Durham 1991), 18
[18] 'Organo-Historica Or the History of Cathedral and Parochial Organs', *Christian Remembrancer* (1833–6), 'X, The Organ at St. Stephen's Walbrook', reprinted in *BIOS Reporter*, 14 (1990), 1, 7–8

in the scaling of the chorus that were to have a far-reaching effect on subsequent generations.

It has already been suggested that the Harris school voiced third- and fifth-sounding ranks differently from unisons, and the large-scale Twelfth at Christ Church Spitalfields indicates a distant memory of French practice. In one of Bridge's last organs, built for St Leonard Shoreditch, London, c1756, the Twelfth is again wider than the rest of the chorus. But here a further modification has taken place: Open Diapason and Principal are to the same scale, but the Fifteenth and Mixture seem to be one note smaller.[19]

With the Englands we have evidence of further experimentation with scaling. At St George, Gravesend there stand the substantial remains of an organ built by George England in 1764, including the earliest surviving English Cornet. While the Cornet is generally larger scaled than the Great chorus, as one might expect, there are three different scales within the one stop: the 4′ rank is the largest, the 2⅔′ two pipes smaller, and the 2′ and 1⅗′ one pipe smaller still.[20]

In George Pike England's organs this gentle variety in the scales of the open fluework has developed into confident manipulation. This fact was known in the nineteenth century, but Hopkins's detailed descriptions of the scaling methods of seventeenth- and eighteenth-century builders[21] is not supported by evidence from surviving instruments[22] (nor, incidentally, can his examples of mixture compositions be assumed to be reliable). To see what was actually going on it is informative to look at the most intact of G. P. England's organs at Blandford Forum in Dorset (see plate 43, p. 182). This instrument was built in 1794. An early account of it gives the specification, which, apart from the lack of a Choir Cremona or Vox Humana, is in every way typical of a parish church organ of the period.[23]

Blandford Forum Parish Church: George Pike England 1794

Compass: Great & Choir GG,AA–f‴ (58 notes), Swell g–f‴ (35 notes)

Great Organ	Choir Organ	Swell Organ
Open Diapason	Stopt Diapason	Open Diapason
Stopt Diapason	Dulciana	Stopt Diapason
Principal	Principal	Principal
Twelfth	Flute	Cornet III
Fifteenth	Fifteenth	Trumpet
Sesquialtra III		Hautboy
Mixture II		
Trumpet		
Cornet IV		

---

19 D. Gwynn, *St. Leonard Shoreditch*, Harley Foundation Technical Report 1990
20 D. Gwynn and D. C. Wickens, *St. George Gravesend*, Harley Foundation Technical Report 1990
21 Hopkins and Rimbault, *The Organ*, part II, 154–6
22 D. C. Wickens, unpublished paper, 'A Comparison of the Scaling Practice of Father Smith, at the End of the 17th Century, with that of G. P. England, at the End of the 18th Century; with Some Comments about Scaling in the Intervening Years', 1992   23 Royal College of Organists Library; Sperling Manuscript II, 84

As David Wickens has observed, the scale of the Choir Principal is to all intents the same as Bernard Smith's Choir Principal of 1698 at Great St Mary's, Cambridge,[24] but the Choir Fifteenth is smaller. The Great Open and Principal are larger, the Great Fifteenth similar to that on the Choir, and the Twelfth, Sesquialtera and Mixture to the same scale as each other, but smaller than the fifteenths. On the Swell the Open is the same scale as the Great Open, and the Principal is the same scale as the Great and Choir fifteenths. The Choir Dulciana is not a string-toned stop as introduced by Snetzler, but rather a small-scaled open diapason. The four ranks of the Cornet are broader than the chorus but with narrower mouths; they are all to different scales, the highest-pitched rank being the smallest.[25]

The sophistication of this method is entirely borne out in the sound of the organ: gentle but sparkling, and notable for its impeccable blend. In its obvious under-statement it mirrors English aesthetics in architecture and design. This is the musical equivalent of an Adam interior, by any criteria rich and sumptuous, but marked by very considerable restraint and a conscious desire to avoid bold state-ment. We have seen this tendency towards refinement growing during the eigh-teenth century, and with G. P. England it appears at its most elegant and cultured. In the light of this and the fact that England's organs are clearly rather soft in tone (the present pressure at Blandford is 71mm; the footholes in the pipes are smaller than in earlier builders' work, the cut-ups are uniformly around $\frac{1}{4}$ of the mouth width in the large basses, rising to $\frac{2}{7}$ in the trebles of the upperwork; the nicking has now become fine and regular) it seems at first difficult to account for the *Christian Remembrancer*'s impression of 'devil' in the chorus. However, given that the upper-work was narrower in scale than in older organs and that, with the movement towards refinement, the pipework was being voiced more keenly than might have been the case a hundred years before, the England choruses would have had a sparkling brilliance none the less telling for being modest in output.

If, in the work of the Englands, understatement, moderation and a general con-tentedness to follow the established pattern of stop-lists characterised the modest and self-effacing taste of the Britain of Jane Austen, then the innovations of Samuel Green reflected the other Britain: one of growth, social change and embryonic industrial revolution.

Samuel Green was born in Oxfordshire in 1740. In 1754 he was apprenticed to the organ and clock maker George Pyke and he later became a freeman of the Clockmaker's Company. Between 1761 and 1768 he was in partnership with the youngest of the three John Byfields. Studies by David Wickens suggest that he may also have worked with Snetzler. He set up his own business in London in 1772.[26]

Green enjoyed the patronage of George III, and during his career he secured many contracts in cathedrals and collegiate churches: this was the area of work which seems to have eluded Snetzler and the Englands. In the *Gentleman's Magazine*

---

[24] Thistlethwaite, 'Organo Pneumatico'   [25] Wickens, 'A Comparison of the Scaling Practice of Father Smith'
[26] D. C. Wickens, *The Instruments of Samuel Green* (London 1987)

◀ *Plate 43* The organ in the parish church of Blandford Forum, Dorset, built by George Pike England in 1794. The centre of town was destroyed by fire in 1731, and was rebuilt with a new parish church. Blandford still retains much of its eighteenth-century character. The organ has been relatively little altered, and retains the refined and sophisticated voicing practised by England and others towards the end of the century. The case shows English builders' continuing indebtedness to the art of the cabinet maker. Mouldings and details have become thinner and lighter than in the preceding generations, but elegant proportions and excellent standards of joinery ensure the success of the design.

of June 1814 a list of his work is given, allegedly taken from his own account book. This includes new or substantially new organs for the cathedrals at Canterbury, Wells, Lichfield, Salisbury, Rochester, Bangor and Cashel in Ireland; the organs at St George's Chapel, Windsor, the Royal Hospital, Greenwich, New College, Oxford; and many for parish churches in London and the provinces.[27]

A typical larger instrument is that for Rochester Cathedral, ordered in March 1790 and completed in November 1791, for which the agreement with the Dean and Chapter survives.[28]

Rochester Cathedral: Samuel Green 1790–1

Compass: Great and Choir GG,AA–e''' (57 notes); Swell g–e''' (34 notes)

Great Organ	**Choir Organ**	**Swell Organ**
Open Diapason	Dulciana [from g]	Open Diapason
Open Diapason	Stop Diapason	Dulciana
Stop Diapason	Principal	Stop Diapason
Principal	Fifteenth	Principal
Great Twelfth	Bassoon	Dulciana Principal
Fifteenth		Sexquialtera III
Sexquialtera III		Trumpet
Mixture II		Hautboy
Trumpet [bass]		
Trumpet [treble]		
Cornet IV [from c']		

The Swell Sexquialtera was named Cornet in the finished instrument. There is evidence that Green provided pedals pulling down the lowest notes of the Great organ, possibly GG,AA–c (seventeen notes).[29] The organ stood on the screen in a rather plain gothic case; the Choir organ was in a separate case in front.

This specification seems ordinary enough apart from the proliferation of Dulcianas and the absence of a Flute. Hidden behind this veneer of convention are numerous developments, both technical and tonal. In an account of the organ at the Royal Hospital, Greenwich in the *Christian Remembrancer*, the anonymous author remarks:[30]

[27] *Gentleman's Magazine* (June 1814), quoted in Hopkins and Rimbault, *The Organ*, part I, 151–3
[28] P. Hale, *The Organs of Rochester Cathedral* (Rochester 1989), 13–14   [29] Wickens, *The Instruments of Samuel Green*
[30] 'Organo-Historica, Or the History of Cathedral and Parochial Organs', *Christian Remembrancer* 1833–6, 'IX, The Organ at the Royal Hospital Chapel, Greenwich', reprinted in *BIOS Reporter*, 13 (1989), 3, 10–11

Plate 44 The organ in St Olave Hart Street, built by Samuel Green in 1781 (photograph c1910). The case is conservative in design, though the lightness of the carving and mouldings reveal its late eighteenth-century date. The case has been integrated into the panelling of the west wall of the nave. The two doorways on either side of the organ indicate the dawn of a realisation that church furnishings might be able to mirror the style of the building in which they stood, soon to blossom in a full exploration of the gothic. The church and organ were destroyed in the Second World War.

[Green's] zeal for the mechanical improvement of the organ consumed much of his valuable time in experimental labours, which to him produced little or no emolument.

On the tonal side Green seems to have adopted the trend towards delicacy and developed it still further. The *Christian Remembrancer* recorded that 'The organs built by this artist are characterised by a peculiar sweetness and delicacy of tone, entirely original; and, probably, in this respect, he has never been excelled.'[31] For Sir John Sutton, writing in the 1840s, this seemed to be less of a virtue:[32]

He certainly carried his system of voicing the pipes to the highest degree of delicacy; but what he gained in that way he lost in the general effect of the instrument. In his Diapasons, though the quality of tone is sweet, at the same time, it is very thin, and his Chorus is entirely destitute of either fulness or brilliancy of tone. His Choir organs are pretty toned, and would make nice chamber Organs, but they want firmness. One would suppose that Green was anxious in his instruments to emulate the tone of a musical snuff box, rather than that of an Organ.

Green's first line of development in securing the effect he desired was to experiment, perhaps even before the Englands, with the scales of the chorus. At St Katherine by the Tower in 1778 he was already varying the scales of the mixture ranks; at St Thomas, Ardwick in 1788 the Open Diapason is larger than the rest of the chorus. In the organs at Rochester and Lichfield evidence from surviving pipework shows a greater degree of experimentation. The appearance of extra pipes in some ranks, definitely by Green and contemporary with the instruments themselves, together with re-marking of the pipes, suggests that Green took spare pipes with him to the site and rescaled stops during the tonal finishing in the building.[33] This is considerably removed from the standardised scaling and voicing adopted by, for example, Snetzler. The attempt to consider blend and balance in detail is distinctive and novel.

The reasons for this become clearer when one understands that Green's voicing broke new ground in other respects as well. Delicacy was achieved partly by reducing the size of the pipe foot and by increasing the amount of nicking. The loss of grandeur in the chorus was made up for by increasing the scales of the extreme basses. This had the effect of tipping the overall tonal balance: the basses became strong and the trebles relatively weak. At Armitage in Staffordshire, where a large part of Green's Lichfield Cathedral organ of 1789–91 now resides, one can easily distinguish the innovatory quality of the ponderous large diapason pipes.[34]

With such a significant alteration in the balance of the chorus it is not surprising that Green needed to experiment on site to secure blend, especially given that his goal was a rather refined sound. In the earlier straight-line chorus of Smith or Snetzler the voicing of the foundation stops and the effect of the strong mixtures conspires to make the bass articulate and brilliant, and the treble solid and foundational. Blend between bass and treble looks after itself, and grandeur in the tutti is

[31] *BIOS Reporter*, 13 (1989), 3, 10–11   [32] Sutton, *A Short Account*, 81–2
[33] Information on Green's scaling techniques kindly provided by D. C. Wickens   [34] Author's examination

achieved throughout the chorus, rather than depending on the large bass pipes alone. By refining the upperwork and developing grandeur in the basses the question of balance becomes more critical, and depends much more on how the organist plays. This general trend is observable in music of the late eighteenth century and early nineteenth century. By the time we get to the voluntaries of Samuel Wesley and William Russell a characteristic pattern has developed. In full passages the left and right hands are occupied independently: the bass exploits the foundation of the organ, often in octaves (making up for the absence of a Pedal organ in England), and the treble parts move high up the keyboard with a thicker texture of three or even four parts, providing brilliance.

This change has been described fully because of its importance to understanding a certain English attitude to the relationship between foundation stops and the chorus that they support; an attitude that heavily influenced the builders of the nineteenth century and is still largely prevalent today. In this respect Samuel Green is an important pioneer, and we will see further developments of this trend in later chapters.

Green's innovation extended to other areas as well. At a time when English manufacturing was noted for technical invention and the appearance of machinery, Green introduced or developed numerous refinements to the mechanism. He often arranged the pipes from f♯ up in chromatic order on the soundboards, even in large organs. This reduced the extent to which rollerboards were required: splayed backfalls now effected the change from keyboard spacing to the spacing of the pipes on the soundboards, and there was less friction. Where rollers were needed, for example for the basses up to f, the axles were bushed with leather for quietness. To make the key action readily adjustable the ends of the trackers were fitted with tapped wires and leather buttons. The appearance of Green's consoles was enhanced by the use of ivory inserts screwed into the heads of the stop knobs, engraved with the name of the stop; this was easier to read than a paper label stuck alongside and far less confusing in a large organ. Green also usually made keyboards with white naturals and black sharps (a scheme more characteristic of harpsichords and fortepianos), though he was not necessarily the first to do so. In chamber organs the mechanism of shifting movements was simplified by springing the affected slides in the 'on' position, with a notch in the stop knob holding them 'off': the pedal operated directly on the ends of the slides and no duplicate slides were required. The harpsichord maker Shudi had developed and patented a swell for the harpsichord consisting of hinged shutters rather like a venetian blind. Green adapted the venetian swell to the organ, at first in chamber organs, and later on a large scale in his bigger instruments. At St George's Chapel, Windsor the whole organ was enclosed in a swell box, with the Swell Organ in a further swell inside. Winding systems were modified: instead of the traditional diagonal bellows, lifted alternately to provide the organ with wind, Green (together with some of his contemporaries) began to use a horizontal-rise reservoir fed by a diagonal feeder or feeders. This, together with the inverted ribs whose invention is traditionally attributed to the clock maker Alexander Cummings, was to become the standard winding system for organs all over the world in the next century. Green also used new pipe alloys, including a 'spotted' metal of about 60 per cent tin and 40 per cent lead; this has a mottled appearance that forms during cooling of the freshly cast sheet and only needs to be planed on one side. Green's organs stand on an independent building frame with the case erected round it, rather than being supported by the structure of the case itself.[35]

Many of Green's developments in mechanism were to spread from England to other areas in the work of subsequent generations. When the French speak of the *mécanique anglaise* that became popular in the 1840s they refer to a combination of new techniques and devices, many of which can be seen for the first time in Green's instruments.

The last major London builder of the eighteenth century to be noticed is John Avery, a contemporary of George Pike England. Little of his work survives, though his instruments were evidently highly respected and he deserves more attention than is possible on the basis of the available evidence; the most often repeated information about his activities is that he was a 'shocking drunken character', 'generally drunk and often in prison for debt'.[36] His new instruments included Winchester Cathedral, Carlisle Cathedral, and King's College, Cambridge.[37]

The rapid growth of population and wealth in Britain supported the famous London builders but also encouraged activity in many regional centres. We have seen how a town like Cambridge could support its own school of craftsmen, even on the small scale of Thamar and Quarles. But the larger provincial cities were growing rapidly, and some, like Bristol and Dublin, could rival the capitals of continental Europe in size and wealth.

In Bristol and the west country we have already seen the rise and fall of independent organ makers: the Haywards of Bath and Taunton of Bristol in the seventeenth century, and the work of Renatus Harris after his departure for Bristol in the early eighteenth century. Thomas Swarbrick worked extensively in the West and Midlands. To this list of provincial craftsmen should be added Brice and Richard Seede of Bristol, whose activity covers the period 1752–1823. Their work, which is clearly related in some way to that of the Harrises and Swarbrick, is represented today by the organs at Powderham Castle, Devon (Brice Seede 1769) and Lulworth Castle Chapel, Dorset (Richard Seede, installed c1785), and the remains of other larger instruments.[38] The organ at Lulworth, restored in the 1980s, is notable for its reversed console and for having two Open Diapasons amongst only eleven stops, an unusually grand scheme for such a small instrument (see plate 45, p. 188).[39]

Mark Anthony Dallam, a grandson of Robert Dallam,[40] settled in York, where

[35] Wickens, *The Instruments of Samuel Green*   [36] Sutton, *A Short Account*, 86   [37] Ibid., 88
[38] C. Kent, 'An Introduction to Brice and Richard Seede, Organ Builders of Bristol', *BIOS Journal*, 5 (1981), 83–97
[39] C. Kent, 'The Organ of St. Mary's Chapel Lulworth Castle – A Symposium, An Historical Survey', *BIOS Journal*, 11 (1987), 8–20   [40] M. Cocheril, 'The Dallams in Brittany', *BIOS Journal*, 6 (1982), 63–77

Plate 45   The organ at Lulworth Castle Chapel, Dorset installed here by Richard Seede c1785, possibly
incorporating parts of an earlier instrument, and now restored. This is an unusual instrument in several respects.
First, it has only one manual, though very fully developed to give a full church organ sound. Secondly, it has a
reversed console occupying the dummy Chaire case at the front of the gallery, the only English example surviving
from the eighteenth century. The case is that of a large chamber organ, though owing something to the style
introduced to the west country of England in the Harris & Byfield organ at St Mary Redcliffe, Bristol in 1726.

he died in 1730.[41] He was followed in York by Thomas Haxby, a maker of stringed instruments, harpsichords, fortepianos and organs, who worked from 1756 and died in 1796.[42] Then came John Donaldson, who worked in Newcastle from c1783 to 1790, and in York from 1790 until his death in 1807.[43] Both Haxby and Donaldson seem to have had connections with Snetzler, who built several organs in Yorkshire. Haxby certainly knew Snetzler; a long-standing rumour has it that Donaldson was trained by Snetzler, and his first appearance within a few years of Snetzler's retirement may be significant. Donaldson's major surviving work was built for Belvedere House, Dublin in 1790, and is now at the Holywell Music Room, Oxford. It is a two-manual instrument; it reveals its indebtedness to Snetzler in a Dulciana and a unique octave-sounding Violincello, but also shows varied scaling and a delicacy of tone more characteristic of George Pike England or even Green.

In Dublin the post-Restoration organ was introduced by Lancelot Pease; a case by him survives in the Public Theatre in Trinity College, Dublin;[44] another old case from Waterford Cathedral, now at Errigal Keeroge in County Tyrone, may also be by him.[45] Later in the seventeenth century there appeared one John Baptist Cuvillie (properly Jean-Baptiste Cavaillé?),[46] initially, it seems, working as a site foreman for Renatus Harris, but later establishing a reputation of his own. He was clearly French; making alterations to the organ at Christ Church Cathedral, Dublin in 1696–7 he added a 'tramblen' (Fr. *tremblant*, Eng. tremulant) to improve the effect of the Vox Humana, observing that it was a feature:[47]

which no organ in England can show the like, for they have not found out how to make the tramblen stop; and for want of that stop all their vox humanas are deficient, whereas I have made this stop . . . as perfect as any organ beyond the sea.

In the eighteenth century the Dublin school was represented by four members of the Hollister family, covering three generations: Robert, Thomas, Philip and William Castles Hollister.[48] Philip Hollister's organ for St Colomb's Cathedral, Derry was notable for eschewing the uniform use of plain metal for the pipework: the contract of June 1748 specifies 'finest mettal', 'middle finest mettal' and 'least finest mettal' for the various stops, as well as red deal for stopped diapason and flute basses.[49]

[41] B. B. Edmonds, 'Yorkshire Organ Builders, the Earlier Years', *BIOS Journal*, 9 (1985), 42–50
[42] D. Haxby and J. Malden, 'Thomas Haxby of York (1729–1796): an Extraordinary Musician and Musical Instrument Maker', *BIOS Journal*, 7 (1983), 59–76
[43] S. Bicknell, 'The Donaldson Organ in the Holywell Music Room Oxford', *BIOS Journal*, 11 (1987), 32–49
[44] J. Holmes, 'The Trinity College Organs in the Seventeenth and Eighteenth Centuries', *Hermathena*, 113 (1972), 40–8
[45] P. McSweeney, 'The Organ and Harpsichord in Ireland before 1870' (MA thesis, University of Cork, 1979)
[46] A. Freeman, 'Records of British Organ Builders' (Second Series), in *Musical Opinion* 1922–5, paragraph 244; N. M. Plumley, 'The Englishness of the English Organ Case, Some Thoughts on Organ Case Design in England 1660–1800', *BIOS Journal*, 4 (1980) 6–18
[47] W. H. Grattan-Flood, 'The Organs of Christ Church Cathedral Dublin', *Musical Opinion*, 40 (1916–17), 659
[48] Freeman, 'Records of British Organ Builders' (Second Series), paragraph 236–9
[49] M. E. Callender and M. E. Hoeg, 'The Philip Hollister Organ of Derry Cathedral', *The Organ*, 58 (1979–80), 58–66

London builders set the pattern both for immigrants like Snetzler and for organ making in the provinces; they also established the English organ type in the colonies of the New World. Though North America offered a home to craftsmen from continental Europe, such as the famous David Tannenberg, it was the English exports to the towns of the Eastern seaboard that set the standard for the future development of the craft in the United States. Tannenberg's influence was mainly restricted to the German-speaking settlements of Pennsylvania and Philadelphia.

Bernard Smith had sent an organ to Barbados in 1699,[50] and both English and German settlers in the North American colonies had chamber organs around 1700. Regular imports started with Richard Bridge's organ of 1733 for Trinity Church, Newport, Rhode Island; the case survives. This instrument was set up by Karl Theodore Pachelbel, son of the composer.[51] Bridge sent another instrument in 1756 for the King's Chapel, Boston, and Abraham Jordan (junior) built an organ for Trinity Church, Boston in 1744, which was approved by Handel before it left London. Snetzler built several organs for North America, including one of his largest instruments for Trinity Church, New York City in 1764 (with the advice of the composer John Stanley), and a smaller one for St Michael, Charleston, South Carolina in 1768. Barbara Owen writes:[52]

With the Declaration of Independence in 1776 the colonial period came to an end, but not so the importation of English organs. Although a prolific American school of organ building (which at first based its work largely on English models) began in the later part of the eighteenth century and continued with growing vigor throughout the nineteenth century, a small number of instruments continued to be imported.

These included organs by Samuel Green, his contemporary Henry Holland, John Avery and several by George Pike England. By the beginning of the nineteenth century the number of imports had dwindled in the face of the confident activity of native craftsmen. However, it is interesting to note the arrival in New York of one John Geib around 1798.[53] He arrived from England (where he made pianos and had built an organ in St Mary, Stafford, in 1789–90[54]) and worked in a broadly English style, but is in fact almost certainly from the Geib family who worked in Saarbrücken, Germany, in the period 1760-90.[55] After some significant instruments by Thomas Elliot and Robert Gray (and some less notable by Bevington and Bates) in the period 1800–40, English imports were effectively suspended until recent times.

It is not an overstatement to claim that American organ building was founded on the English model, and a comparison between builders on opposite shores of the Atlantic is perfectly reasonable. To quote Barbara Owen again:[56]

[50] *London Post* 4 October 1699   [51] O. Ochse, *The History of the Organ in the United States* (Bloomington 1975), 28
[52] B. Owen, 'Colonial Organs, Being an Account of Some Early English Instruments Exported to the Eastern United States', *BIOS Journal*, 3 (1979), 92–107   [53] Ochse, *The History of the Organ in the United States*, 81–5
[54] H. Snow, 'The Organ of St. Mary Stafford', *The Organ*, 16 (1936–7), 239–43
[55] H. Fischer, *100 Jahre Bund Deutscher Orgelbaumeister* (Munich 1991), 93   [56] Owen, 'Colonial Organs'

... the influence of the early imported instruments loomed very large in proportion to their numbers. In a very real sense they provide the earliest American builders with a readily accessible textbook to their craft, and until continental influences began to be felt in the 1850s and 1860s the American organ remained solidly in the mainstream of the eighteenth century English tradition – even, paradoxically, some decades after that tradition had been largely superseded in the British Isles.

By the close of the eighteenth century we can build up a very full picture from the many surviving instruments of how the English organ worked and sounded. Fortunately this evidence is amply supported by published organ music and by two contemporary organ tutors.

The many solo organ voluntaries published during the eighteenth century give a clear idea of how the art of registration had developed in England, indicating a formalised repertoire of sounds available through the correct choice of stops. How these choices work musically on an organ of the period is an excellent way of cross-referencing the tonal qualities of the different builders and of assessing the authenticity of surviving material in instruments that have been altered in some way. Some explanation of the English music publishing business helps put the voluntaries in context. In many other parts of the world the appearance of compositions in printed form indicated the high reputation of the composer and was often the result of patronage. Such printed editions were often representative of the composer's best or most typical work. In England in the eighteenth century the printing of music was a commercial operation depending on wide sales for its financial success. Thus the organ voluntaries were written to a moderate technical difficulty. Compositions written down for private use (and indeed improvisations) may have been more complex and demanding. This is certainly suggested when one compares the published voluntaries of John Stanley, which are effective but musically simple, with the more advanced writing in the organ concertos and his reputation as an extempore performer.

Stanley's three volumes of organ voluntaries sum up the developments in registration in the first half of the eighteenth century, and illustrate excellently the ground rules that formed the basis for English organists to follow until the radical changes in organ building and playing in the 1840s.[57] These rules are set down formally in the treatises of John Marsh[58] and Jonas Blewitt,[59] and confirmed in other collections of voluntaries.

The slow introductions to most voluntaries are played on the Open and Stopped Diapasons together; the Open Diapason is never used singly. Full Organ consists of the entire Great organ, including mixtures and reeds (but not the Cornet), though sometimes qualified by the instruction 'with the Trumpet' or 'without the Trumpet'. The Cornet and the unison sounding reed stops (Trumpet, French Horn,

[57] J. Stanley, *Thirty Voluntaries*, Op. 5 (London 1748), Op. 6 (1752), Op. 7 (1754)
[58] J. Marsh, *Eighteen Voluntaries for the Organ . . . To which is prefix'd an Explanation of the . . . Stops etc.* (London 1791)
[59] J. Blewitt, *A Complete Treatise on the Organ to which is added a Set of Explanatory Voluntaries etc.* (London c1795)

Cremona, Vox Humana) are used in solos for the right hand, accompanied by suitable registration on the Choir organ and with echoes on the Echo or Swell organ (the Cornet may well also have been used for announcing the tunes of the psalms). The Dulciana and Flute may be used on their own, the Flute sounding an octave higher than written. Where use of the Swell is indicated in the later eighteenth century, it should be assumed that the normal position of the box is closed, and the registration on the Swell should mirror what is drawn on the Great. These categories are rarely departed from before the nineteenth century, though there are a few left-hand solos to be found, and an intriguing voluntary by Stanley which requires the use of three keyboards at once.[60]

Only one notable departure from these guidelines is known, but as it appears on a piece of paper glued to a chamber organ by John Byfield (II) it is of considerable interest. The organ has one manual and six stops: Open and Stopped Diapason, Principal, Flute, Twelfth and Fifteenth.[61]

Directions for compounding the stops of the Organ properly:-
1. Open Diaphason & flute together
2. Open and Stop Diaphasons together
3. Diaphasons & Fifteenth
4. Diaphason & Principal
5. Stop Diaphason & Flute
6. Diaphasons, Fifteenth & Flute
7. Diaphasons & Twelfth
8. Diaphasons, Principal & Flute
In drawing of the stops, take care that they be put as far out or in as they will go, or else the Organ will appear out of tune.

This is a remarkably inventive list, and it includes some unexpected combinations that work very well in practice. Less conservative than registrations suggested by composers and theorists, these recipes suggest an organ builder's acquaintance with the many possibilities offered by only a few well-voiced ranks of pipes.

The relative rigidity of the customary suggestions for drawing the stops is somewhat reminiscent of the situation in France, and though the music that resulted is quite different, it encourages one to view eighteenth-century English organs as distant cousins of instruments across the English Channel, especially in view of the continued dominance of descendants of the Dallams and Harrises. While the tasks to be performed by the English organ remained relatively undemanding, as was the case in parish churches or in the Cathedrals and collegiate churches, both the organ type and the sounds it could offer were perfectly adequate, and the builders who made the instruments could satisfy their customers through continual refinement of the basic idea. However, by the end of the century certain other uses for the organ

---

[60] Stanley, *Thirty Voluntaries*, Op. 7 no. 4
[61] Instructions glued to the 1766 John Byfield organ from Cullen House, Banffshire, Scotland and now at Finchcocks, Goudhurst, Kent.

were emerging, and some of these presented demands which could not be met without a major shake-up in organ tone and design.

Public appetite for music had become almost insatiable. It was not simply congeniality which led Handel and J. C. Bach to settle in London: there were very considerable financial rewards to be had. The organ had its place in the world of secular performance; though originally it may have been chamber organs that were needed to provide continuo to consorts of viols or singers, before long larger instruments were needed and used (this fact should be taken into account by today's performers, who all too often believe that a tiny three-stop box organ is adequate for their purpose). The pleasure gardens of London may have started the trend.

The pleasure gardens were commercial enterprises offering a wide variety of entertainment in an attractive public park: a fairground whose rough edges had been softened by a generous dose of civilised gentility. In the three major establishments of Ranelagh, Vauxhall and Marylebone, a pavilion for the performance of concerts was the centrepiece, and in the 1730s and 40s all three were fitted with organs.[62] These buildings were the true precursors of the secular concert hall of modern times.

Handel's contribution to the establishment of popular concert-going was considerable. Initially his attention was devoted to the introduction of Italian opera, but after the vogue for this subsided he turned to the oratorio. This was the musical contribution which most endeared him to the English public and for which he is still remembered today in countless reverent performances of *Messiah*.

The extraordinary status of the oratorio became apparent in the Handel Commemoration Festival of 1784 (see plate 40, p. 173). Held in Westminster Abbey, it drew together five hundred performers, and required the construction of special seats and staging. The organisation required to bring the musical part of the proceedings to a successful conclusion was on an unprecedented scale. For the occasion the new Samuel Green organ destined for Canterbury Cathedral was temporarily erected on the stage in the Abbey. It was fitted with a remote keyboard, which seems to have acted on a harpsichord as well; these 'keys of communication with the harpsichord' were detached nineteen feet (5.8m) in front of the organ. According to Burney, such detached consoles were introduced by Handel for his oratorios (but see the reference to Jordan's reversed console in Chapter 9), but to remove the keys quite so far from the instrument was a remarkable technical feat.[63]

Once the taste for the mammoth musical event was acquired, it was never to be shaken off. In the accompaniment of large bodies of singers the English found a new sublime use for the organ. In the next century the demands this placed on the design and mechanism of the instrument were to stretch the ingenuity and patience of the builders to the limit, and were to usher in a new age.

[62] B. Matthews, 'The Organs of the London Pleasure Gardens', *The Organ*, 48 (1968–9), 35–40

[63] C. Burney, *Account of the Musical Performances in Westminster Abbey & The Pantheon on May 26, 27, 29 and June 3, 5, 1784 in Commemoration of Handel* (London 1785)

CHAPTER ELEVEN

INTERLUDE – THE CHAMBER ORGAN
1600–1850

So far this work has largely been concerned with the development of the organ in the English church. However, a second thread of the story is that of the chamber organ. Small organs for domestic use are a characteristic part of the output of the English craft and, surviving in large numbers, these charming instruments offer one of the most accessible and rewarding ways of exploring the historic English organ.

Modern appreciation of them can be said to have begun with Sir John Sutton who, in his *Short Account of Organs* (1847), described two late seventeenth-century instruments that belonged to him and which he attributed to Bernard Smith.[1] Both are still in existence. The smaller of the two, now the property of N. P. Mander Ltd and standing in their workshops in London, is a one-manual instrument.[2]

Chamber organ formerly the property of Sir John Sutton, now at the workshops of N. P. Mander Ltd, London: anon., late seventeenth century

Compass C–c''' (49 notes: C# originally played AA?)
Stop names modern (no original labels)

Stopped Diapason	8
Principal	4
Fifteenth	2
Mixture	II

Sutton had the organ restored in 1845 by Bishop, and the mixture pipes date from then.[3] Of the remaining stops, the Stopped Diapason and Principal are of pine with oak caps and the Fifteenth, standing partly in the front, is of metal rich in tin.

Several features of this instrument are common to English chamber organs of all periods. First, its appearance and external construction belong firmly to the furniture making tradition of the period in which it was made. With the double doors shut over the keys, stops and front pipes the instrument appears to be a small oak press or cupboard. Secondly, the generally small dimensions of the organ require a

---

[1] Sir J. Sutton, *A Short Account of Organs Built in England* (London 1847), 54–5   [2] Author's examination
[3] A. Freeman and J. Rowntree, *Father Smith* (Oxford 1976), 166

Plate 46   A chamber organ, probably dating from the second quarter of the seventeenth century, once at Hunstanton Hall, Norfolk and now in Smithfield, Virginia, USA. The visual conceit of receding perspective common in seventeenth-century casework is here elaborated to a complete view of the interior of a vaulted hall, in which the wooden front pipes are made to appear as pilasters lining the walls. The fine mouldings and channelled details are typical of mid seventeenth-century joinery of the first class. As with many early English chamber organs the pipes are entirely of wood. The bellows are in the roof of the organ.

degree of ingenuity in the layout of pipes and mechanism. Thirdly, the presence of wooden pipes is typical, and the ability of the maker to produce a consistent and finely voiced principal tone out of small-scale open wooden pipes is a notable feature.

It is now clear that a number of very similar instruments survive. Amongst them are those at Canon's Ashby, Northamptonshire; Canterbury Cathedral (the Galpin Organ); St George in the Meadows, Nottingham and the Royal College of Music, London. In all there is considerable use of wooden pipes, and in some all the pipes, including the mixture, are of wood (mostly pine with oak caps).

Plate 47   A chamber organ attributed to Bernard Smith and dating from the second half of the seventeenth century, now in the collection of the organ builders N. P. Mander Ltd in London. In the nineteenth century this organ was found at New College, Oxford by Sir John Sutton, who had it restored for his own use. It is one of several similar instruments surviving. All have wooden pipes, continuing a style of manufacture that appears to have been established long before Smith arrived in England. These instruments may belong to a long-standing tradition in the making of small organs.

The attribution of these small organs to Bernard Smith cannot be traced back to an authentic source: none of them are signed, nor are they marked in any manner that invites comparison with the few remains of Smith's larger instruments. That near contemporaries thought that there were Smith chamber organs is illustrated in an excerpt from a letter, thought to have been written by Handel:[4]

Father Smith's chamber organs generally consist of a stop diapason of all wood. Sometimes there is an open diapason of wood. Down to Cefaut, an open flute of wood, a fifteenth of wood, a bass mixture of wood: that is to the middle C. of two ranks, the cornet of wood of two ranks to meet the mixture in the middle. Sometimes the mixture is of mettle, as is the cornet. N.B. – if it is stiled "a furniture" it is *not* one of his, that is *if* the mixture is stil'd so *it is not*. Remark that the wooden pipes are all of clean yellow deal.

The earliest positive attribution to Smith is in the label attached to the organ in Dingestow Court, Monmouthshire, by Robert Gray in 1775, who rebuilt it with a new case and mechanism in that year.[5] The next claim is Sutton's, concerning the two chamber organs that belonged to him. However, it is clear from the larger of the two that this is not the end of the story. This second instrument is now at Compton Wynyates, Northamptonshire.

Chamber organ formerly the property of Sir John Sutton, now at Compton Wynyates, Northamptonshire: anon., late seventeenth century

Compass originally AA,C,D–c''' (49 notes)?
Stop names modern (no original labels)

Lower manual

Open Diapason	8 wood
Stopped Diapason	8 wood
Principal	4 wood

Upper manual

Stopped Diapason	8 (from lower manual)
Stopped Flute	4 metal
Fifteenth	2 metal
Mixture	II metal

Coupler lower manual to upper manual

The appearance and construction of this organ leaves one in no doubt that it is by the same builder (or at least comes from the same sphere of influence) as the smaller instruments. However, the note marks on the pipes are in the form characteristic of the Dallam/Harris line of builders and are not like Smith's. And, in the words of the organ builder Dominic Gwynn, 'The most suggestive evidence is that on the Fifteenth AA [pipe] has been written *Cart* . . . "Cart" (Anglicisation of the French *Quarte de Nazard*) is unlikely to have been used by anyone but a Dallam or Harris

---

[4] Mrs. Delany, *The Autobiography and Correspondence of Mary Granville, Mrs. Delany*, ed. Lady Llanover, 6 vols., 2 series of 3 (London 1861–2), 2nd series, I, 568n.   [5] Freeman and Rowntree, *Father Smith*, 176–7

after the return from Brittany'.[6] Furthermore, it is clear from the evidence of other surviving chamber organs that these instruments are the successors to a lively local tradition that was already flourishing long before Smith arrived in England.

Four important chamber organs survive from the half century before the probable date of the so-called 'Father Smith' instruments. That at Knole, Kent is believed to have been built in the 1620s. It is in the form of a low chest, and has four stops, all of oak.[7]

Chamber organ at Knole, Kent: anon, early seventeenth century

Stop names modern (no original labels)

Stopped Diapason	8
Principal	4
Twelfth	$2^{2}/_{3}$
Fifteenth	2

There may once have been other instruments of this kind. In 1513 Brasenose College, Oxford was bequeathed 'a payre of orgaynes bought at London of the facion of a countyngborde or lowe table'.[8]

Fragments of another early instrument survive at Canterbury Cathedral; this was bought in London in 1629 for Dean Isaac Bargrave. Here the organ stands on a table-like frame. Unplayable and lacking any pipes, it is more of archaeological than musical significance. However, the survival of another instrument standing on a four-legged frame or table suggests that this was a recognised type in the earlier seventeenth century. Built for the Le Strange family of Hunstanton Hall, Norfolk, it now stands in a church at Smithfield, Virginia, USA (see plate 46, p. 195). Again the pipes are entirely of wood, and the comparison with contemporary furniture is apposite. The display of front pipes revealed by opening the doors of the case is especially remarkable. What appears is a richly painted *trompe l'œil* scene of an architectural setting, with a colonnade and chequered pavement arranged in imitation of receding perspective. The comparison between this and certain full-sized cases made by members of the Dallam family is obvious.[9]

The ex-Hunstanton organ is undated and unsigned, but the comparison between the painted front and part of another chamber organ, dated 1643 and signed Christianus Smith, indicates a date of c1630–40. In this latter instrument the front panel again displays an architectural interior, here with the addition of two musicians in royalist dress standing on the painted pavement: one is playing a sackbut, the other a cornett (I would suggest that the façades of both are painted by the same artist). The Christianus Smith organ is the property of N. P. Mander Ltd and is in store at their workshop in London. At a time when all the seventeenth-century

---

[6] C. H. Davidson, *Sir John Sutton, A Study in True Principles* (Oxford 1992), 72
[7] M. Renshaw, 'An Early 17th Century British Organ, a Preliminary Study', *BIOS Journal*, 4 (1980), 34–42
[8] A. V. Butcher, 'Two Small Hill Organs', *The Organ*, 27 (1947–8), 18–22   [9] Author's examination

chamber organs were assumed to be by Father Smith it was naturally assumed that Christianus Smith was a relative, and this was in turn used to cement the theory that Bernard Smith came from an English family.[10] It must now be admitted that there is no evidence to support this point, and for the time being Christianus Smith remains an isolated figure. A recent assessment of the remains of this organ suggests that it has been quite radically altered at some point in its past.[11] The original specification has not been discovered and for the time being there are no plans for its restoration.

Surviving pipes at Nettlecombe Court, Somerset (John Loosemore 1665) show that there were other builders able to make small-scaled open wooden principals before Bernard Smith came to England.[12] In the Cathedral Song School at Exeter, there once stood another chamber organ by Loosemore, again with wooden pipes. This has now disappeared.[13] The case and part of the soundboard of an early chamber organ survive at Lichfield Cathedral, the detailing of the case being similar to the ex-Hunstanton organ;[14] the instrument is anonymous, but it may be significant that Robert Dallam was employed at Lichfield in 1639–40.[15]

There is enough evidence here to show that there was a tradition of chamber organ building right through the seventeenth century, and their existence is confirmed by John Aubrey and Samuel Pepys, amongst others. The uses of these instruments must have been varied: in the Song School at Exeter for choral practice; in a private house such as Hunstanton Hall for solo or consort use. The so-called Father Smith chamber organs follow naturally on from this earlier tradition. The question of who actually made them must remain open for the time being.

As with church instruments, there is a distinct lull in activity in the early eighteenth century. Some chamber organs from this period may have been absorbed in the Father Smith legend; for example, that at St Paul's Presbyterian Church, Liss, Hampshire, formerly attributed to Smith,[16] is now likely to be redated to the period 1710–50.[17] Organ builders of the period 1700–40 were certainly capable of making small organs, but the fact that so few survive (in marked contrast to the substantial group of instruments from the seventeenth century) suggests that the chamber organ had fallen out of fashion.

The reasons for this, as with the lull in the building of church organs at roughly the same time, may be partly economic. The country was at war for most of Queen Anne's reign. The attempt to reduce the national debt through the South Sea Company led to a wild outburst of speculation until the bubble burst in 1720. The market for domestic musical instruments must have suffered in the wake of these events.

[10] C. Clutton and A. Niland, *The British Organ* (London 1963), 58–9
[11] Examined by the author while employed with N. P. Mander Ltd; interim report lodged in the company's files
[12] Author's examination
[13] E. J. Hopkins and E. F. Rimbault, *The Organ, Its History and Construction*, 3rd edn (London 1877), 63; Letter from J. C. Hele to A. Freeman 28 October 1896, quoted in *The Organ*, 6 (1926–7), 192   [14] Author's examination
[15] R. Greening, *The Organs of Lichfield Cathedral* (Lichfield 1974), 5–8
[16] Freeman and Rowntree, *Father Smith*, 53, 156–7   [17] Conversation with the organ builder Dominic Gwynn

Revival takes place in the 1740s, and within a few years there is a marked boom in the production of small organs of various types. Renewed financial security is certainly one reason for this revival, but we should not ignore the revolution in public music making which also played a part. The Civil War and the Glorious Revolution ended a society in which the arts were dominated by the court and the aristocracy, and in England church patronage had long since declined. But, with cities as large as London, Bristol and Dublin, there were significant opportunities for the arts to flourish on a commercial basis. The playhouses of Shakespeare's London illustrate the emergence of arts in the public, profit-making arena from 1600 or even earlier. In the early eighteenth century English towns were bustling with wealthy men of commerce; music could be organised to entertain this new class and to make a profit.

From this we understand why George Frederick Handel is such an important figure in English music: quite apart from his talent as a composer and performer, it was his flair as a musical entrepreneur and impresario which made such an impact. It is quite possible that we should attribute the revival of the chamber organ in part to his influence. Handel introduced organ concertos in the intervals of his operas; Burney remarks that he introduced a detached console from which he could direct the orchestra;[18] Handel is supposed to have taken an organ with him to Dublin for the first performance of *Messiah*.[19] In 1749 he advised his librettist Charles Jennens on the purchase of a small organ:[20]

Sir,

Yesterday I received your letter, in answer to which I hereunder specify my opinion of an organ which I think will answer the ends you propose, being everything that is necessary for a good and grand organ without reed stops, which I have omitted because they are continually wanting to be tuned, which in the country is very inconvenient, and should it remain useless on that account, it would still be very expensive althou' that may not be your consideration. I very well approve of Mr. Bridge, who without any objection is a very good organ builder, and I shall willingly (when he has finished it) give you my opinion of it. I have referr'd you to the flute stop in Mr. Freeman's organ being excellent in its kind, but as I do not refer you in that organ, The system of the organ I advise is (Vizt. The Compass to be up to D and down to Gamut, full octave, Church Work).

One row of keys, whole stops and none in halves.

Stops
An Open Diapason – of Metal throughout to be in front
A Stopt Diapason – the Treble Metal and the Bass Wood
A Principal – of Metal throughout
A Twelfth – of Metal throughout

[18] C. Burney, Account of the Musical Performances in Westminster Abbey & The Pantheon on May 26, 27, 29 and June 3, 5, *1784 in Commemoration of Handel*, (London 1785)
[19] H. C. Robbins Landon, *Handel and his World* (London 1984); C. Hogwood, *Handel* (London 1984)
[20] W. L. Sumner, *The Organ, Its Evolution, Principles of Construction and Use*, 4th edn (London 1973), 170

A Fifteenth – of Metal throughout
A Great Tierce – of Metal throughout
A Flute Stop – such a one as in Mr. Freeman's Organ

I am glad of the opportunity to show you my attention, wishing you all health and happiness, I remain with great sincerity and respect, Sir,

Your most obedient and humble Servant,

George Frederic Handel

The organ, built by the Bridge pupil Thomas Parker, and with a small second manual added either during construction or early in its life, is now at Great Packington Church, Warwickshire.[21]

With the arrival of John Snetzler in London around 1740 there is a turning point in the history of the chamber organ. In Chapter 10 we saw that he seems to have concentrated on small organs at the beginning of his career in England, and the form that these took is of some importance. One of the earliest surviving is that now in the Belle Skinner collection of musical instruments at Yale University, USA. It is signed and dated 1742.[22]

Chamber organ in the Belle Skinner collection, Yale University USA: John Snetzler 1742

Compass C–d''',e'''
Op. Diapason	metal
Diapaison [stopped]	wood
Flauta	wood
Fiffteenth	metal
Sesquialtra [C–b]	metal
Sesquialtra [c'–e''']	metal
Cornet [c'–e''']	metal

In its original form the organ seems to have been in the shape of a desk or bureau. Early in its life the Open Diapason was added by Snetzler and the case enlarged. The case is painted with florid and colourful scrolls and garlands.

The bureau organ was characteristic of Snetzler and a number of them survive. The Yale organ was an early example, and its significance is twofold: first, it introduced a new variety of extremely compact, even portable, instrument of immense practical use with other performers; secondly, the form of the organ allied the chamber organ to the construction and style of contemporary furniture. This becomes a feature of Snetzler's chamber organs, and spreads during the later eighteenth century to organs of all sizes, the cabinet-maker's casework of later Georgian organs being a particular feature of the English craft. In Snetzler's work the connection with the decorative arts was probably established through his brother

---

[21] B. B. Edmonds, 'Notes and Queries', *BIOS Reporter*, 12 (1988), 3, 15
[22] Author's examination during restoration by N. P. Mander Ltd in 1984

Leonard, a carver and plasterer, who may have been responsible for the elegant and fashionable cases.[23] These distinguish themselves from the work of earlier builders, whose cases had followed fashions in architectural woodwork. With Snetzler's organs the connection with contemporary furniture is made much more obvious, not least in the use of the newly fashionable mahogany rather than oak, and the new aesthetic is developed in the designs of Green and the Englands.

The enlargement and redecoration of the Yale organ is also intriguing. When the organ was restored in 1984 the painted decoration of the case was conserved by Anna Hulbert, who expressed the view that the character of the work was similar to theatrical scenery painting.[24] There is a persistent tradition that this organ actually was the instrument used by Handel for the first performance of *Messiah* in Dublin in 1742;[25] the link is a tenuous one and has not been proved, but the way the instrument has been dressed up as though for the stage is a suggestive link with the new kinds of performance practice introduced by Handel.

In Snetzler's oeuvre we also find a considerable number of larger chamber organs, many built to standard patterns, again resembling the best furniture of the period. That now at St Andrew-by-the-Wardrobe, London, built for Teddesley Hall, Staffordshire in 1769, is typical.[26]

Chamber organ formerly at Teddesley Hall, Staffordshire, now in the church of St Andrew-by-the-Wardrobe: John Snetzler 1769

Compass GG,AA–e'''
Open Diapason [GG–B from St. Diap. with 4' helpers]
Stop Diapason [wood]
Dulciana [GG–B from St. Diap]
Principal
Flute [wood]
Fifteenth
Sesquialtera [GG–b]
Cornet [c'–e''']

An almost identical organ built in the same year survives in private hands in Somerset.[27] In both instruments the natural keys are of ivory and the sharps plated with ebony, and the stops are identified by engraved labels let into the heads of the stop knobs: these are early appearances of these features. The Somerset organ has louvres in the sides and roof connected to a pedal: other slightly haphazard swelling devices can be found in Snetzler organs. A larger two-manual version of this design was built for Cobham Hall, Kent in 1778–9 (see plate 49, p. 205). This has a very rare surviving example of wind supplied by two diagonal bellows.[28]

To claim that Snetzler cornered the market in chamber organs would be an

---

[23] A. Barnes and M. Renshaw, *The Life and Work of John Snetzler* (Aldershot 1994), 5–6
[24] Report on conservation work during the restoration of 1984 lodged with N. P. Mander Ltd
[25] Barnes and Renshaw, *The Life and Work of John Snetzler*, 60–4   [26] Author's examination
[27] Barnes and Renshaw, *The Life and Work of John Snetzler*, 157–8   [28] Ibid., 182–4

Plate 48   The organ in Danson Mansion, Welling, Kent (at present in Hall Place, Bexleyheath, Kent), built by George England in 1760. This is an unusually grand example of a chamber organ, housed in a mahogany case designed to form a part of the decorative scheme of the room in which it stood. The quality of the cabinet making is superlative, extending to herringbone veneers on the borders of the console doors, stop jambs and music desk panel. The organ is mounted on wooden rollers so that it can be drawn forward for tuning and maintenance.

exaggeration, although it is difficult to escape the conclusion that he led the field in re-establishing their popularity. His contemporaries were busy too, and notable surviving examples are at Finchcocks, Goudhurst, Kent by John Byfield (II) 1766 (built for Castle Grant, Banff, Scotland, with a case apparently designed by John Adam),[29] Hall Place, Bexleyheath, Kent by George England 1766 (built for Danson Mansion, Kent) (see plate 48, p. 203),[30] Wardour Castle, Wiltshire by John England 1767,[31] and Powderham Castle, Devon by Brice Seede 1769.[32]

Snetzler's small organs have all the forthright brilliancy that reputedly distinguished his larger instruments. This is plain enough in the larger chamber organs, such as those now at Eton College and St Mary's Church, Hillington, Norfolk, and the organ at St Andrew-by-the Wardrobe, London.[33] However, in the bureau organs the effect is still more remarkable. The most original of these instruments known to the author is that now in the town museum at Schaffhausen, Switzerland where Snetzler was born. It was acquired in England in 1982 by a descendant, Dr Barbara Schnetzler, and was restored by N. P. Mander Ltd. It was probably made for the Chandos Pole family of Radburne Hall, Derbyshire and is dated 1763.[34]

Bureau organ formerly at Radburne Hall, Derbyshire, now in Schaffhausen, Switzerland: John Snetzler 1763

Compass C,D–e'''
Stopped Diapason	8 wood
Flute	4 wood
Fifteenth	2 metal
Sesquialtera [bass, $1\frac{3}{5}$ + $1\frac{1}{3}$]	II metal
Cornet [treble, $2\frac{2}{3}$ + $1\frac{3}{5}$]	II metal

A pedal raises and lowers the lid of the organ to provide a simple swelling device. In 1982 the organ was very clean and well preserved and still retained most of its original leather work. The pipes had been crudely torn to alter the tuning, but once repairs had been made it became clear that the instrument had been tuned in ¼-comma meantone temperament or something very close to it. The effect, in the home keys, of the Fifteenth and the strong quint and tierce in the Sesquialtera and Cornet is astonishingly bold. The effect of playing a chord of C major, with the tutti very strongly coloured by dissonant intervals in the upperwork, is disconcerting. Moreover the Stopped Diapason and Flute sound the unison rather weakly, with a very strong first harmonic (the octave quint). The result is that the notes of a G major triad are represented almost as strongly as as those of C major. To analyse a chorus in this way is to challenge the very principles of organ tone, and

[29] N. M. Plumley, 'The Harris–Byfield Connection, Some Recent Findings', *BIOS Journal*, 3 (1979), 111–15; a fuller description of this instrument is given in Chapter 9.   [30] Author's examination
[31] Author's examination
[32] C. Kent, 'An Introduction to Brice and Richard Seede, Organ Builders of Bristol', *BIOS Journal*, 5 (1981), 83–97
[33] Author's examination of all three instruments
[34] Analysis of the tuning carried out by the author in consultation with John Mander during the restoration of this organ by N. P. Mander Ltd in 1982. Restoration report kept in the files of N. P. Mander Ltd

Plate 49 The organ in Cobham Hall, Kent, built by John Snetzler in 1778–9. This two-manual instrument is housed in a case typical of Snetzler's chamber organs, owing something to the delicate classical taste introduced by the brothers Adam (although the Music Room in which it stands is actually the work of William Chambers).

it has to be accepted that the multiple dissonances and consonances found in a principal chorus actually produce a musical effect full of interest and colour. But here,
with such a Spartan distribution of the harmonic components and heard at very
close quarters the tonality of this or any other chord is highly ambiguous. However,
as soon as it is put into a musical context, all becomes clear, and the vigour and
daring of Snetzler's method is suddenly justified. The combination of boldly voiced
mutations and shifting patterns of consonance and dissonance (always a part of a
performance on a keyboard instrument tuned to meantone temperament) high-
lights the harmonic structure of the composition played, and in particular emphasises modulations away from the home key. That home key will itself have its own
colour, depending on how many sharps or flats it has. This tonal world is one that
is almost completely unfamiliar to modern ears, despite the early music movement
and interest in authentic performance: the insights it provides are well worth pur-
suing.

   This full description has been given because of the ease of analysing and describing the chorus of such a small organ. But we can pause to remind ourselves that the
use of the tierce in chorus mixtures is a particular feature of English organ building. Introduced, perhaps, by Bernard Smith, by 1700 it seems to have filtered into
the work of Renatus Harris too (see Chapter 8). From then on it is universally
accepted until the arrival of alternative recipes in the 1850s, and for some builders
it has survived into modern times. In other countries it was possible to use a tierce
in the chorus, and in the organs of Arp Schnitger or of the Netherlands in the eighteenth century this is usually an option. However, only a few builders made the
tierce a compulsory part of the chorus (e.g. Ludwig König at Nijmegen in 1776). In
England the almost universal presence of the tierce is probably an answer to the
question of why contemporary organ music has such a thin layout (the voluntaries
of Stanley, for example, are written mostly in two or three parts): the tierce rank fills
in some of the missing texture. Thus the chamber organ provides an easily understood clue to the whole nature of English organ aesthetic in the eighteenth and early
nineteenth centuries.

   In the following generation the most prominent figure in the making of chamber
organs is Samuel Green. This may strengthen the hypothetical link between the two
builders mentioned in Chapter 10. If Snetzler's method was uncompromising, then
it is hardly surprising that Samuel Green's work shows a reaction. The manufacture
of small organs seems to have absorbed much of Green's aptitude for invention and
perfectionism. Hence Sir John Sutton's laconic assessment: 'His Chamber Organs
are very nice instruments, (in short all his Organs are Chamber Organs on a large
scale,) . . .'[35] Perhaps Green's tonal and mechanical outlook can be interpreted as a
direct reaction to Snetzler's work in the same field. Where Snetzler built organs that
were mechanically simple (and probably cheap to make), Green went to great
lengths to make the mechanism silent and precise, to make the wind supply steady,

---

[35] Sutton, *A Short Account*, 83

and to make an effective swell – all features that are handled with comparative crudity by Snetzler. Where Snetzler provided a chorus of startling boldness and with all the open metal ranks of equal power, Green introduced refinement and delicacy and modified the power of the off-unison ranks to secure a new kind of blend.

If Green did indeed find a fascination in detail, then the chamber organ must have provided an ideal outlet for his skills: unhampered by the practical difficulties encountered in large organs and the vicissitudes of adapting a tonal scheme to unpredictable acoustic conditions in a large building, the one-manual organ must have offered the nearest that a perfectionist could get to creating an instrument that was truly satisfactory in every detail. In Green's work the chamber organ suddenly attains a level of sophistication and maturity that it will retain until its demise in the middle of the nineteenth century. This can be seen in several surviving instruments, those at Attingham Park, Shropshire (1788) and Edith Weston Parish Church, Northamptonshire (1787) being typical examples.[36]

Chamber organ at Edith Weston Parish Church, Northamptonshire: Samuel Green 1787

Compass GG, AA–f'''

Open Diapason [from c]	8
Stop. Diap. Bass [GG–b]	8
Stop. Diap. Treb. [c'–f''']	8
Dulciana [c'–f''']	8
Principal B. [GG–b]	4
Principal Treb. [c'–f''']	4
Flute [c'–f''']	4
Fifteenth	2
Sesq. Bass [1⅗, 1⅓, 1]	III
Sesq. Treb. [2⅔, 2, 1⅗]	III

General swell with venetian shutters
Shifting movement reducing to Open Diapason, Stopped Diapason and Dulciana

By the end of the eighteenth century the chamber organ was firmly established as the instrument of choice for a well-to-do household, challenging both the harpsichord and the emerging fortepiano. The relative stability of tuning compared to a stringed keyboard instrument must have been an advantage, but it should also be noted that a small organ is a good vehicle not just for keyboard music, but also for transcriptions of instrumental works, and could readily be used for the accompaniment of family prayers. These qualities of reliability, versatility and dignity must account for its popularity.

Other builders were no less enthusiastic to build their own versions, and there are instruments surviving by George Pike England, John Avery, Hugh Russell, Flight &

---

[36] Author's examination

Robson, Thomas Elliot, James Davis, Robert and William Gray (separately and together), James Hancock, Henry Holland, Henry Lincoln and many other builders, both named and anonymous. Many of these are housed in exquisite cabinet-maker's cases, reflecting in their endless variety and sophistication the changing fashions and inventions of English domestic taste. An especially pretty example, built by Thomas Elliot in 1819, stands in East Marden Parish Church in West Sussex, its case decorated with a delightfully informal group of Regency motifs and details. Others by Elliot are gothic: that at Tewkesbury Abbey (1818) is a composite of Regency classical form with fanciful gothick detail; at Lewannick in Cornwall (1827) the organ is dressed in the slightly more hard-edged style of the early scholarly gothic revival.[37]

While organ builder's casework could reach a pinnacle of quality and elegance (to which the chamber organs of Elliot are a witness) the field was inevitably of interest to the army of architects, designers and cabinet makers who were the arbiters of English domestic taste in the eighteenth century.[38] For example, there are organ cases amongst the work of William Kent.[39] Robert Adam's output includes several designs for chamber organs, and executed examples exist at Newby Hall, Yorkshire and Kedleston Hall, Derbyshire (containing an organ by Snetzler of 1765–6[40]). James Wyatt provided a case for Samuel Green's organ of 1790 for Heaton Hall near Manchester.[41] In 1762 the celebrated cabinet maker Thomas Chippendale included designs for six different organ cases in the third edition of his *The Gentleman and Cabinet-Maker's Director;*[42] other designs appeared in similar works by Thomas Johnson,[43] and William Ince and John Mayhew,[44] also amongst the drawings of John Linnell.[45]

Alongside the straightforward chamber organ there appeared in the late eighteenth century large numbers of barrel organs, where tunes could be played by turning a cylinder fitted with a pattern of raised pins and wire staples that moved the appropriate notes. These might be fitted with a keyboard as well, in case a live performer was to hand. Though nothing new in principle – Thomas Dallam's organ for the Sultan of Turkey was surely of this type – the barrel organ suddenly became popular after 1800. Flight & Robson were the specialists in the field: a spectacular example survives at Leigh Court, near Bristol, Avon. It is divided on either side of a doorway in the staircase hall of a splendidly severe Greek-revival house: the case is a rare and fine example of austere neo-classical taste.[46] The complex barrel organ by Bishop at The Argory, Co. Tyrone, is described in Chapter 12.

---

[37] B. B. Edmonds and N. M. Plumley, 'Thomas Elliot, Organ-Builder', *BIOS Journal*, 12 (1988), 56–71

[38] M. Wilson, *The English Chamber Organ* (Oxford 1968), 15–20

[39] J. Vardy, *Some Designs of Mr. Inigo Jones and Mr. Wm. Kent* (London 1744)

[40] Barnes and Renshaw, *The Life and Work of John Snetzler*, 140–2

[41] D. Wickens, 'The Samuel Green Organ at Heaton Hall', *BIOS Journal*, 4 (1980), 51–65

[42] T. Chippendale, *The Gentleman and Cabinet-Maker's Director*, 3rd edn (London 1762)

[43] T. Johnson, *One Hundred and Fifty New Designs* (London 1761)

[44] W. Ince & J. Mayhew, *The Universal System of Household Furniture* (London c1762)

[45] Victoria and Albert Museum, Prints and Drawings 92.D.26   [46] Author's examination

Plate 50 The organ in the chancel of Hillsborough Parish Church, County Down, Northern Ireland, built by George Pike England for Hillsborough Castle in 1795. This is a typical domestic instrument of the late eighteenth century, housed in a mahogany case following the pattern of contemporary glass-fronted bookcases and representing the complete appropriation of chamber organ design by cabinet makers.

During the early nineteenth century, when there was a gradual revival in interest in music in the parish church, many barrel organs were installed in country churches to play tunes for the accompaniment of metrical psalms, often ousting the village orchestras that had fulfilled the task hitherto.

This marks the migration of the small organ from the domestic sphere into the church, and indicates the demise of the chamber organ as a genre. Though there are still fine examples by the builders who lived into the Victorian age (Bishop, Hill, Walker, Holdich), by 1850 interest in small instruments was mainly devoted to considering how they could be adapted for ecclesiastical use. At home – perhaps owing in part to the playing, influence, and business acumen of Muzio Clementi – the grand piano established its pre-eminence. Over the succeeding two or three generations the countless chamber organs in private houses in England were either disposed of or found their way into local village churches, where many of them are still to be found and enjoyed.

In modern times there has been a revival of interest in specialist small organs, but these have had varied uses – many standing in churches – and there has been no significant revival of the chamber organ as a genre in its own right. However, the movement towards more authentic performances of pre-classical music has led to the re-introduction of the small organ as a continuo or consort instrument in the appropriate repertoire. Here the pre-eminent type is the box organ: a tiny instrument, usually of three stops, that can be transported easily (often in the back of an estate car) and set up and tuned at the concert venue in a matter of half an hour or so (whether such a tiny instrument is really suitable for continuo in, say, the Bach Passions, is a problem that has yet to be addressed). Those by Peter Collins (seventeen similar instruments were built by him between 1973 and 1989[47]) have set a pattern for effective, functional simplicity, but there are many variations on the theme and examples by other makers (amongst them Nigel Church, William Drake, Peter Hindmarsh, Kenneth Tickell, J. W. Walker & Sons Ltd.[48]) are to be found. In a handful of instruments (some of box organ form and others chamber organs that divide into sections for easy transport) the highest standards of classical casework design and decoration have been revived, especially in those by N. P. Mander Ltd[49] and Martin Goetze and Dominic Gwynn.[50]

---

[47] J. P. Rowntree and J. F. Brennan, *The Classical Organ in Britain*, vol. I: 1955–1975 (Oxford 1975), 26; vol. II: 1975–1978 (Oxford 1979), 26; vol. III: 1979–1990 (Oxford 1993), 26

[48] Rowntree and Brennan, *The Classical Organ in Britain*, vols. I–III

[49] Rowntree and Brennan, *The Classical Organ in Britain* , vol. III, 32, 43, 131

[50] Ibid., 27, 37, 38, 44, 133, 129, 132

CHAPTER TWELVE

THE INSULAR TRADITION
1800–1840

The technical and tonal innovations of Samuel Green and the demands placed on
the organ by ambitious choral concerts suggested possibilities for extensive change.
By 1800 Britain was already in the throes of major industrial expansion, accompanied by rapid growth in population and the expansion of towns and cities.
Successive waves of change in the transport system illustrate the radical transforma-
tion of the structure of the nation. The building of the turnpike roads, the labours
of Telford and Macadam and the construction of the canal network reduced
journey times considerably and allowed the easy transportation of heavy goods;
within a generation the appearance of railways would work a further revolution.

Similar change and growth would be reflected in the organ before long. The fact
that it got off to a slow start is not hard to understand. In politics reform was in the
air and was to be much discussed, but stagnation was the rule for the time being.
Taste in art and architecture had entered a phase of understatement and restraint
severe even by English standards: the astonishingly spare buildings of John Soane
are a witness to this austerity, reflected on a smaller scale in the plain terraces of
middle-class houses in London and other cities. The Church of England was complacent: relaxed and confident after the upheavals of the sixteenth and seventeenth
centuries, it was not in the van of progress. Many of the coming changes in organ
building were the result of nonconformist or secular influences. A general tendency
to neo-classical coolness in art was perhaps cherished by those who still distrusted
the florid exhibitionism of foreign taste. In the period immediately after the French
Revolution a conservative attitude in politics and art was an understandable reaction: sudden change had been seen to bring chaos and terror. Furthermore the long
struggle with France put a severe strain on the economy, and while money was tight
developments in organ building had to wait.

Thus the typical church organ described and illustrated in Rees's *Cyclopaedia* of
1819 (see plate 52, p. 214) is of a kind with which we are already familiar (not least,
perhaps, because the article in question is partly written by the now elderly Charles
Burney).[1] The only difference one can immediately spot is that the mounted Cornet

---

[1] Ed. A. Rees, *The Cyclopaedia, or Universal Dictionary of Arts, Sciences, and Literature* (London 1819)

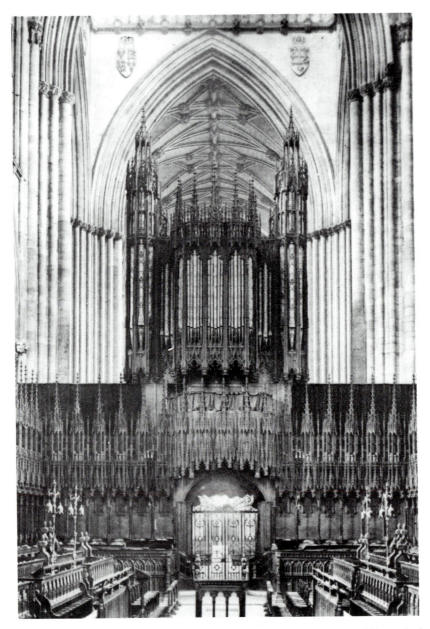

Plate 51   The organ in York Minster, built by Elliot & Hill after the disastrous fire of 1829. This was the first English attempt to build a really large organ, and the instrument was not entirely successful, though it opened the way to the more confident execution of major projects in the next generation. The case is descended from the first experiments in gothic met in the cases of organs by Samuel Green. Because of limited space on the screen the upper section overhangs on all four sides, supported by iron cantilevers. The appearance is of a large gothic tabernacle in which the pipes, gilded and decorated as they often were in the seventeenth century, have become incidental to the overall design.

has disappeared; in many organs it more or less duplicated the treble portion of the Great Sesquialtera, and a mixture stop combining a Sesquialtera Bass and a Cornet Treble, sometimes on separate knobs, is common between 1800 and 1840. In any case a feeling had arisen that the frequent use of the Cornet (and other solo stops) in showy voluntaries had led to what the Rees *Cyclopaedia* article describes as a 'trifling and vitiated style of performance', lacking the gravity appropriate to church music.

Though the English church organ of 1800 had developed from the combined French and Dutch influences of the late seventeenth century, throughout the eighteenth century it had remained isolated from the rest of Europe. As we have seen, the work of a foreign builder like Snetzler had surprisingly little impact on the local tradition. The English organ had perhaps never been noted for its cosmopolitan outlook, but at this period its insularity – to use a word so successfully applied by N. J. Thistlethwaite in his definitive history of the development of the Victorian Organ[2] – was especially startling. Thanks to the increasing refinements adopted by the Englands and Samuel Green, these were perhaps amongst the quietest organs in the world. Nor were they very large, especially compared to the four- and five-manual instruments of F.-H. Clicquot in France, or the great 32'-fronted organs of northern Europe. The tonal palette was narrow, they lacked all but the most rudimentary pedals, they retained an eccentrically long compass for the keyboards, and eschewed the use of all but the most homely materials: pipe metal poor in tin, pine and oak, with mahogany for only some of the increasingly plain and understated cases. But they were, in their way, very sophisticated: mechanically orderly and accomplished, well made and very carefully voiced, and with a relaxed fitness for their musical purpose which rendered them capable of producing sounds of great beauty. Their qualities were indeed such as to render those who were used to them quite blind to the supposed merits of larger and outwardly more impressive instruments overseas – at least for the time being. Burney was one of few Englishmen who had played organs abroad in the eighteenth century, but his conclusions are probably no more complacent than any other English visitor's would have been.[3]

It is very extraordinary that the swell, which has been introduced into the English organ more than fifty years, and which is so capable of expression and of pleasing effects, that it may well be called the greatest and most important invention that ever was made on any keyed instrument, should be still utterly unknown in Italy. The *touch* too of the organ, which our builders have so much improved, still remains in its heavy, noisy state; and now I am on this subject I must observe that most of the organs which I have met with on the Continent, seem to be inferior to ours built by Father Smith, Byfield, or Snetzler, in everything but size. As the churches there are often immense, so are the organs; the tone is indeed somewhat softened and refined by space and distance; but when heard near, it is intolerably coarse and noisy; and though the number of stops in these large instruments is very great, they afford

[2] N. J. Thistlethwaite, *The Making of the Victorian Organ* (Cambridge 1990)
[3] C. Burney, *The Present State of Music in France and Italy*, 2nd edn (London 1773)

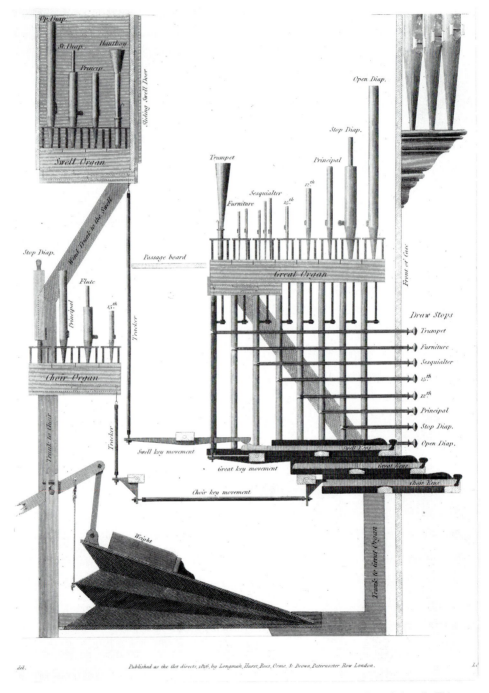

Plate 52 'Interior profile of an English Church Organ'; engraving dated 1816 from *Rees's Cyclopaedia*. This illustration sums up the development of the English organ up to this date; only a Great Organ Cornet is missing, this stop having fallen out of fashion in the early years of the nineteenth century. Otherwise the technical details, including the style of the pipework, the key action and the bellows, are all typical of organs from 1715 to 1815.

but little variety, being for the most part duplicates in unisons and octaves to each other, such as the great and small 12ths, flutes and 15ths: hence in our organs not only the touch and tone, but the imitative stops are greatly superior to those of any organs I have met with.

The expanding population made considerable demands on existing church build-ings: many were fitted with galleries to provide more seats, and organs were fre-quently installed on them. New churches were erected to meet the increasing demand, some funded by Parliament, others by local associations or by individuals, setting a pattern of enthusiastic new building that was to last for a century. Whereas in the eighteenth century the provision of an organ in an Anglican church was often a matter of debate, it was now taken for granted that new town churches would be provided with organs. The proliferation of nonconformist places of worship was no less striking, opening a further potential market for new instruments.

Once the financial stringency forced on the country by the long struggle with France had ceased, numbers of organ builders were able to pursue their craft successfully. Such, in fact, was the expansion in the craft after 1815 that it is no longer possible to trace the lineage of the descendants of Smith and Harris with such clarity as before. We are rapidly entering the age of the organ building company, rather than of the master craftsman operating a workshop with a number of assistants.

The builders competing for the spoils were numerous. Starting with London's major builders (ignoring many smaller concerns): the Renatus Harris line, repre-sented by Bridge and the Englands in the eighteenth century, was continued after G. P. England's death in 1815 by Nicholls, and then by Joseph William Walker, who founded his business in 1827 and is traditionally claimed to have been England's apprentice.[4] John England's former partner Hugh Russell set up on his own around 1784, and was followed after his death in 1825 by his son Timothy.[5] Descent from Snetzler was claimed by Thomas Elliot, who is first recorded in 1790. He was joined in 1815 by William Hill, who later married his daughter. Elliot died in 1832, and Hill was briefly in partnership with Frederick Davison (1837–8), afterwards contin-uing to work under his own name.[6] Robert Gray set up business in the 1770s and was later joined by William Gray. Robert died in 1796, William in 1821, the firm being taken over by John Gray. After his short-lived association with Hill, Frederick Davison married John Gray's daughter, and Davison assumed control of the company, now Gray & Davison, after John Gray's death in 1849.[7] Benjamin Flight was building barrel organs in the 1770s. His son, also Benjamin, was joined by Joseph Robson around 1806. The partnership of Flight & Robson continued to be particularly well known for their barrel organs: these included the 'Apollonicon' organ of 1817, which played from three barrels or from keyboards accommodat-ing up to six organists at once. After bankruptcy in 1832 John Flight and Joseph Robson both operated on their own.[8] James Chapman Bishop left Flight &

[4] Thistlethwaite, *The Making of the Victorian Organ*, 57   [5] Ibid., 51   [6] Ibid., 55–6   [7] Ibid., 55
[8] Ibid., 58–9

Robson to set up on his own in 1807.[9] John Lincoln was working from 1789. His son, Henry Cephas Lincoln was apprenticed to Flight & Robson. The company was known as Lincoln & Son until about 1819, after which H. C. Lincoln continued to work on his own.[10] Mention should also be made of James and David Davis: David was a partner in the music publishing house Longman & Broderip, and the brothers seem to have built organs on their own account and under the Longman & Broderip title between 1793 and 1822.[11]

In the provinces activity was no less impressive. In Bristol the Seedes had been succeeded by the John Smiths, father and son.[12] In Yorkshire John Ward of York, the Booths and the Greenwoods held sway.[13] In Manchester Samuel Renn founded a flourishing business; he had been foreman to James and David Davis.[14] Liverpool had Bewsher & Fleetwood, Kendal had William Wilkinson, Edinburgh had James Bruce.[15] By 1850 dozens of towns and cities had their own organ manufactories, and this was the first generation to mount a serious challenge to the supremacy of the London makers.

The temptations and rewards were comparatively much greater than before. When David Davis died in 1822, having risen from a childhood in a Lancashire cottage to the position of one of London's leading makers (as well as holding an interest in Longman & Broderip), he left a fortune of £12,000.[16] An inventory of the manufactory of Flight & Robson, made at the time of their bankruptcy in 1832, describes organ building premises arranged on a scale unknown before: nine workshops, a yard, 'piazzas and warehouses', gallery, counting house, and a 'Great Room' open to the public containing sixteen organs and pianos. There were also about forty organs complete or under construction.[17] Thistlethwaite has discussed the work of John Gray, for whom accounts survive from the 1820s and 1830s.[18] In 1825 the accounts record work to the value of £2,513 passing through the workshops in the form of new organs, rebuilds and repairs – to which should be added, presumably, fees accruing from tuning and maintenance and from the hire of organs (a significant sideline of Gray's operation). The profit for the year was an astonishing £1,516. In 1826 the work in progress was valued at £3,759 and the profit was £995.

Gray's extremely healthy position was supported by a manufacturing method quite different from anything we have encountered before and probably more industrial and more advanced than anything to be found on the Continent at this time. He may only have employed between fifteen and twenty staff, but it is clear

[9] Thistlethwaite, *The Making of the Victorian Organ*, 52–3; L. Elvin, *Bishop & Sons, Organ Builders* (Lincoln 1984)
[10] Thistlethwaite, *The Making of the Victorian Organ*, 51
[11] M. Sayer, *Samuel Renn, English Organ Builder* (London 1974), 1–4
[12] Thistlethwaite, *The Making of the Victorian Organ*, 155
[13] B. B. Edmonds, 'Yorkshire Organ Builders of the Nineteenth Century', *BIOS Journal*, 8 (1984), 4–17; Thistlethwaite, *The Making of the Victorian Organ*, 50   [14] Sayer, *Samuel Renn, English Organ Builder*
[15] Thistlethwaite, *The Making of the Victorian Organ*, 50   [16] Sayer, *Samuel Renn, English Organ Builder*, 1–4
[17] A. W. J. G. Ord-Hume, *Barrel Organ* (London 1978), 494–503
[18] Thistlethwaite, *The Making of the Victorian Organ*, 59–65

that they were involved in continuous and methodical production. For example, in 1827 the extensive stock of pipework made to standard scales included 15 Open Diapasons, 10 Stopped Diapasons, 7 Principals, 6 Twelfths, 8 Fifteenths, 7 Sesquialteras, 6 Trumpets, 2 Flutes, a Dulciana, a Cremona and an Hautboy.[19] His premises were substantial enough to allow organs to be erected, voiced and tuned before they left for their destination, and public performances were arranged on the larger new instruments. Machinery may also have played a part in efficient manufacture: M. Sayer has illustrated this in respect of the Manchester builder Samuel Renn, observing his proximity to the inventor of a metal-planing machine;[20] he has also pointed out the extensive standardisation that Renn adopted in specifications, pipe scales, layout and mechanism and the effect this had in keeping his prices keen.[21] The inventory of Flight & Robson's plant mentioned above describes three lathes, a sawing machine, a screw making machine and a machine for cutting brass, as well as two voicing machines – small skeletal organs on which pipes could be mounted and voiced before installation in the instrument for which they were destined.

This extensive use of early factory methods may well have been an excellent preparation for the massively ambitious organ building projects of the next generation, and the benefits of new efficiency are worth heralding; however, combined with the knowledge of substantial profits and the fact that the English organ at this time was particularly plain and simple, there is a question to be asked about quality. For example, is the fact that English pipework from the period 1800–40 is made of an unusually thin plain metal (desperately prone to damage or even collapse) a sign of the legitimate artistic pursuit of a particularly refined and delicate tone, or is it merely cheap?

It is certainly true that in a period of rapid growth competition amongst organ builders was fierce. When the authorities at Christ's Hospital School in the City of London needed a new organ they were able to invite tenders for three different schemes from 'four of the most eminent Organ Builders'; they accepted the lowest bid, from Messrs Elliot & Hill.[22] Elliot was concerned: 'I am confident the organ we have in hand for Christ's Hospital, will not pay us as it ought; Hill being so very desirous of obtaining business at a very little profit, sooner than lose it.'[23] As well as paring their prices to the bone, organ builders frequently had to pay substantial commissions to organists and agents for orders received. Hill was accustomed to paying 10 per cent.[24] With such financial pressures it is quite certain that quality suffered.

A few instruments representative of the more conservative style of the early nineteenth century survive. Individual instruments by Flight, Davis, Russell, Bishop and Renn are still standing. Thomas Elliot's work is represented by two manual organs

[19] Ibid., 62   [20] M. Sayer, 'English Organ Design in the Industrial Revolution', *BIOS Journal* 4, (1980), 90–9
[21] M. Sayer, 'Industrialized Organ Building, A Pioneer', *Organ Yearbook*, 7, (1976), 90–100
[22] N. M. Plumley, *The Christ's Hospital Papers I, The Organs and Music Masters* (Christ's Hospital 1981), 24
[23] Thistlethwaite, *The Making of the Victorian Organ*, 65   [24] Ibid., 65

at Scone Palace, Perthshire (1813), Ashridge, Hertfordshire (1818) and by the organ he built for the Chapel Royal, St James's Palace, London in 1819, now at Crick Parish Church, Northamptonshire.[25] In 1820 William Gray built an organ for the new Church of St Mary Bathwick, Somerset. The instrument was built with a relatively rare late example of a Choir organ in a separate case. The trustees of the church provided a glowing testimonial stating that it was:[26]

an Instrument so externally correct and beautiful, and has been pronounced by the best judges, to be so truly rich and harmonious in its various Tones, that in our opinion, it will be a lasting record of exquisite workmanship, and ever speak for itself the superior abilities of its builder.

These remarks are rather poignant in light of the fact that, after various vicissitudes, the organ now stands restored in a museum in Berlin.

Perhaps most indicative of the state of play is the organ now at Thaxted Parish Church in Essex. It was built by Henry Cephas Lincoln in 1821 for St John's Chapel Bedford Row, London.[27] The names of the stops are familiar enough, and none of the pipes in this organ exhibits the slightest innovation from those made fifty years before. But several features of this organ distinguish it from its eighteenth century forebears and are suggestive of things to come.

London, St John's Chapel Bedford Row (now in Thaxted Parish Church, Essex): Henry Cephas Lincoln 1821

Great Organ (FF, GG–f''')

Open Diapason Front	8
Open Diapason (from C)	8
Stopped Diapason	8
Principal	4
Twelfth	2⅔
Fifteenth	2
Sesquialtra (FF–b)	IV
Cornet (c'–f''')	IV–III
Mixture	II
Trumpet	8

Pedal Organ (FF–c, FF♯ plays F♯)

Pedals	8

Choir Organ (FF, GG–f''')

Dulciana (FF–e from St. Dp.)	8
Stopped Diapason	8
Principal	4
Flute	4
Fifteenth	2
Bassoon	8

Swell Organ (e–f''')

Open Diapason	8
Stopped Diapason	8
Principal	4
Cremona	8
Hautboy	8
Trumpet	8

Coupler Swell (Swell to Great)
Pedals Great (Great to Pedal)
Pedals Choir (Choir to Pedal)

---

[25] Ibid., 9
[26] A List of Church and Chapel Organs Built by W. Gray, c1822, reprinted in *BIOS Reporter*, 15 (1991) 1, 7–10
[27] Thistlethwaite, *The Making of the Victorian Organ*, 8–9

Plate 53   The organ in the parish church at Thaxted, Essex, built by Henry Cephas Lincoln for St John's
Chapel, Bedford Row, London in c1821 and moved here in 1858. This instrument is similar in many respects
to an organ of the eighteenth century, though with some important modifications. The keys of the Great and
Choir organs now extend to FF, and an FF-compass pedalboard has been added, together with one rank of
open wooden pedal pipes at unison pitch and a number of couplers. The case is in the regency style and,
although well executed, it does not show as confident a hand as those designed fifty years or more earlier.

Key compass continued to expand. We have seen that certain seventeenth- and eighteenth-century organs had keyboards descending to FF or even CC, but these were exceptional. In the early nineteenth century the subject is taken up again: here is a modest-sized instrument of FF compass. Samuel Green had built Swell organs with longer compass than before: at Thaxted the Swell descends below the usual g to e, and later organs will push still further. The Swell division is gradually becoming more complete and therefore more useful, by 1850 relegating the Choir Organ in a three-manual instrument into third place, and becoming a distinctly useful part of a two-manual scheme. The presence at Thaxted and elswhere of a Swell-to-Great coupler – operated by a stop knob – allows the expressive power of crescendo and diminuendo to be added to the main foundation stops. This is an effect central to the nineteenth century English view of organ tone and build-up, and a knowledge of its importance is vital in understanding the role of the Swell in the Victorian organ.

Finally, the pedal organ was taking on a degree of independence. The occasional pedalboards of the eighteenth century, pulling down the bass keys of the Great Organ (but with no pipes of their own) were of many varieties. Avery seems to have pioneered the idea of independent pedal pipes in the 1790s, providing one rank of unison basses in several instances.[28] By the early nineteenth century larger organs could boast pedal divisions of various types. The pedal board might offer a row of short pedals hinged at the toe, or a full-sized pedal board with the keys hinged at the heel ('German Pedals'). The compass might be anything from one octave to seventeen notes. Where pedal pipes were provided they might be at unison or sub-octave pitch, always of wood.

Lincoln's specific treatment of the Pedal division in the Thaxted organ is significant in that it shows the dawning of a dim realisation of the existence of other organ building traditions overseas. Lincoln is known to have had a copy of the great organ building treatise of Dom Bédos,[29] and he annotated it with comments about the suitability of the various pipes scales given and with some scales of his own: '*Doublette et dessus de Bourdons à Cheminée* – "these scales are excellent & require to be transposed ½ a note [to account for the difference between French and English pitch]"'; '*Nasard* – "the small scale best calculated for ordinary purposes"'; '*Cromorne 4e taille* – "used at Camberwell new church 1824"'.[30] The arrangement of the unison Pedal pipes and their action in the Thaxted organ is exactly *à la Française*, though the pedal board itself is of the German type.

The innovations regarding key compass, the introduction of pedal pipes and the provision of a few couplers were shared amongst many of the builders of this period, and they are important in laying the ground for more radical change in years to come. The potential for further inventiveness is obvious in, for example, the various *tours de force* performed by Flight & Robson in their self-playing organs. An

[28] Ibid., 16–18   [29] F. Bédos de Celles, *L'Art du Facteur d'Orgues*, 4 vols. (Paris 1766–78)
[30] Copies of the pages annotated by Lincoln in Reading University, Department of Music, Susi Jeans Papers, File 40. The whereabouts of the original is not now known.

example of such an instrument, though actually built by J. C. Bishop in 1824, survives at The Argory, Co. Tyrone, Northern Ireland. The organ itself is unremarkable (apart from its rather startling Egyptian-style case and its position on the staircase landing of a sumptuous private house), but the clockwork barrel mechanism which operates it (in addition to the normal keyboard) is spectacular. The weights driving the clockwork descend from the ceiling of the first floor to a pit below the ground floor of the house, allowing twenty minutes of uninterrupted playing. The barrels, about 1650mm long and 400mm in diameter, operate the keys and also the stops of the organ – the latter from 'on' and 'off' pins on the barrel through linkages to a duplicate slide for every stop. Bishop had originally intended that the barrel should also open and close the swell box, one shutter at a time, but the mechanism for this appears not to have been completed. The arrangements of the music on the barrels was by the composer and organist Samuel Wesley (correspondence with him survives), and presumably he was responsible too for the highly innovative registration used. For example, a choir organ effect is obtained by the use of Dulciana 8, Flute 4, and Fifteenth 2. Still more remarkable is the use – in the Overture to Mozart's *Magic Flute* – of a full Rossini crescendo, from Dulciana alone to full organ and back again, in the space of a few bars.[31]

If this suggests an ability to experiment successfully when the opportunity arose, it is not surprising that it is in the work of Bishop that we find the first serious technical innovations of the nineteenth century. He adapted and simplified the old shifting movements, producing instead the composition pedal, which operated directly on the stop action and brought into play pre-determined selections of stops.[32] Though this appears restricting at first sight, it was now easy to provide several composition pedals on one department (three for the Great Organ, as well as a pedal operating the Swell-to-Great coupler and a shifting movement to the Swell Organ, at St James' Bermondsey in 1829 – an arrangement offering unrivalled flexibility).[33] Increase in compass, the stress now placed on the importance of the bass, the arrival of pedal pipes, and a style of playing which envisaged marching octaves in the bass against held chords in the treble all conspired to show up any weakness in the wind system. The development of the horizontal reservoir with separate feeders had gone some way to addressing this problem. Bishop introduced the concussion bellows, a small sprung bellows mounted on a wind trunk and acting as a damper to any shock waves generated by sudden demands on the wind system. At St John Waterloo Road, London in 1824 Bishop went further, providing a separate bellows for the pedal pipes.[34] If these inventions suggest that Bishop was to the 1820s what Samuel Green was in the 1790s, then this is borne out by his approach to voicing. At Bermondsey a report found that[35]

The swell is of a very sweet quality; the reeds are very smooth and equal, particularly the Cremona. The choir organ is silvery in its tone, and the soft stops throughout are voiced

---

[31] Author's examination of the organ during assembly after restoration by N. P. Mander Ltd in 1984
[32] Thistlethwaite, *The Making of the Victorian Organ*, 54   [33] Ibid., 446   [34] Ibid., 54
[35] *The Examiner* (26 May 1829), 264; quoted in Thistlethwaite, *The Making of the Victorian Organ*, 52

Plate 54 The organ in St James Bermondsey, London, built by James Chapman Bishop in 1829 (photograph c1910). This instrument illustrates the development of the insular style in the 1820s: to the traditional recipe there has now been added a three-stop pedal organ. The case was designed by James Savage, the architect of the church, in a severe neo-classical style. Savage's church has a certain spartan grandeur; the organ case is lumpy and uncertain; other designers were able to apply the grecian style to organ cases with greater success.

with the utmost delicacy: in a word, Mr. Bishop has eminently succeeded in the difficult task of combining sweetness and power.

Bishop is traditionally supposed to have invented the closed shallot for reeds,[36] in which the (usually tapered) shallot has been cut at such an angle that only a small

[36] For example in T. Willis, 'Recollections of my Father' (undated and unpublished biographical note on the subject of Vincent Willis)

opening in the bottom end is revealed, and certainly these can be found in organs built by him in the 1820s. This small detail of his practice is worth noting, as it is to bear a rich crop of fruit later and in other hands. He also invented the Claribella in or before 1819,[37] an open wooden flute of 8′ pitch, heralding further experiments with pipe forms and new stops in years to come.

Technical improvements in key action, stop action and winding were taken up by all the leading builders and are England's most notable contribution to the craft in the early nineteenth century. It is not often realised that the distinctively English approach to the mechanical side of the organ was influential overseas, partly as a result of the emigration of John Abbey to France in the 1820s. Abbey was apprenticed to James and David Davis, and then worked for Hugh Russell after 1818. He was invited to Paris around 1826 by Sébastien Erard, the piano maker, to help in the construction of three new organs. Erard had spent time in London during the French Revolution and was aware of the skills of English instrument makers. He was now old and in poor health. French organ building had suffered badly from the effects of revolution and war and was in a parlous state. Erard was inventive and progressive; he saw in the English approach to organ building the possibility of introducing new ideas.

The entire package of radical innovations then unfamiliar in mainland Europe needs to be listed to be appreciated: the swell box; a balanced key action (suspended action was still the norm in France) adjustable by tapped wires and buttons and made silent by bushing; couplers operated conveniently by stop knobs; long-compass keyboards; keys with long ivory-covered naturals similar to those of the piano; the horizontal reservoir with compensating folds and separate feeders; extra reservoirs for the pedal organ or other sections of the instrument; concussion bellows to steady the wind; consoles with the stop knobs themselves clearly labelled and arranged in logical order within easy reach of the player; composition pedals allowing rapid changes of registration without the hands leaving the keys; and finally the exquisite delicacy of voicing in the softer stops.

Abbey found plenty of work in France, though there is good evidence to suggest that the experience of building large organs to suit French taste extended his abilities and his financial acumen to their limits. However, the extent to which he made *la méchanique anglaise* one of the basic ingredients of the French romantic organ is undeniable, and in his instruments the English flavour is obvious. In June 1834 Abbey was declared the winner of a competition to build a new organ for the Abbey of St Denis, near Paris. As is well known, after much further traffic in proposals and counter proposals the organ was eventually built by the young Aristide Cavaillé-Coll and completed in 1847, founding the career of one of the greatest organ builders the world has seen. The extent to which his success depended on the innovations of Abbey (and later of another Englishman, Charles Spackman Barker) should not be overlooked.[38]

---

[37] M. Sayer, letter to the Editor, *The Organ*, 54 (1974–5), 97

[38] J.-A. Villard, 'John Abbey, Organ Builder, his Work in France', part I, *BIOS Journal*, 10 (1986), 7–19; part II, *BIOS Journal*, 12 (1988), 20–30

Meanwhile the leading English builders were attempting to meet the challenges presented by the Handel Commemoration Festival of 1784. If the giant oratorio performance indicated in simple terms the desire to experiment with massive effects, it also marked the advent of romantic taste in art. Music could now express the sublime, the terrible, the dramatic; it could exploit contrasts of tone and dynamics; it could stir the emotions as well as reflect them. The English organ builder's response at first followed lines already established. The development of the swell organ and composition pedals offered expression and rapid contrast. The long compass and the embryonic pedal organ extended the organ's range to new rumbling depths. Finally the effect of many performers could be simulated on the organ by duplicating the ranks of the chorus – or, indeed, in one or two instruments (Flight & Robson's Apollonicon being only one such organ) by actually adding the other performers seated at additional keyboards! From the 1820s onwards large organs would often exhibit innovations in one or more of these areas, sometimes in a highly experimental manner and operating at the limits of the technology then available.

At York Minster the organ was completely reconstructed in 1802–3 by Benjamin Blyth, formerly foreman to Samuel Green's widow Sarah. The organ followed the pattern of Green's larger instruments with the novelty of three Open Diapasons on the Great Organ. The organ was not a success, and over the years that followed the organist, John Camidge, pursued a programme of enlargements and alterations with the York builder John Ward. The wind pressure was raised, an extra manual division was added (called Nave Organ, and eventually finding a home on the west face of the screen mounted instrument, enclosed in its own swell box), and a remarkable Pedal Organ was built, its pipes divided on either side of the main instrument and hidden in the pulpitum.[39]

York Minster: rebuilt Benjamin Blyth 1802–3 and subsequently enlarged by John Ward – Pedal Organ

Pedal Organ, left side (FF–c)		**Pedal Organ, right side** (FF–c)	
Double Stop Diapason (wood)	16	Double Stop Diapason (wood)	16
Double Open Diapason (wood)	8	Double Open Diapason (wood)	8
German Stop Diapason	8	German Stop Diapason	8
German Principal	4	German Principal	4
Sackbut (wood)	16	Sackbut (wood)	16
Trombone (wood)	8	Trombone (wood)	8
		Shawm (wood)	4

Camidge may have visited the Continent around 1820, and this extraordinary scheme suggests a part-understood attempt to imitate the north European independent pedal chorus.

If the chaotic enlargement of the York organ represented one attempt to extend the range and power of the English organ, then the organ at St Luke Chelsea stated

---

[39] Thistlethwaite, *The Making of the Victorian Organ*, 118–22

even more clearly the desire for a massive effect created by extensive duplication. Begun by William Nicholls, it was installed by John Gray and finished in 1824. The church was large; a pioneer of the serious gothic revival and a showpiece of the new church building movement.[40]

London, St Luke Chelsea: William Nicholls, completed by John Gray 1824

Great Organ (GG–f''')		**Choir Organ** (GG–f''')	
Open Diapason	8	Stopped Diapason	8
Open Diapason	8	Dulciana	8
Open Diapason	8	Principal	4
Stopped Diapason	8	Flute	4
Stopped Diapason	8	Fifteenth	2
Principal	4	Bassoon & Cremona	8
Principal	4		
Twelfth	$2\frac{2}{3}$	**Swell Organ** (f–f''')	
Fifteenth	2	Open Diapason	8
Fifteenth	2	Open Diapason	8
Tierce	$1\frac{3}{5}$	Stopped Diapason	8
Sesquialtra	IV	Dulciana	8
Trumpet	8	Dulciana	8
Clarion	4	Principal	4
		Principal	4
Pedal Organ (GG–c)		Flute	4
Pedal Pipes		Cornet	III
(Basses GG–BB? unison, then 16')		Trumpet	8
		Hautboy	8
		Clarion	4

Couplers not recorded

This scheme shows duplication carried out to what seems now an eccentric extent: there is no real evidence that ranks of similar name were voiced in any significantly different way from each other, and apart from a slightly thicker texture (coloured by the inevitable problems caused by the fact that ranks of similar construction and pitch will not easily stay in tune with each other) it is difficult to see how the result can have justified the considerable extra expense. Nevertheless, duplication remains a hallmark of English organ schemes for some time to come. Part of the reason for this lies in the contemporary taste for the effect of the Open and Stopped Diapasons together: since they were frequently singled out for praise as one of the most dignified and solemn effects that the organ could offer (and therefore appropriate to church music), one could therefore argue that one could hardly have enough of them.

Other instruments were not quite as single-minded as this one, but many exhibited other innovations. In the 1820s organs began to acquire manual doubles on a

[40] Ibid., 451–2

regular basis. These were sometimes on the Swell (and therefore of short compass, avoiding the space consuming and expensive bottom notes), but also appeared on the Great Organ of some larger instruments.[41] Pedal organs became gradually more ambitious: at St James Bermondsey in 1829 Bishop provided two octaves of Pedals from GG, with a Double Diapason, a Unison Diapason and a Trombone (unison).[42] In case the deployment of these forces proved too arduous for one artist, the Pedal Organ could be played by another performer from a small keyboard to the left of the manual keys (and was used thus at the opening).[43] Several instruments exhibited manuals descending to CC: the Elliot & Hill of 1829 at Christ's Hospital School, London combined CC compass for the Great and Choir with a Swell descending to G, two octaves of pedals from CC with a set of unison pedal pipes, a keyboard operating the pedal organ (as at Bermondsey), and no less than five couplers (Great to Swell [sc. Swell to Great?], Choir to Swell [sc. Swell to Choir?], Choir to Great, Great to Pedal and Choir to Pedal).[44]

Other examples of the trends can be found in the work of most builders of the period, both in London and the provinces. But it is to Elliot & Hill we return to observe the construction of England's first Leviathan organ, the true parallel, in this age of industrial pioneers, to the ambitious and ultimately ill-fated steamships of Brunel.

The organ at York Minster burnt in the catastrophic fire of 1829. John Camidge, having established a pattern of experiment and enlargement with the Blyth/Ward organ, was no less ambitious regarding its successor. The contract went to Elliot & Hill. Elliot died in 1832 and the perseverance and inventiveness of Hill saw it through to completion (see plate 51, p. 212). The problems he faced were on a scale unknown in England at the time; that the organ was not a success and was repeatedly altered and modified until its first major rebuild in 1859 is an indication more of the failings of the scheme and the scale of innovation required to make the instrument work at all than a criticism of its builder. The original scheme is impossible to determine, but a likely synopsis is as follows:[45]

Great Organ West (CC–c'''')	8. 8. 8. 4. 4. 2⅔. 2. 2. III. IV. 8. 8.
Great Organ East (CC–c'''')	8. 8. 8. 4. 4. 2⅔. 2. 2. III. IV. 8. 8.
Choir Organ (CC–c'''')	8. 8. 8. 4. 4. 4. 2. 2. 8. 4.
Swell Organ (C–c'''')	8. 8. 8. 8. 8. 4. 4. 4. V. 8. 8. 8.
Pedal Organ (C–c')	32. 32. 32. 16. 16. 16. 32. 16.

Note that as the Great and Choir descend to CC (an octave below the lowest note of a modern organ keyboard) the manual unisons started with pipes 16′ feet long. The Pedal 32′ ranks were the first pipes in England made on such a scale.

As the arguments developed about the shortcomings of this ill-conceived instrument, Hill was already engaged on the construction of another similar monster at Birmingham Town Hall. As an indication of the importance of music in public life

[41] Ibid., 108   [42] Ibid., 446–7   [43] Ibid., 173
[44] Plumley, *The Christ's Hospital Papers I, The Organs and Music Masters* , 29
[45] Thistlethwaite, *The Making of the Victorian Organ*, 122–27

Plate 55 The organ in St John Waterloo Road, London, built by James Chapman Bishop in 1824 (photograph c1910). Double cases were not uncommon, even if rare by the early nineteenth century, but were usually restricted to cathedrals and the occasional collegiate church. This is a relatively late example, in a church built to ease overcrowding in a rapidly expanding city. The confident application of the grecian style is by Francis Bedford, the architect of the church.

and the high prices that seats could command, it needs only to be remarked that the Musical Committee of Birmingham's General Hospital erected the Parthenon-like hall and built its 32′-fronted organ in order to *raise* money for the hospital, in which aim it was a complete success. The organ was completed in 1834. Again the original stop-list is difficult to determine, but a likely synopsis is as follows:[46]

[46] N. J. Thistlethwaite, *Birmingham Town Hall Organ* (Birmingham 1984), 9

Great Organ (CC–f‴)   16. 8. 8. 8. 8. 8. 4. 4. 4. 2⅔. 2. 2. V. III. 8. 8. 4. 2.
Choir Organ (CC–f‴)   8. 8. 8. 8. 4. 4. 4. 2. 8.
Swell Organ (C–f‴, CC–BB
acting on Choir)   16. 8. 8. 4. 4. 2. 8. 8. 8. 4. Carillon (bells)
Combination organ (fourth manual, stops derived from other departments)
from Choir Organ: 8. 8. 8. 4. 4.
from Swell Organ: 8. 8. 4. 4. 2. 8. 8. 8. 4.
Pedal Organ (C–c′)   32. 32. (flues) 16. (reed)

Swell to Great, Choir to Great, Pedals to Great [sc. Great to Pedal], Pedals to Choir [sc. Choir to Pedal]

Two octaves of keys to the left of the manual keyboards to act on the Pedal Organ

The purpose of the organ reflected a direct line of descent from the Handel Commemoration of 1784: it was intended to support 'those great choral effects, which have hitherto rendered the Birmingham Festivals so attractive'.[47] In this limited purpose it can claim to have been successful. However, the obvious splendours of so large an instrument invited its use as a solo vehicle, and in this role its shortcomings were exposed. In this respect it suffered from the same faults as the organ at York.

In both organs the key action was intractably heavy. When Mendelssohn was asked to play at the 1846 Birmingham Festival he commented 'as for the heavy touch, I am sure that I admired your organist very much who was able to play a Fugue. I am afraid that I would not have strength enough to do so . . .'[48] In both organs the attempt to secure power, or at least grandeur of effect, through wholesale duplication of ranks was wasteful and lacking in variety. Though Hill increased the scales of the pipes, especially at Birmingham, much of his efforts were devoted to the bass and Pedal pipes, further increasing the emphasis on the bass which had commenced in the work of Samuel Green, arguably to the neglect of the chorus. Power was limited by the thin plain metal pipes characteristic of all English builders at the time, which were incapable of being blown hard: this is still a problem with the surviving 1834 pipework at Birmingham.[49] Finally, the provision of the long CC manual compass accompanied by a relatively rudimentary Pedal Organ (at least at Birmingham) confused the pitch status of the manual choruses, and prevented a real appreciation of the greatly increased solidity and apparent power that might have been offered by a chorus based on a manual sub-unison. At York the problems were made worse by the difficult acoustics of the building. The organ stood on the choir screen at the east side of the crossing; there was little chance of it being fully appreciated in the nave: the sound went straight up the tower.

These significant musical lacunae do not obscure the extent of Hill's daring and

---

[47] *Mechanic's Magazine*, 20 (1834), 403; quoted in Thistlethwaite, *The Making of the Victorian Organ*, 129
[48] Thistlethwaite, *The Making of the Victorian Organ*, 134
[49] Observations made by the author during the rebuilding of the Birmingham Town Hall Organ by N. P. Mander Ltd in 1984

Plate 56   William Hill's organ in Birmingham Town Hall, completed in 1834, and shown here in an engraving depicting the Music Festival of that year. This, with the contemporary instrument at York Minster, represent the most ambitious attempts to build a large and powerful organ within the constraints of the insular tradition. The display of front pipes, the largest with a speaking length of 32′ and speaking the note CCC (made of zinc), dominates the hall, and dwarfs the slightly half-hearted attempts at a surround of quasi-grecian casework.

his many innovations. The sheer size of the two instruments required use of the latest technology: in both the massive building frames incorporate cast iron members. At York, brackets support the cantilevered overhang on all four sides of the case; at Birmingham, a cast iron bridge supports about three tonnes weight of 32′ pipes where they stand over the action trench behind the console.[50] To make the 32′ metal Diapason and other large basses at York, Hill resorted to thick sheet zinc (the possibility of an alloy rich in tin being either unknown in England at this time or simply too expensive to contemplate). To bend it into shape he invented a rolling machine of a type widely used in industry ever since. Less successfully, the 32′ wooden pipes at Birmingham were made of frames and panels, rather than solid timber. Coupled with a preposterously large scale, this construction rendered them almost useless. Hill was perfectly well aware of the problems such large organs presented as far as the key action was concerned. His experience was inadequate for the resolution of the difficulty, and his provision of several multiple-palletted soundboards for the Great Organ at Birmingham suggests only a partial grasp of where the difficulties lay. However, for the large pipes he developed an ingenious and reliable square-drop or 'box' pallet, supplying ample wind but offering little resistance or 'pluck' when opened. Some of those provided at Birmingham are still in working order.[51]

Even if Hill's first attempts at large organs were only partly successful, they were undeniably impressive and were the foundation of a long and distinguished career in which innovation and improvement were consistent themes. In addition, though the organs at York and Birmingham were by no means perfect, they gave Hill an opportunity to experiment fruitfully with new pipe forms and new voicing techniques. At York a number of unusual ranks, mostly wooden flutes, exhibit a new line of thinking: there was a wooden Dulciana and Celestina at unison pitch, wooden Harmonica, Principal, German Flute and Claribella at 4′, and a wooden Flageolet at 2′. The Clarino, Shawm and Sackbut extended the interest in variety into the reed family. Hill's experiments with reed construction and voicing were to go much further, especially at Birmingham.[52]

In this organ there is a reed stop called the *Posaune* or Trombone, which all who are acquainted with the organs of the continent consider to be the most powerful and richest in tone of any existing.

The next step was to develop the idea of unusually powerful organ tone for a surprising new purpose:[53]

Mr. Hill has designed . . . for the use of the newly-formed railroads at Birmingham . . . an instrument which is constructed altogether without the introduction of either wood, leather, or any of the ordinary materials of an organ. The whole is of iron or brass. The bellows, wholly iron, blown by steam; the wind chests, also iron, and the pipes brass, so that the power of tone is rendered (by the force of wind and quality of the metal) extremely penetrating.

---

[50] Author's examination of both organs   [51] Author's examination
[52] *Penny Magazine* (8 November 1834); quoted in Thistlethwaite, *The Making of the Victorian Organ*, 131
[53] *Musical World*, 6 (1837), 76; quoted in Thistlethwaite, *The Making of the Victorian Organ*, 132

Signalling arrangements on the early railways were extremely primitive and hap-hazard; though Hill's device seems fanciful today, its intention was undoubtedly serious. It also led him to consider the possibility of incorporating high-pressure reeds in an organ, and in 1840 just such an addition arrived at Birmingham Town Hall.[54]

Mr. Hill has just finished the last octave of a set of magnificent reeds for this organ. They are voiced on about 15 inches of wind [380mm] – from two-and-a-half to three inches being the usual weight for church organs) and approach as near to the effect of a brass band as anything we have ever heard. They are to be placed in their situation immediately. . . .

The Grand Ophicleide, later renamed Tuba Mirabilis, was an instant triumph. Its pipes survive in the Birmingham organ, and though there has been alteration and revoicing over the years, the principles of the stop are largely clear: with large-scale tubes and the high pressure it would have been possible to produce a clear trumpet tone of great power and body with comparative smoothness.

Hill's introduction of the high-pressure reed is of incalculable importance, and English taste was to encourage the development of this idea in all the larger organs of the Victorian age. After such challenges and at least some success, one would have forgiven Hill for resting on his laurels. But in fact he was in the grip of an indomitable desire to change and improve the English organ, and in 1840 he stood on the threshold of a complete revolution in organ design, in which he was to play a vital part. If England had, in the early nineteenth century, struggled with the implications of its industrial growth, with the pressure for political and social reform, and with the national tendency to be circumspect and independent, it was by 1850 to establish itself as a truly modern nation and a world leader in the development of industry. Hill was the man to bear the standard of organ building in the new age.

[54] *Musical Journal* (January 1840); quoted in Thistlethwaite, *The Making of the Victorian Organ*, 132

CHAPTER THIRTEEN

THE GERMAN SYSTEM
1840–1865

After about 1840 the structure and use of the organ in Britain changed completely and permanently. From being the instrument found in the churches of a largely agrarian island nation, it suddenly emerged as a flag bearer of the new industrial empire, able to sound its triumphant message in sacred and secular contexts alike. The reasons for further rapid change are many.

The English organ had become confused. The experiments of the 1820s and 30s had produced instruments of varied and therefore unpredictable compass. The emergence of the pedal organ provided a department that competed with the Great organ for the provision of a solid bass line, but too inconsistent in layout from one organ to another to allow either the development of any conventions of pedal technique or the performance of organ music from other countries. Furthermore, to provide an organ with both long compass (to GG, FF or even CC) and a pedal organ in addition was expensive, and the duplication of resources in the pedal section and manual basses must have led some to enquire whether there was not a more economical and practical way of doing things.

The answer was found abroad, hence the use of 'The German System' as a term to describe the new method. Thanks to the advent of faster travel (at first by road but then, in the 1840s, with the added speed offered by England's railways and steamships across the Channel) the Continent of Europe was brought within easy reach. With a new desire to build organs on the grand scale, attention naturally turned to the great organs of Holland and Germany and, in due course, to the remarkable instruments being produced by builders such as E. F. Walcker (Ludwigsburg) and A. Cavaillé-Coll (Paris). According to Thistlethwaite, the Grand Tour was undertaken at various times by Camidge (in connection with his plans for the York Minster organ), Jonathan Gray (1824, possibly with Camidge), Vincent Novello (1829), Cramer (before 1831), H. J. Gauntlett (c1836), Joseph Moore (early 1830s, in connection with plans for the organ at Birmingham Town Hall), J. W. Fraser (1830s), Josiah Pittman (1839), William Rea (early 1840s), George French Flowers (late 1830s) and Adam Hamilton (brother of the Edinburgh builder David Hamilton, before 1842). Extensive travels were also undertaken by E. J. Hopkins

Plate 57 William Hill's organ of 1841 in the Great George Street Chapel, Liverpool. This instrument introduced the principles of the German System on a grand scale: the manual divisions all commenced at C, there was a fully developed C-compass Pedal Organ, and the stop list included many of Hill's novelties, including a Tuba Mirabilis. The case seems to owe something to that designed by Chalgrin for the church of St Sulpice in Paris, built in 1776–81 to house a monumental organ by François-Henri Clicquot, and shows the willingness to explore continental ideas at this time. The organ was vandalised in the 1970s and subsequently broken up and removed.

(1844, 1852 with Jeremiah Rogers of Doncaster, and on subsequent occasions), J. Rogers on his own (before 1843), Gauntlett again (1842), Samuel Sebastian Wesley (in connection with the organ for St George's Hall, Liverpool), Henry Smart (1852 and subsequently) and, the most widely travelled of all, Sir Frederick Gore Ouseley.[1]

For some the journey was as unenlightening as it had been for Burney; two English builders who visited Cavaillé-Coll's organ at La Madeleine in Paris pronounced it 'altogether beastly . . . a big brass band and nothing more',[2] but many realised that they were visiting instruments which spoke from the pinnacle of a great tradition and offered hitherto undreamed-of possibilities of scale, variety and power.

That there was something to be listened to in the continental tradition was made even more plain by the visits to England of Felix Mendelssohn-Bartholdy and the discovery of the music of J. S. Bach. Some of his works may have come to England via C. P. E. Bach; it is reported that Burney had some manuscripts from him and that he asked Samuel Wesley to play them.[3] Sporadic publications of Bach's works, sometimes as arrangements, appeared in the first years of the nineteenth century, and Samuel Wesley started performing his music (at first probably selections from the 48 Preludes and Fugues) in 1808. It seems not to have been until 1827 that any of the major organ works were heard in public, played by Samuel Sebastian Wesley and H. J. Gauntlett. However, the arrival of Mendelssohn in 1829 (the first of many long visits) revealed the mastery of Bach's music played by a performer fully acquainted with them. Further enthusiasm followed. By the late 1830s performances by Mendelssohn and others established the importance of the organ works at the core of the organist's repertoire.[4]

These cultural influences are important, but underlying them is the simple need for the organ to grow in size and scope to meet the pretensions of the industrial era. This was an age in which new bridges leapt across chasms in a single suspended span, in which great iron ships plied across the ocean under their own power, and in which men hurtled across the land at terrifying speed in the comfort of the railway carriage. It was for the organ builder to respond to this challenge in an appropriate way. In order to do so he had to be confident in the design and creation of the largest instruments; he had to have the resources to carry out work on such a scale with reasonable speed and efficiency; he also had to be certain of a reception that would keep his work in the public eye. The need to be novel and daring is clear enough, but one should also stress the way in which the image of the organ developed in the secular world. Hill's instrument in Birmingham Town Hall paved the way for many more in concert halls and public meeting places in Britain. These, amongst the largest and grandest of English organs, were to stimulate public

---

[1] N. J. Thistlethwaite, *The Making of the Victorian Organ* (Cambridge 1990), 178–80
[2] *Musical World*, 31 (1853), 594   [3] *Musical Standard*, 39/6 (1889)
[4] Thistlethwaite, *The Making of the Victorian Organ*, 164–75

interest in music, often introducing, in transcription form, orchestral works that would not otherwise have been heard by the majority.

The German System proved to be an ideal model to pursue; replete with cultural authority and convenient for the organ builder, instruments built in the new manner consistently offered the fullest range of tone and power from a relatively econom- ical distribution of resources.

The principles to be followed are set out in *The Organ* by E. J. Hopkins and E. F. Rimbault (London 1855).[5] This followed the publication in English of Seidel's *Die Orgel und ihr Bau* (Breslau 1842)[6] and the important new works of Töpfer[7] and Hamel.[8] Organs were now to have manuals of the same compass as each other, all starting at C; the notes below this, common on English Great organs, were to be omitted and the short-compass Swell extended. Each manual division was to have its own independent chorus structure (although in practice this was very rarely applied beyond the Great and Swell organs). The bass was to be provided by a fully independent Pedal organ, again starting at C but at 16′ pitch, so sounding an octave lower than the manuals, with its own chorus. The construction of the stops was to be varied extensively, with the help of the introduction of many new pipe-forms from Germany and France, thus avoiding the duplications of tone found in the large English organs of the 1820s and 1830s. Finally, England still clung to unequal temperament: the theoretical compromises of the seventeenth and eighteenth cen- turies had passed unnoticed, and it seems likely that modified meantone tuning was the norm. This was a serious obstacle to the progress required according to the taste of the day – keys with more than three sharps or flats were barely usable, and there- fore endless tracts of contemporary repertoire were out of bounds. 'Why', wrote the organist Chevalier Sigismund Neukomm, 'do the English organists continue to follow a barbarous system no longer adequate to the improved state of modern instrumental music, and which renders the organ unfit for accompaniment when in concert with other instruments?'[9]

Reform started in several places independently. In Bristol the organist Edward Hodges promoted C-compass organs between 1821 and 1837, though more out of a desire for logical consistency than with a view to bringing the instrument into line with those on the continent.[10] In Edinburgh the organ builder David Hamilton started work in 1824 after training in Germany (it is not known where); his instru- ments included many tonal and technical innovations, though it was not until the 1840s that he was consistently using the new C compass.[11]

[5] E. J. Hopkins and E. F. Rimbault, *The Organ, Its History and Construction*, 1st edn (London 1855); 2nd edn (London 1870): 3rd edition (London 1877)

[6] J. J. Seidel, *The Organ and its Construction, a Systematic Handbook for Organists, Organ Builders, etc.* (London 1852) (English translation of *Die Orgel und ihr Bau*, Breslau 1842)

[7] J. G. Töpfer, *Die Orgelbaukunst* (Weimar 1833); J. G. Töpfer, *Lehrbuch der Orgelbaukunst* (Weimar 1855)

[8] P. J. Hamel, *Nouveau Manuel Complet du Facteur d'Orgues* (Paris 1849)

[9] Hopkins and Rimbault, *The Organ*, 3rd edn, part II, 182

[10] Thistlethwaite, *The Making of the Victorian Organ*, 150–59

[11] A. Buchan, 'The Hamiltons of Edinburgh, A Preliminary Investigation', *BIOS Journal*, 15 (1991), 4–29

But it was in London that the German System was developed thoroughly, thanks to the eager promotion of H. J. Gauntlett coupled with the inventiveness and skill of the organ builder William Hill.

The organ hired by Gray & Son for the Exeter Hall Festival in 1836 seems to have introduced the 'German mode' to the capital,[12] and in 1838 Hill, then briefly in partnership with Frederick Davison, built a small 'German scale' organ at Turvey, Bedfordshire, in collaboration with Gauntlett.[13] Another instrument, apparently planned by Davison, was 'to afford every facility for the easy as well as just performance of the organ music of Bach and Mendelssohn';[14] destined for St John, Chester, it appeared in part in Westminster Abbey for Queen Victoria's Coronation in June 1838. On delivery to Chester it was Gauntlett who played at the opening.[15]

Henry John Gauntlett (1805–76) was a lawyer by profession with an extensive musical ability (and strong opinions on the subject) unhampered by formal training. As Editor of the *Musical World*, as a pioneer of travel to see organs abroad, as a close friend of Mendelssohn and as a persistent proponent of his own views, he was ideally placed to exert a considerable influence on the path of organ building. Between 1838 and 1849 he designed instruments built by Lincoln, Bevington, Flight and, especially, Hill; all had C compass and almost all had two octaves of pedals with their own pipes.[16] At Christ Church Newgate Street, London, Gauntlett supervised the reconstruction of the organ by Hill, the impressive scheme of this influential organ included three manuals from C to f''' (fifty-four notes) and Pedals from C to g' (thirty-two notes); the Pedal Organ had a complete chorus:

16. 16. 16. 8. $5\frac{1}{3}$. 4. V. V. 16. 8.

– though its potential was limited as all the stops were of restricted compass, one octave only for the most part.[17]

Hill and Gauntlett continued to move forward, collaborating on organs for St Luke Cheetham Hill, Manchester and St Peter upon Cornhill, London in 1840.[18] In 1841 came a large new instrument for Great George Street Chapel, Liverpool. The confident and original scheme, bristling with daring novelties, illustrates just how far things had moved since the organs of York and Birmingham only a few years before (p. 237).[19]

Almost all the vital elements of the Victorian organ are present. Within a framework which includes the traditional English chorus from diapasons to mixtures (including tierce ranks) we see the development of balanced provision of stops on the two main departments, the arrival of a complete and independent pedal division (based, as in all English pedal organs from their origins until the 1950s, on a wood Open Diapason 16 of large scale), and the appearance of the many tonal novelties concocted by Hill over the preceding decade. Most significant is that it is the Swell Organ, not the Choir, which has been upgraded to the level of partnership with the Great, even overtaking it in the provision of chorus reeds at 16', 8', and 4'

[12] Thistlethwaite, *The Making of the Victorian Organ*, 181–2   [13] Ibid., 182–3   [14] *Musical World*, 9 (1838), 249
[15] Thistlethwaite, *The Making of the Victorian Organ*, 183–4   [16] Ibid., 185–95   [17] Ibid., 463–4
[18] Ibid., 189   [19] Ibid., 467–8

Liverpool, Great George Street Chapel, William Hill 1841

Great Organ (C–f''', 54 notes)

Bourdon [C–B]	16
Tenoroon Open Diapason [c–f''']	16
Open Diapason	8
Open Diapason	8
Stopped Diapason Bass [C–B?]	8
Stopped Diapason Treble [c–f'''?]	8
Quint	5⅓
Principal	4
Stopped-flute (metal)	4
Twelfth	2⅔
Fifteenth	2
Tierce	1⅗
Sesquialtera	III
Mixture	II
Doublette	II
Trombone	8
Clarion	4
Octave Clarion	2

Swell Organ (C–f''', 54 notes)

Bourdon [C–B]	16
Tenoroon Dulciana [c–f''']	16
Open Diapason	8
Stopped Diapason Bass [C–B?]	8
Stopped Diapason Treble [c–f'''?]	8
Dulciana (Echo) [c–f'''?]	8
Principal	4
Suabe-flute	4
Twelfth	2⅔
Fifteenth	2
Flageolet	2
Sesquialtera	III
Mixture	II
Echo Dulciana Cornet [from c or c'?]	V
Contra-fagotto	16
Cornopean	8
Trumpet	8
Oboe	8
Clarion	4
Swiss Cromorne-flute	8

Choir Organ (C–f''', 54 notes)

Stopped Diapason	8
Dulciana	8
Claribel-flute	8
Oboe-flute	4
Wald-flute	4
Piccolo	2
Corno-flute	8
Cromorne	8

Pedal Organ (C–d', 27 notes)

Grand Open Diapason	16
Bourdon	16
Principal	8
Fifteenth	4
Sesquialtra	V
Trombone	16

Solo Organ (playable from the Swell keys)

Tuba Mirabilis	8

Swell to Great
Choir to Great
Great to Pedal
Swell to Pedal
Choir to Pedal
Pedal Octave [?]

4 composition pedals

pitch. This is in contrast to contemporary work abroad: in Germany the Swell was still at an experimental stage; in France the Récit Expressif started as a junior partner to the Grand Orgue and Positif, only in later and larger organs approaching the size and scope favoured in England. The decision to turn the Swell into a large independent department, able to match the resources of the Great Organ, may have been influenced by a desire to imitate the large Oberwerk divisions found in Germany and Holland, and in some instruments (St Peter upon Cornhill, London, 1840;[20] St Mary at Hill, London, 1848[21]) the Swell box was above the Great pipes rather than above and behind them. Whatever the reasons, it set the English organ on a distinctive and independent path that has had widespread influence to this day.

It is probable that Hill's practical common sense went some way to restraining Gauntlett's wilder flights of daring: experience at York and Birmingham had illustrated all too clearly the limits of what was possible. At St Olave Southwark the organ builder H. C. Lincoln embarked, in consultation with Gauntlett, on the construction of an instrument with a Great Organ of no fewer than twenty-seven stops; it appears to have driven him to despair, and Hill was called in to finish the instrument.[22]

In the building of his own German System organs it was Hill's musical sense no less than his practical ability that contributed to their outstanding success. Elliot's and Hill's claim to descent from Snetzler is borne out in part by their attitude to pipe scales. There is less consistent sign of the attenuation of the upperwork introduced by Green and England in order to secure refinement and delicacy. In some Great choruses Elliot & Hill (or, later, Hill on his own) would make the Principal, Twelfth, Fifteenth and Mixtures to the same scale. The Open Diapason(s) might be larger (Ashridge, Elliot & Hill 1818; St Peter upon Cornhill, Hill 1840; Kidderminster Town Hall, Hill 1855[23]). Thus the chorus was bolder than Green's or England's (but still less powerful than customary in the rest of Europe) though arguably less sparkling. This treatment lent itself admirably to the extension of the chorus by the introduction of manual 16′ stops, additional mixtures and the occasional Quint 5⅓ or even Tierce 3⅕ (harmonics of the 16′ series), and must have contributed significantly to the success of Hill's first large German System organs. Equally his experience with different kinds of reed stops helped contribute to the grandeur of these instruments: the Posaune and its newly introduced relative the Cornopean appeared frequently, providing a thicker and richer Trumpet tone than had been possible before. In the largest instruments the family was extended to include the now celebrated Tuba Mirabilis. Some of the effect was achieved by the use of very large scales for the resonators, but the ability to make musical sounds from these novel scales was entirely a question of Hill's undoubted skill as a reed voicer. In addition, thanks to Hill's love of experiment, he was able to offer a wider menu of new flute and solo stops than any of his contemporaries, as the scheme for

---

[20] Ibid., 230–1   [21] Author's examination of the organ before the fire of 1988
[22] Thistlethwaite, *The Making of the Victorian Organ*, 190–91, 508–10   [23] Ibid., 46, 240, 242

Great George Street shows. Some of these sank back into obscurity again – no one now knows quite what, for example, a Swiss Cromorne-flute might have been. Finally, from 1843 onwards Hill started experimenting with string-toned stops, usually of open metal. The Viola da Gamba or Cone Gamba (and Gemshorn at 4′ pitch) were tapered, the Salicional and Hohl-flute (not in fact a flute at all) were cylindrical. This (and the introduction of the Keraulophon by Gray & Davison in 1843) started a popular vogue for delicate narrow-scaled registers.[24]

At first Hill monopolised the 'principles adopted by the celebrated Organ Builders of Germany, in the compass of the manuals, and the mode of the blending of the stops',[25] and by 1842 the system penetrated the inner sanctum of English music making, when a fine example of Hill's latest work was erected in Worcester Cathedral.[26] But, before long, Gray & Davison joined the fray, no doubt with the keen interest of Frederick Davison, Hill's erstwhile partner. In 1843 the firm built a 'Model Organ on the German Plan'[27] for St Paul Wilton Place, Knightsbridge, London. It was an immediate success; though in some ways not as innovative as Hill's latest organs, it was perhaps better balanced, with its resources economically spread over three manuals where Hill and Gauntlett would often compress them into two rather unwieldy departments. The organ was very well received, its new Keraulophon especially so (p. 240).[28]

Other builders gradually followed: Robson at St Michael Chester Square, London in 1847, Bevington (with Gauntlett) at the Mechanics' Hall, Nottingham, in 1849,[29] and others in their wake. As early as 1852, when Gray & Davison built a new organ for Eton College Chapel with the old GG compass it was denounced as 'old-fashioned, expensive and ineffective':[30] England was now converted to the German System.

As had been proved at York and Birmingham, the large new organs demanded at the beginning of Victoria's reign were difficult to play: these grand instruments had reached the limit of what was possible with the mechanical key action of the period. Ways of lightening the touch developed slowly, and centred round the application of pneumatics, harnessing the copious supply of air under pressure already available in the organ. As early as 1827 Joseph Booth of Wakefield had used pneumatic 'puffs' to draw down individual pallets under the largest pipes.[31] The Edinburgh builder David Hamilton, by his own account, went further. He claimed to have incorporated a pneumatic lever key action in the organ at St John's Episcopal Church, Edinburgh in 1835. Here the tracker from the key simply opened a small valve that admitted wind to a power bellows: this inflated and opened the larger pallet in the soundboard.[32] Whatever the alleged precedence of

[24] Ibid., 196–201
[25] Circular issued by Hill in 1841, quoted in Thistlethwaite, *The Making of the Victorian Organ*, 510–11
[26] Thistlethwaite, *The Making of the Victorian Organ*, 460–1   [27] *Musical World*, 18 (1843), 140
[28] Thistlethwaite, *The Making of the Victorian Organ*, 472–3   [29] Ibid., 257–8
[30] Henry Smart in *Musical World*, 30 (1852), 497   [31] Hopkins and Rimbault, *The Organ*, 1st edn, part II, 59
[32] Thistlethwaite, *The Making of the Victorian Organ*, 353–3

London, St Paul Wilton Place, Knightsbridge, Gray & Davison 1843

Great Organ (C–f‴, 54 notes)		Swell Organ (C–f‴, 54 notes)	
Double Diapason bass [C–B?]	16	Double Diapason bass [C–B?]	16
Double Diapason treble [from c?]	16	Double Diapason treble [from c?]	16
Open Diapason	8	Open Diapason	8
Open Diapason	8	Stopped Diapason	8
Stopped Diapason	8	Principal	4
Principal	4	Flute	4
Twelfth	$2\frac{2}{3}$	Fifteenth	2
Fifteenth	2	Sesquialtra	III
Sesquialtra	IV	Mixture	II
Mixture	II	Cornopean	8
Furniture	II	Trumpet	8
Trumpet	8	Hautboy	8
Clarion	4	Clarion	4

Choir Organ (C–f‴, 54 notes)		Pedal Organ (C–e′, 29 notes)	
Stopped Diapason bass [C–B?]	8	Open Diapason	16
Stopped Diapason treble [from c?]	8	Stopped Diapason	16
Dulciana [from c?]	8	Principal	8
Keraulophon [from c?]	8	Fifteenth	4
Clarabella Flute [from c?]	8	Sesquialtra	IV
Principal	4	Trombone	16
Flute	4		
Fifteenth	2		
Piccolo	2		
Mixture	II		
Clarionet	8		

Swell to Great
Swell to Choir
Great to Pedals
Swell to Pedals
Choir to Pedals

4 composition pedals to Great
2 composition pedals to Swell
2 composition pedals to Pedal

A separate keyboard was provided to the left of the Choir keys from which the Pedal might be played.

---

various inventions, it is Charles Spackman Barker who is usually given the credit for the pneumatic lever as popularised after 1841; indeed it is often referred to as the Barker Lever. Barker claimed to have developed his device in 1832 and to have offered it to Camidge at York Minster in 1833 and to Hill in connection with the Birmingham organ. It is possible that, at this stage, Barker's lever was either faulty or impractical; at any rate he met with no encouragement at first. He approached the French builder Aristide Cavaillé-Coll (1811–99) in 1837, travelled to France at his invitation, and the Barker Lever made its first appearance to wild acclaim at the Abbey of St Denis in 1841.

St Denis was to Cavaillé-Coll what York was to Hill: as a very young man Cavaillé-Coll had won the competition for the new organ with a proposal for the first large modern instrument to be built in France, learning much from the work of John Abbey and introducing the German System in all its glory. The organ was hair-raisingly ambitious: the offer from Barker to solve the inevitable problems of weight of touch was clearly a godsend and Cavaillé-Coll lost no time in working with Barker on a practical and entirely successful version of the Barker Lever, oper-ating on exactly the same principle as the Hamilton lever described above. To the incredulous amazement of the public the touch of this mighty instrument was ren-dered as light as that of a pianoforte.[33] The St Denis organ became celebrated over-night, and was probably the most highly praised new organ in Europe. Its fame spread to England, and with it the possibility of the use of the pneumatic lever to lighten the touch of large instruments.

Hill proposed the use of the pneumatic lever to the organ committee at St George's Hall, Liverpool in 1847, and in 1849 it was applied to his organ at Birmingham Town Hall. But the first use by an English builder seems to have been by Walker early in 1849 at the Exeter Hall, London.[34]

The building of the St Denis instrument marks a new wave of interest in organs on the Continent. It must be remarked that, despite the avowed intentions of proponents of the German System to follow a method illustrated in instruments overseas, and despite their keenness to compare the latest English organs to 'the noble instruments of Haarlem, Dresden, Strasburgh, Hamburg, and other large continental towns',[35] the resemblance is not one that would have forcibly impressed itself on the inhabitants of those places. Hill's voicing, for example, though reaching into a new sphere of grandeur and brilliance, still retained much in the way of English refinement and modesty; his many newly invented stops often bore no physical resemblance to their namesakes abroad, the Hohl-flute in particular (Hill's answer to Gray & Davison's Keraulophon) was the very antithe-sis of the large-scaled stopped metal flutes appearing under that name in Holland and Germany.

At the Great Exhibition of 1851 Britain opened its doors to the world, and the world came flooding in. No event before or since has managed to make it so clear to the people of these islands that they belong to a wider human community capable of the same ideals and achievements as themselves. Under the towering roof of Paxton's astonishing Crystal Palace – constructed, with typical Victorian

[33] C. and E. Cavaillé-Coll, *Aristide Cavaillé-Coll, ses Origines, sa Vie, ses Oeuvres* (Paris 1929)
[34] Thistlethwaite, *The Making of the Victorian Organ*, 356
[35] H. J. Gauntlett's review of the Hill organ in Great George Street Chapel, Liverpool in the *Morning Post* (1 January 1842).

aplomb, from first sketch to opening ceremony in only seven months – some five million people saw at first hand the very goods and inventions that counted for progress in other nations. Organs were well represented; two of those exhibited showed that the instruments actually made in Germany or France were of a quite different calibre to even the best of the latest English work.

The organ by Ducroquet of Paris (built under the superintendence of Charles Spackman Barker) was notable for sheer quality of manufacture, as well as placing under the public eye many of the innovations and much of the grandeur established by Cavaillé-Coll at St Denis. It had a reversed, detached console with keyboards of five complete octaves from C to c'''', reeds on high wind pressure, the Barker Lever applied to the Grand-orgue, couplers uniting the Récit to the Grand-orgue at unison, octave and sub-octave pitches, and it glittered with pipes of nearly pure tin in the French tradition. Included were stops that had not appeared on English shores before: the Flûte à Pavillon, the Flûte Harmonique and the French Viola da Gamba, as well as a chorus of the trenchant and brassy Trompettes for which the French were famous.[36] 'No English builder ever did make such an organ' gasped the *Musical World* a few years later;[37] nor would they thereafter, for with a price tag of £1,200 for only two manuals and twenty stops this was simply too expensive to sell in the cut-throat climate of English organ building. However, it summed up the kind of qualities that English travellers admired so much in the new organs of Cavaillé-Coll and helped the French organ to become established in the public mind as a product of the highest artistic quality.[38]

The influence of Prince Albert on the contents of the exhibition was shown in his invitation to the firm of Schulze of Paulinzelle to send an organ; the recent works of this small family concern were presumably known to him and to Mendelssohn from their student days in Leipzig.[39] Where the French organ doubt-less achieved much of its impact from its *batterie* of Trompettes and Bombardes, Edmund Schulze's instrument derived from his own Saxon traditions and displayed a flue chorus (Principal 8, Octave 4, Mixtur V) that seems to have stopped listeners in their tracks. Schulze used large scales, wide mouths for the pipes and copious amounts of wind, unleashing the kind of power and brilliance from the flue work that had not been encountered in England since the days of Father Smith. Jeremiah Rogers, the organist of Doncaster parish church, was deceived: 'The man has got some old pipes in his organ!' he exclaimed at first, only being convinced that the organ was indeed new when he climbed up and looked inside.[40] As well as this splen-did chorus, Schulze's organ exhibited characteristic German flutes and solo stops: the Gamba, Hohlflöte, Lieblich Gedackt, Geigen Principal and Flöttraverso. Where Ducroquet's organ was to lead to no further orders for Barker, Schulze would return to execute several decisively influential projects.

[36] W. L. Sumner, *The Organ*, 4th edn (London 1973), 230, 411–12   [37] *Musical World*, 42 (1864), 137
[38] Thistlethwaite, *The Making of the Victorian Organ*, 275, 296–7
[39] J. H. Burn, 'Edmund Schulze's Exhibition Organ', *The Organ*, 10 (1930), 100–3   [40] Ibid., 101

Nor were English builders idle. Hill, perhaps confident of his position at this time, showed only a small organ of sixteen stops. Even so, he included an example of his celebrated Tuba Mirabilis and provided a pneumatic stop action, in which the registers were brought on and off by pressing levers arranged like a diminutive keyboard.[41] Gray & Davison were able to show the new organ destined for the London church of St Anne Limehouse. This was a true successor to the 'Model Organ' for St Paul Wilton Place, and was about the same size. It stands at Limehouse to this day and speaks with all the authority of one of the finest early German System organs existing, as well as having the distinction of being the largest exhibit from the Great Exhibition to have survived (see plate 58, p. 244).

In some ways it is still a traditional organ. Apart from the C compass and the appearance of a Keraulophon, the only distinctively new sound to be obtained from the fluework is thanks to a Double Open Diapason 16 and two Open Diapasons 8 on the Great Organ: these give a fullness that could barely have been achieved even by the most adept performer on an earlier organ with long compass but no Double. The two Open Diapasons are now different from each other: one large in scale, the other smaller, but still only slightly differentiated in volume. The Swell Organ is not as fully developed as in a Hill organ, and retains its short compass (here the pipes start at c with the lowest octave of keys acting on the bass of the Choir Organ); the Swell box is at the back of the instrument and the department does not in any way challenge the supremacy of the Great. On the other hand the Choir Organ is fully developed, with a number of solo stops and a sprightly chorus of its own including a Mixture II. There is still no attempt to generate sheer power from the fluework; this task is left to the reeds. The Great Posaune 8 and Clarion 4 and the Pedal Grand Bombarde 16 live up to any military expectations generated by the names engraved on the knobs: they are startlingly powerful and commanding compared to the rest of the instrument and never fail to make a deep impression on the visitor. This instrument also shows a novelty in the form of its casework. Gone is the superstructure of towers, flats and cornices that marked all large cases before this time: above the console and wooden substructure of the organ rise pipes and pipes alone, a semi-functional display of the very machinery that makes an organ an organ, inviting comparison with the chimneys of a factory or steam engine. In 1851 this was an instrument with a truly modern look: few builders would now build traditional cases with any sense of confidence and within twenty years the organ case was all but dead.

However, the most ambitious organ shown in the Crystal Palace was that built by the young Henry Willis. Willis was born in London in 1821 in a family with musical connections. He was apprenticed to John Gray in 1835, but had moved to Cheltenham by the early 1840s. He returned to London to set up shop on his own account around 1845, and carried out significant rebuilds at Gloucester Cathedral (1847) and Tewkesbury Abbey (1848). He had by this time already made the

---

[41] Thistlethwaite, *The Making of the Victorian Organ*, 296, 356, 511–13.

Plate 58   The organ in St Anne Limehouse, London, built by Gray & Davison in 1851 and exhibited in the Crystal Palace at the Great Exhibition of that year (photograph c1930). The case, by Albert Howell, is a radical departure from all previous designs. The superstructure of woodwork above impost level has been omitted altogether, leaving exposed the very machinery of the organ – its pipes. The motifs – chimney-like pipes, a panel reminiscent of a wheel above the keys – are emphatically those of the steam age, designed to emphasise the mechanical complexity of the instrument and the manufacturing ingenuity of its makers. From this date onwards few Victorian organs had any substantial upper casework.

acquaintance of Samuel Sebastian Wesley. For the Great Exhibition he built an organ of no fewer than seventy stops: Willis was a man of indomitable ambition and there is little doubt that he hoped to be as famous for his organs as I. K. Brunel was for his engineering.[42]

It is not known for certain how Willis financed the construction of this huge instrument, but the name of Sir James Tyler is traditionally mentioned.[43] Willis announced, with characteristic freedom from the constraints of modesty, that 'it is presumed by its builder to be the first successful large organ yet constructed in England'. It certainly allowed the performer an ease of control that was to make a deep impression. Willis used the Barker Lever to lighten the touch of the keys. He also applied pneumatics to the stop action, and introduced his patented thumb pistons: a row of small brass buttons was placed in the key slips between one manual and the next to be pressed by the thumbs, perhaps even while playing. These acted, via the agency of the pneumatic stop action, in the same way as composition pedals, bringing on fixed combinations of stops.[44]

By the death of Willis in 1901 his firm had become the most famous in England, and in the early twentieth century it was customary to look back on Willis's career as an unbroken succession of triumphs. Certainly the committee appointed to decide on a builder for the large new organ in St George's Hall, Liverpool were deeply impressed by the Exhibition organ, and their order went to Willis. The Liverpool instrument was completed in 1855 (see plate 59, p. 246). The intervention of Samuel Sebastian Wesley, the Corporation's adviser, was critical. Hill and Gray & Davison were committed to the German System and the introduction of equal temperament; Wesley was not. In putting forward Willis to build the Liverpool organ he was able to insist on the retention of GG compass for the manuals and meantone tuning, in addition developing an eccentric stop-list full of the kind of duplication and repetition that had bedevilled the large organs of the 1830s. Willis attempted high-pressure reeds and a 32′ Diapason made of cast iron but, judging by the fact that these were swept away and replaced as early as 1867, they were not a complete success.[45] The retention of several archaic features invited criticism from the rest of the organ world, and blinded commentators to Willis's ability; hostile notices appeared in the *Musical Gazette* and *Musical World*.[46] The diapasons were 'universally regarded as the weak point of the instrument'.[47] A remarkable summary of this instrument was written retrospectively in 1891: it was 'perhaps the most disappointing large organ erected in modern times'.[48] (The organ enjoys a considerable reputation today; it is likely that this is thanks to work carried out in 1867 and 1897.) Willis would have to wait before he could establish his position as a leading figure.

Meanwhile Hill and Gray & Davison continued to divide the major spoils between them. Both firms and their respective partisans remained acutely aware of

[42] W. L. Sumner, *Father Henry Willis, Organ Builder, and his successors* (London 1955)
[43] Information kindly passed to the author by B. Q. S. F. Buchanan, Esq.   [44] Sumner, *Father Henry Willis*
[45] Thistlethwaite, *The Making of the Victorian Organ*, 135–49   [46] Ibid., 139–40
[47] *The Ecclesiologist*, 26 (1865), 113   [48] *Musical Standard*, 40 (1891), 99

Plate 59 The organ in St George's Hall, Liverpool, built by Henry Willis in 1855 under the direction of Samuel Sebastian Wesley. In contrast to the Panopticon organ, this instrument retained many features of the insular tradition: keyboards to GG, unequal temperament, and extensive duplication in the stop-list. It failed to bring Willis the success that he considered to be his due, and was extensively altered in 1867 and 1897. The case, by C. R. Cockerell, follows the principles introduced at St Anne Limehouse: the upper part of the organ is left exposed decorated only by finials on the larger pipes and decorative bands appearing to hold them up, although the detailing is still lavish.

Plate 60   The organ in the Royal Panopticon of Science and Art, Leicester Square, London, built by William
Hill in 1853. Despite some eccentric features – the moorish case, a hole through the centre of the instrument to
allow the projection of lantern slides, and the provision of keyboards for three players – this was, by all accounts,
the first really successful large German System organ. At the top of the organ can be seen the exposed Solo
division, with its Tubas mounted horizontally after the manner of the *Trompeteria* of Spanish organs. After the
closure of the Panopticon the organ stood for some years in the South Transept of St Paul's Cathedral, before
being moved to the Victoria Rooms, Bristol c1872. It does not survive.

the need to move forward and to take account of the latest information brought back by travellers on the continent. Interest had been excited in the work of Schulze, and further foreign trips were necessary. E. J. Hopkins, organist at the Temple Church and co-author of the standard Victorian text on the organ, visited the Schulze in Bremen Cathedral and was overwhelmed: 'I never at any organ, in the whole course of my life, felt myself under such a species of enchantment. Indeed the excitement was so great that I had two or three times to leave the church in the most urgent state.'[49] Others, such as the organist and engineer Henry Smart, became equally enthusiastic about the works of Cavaillé-Coll.[50] Hill's four-manual organ for the Royal Panopticon of Arts and Sciences (1853) had moved away from the insular manner of his early work towards a confident expression of the continental style, albeit still using fundamentally English ingredients (see plate 60, p. 247):[51]

Great	16. 8. 8. 8. $5^{1}/_{3}$. 4. 4. $2^{2}/_{3}$. 2. III. III. III. 16. 8. 8. 4.
Swell	16. 8. 8. 8. 4. 4. $2^{2}/_{3}$. 2. IV–V. 8. 8. 8. 4.
Choir	16. 8. 8. 8. 4. 4. $2^{2}/_{3}$. 2. 2. II. 8. 8.
Solo	8. 8. 4. 2. II. 8. 8. 8. 4
Pedal	32. 16. 16. 16. 8. $5^{1}/_{3}$. 4. V. 16. 8.

The last two stops of the Solo Organ, the Grand Tuba Mirabilis 8 and Grand Clarion 4, were mounted horizontally at the top of the organ (horizontal reeds are a feature of Spanish organs) no doubt to devastating effect (see below). Hill also adopted the idea of Cavaillé-Coll (much quoted but in practice rarely carried out) for increasing the pressure in the trebles of the Great reeds,[52] and they were in any case on a higher pressure than the fluework. This instrument, its one archaic oddity being the provision of extra keyboards for a second and third performer, was an important success. Smart pronounced it 'without equal in this country';[53] it was perhaps the 'first successful large organ to be built in England', receiving exactly the accolades that Willis sought at the Great Exhibition, and establishing a positive new rôle for the organ in a place of public entertainment.

Gray & Davison were, again, not far behind. The organ for Glasgow City Hall was built to the designs of Smart, who introduced sub- and super-octave couplers, Harmonic Flutes and other features derived from French practice,[54] including reeds on a high pressure of wind, just pre-dating Hill's similar treatment at the Panopticon.[55] Smart's opening recital included organ music by Bach but was dominated by transcriptions from the orchestral works of Handel, Weber, Mendelssohn, Rossini and Meyerbeer.[56] This instrument, and the way it was first played, set the tone for the English concert organ for the next hundred years. Its success was confirmed in organs at Birmingham Music Hall (1856), where the wind pressures were increased in the treble, à la Cavaillé-Coll,[57] and then at the

[49] C. W. Pearce, *The Life and Works of Edward John Hopkins* (London 1910), 66
[50] Thistlethwaite, *The Making of the Victorian Organ*, 277–90
[51] Ibid., 212–14   [52] Ibid., 208   [53] *Musical World*, 32 (1854), 475–7; 533–5
[54] Thistlethwaite, *The Making of the Victorian Organ*, 278–9, 476–7   [55] Ibid., 279–80   [56] Ibid., 281
[57] Ibid., 278–80

Crystal Palace (which had now been moved to its new home at Sydenham, south of London) (1857).[58] At Leeds Town Hall in 1859 the firm again joined forces with Smart, who contributed his knowledge of continental organs and his engineering skill to a landmark instrument.

Great
Front   16. 8. 8. 8. 4. 4. $2^2/_3$. 2. IV. V. 8. 4.
Back   16. 8. 8. 8. $5^1/_3$. 4. 4. 2. III. IV. 16. 8. 8. 4.
Swell   16. 8. 8. 8. 8. 4. 4. 4. $2^2/_3$. 2. 2. IV. III. 16. 8. 8. 8. 8. 4.
Choir   16. 8. 8. 8. 8. 8. 4. 4. 4. $2^2/_3$. 2. 2. V. 16. 8. 4.
Solo   8. 8. 4. 2. 8. 8. 8. 8.
Echo   (added 1865) 16. 8. 8. 4. 4. IV. Carillon
Pedal   32. 32. 16. 16. 16. 16. $10^2/_3$. 8. 8. $5^1/_3$. 4. IV. 32. 16. 16. 8.
4 manual keyboards (Echo played from Solo or Choir through couplers)
15 couplers, including Back Great to Swell
Swell and Solo enclosed in swell boxes
Crescendo and diminuendo pedals
4 adjustable composition pedals, each with an index for setting to desired combination of stops

Not only was the Solo Organ enclosed, but both flue and reed pipes were mounted horizontally. The stops of this division were avowedly orchestral in character: imitative flutes (harmonic, after the French pattern), Clarinet, Oboe, Bassoon and Cor Anglais. Standing on a complex soundboard with one pallet to every pipe, the division could produce special orchestral effects from these stops by 'mechanical combination': 'Clarinet and Flute, in octaves . . . Oboe and Bassoon, in octaves. . . . Flute, Clarinet and Bassoon, in double octaves', and so on. The adjustable combination pedals and the crescendo device offered further flexibility to the performer.[59]

Other builders were soon as confident with the German System as their more famous brethren. A notable example appeared at Worcester Music Hall in 1854, built by John Nicholson of Worcester. Nicholson's organ was remarkable for having the Choir and Swell enclosed in swell boxes, the latter housed in a large chamber to one side of the stage. The influence of an outside consultant is likely.[60] Kirtland & Jardine, the successors to the business of Samuel Renn,[61] were also progressive, thanks partly to the persuasive advocacy of new methods by Benjamin Joule: 'Messrs *Kirtland & Jardine* have made personal examination of some of the finest specimens of the German and French Schools of Organ Building.'[62] At St Peter, Manchester (1856) the result was an eclectic mixture of French and German influence both tonally and mechanically. In a further instrument for the Free Trade Hall, Manchester (1857) Kirtland & Jardine introduced the scaling system proposed by

[58] Ibid., 282–3, 477–8   [59] Ibid., 284–90, 480–82
[60] M. Sayer, *Samuel Renn, English Organ Builder* (Chichester 1974), 49–59
[61] Sayer, *Samuel Renn, English Organ Builder*, 111; M. Sayer, 'Kirtland and Jardine of Manchester', *The Organ*, 54 (1976), 169–76   [62] Hopkins and Rimbault, *The Organ*, 1st edn, part II, 599

Professor Töpfer of Weimar,[63] in which the pipe diameter halved on the seventeenth note (scale A) or eighteenth note (scale B) of the keyboard, continuing in like proportion to the top of the compass.[64] J. W. Walker, mainly known for small organs and late to adopt the German System, built a solid and extremely musical three-manual organ for Romsey Abbey (1858). The organ by G. M. Holdich of London for Lichfield Cathedral (1861) was more conservative than some[65] but included a splendid ten-stop Pedal Organ. The organist, Samuel Spofforth, was of the old school, and viewed the pedals coolly: 'You may put them there, but I shall never use them!'[66]

Meanwhile a new organ of monumental size and considerable importance was in the course of construction for Doncaster parish church. The old church had burnt in 1853. As the new building by Scott rose from the ashes, the organist, Jeremiah Rogers, turned to Edmund Schulze for the new instrument, placing an order in 1857. The organ was completed in 1862 to the following scheme:[67]

Great   32 (from c). 16. 16. 8. 8. 8. 8. 5⅓. 4. 4. 4. 2⅔. 2. V. III–V. V. 16. 8. 8. 8. 4.
Swell   16. 8. 8. 8. 8. 8. 4. 4. 4. 4. V. III. IV. 16. 8. 8. 8. 8. 4.
Choir   16. 8. 8. 8. 8. 8. 4. 4. 4. 4. 2. III. 8.
Solo   (largely borrowed from the Swell) 8. 8. 8. 4. 4. 16. 8. 8. 8.
Echo   16. 8. 8. 8. 8. 4. 4. II.
Pedal   32. 16. 16. 16. 16. 16. 10⅔. 8. 8. 8. 8. 6⅖. 5⅓. 4. 3⅕. II. II. 32. 16. 16. 8. 8. 8. 4.

Technically the organ was mixed. It was built on the 'simplification system', a technique advocated by Vögler in the eighteenth century and used by Kirtland and Jardine (and later by Brindley and others) in England. The pipes were arranged in strict chromatic order on the soundboards, permitting, in theory, a simple mechanical linkage with no rollerboards, much as used in a previous generation by Samuel Green. Partly because of the chromatic layout, and partly because of Schulze's belief in supplying copious amounts of wind to the pipes, the soundboards were vast in size, and to this day those at Doncaster are among the largest in Britain. The arrangements for raising the wind were old-fashioned by English standards, consisting of a row of twelve diagonal bellows, and needing four men to operate them when the full resources of the instrument were in use. The stops of the Pedal Organ were derived from thirteen ranks, each one appearing at two pitches an octave apart from each other. Much of the organ had, and still has, a rough appearance, and the original key action (tracker, with Barker Lever to the Great Organ) and stop mechanism (both now removed) led to some criticism.[68]

Schulze's workshop was 'a rustic building with a small water-wheel, little more than a roomy carpenter's shop',[69] and it is unlikely that he made any metal pipes.

[63] Hopkins and Rimbault, *The Organ*, 2nd edn. part II, 508–9   [64] Töpfer, *Lehrbuch der Orgelbaukunst*
[65] R. Greening, *The Organs of Lichfield Cathedral* (Lichfield 1974)
[66] Traditional, quoted in C. Clutton and A. Niland, *The British Organ* (London 1963), 94
[67] Hopkins and Rimbault, *The Organ*, 2nd edn, part II, 530–1
[68] Thistlethwaite, *The Making of the Victorian Organ*, 387
[69] T. C. Albutt, 'Reminiscences of Edmund Schulze and the Armley Organ', ed. A. Gray, *The Organ*, 2 (1925), 78

The fluework for Doncaster seems to have been largely the work of the trade pipe-maker Violette, of London.[70] There was, in compensation, a lively interest in the making of wooden pipes. Some were intriguing and clearly excellent, such as the wooden Violones and Principal basses. Others, such as the cylindrical and tri-angular wooden flutes, the flutes with circular mouths transversely blown from an angled external windway (the Harmonica) and the Terpodion (named in honour, if not actually in imitation, of a contemporary experimental keyboard glockenspiel), were simply intriguing.

Schulze's artisan background had a strong appeal to those English commenta-tors already wary of the factory practices of English builders; more importantly, lack of workshop space, and the arrangements concerning the provision of metal pipework, forced Schulze to voice his organs on site. This process clearly fascinated his admirers, and contributed to the image of him as an artist and craftsman, as well as giving each instrument a tonal individuality and freshness perhaps lacking in factory-voiced organs.

Whatever quibbles there may have been about its construction, the musical effect of Doncaster was a revelation. Here was 'the noblest work of organ-building art that England has ever heard or seen',[71] 'a great big German fact to say for itself what a fine German organ is reputed to say'.[72] William Spark (a friend of Henry Smart and therefore normally a Francophile) later wrote, [73]

The flue-work of the great and choir organs, as far as the 4-feet tone, is truly superb, and I have never heard – not even from the finest of Silbermann's famous instruments in Germany – a finer variety, beauty, and rich distinctive character [of] tone . . . The player . . . sits with a flood of sound ready to the touch of his fingers, and a store of thunder lying harmless at his feet. The thickness, depth, and independence of the pedal organ here vin-dicate supremely the ascendancy of this important section; where, especially in slow sub-jects, when the bass rolls in its ponderousness – there is no disputing it – it is like the *fiat* of the Omnipotent. The swell, solo, and echo organs have also their gems, especially the har-monic flutes, and many other delicately voiced stops.

Several aspects of the voicing style were new to England. The astonishing variety of pipe-forms, some of them downright eccentric, was fascinating, but it was on the foundation stops and chorus that attention was focused. An organ builder who saw Schulze's Great Exhibition organ many years after it had migrated to Northampton noted that 'The Open Diapason [pipes] had no tips, the pipes were cut off and *inserted* in the upperboards, not resting in a countersunk hole as we placed them and still do . . . The strength of tone &c. was adjusted at the flue which was very narrow. The wood pipes were also regulated in the same way and the bore of the foot was not stopped.'[74] This technique is now known as 'open-foot' voicing. Schulze also

[70] J. H. Burn, 'St. George's Church Doncaster, and its Organs', *The Organist and Choirmaster*, 20 (1913), 261
[71] *The Ecclesiologist*, 25 (1864), 22 (possibly from the pen of T. C. Lewis)   [72] *The Musical World*, 41 (1863), 733
[73] W. Spark, *Musical Reminiscences, Past and Present* (London 1892), 187
[74] Letter from E. H. Suggate of Bishop and Sons to B. B. Edmonds (c1930s); quoted in Thistlethwaite, *The Making of the Victorian Organ*, 383–4

introduced Principal pipes with wide mouths, in the proportion of two-sevenths of the circumference. These are characterised by their power. By using heavier metal than was customary in England, and richer in tin, this power could be maintained without any tendency to unsteadiness. Schulze also voiced his fluework to speak slowly, contrasting with the quick but bland attack practiced by the English. This not only changed the quality of attack, but encouraged the pipes to speak with a brighter tone not heard in England since the days of Snetzler, and never before in the context of a twenty-one stop Great Organ including a Bourdon 32′ and fourteen ranks of mixtures. The resulting flood of 'pure *ah* vowel'[75] – as one writer put it – was a lively contrast to the flutier choruses of Hill and others.

The significance of this organ was great, leading to some further orders for Schulze and inspiring many imitators in England, some of whom will be dealt with in the next chapter. But it also marks a development in the taste for the continental organ. According to the *Musical World*:

The arrival of this great German instrument amongst us has administered such a sharp stimulant to the well-nigh defunct corpus of English organ-building art that, already, the patient gives sign of at least exerting itself towards the recovering of a healthy life. [76]

In view of the total revolution in English organ building undertaken in the previous thirty years this is at first a surprising statement, but in fact the public wanted still more in the way of improvements. The *Musical World* set the scene for further debate, elegantly summarising the progress made since the 1830s:[77]

We well remember that, not more than thirty years since, it was the settled habit of organ-builders, professors, and amateurs to think and speak of the merit of foreign organs as a complete delusion. Not that they had any proper means of forming an opinion on the matter. They were at no pains to see and hear for themselves what the continental artists were doing at the time. They were simply content to believe that their own performances were the best in the world, – that no German could equal them – especially, that no Frenchman could make an organ at all, – and to put down all accounts to the contrary as the result of travellers' ignorance. This was in the days when one heard of nothing but fine diapasons and monstrous pedal pipes; and, beyond these, not the faintest notion existed as to what truly constituted the plan and characteristics of a large organ. Within the last few years, however, English opinion on this subject, as on many others, has undergone a vast change. A flying speed by land and sea, cheap fares, and all manner of voyaging facilities, have sent Englishmen by shoals to the Continent . . . Our organ builders, unfortunately, have not generally availed themselves of these privileges; but our organ players have, and it is interesting to watch the effect of experience as reflected in their totally changed habit of thought. From the more enthusiastic of these, indeed, it is now very common to hear the avowal that an organ-hunting expedition to the continent has satisfied them that there is not an English organ worth playing on! Now, allowing for the dazzle of novelty and some trifle of exaggeration, there must be a little truth in all this.

---

[75] T. E. Pearson, 'The Schulze Organ in St. Bartholomew's Church, Armley, Leeds, A Critical Estimate', *The Organ*, 1 (1922), 25

[76] *Musical World*, 41 (1863), 733   [77] 'Good Reasons for Bad Organs', *Musical World*, 42 (1864), 136–8

In the pages of the *Musical World* and the *Ecclesiologist* correspondents made it clear where they thought the shortcomings lay. First, lack of power. Those who knew French organs may well have been aware of the terrific impact of the fiery French trompettes and bombardes. Anyone who could afford a train ticket could visit Doncaster and listen to the flood of tone emitted by the flue pipes of Schulze. Secondly, poor standards of workmanship. The practices of competitive tendering and generous commissions were still the norm. It should not be forgotten that the German System had been adopted by organ builders partly because it was *cheaper*. There was no encouragement, in such circumstances, to adopt some of the downright luxurious constructional details of, say, a fine French organ, and thus materials, layout and manufacture still owed much to the cut-throat 1820s.[78]

Response to these criticisms was limited by the uneven economic climate of the 1860s. A typical Gray & Davison of the period was the organ built for Llandaff Cathedral in 1861, in consultation with Sir Frederick Gore Ouseley, now standing in Usk Parish Church, Monmouthshire.[79]

Llandaff Cathedral (now at Usk Parish Church, Monmouthshire): Gray & Davison 1861

Great Organ (C–f''', 54 notes)

Bourdon [wood]	16
Open Diapason	8
Gamba	8
Stop Diapason [wood]	8
Principal	4
Harmonic Flute [from c]	4
Twelfth	2⅔
Fifteenth	2
Mixture	IV
Trumpet [horizontal]	8

Swell Organ (C–f''', 54 notes)

Double Diapason [wood]	16
Open Diapason	8
Keraulophon [bass from St. Diap.]	8
Stop Diapason	8
Principal	4
Fifteenth	2
Mixture	II
Cornopean	8
Oboe	8
Clarion	4

Choir Organ (C–f''', 54 notes)

Double Diapason [wood]	16
Spitz Flute	8
Dulciana [from c]	8
Stop Diap bass [to B]	8
Clarionet Flute [from c]	8
Gemshorn	4
Flute [wood]	4
Piccolo [wood]	2
Clarinet [from c]	8

Pedal (C–e', 29 notes)

Open Diapason [wood]	16
Bourdon [wood]	16
Principal [wood]	8
Trombone [wood]	16

---

[78] Thistlethwaite, *The Making of the Victorian Organ*, 374–6
[79] British Organ Archive, Gray & Davison Shop Book 6, no. 10119

Couplers
Great to Pedal
Swell to Pedal
Choir to Pedal
Swell to Great
Choir to Great
Swell to Choir

4 composition pedals to Great, 2 to Swell
Key and stop action mechanical

This scheme is a considerable advance on Wilton Place or St Anne Limehouse. The amount of colour obtained by the imaginative use of pipes of various different constructions is a feature, especially striking in the case of the Great Trumpet, the pipes of which are mounted horizontally over the player's head. The Choir Organ is fully developed, with its own chorus based on stops of tapered construction (spitzflute, gemshorn). Moreover it stands immediately over the Great, in the Oberwerk position: this prominent location gives the department added bite and clarity. Against this the Swell seems quite retiring: it contains stops of normal power enclosed in a swell box which does much to render them more delicate, but little to project the sound towards a distant listener. The organ is physically small and cramped in layout; it is solid enough but perhaps a little lacking in sophisticated detail or polish, and the metal pipes are made with a high percentage of lead. Despite the seemingly advanced stop-list, and a very accomplished and musical tone especially well suited to the French romantic repertoire, this organ might well have been amongst those criticised on the grounds of lack of power and indifferent quality of materials. Whether Gray & Davison responded to the challenge is difficult to ascertain: from the mid 1860s the firm falls out of the picture somewhat, gradually taking a position in the second rank.

However, William Hill (though now in his seventies) and his son Thomas responded with confidence and determination, effecting yet another revolution in the style of organs built by the firm. From the late 1850s Hill organs were more substantially built and laid out, used thicker and stronger pipe metal (sometimes 'spotted' metal, made of tin and lead in approximately equal quantities and having a characteristic mottled appearance), and were louder. Contemporaries were quick to notice the change, and to observe Hill's indebtedness to lessons learnt from the German organ.[80] At the Ulster Hall, Belfast, Hill & Son built a notable instrument in the new manner, completed in 1862:[81]

[80] Thistlethwaite, *The Making of the Victorian Organ*, 395–6   [81] Ibid., 398–9

Belfast, The Ulster Hall, Hill & Son 1862

Great Organ (C–g''', 56 notes)	
Double Open Diapason	16
Open Diapason I	8
Open Diapason II	8
Gamba	8
Stopped Diapason [wood]	8
Quint	5⅓
Principal	4
Harmonic Flute	4
Twelfth	2⅔
Fifteenth	2
Full Mixture	IV
Sharp Mixture	III
Double Trumpet	16
Posaune	8
Trumpet	8
Clarion	4

Swell Organ (C–g''', 56 notes)	
Bourdon & Double Diap. [wood & metal]	16
Open Diapason	8
Salicional	8
Stopped Diapason [wood]	8
Principal	4
Suabe Flute [wood]	4
Twelfth	2⅔
Fifteenth	2
Full Mixture	IV
Double Trumpet	16
Horn	8
Trumpet	8
Oboe	8
Clarion	4

Choir Organ (C–g''', 56 notes)	
Gedact [wood]	16
Cone Gamba	8
Keraulophon [from c]	8
Stopped Diapason [wood]	8
Octave	4
Lieblich Flöte	4
Gemshorn Twelfth	2⅔
Flautina	2
Dulciana Mixture	II
Bassoon [from c]	16
Clarinet	8

Pedal Organ (C–f', 30 notes)	
Double Open Diapason [wood]	32
Open Diapason [wood]	16
Violon [wood]	16
Bourdon [wood]	16
Octave	8
Violon [wood]	8
Twelfth	5⅓
Fifteenth	4
Trombone [wood]	16
Clarion	8

Solo Organ (C–g''', 56 notes)	
Lieblich Gedact [wood & metal]	8
Harmonic Flute	4
Piccolo	2
Vox Humana [enclosed]	8
Tuba [horizontal?]	8

Couplers

Swell to Great
Choir to Great
Solo to Great
Great to Pedal
Swell to Pedal
Choir to Pedal
Solo to Pedal

Accessories

4 composition pedals to Great & Pedal
3 composition pedals to Swell
Tremulant to Solo
Pneumatic lever to Great and couplers, remainder mechanical

Wind pressures
Great & Swell fluework, Choir, 76mm
Pedal fluework, 89mm
Swell reeds, Solo, 102mm
Great and Pedal reeds, 121mm
Solo Tuba, 305mm

Much of this organ survives, despite a couple of rebuilds and some substantial (and arguably unnecessary) additions made in 1978. This is an organ built in the grand manner (even if the component parts still have a bench-finished look). Everything about it is big and sturdy, including the pipe scales and, more importantly, the sound. The Great chorus, built on two diapasons now differentiated in power as well as tone, is a bold and uncompromising statement of continental chorus building. Principal, Twelfth, Fifteenth and the two Mixtures are all to the same scale, and only slightly smaller than the Open Diapason I. Eschewing the use of Töpfer's regular scaling progression, Hill kept to the patterns established in principle by Snetzler in the eighteenth century: in the upperwork the smaller pipes are especially generously scaled. The effect in individual pipes is inclined to be on the fluty side, encouraged by quick speech and by firm nicking of the languids but, thanks to the complete range of high pitches offered by the two Mixtures, the chorus is strikingly brilliant without any trace of harshness. There are no tierces in the chorus – a further indication of German influence – and thus the sound is clear and free from any reedy tang. Power is there in abundance: even the so-called Dulciana Mixture on the Choir Organ is a telling member of its chorus. The reeds are astonishingly large in scale, and on their slightly elevated pressures contribute a rich and pleasantly brassy effect without swamping the fluework. The Swell comes a very close second to the Great in effect; the Choir offers a sprightly miniature chorus and a number of colourful effects; the Pedal Organ gives ample support.[82]

It is quite clear that Hill & Son had found a recipe that would satisfy their customers' newly informed demands: commanding and bold in a concert hall, appropriately scaled down in a parish church, influenced by German practice but still resoundingly English in effect. After William Hill's death in 1870 his son Thomas and, later, his grandson Arthur were able to continue building in this style to general satisfaction until the eve of the First World War. But they were not to be alone: on the one hand Henry Willis's determination to lead the world of organ building was about to bear fruit; on the other, the English disciples of Schulze were to mount their own minority campaign.

---

[82] Author's examination of the organ before, during and after the rebuild of 1978

CHAPTER FOURTEEN

THE HIGH VICTORIAN ORGAN
1860–1900

In the second half of the nineteenth century England emerged as perhaps the pre-eminent organ building nation in the world. This statement needs some justification, not least because recent histories have either portrayed this period as one of decadence and decline or have simply been unwilling to accord England any importance in an international sphere.

In Germany Sauer (Frankfurt on Oder) was able to reach opus number 1,000 after fifty years of activity;[1] in France Cavaillé-Coll revolutionised the state of the nation's organ building from a workshop that employed fifty-two staff in 1860.[2] By comparison the output of English firms was astonishing. When Norman & Beard of Norwich built a new factory in 1898 it employed three hundred craftsmen and produced over a thousand new organs by the time it closed seventeen years later.[3] Given that the established London firms (Hill, Gray & Davison, Walker, Bishop, Willis and Lewis) were building at a similar pace, and given that the more important provincial firms (Kirtland & Jardine, Forster & Andrews, Brindley (later Brindley & Foster) and many others) were able to match the Londoners for efficiency (in 1898 Harrison & Harrison of Durham claimed to have built 1,100 organs since 1861)[4] and often for quality, the picture emerges of organ building on a scale out of all proportion to the physical size of the country, and quite outstripping the output of any other country except the United States.

Nor were the organs either small or of poor quality. For Cavaillé-Coll an organ with a 32' stop was a landmark instrument. For Willis such an organ was a commonplace, turned out at the rate of one every year or so throughout his life. The surviving corpus of great nineteenth-century English organs, culminating in Hill's leviathan instrument of 1890 in Sydney Town Hall, Australia (five manuals, 127 stops, and including a full-length 64' reed), includes some of the finest instruments

---

[1] W. Walcker-Meyer and R. Raue, 'German Organ Building in the Nineteenth Century', *BIOS Journal*, 8 (1984), 82–95

[2] M. Haine, *Les Facteurs d'instruments de musique à Paris au XIXème siècle, des artisans face à l'industrialisation* (Brussels 1985), 97–8   [3] H. Norman, 'The Normans 1860–1920', *BIOS Journal*, 10 (1986), 53–61

[4] L. Elvin, *The Harrison Story* (Lincoln 1973), 271

Plate 61   The organ in Salisbury Cathedral, built by Henry Willis and completed in 1877 (photograph c1930). Following from the success of his organ in St Paul's Cathedral of 1872, Willis was now able to build large divided organs with a combination of mechanical, Barker Lever and tubular pneumatic actions. Freed from the restraints of traditional casework, Willis was now happy to create the illusion that the zinc front pipes were part of the arcading in which they stand. To the sides and back the mechanism of the organ was not even concealed.

to be found anywhere, embracing a variety of styles equivalent to the different craft schools of half a dozen smaller nations.

English organs travelled the world, and while they may well have made less impact in those countries where French or German was the first language, their influence in the long term is inestimable. The English invented the concert-hall organ. They provided the organ with an array of technical inventions that made life easy for both player and builder. The invention of the swell box seeped into the consciousness of other nations, to the extent that only the most historically authentic of modern instruments has no Swell Organ, and today, where a department is enclosed behind shutters the stops in the box are more than likely to owe something to English practice. The specific debt owed by Cavaillé-Coll and by the early American builders has already been mentioned. These connections were maintained. Cavaillé-Coll was strongly influenced by the handful of organs built for English clients. America remained in contact with the British Isles: individual organ builders headed across the Atlantic to explore the New World, and the large American organ of the late nineteenth century was clearly a first cousin of the English instrument (Great, Swell, Choir, Solo and the inevitable Tuba), albeit speaking with a different accent.

Reasons for the rapid expansion in English organ building are not hard to find. The adoption of the German System meant that every notable organ in England had either to be rebuilt or replaced: by 1900 an old GG-compass instrument was a quaint rarity.

The construction of municipal concert halls in every town of even modest pretensions led to the building of dozens of large flagship instruments, either bought from the illustrious London firms or giving the chance for a local builder to erect his magnum opus (for example the four-manual organ with a 32′ front built by Wilkinson of Kendal for Preston Public Hall in 1882).[5] These instruments were of great importance in introducing high-quality music to a wider public, useful equally for oratorio performances or for mixed recitals of orchestral transcriptions and organ music.

Although nonconformist churches had mixed attitudes to the provision of organs, most were quick to accept their use. The proliferation of different denominations and the extensive building of churches and chapels, especially in the industrial towns, opened a further significant market for new organs. The new freedom enjoyed by Roman Catholics after the Act of Catholic Emancipation in 1829 added to the overall number.

In the Anglican world the building of new churches continued apace. Not only did the population of the country continue to increase at a spectacular rate, but it is clear that the bourgeoisie, made wealthy by industrial expansion, felt a moral obligation to use some of their riches in the performance of good works. The endowment of new churches and the building of organs were ideal objects of their munificence.

---

[5] G. Sumner, 'Thomas Wilkinson of Kendal and the Organ in Preston Public Hall', *BIOS Journal*, 1 (1977), 26–48

In any case, from the 1840s onwards developments in the Anglican church greatly increased the importance attached to church music. The Oxford Movement introduced a new wave of high-church feeling entirely appropriate to the Victorian sense of moral dignity. It viewed with dismay the disorganised and informal arrangements for music that persisted in the great majority of parish churches: a parish clerk leading the singing of metrical psalms, sometimes accompanied by a small band of musicians. The growing preference was for an organ and a choir seated in the chancel, imitating on a reduced scale the traditional practices of the cathedrals and collegiate churches. This led to the gradual introduction of organs in all but the very smallest country churches. It also meant that, where in the eighteenth and early nineteenth centuries a parish church instrument would have stood on a west gallery, a Victorian church organ was usually erected on one side of the chancel, in close proximity to the choir. It was the choir that led the music of the service, and the organ supported the choir. This, and the cramped environment dictated by the chancel position, had a profound effect on the layout, construction and sound of the English organ.

It also had an effect on its appearance. The gothic revival in architecture led to some speculative feeling about how a truly mediaeval organ should look. In the absence of any models to follow the appearance of the ancient portative was a guide, its pipework exposed without the encumbrance (or expense) of any upper casework beyond wooden supports to stop the front pipes from falling out – and happily coinciding with the new functional look adopted first by Gray & Davison at St Anne Limehouse in 1851. Only a few lonely figures were interested in the provision of formal casework that more truly reflected what could be discovered on the subject of authentic mediaeval practice: amongst them were Sir John Sutton and members of his circle (including the architect Pugin). Some gothic revival architects continued to design fine cases well into the late nineteenth and early twentieth centuries: the list includes G. G. Scott, J. O. Scott, G. G. Bodley, J. L. Pearson, T. G. Jackson and the Scott-trained organ builder A. G. Hill.

For the organ building profession the spoils were enormous and trade flourished. The market for new organs was large enough to encourage stiff competition in price *and* quality – a hallmark of economic growth. In an age that encouraged invention and daring one might well scan the horizon for a figure of more than usual stature, a Great Victorian who could use his genius to transform the craft and realise his own personal triumph. Such a character has already been introduced: Henry Willis.

Willis's ambition and his unshakeable confidence in his own powers were already apparent at the Crystal Palace in 1851, but it took him some time to convince the world at large to agree with his own opinion of himself. He was snubbed at first: 'Mr. Willis is . . . a very young man, and not yet entitled – whatever he may think to the contrary – to rank with the greatest organ builders of the world.'[6] However, the

---

[6] *Musical World*, 32 (1854), 566; quoted in N. J. Thistlethwaite, *The Making of the Victorian Organ* (Cambridge 1990), 309

impression he made at the Great Exhibition was to win him important work. With S. S. Wesley's influence Willis secured not just the contract for St George's Hall, Liverpool, but also the order to rebuild the Exhibition organ in Winchester Cathedral (completed 1854). This was followed by a new organ at Carlisle Cathedral (1856), in consultation with W. T. Best (for whom Willis had secured the post of municipal organist at Liverpool); then a complete rebuild at Wells Cathedral (1857), with Sir Frederick Gore Ouseley advising. At Wells, Willis's cavalier attitude both to the opinions of the consultant and to the value of the old material (mostly Samuel Green, 1786) was characteristic: Ouseley carefully specified which stops were to be retained and advised that Willis should be told 'not to alter in any wise the voicing of the Diapasons and Mixtures of the Great Organ, which are *very* good'. Willis took no notice and melted down much of the Green material and altered the rest. Despite his dismay at being treated so, Ouseley was obliged to admit that the result was excellent.[7]

Over the competition for the new organ at Leeds Town Hall in 1856 Willis made himself look foolish: having failed to win the contract he wrote, to the *Musical Gazette*, a letter making thinly veiled accusations and generally giving vent to his disappointment. He received a public rebuke.[8] Yet by the end of his career he was described as 'the greatest organ builder of the Victorian Era' and, in the same article, it was suggested that, like John Howe and Bernard Smith before him, he should be known as 'Father' Willis.[9]

Father Willis's eventual success stems from the effort he made in the 1850s and 1860s to match or even surpass the achievements of Hill and Gray & Davison and to satisfy the public demand for organs that were more powerful and better made. The route he took was unique, and the mature Willis organ is an individual creation unlike any other. The solitary path is well illustrated in his approach to reed voicing. In the 1850s Willis seems to have relied on the skills of his brother George, who had trained with Bishop. This was probably the means by which the closed shallot was introduced to the Willis organ, together with a taste for smooth reed tone. We are probably indebted to George Willis for the introduction of two characteristic Willis voices, the Corno di Bassetto (a bold, woody imitation of the Bass Clarinet) and the Orchestral Oboe, and also for the first Willis high-pressure reeds. But the Tuba remained the speciality of Hill. George Willis voiced a Tuba for the organ exhibited at the International Exhibition of 1862 (an event even bigger than the Great Exhibition of 1851, but less well known),[10] but it was not satisfactory and was used only once before it was disconnected.[11] The organ built for Reading Town Hall in 1864 had no Tuba.[12] At the time the St George's Hall organ

---

[7] L. S. Colchester, R. Bowers and A. Crossland, *The Organs and Organists of Wells Cathedral* (Wells 1974), 8
[8] Thistlethwaite, *The Making of the Victorian Organ*, 309
[9] F. G. Edwards, 'Henry Willis', *Musical Times*, 39 (1898), 297–303
[10] B. B. Edmonds, 'The Organs at the International Exhibition 1862', *The Organ*, 42 (1962–3), 16–27
[11] T. Willis, 'Recollections of my Father' (undated and unpublished biographical note on the subject of Vincent Willis). I am grateful to B. Q. S. F. Buchanan for drawing this document to my attention and to the great kindness of the late Miss Ida Willis in allowing her late sister's manuscript to be made public.
[12] Thistlethwaite, *The Making of the Victorian Organ*, 505–6

was altered in 1867, George Willis was indisposed and much of the reed voicing passed to Henry Willis's elder son, Vincent. It was Vincent (not, as is usually assumed, George) who developed the characteristic features of Willis high-pressure reed voicing: the brass weight screwed to the tongue (suggested by his father) to give control of the tongue in the bass; the use of short reed boots and harmonic res-onators in the trebles; the introduction of regulating slots in the resonators and the use of remarkably high pressures where possible. He also devised a device for curving reed tongues, particularly useful in applying precisely calibrated curves to the thick tongues of Tubas.[13] At Liverpool the new Tubas added in 1867 were on a pressure of 445mm in the bass and 572mm in the treble (the organ had been blown by a steam engine since it was first erected): 'their effect was entirely unique in their scorching brilliance'.[14] The practical difficulties and expense of raising such pres-sures meant that after this time 381mm was the normal upper limit for Willis Tubas, though it was quite common, from about 1870 on, for the Great and Pedal reeds of even quite an ordinary three-manual church instrument to be on a pressure of 178mm – still quite beyond the range employed by builders outside England.

As the reeds developed so did the fluework. Much of the pipework for early Willis organs came from the trade pipe-maker Violette. Henry Willis and Violette toured Europe together after the completion of Liverpool, and then started experimental work on the construction of the pipes. It seems likely that the intention was to find a way of blowing the pipes much harder without their overblowing to the first har-monic, so that the organs could be more powerful. For this to be possible the languid of the pipes had to be kept high and the lower lip shaped to restore the quick speech of the pipe. This led to a special dubbed lower lip formed with a punch, another Willis speciality.[15]

These new techniques of reed and flue voicing were incorporated in a tonal scheme of great originality and daring. Like the other London builders, Willis made no use of Töpfer's scientific approach to pipe scaling, using instead a diameter pro-gression developed from more empirical traditional practice.[16] He also continued the pattern established by George Pike England and Samuel Green in making the Principal smaller than the Open Diapason, the Fifteenth smaller than the Principal, the Twelfth smaller again and the mixtures to varied, still smaller scales. He also used narrow mouths, typically ²⁄₉ of the circumference of the pipe for unison ranks and ⅕ for the quints and tierces (¼ of the circumference is more normal). The reduction in power caused by the small scales and narrow mouths was offset by blowing the pipes extremely hard, with wide flues and copious nicking. At various times in his career Willis also slotted the tops of his open flue pipes as an aid to easy tuning. The combination of these techniques encouraged a keen tone, and as the constituent ranks of the chorus were added this keenness developed into a reedy

[13] Willis, 'Recollections of my Father'; C. C. Michell in *Musical Opinion*, 31 (1907–8), 31; 32 (1908–9), 787
[14] C. Clutton and A. Niland, *The British Organ* (London 1963), 100   [15] Willis, 'Recollections of my Father'
[16] Thistlethwaite, *The Making of the Victorian Organ*, 438–41; general information on Willis fluework scales from B. Q. S. F. Buchanan Esq.

brilliance quite unlike the tone preferred by other builders, accentuated by the provision in all Willis mixtures of a strong tierce rank.

Indeed build-up – the gradual crescendo from *piano* to full organ achieved by adding stops one by one – became the characteristic feature of these instruments. As the flues approached a reedy tone, so the new smoother reeds fell more into line with the fluework, encouraging blend between the two. The addition of stops one by one could be masked effectively by use of the Swell-to-Great coupler and the smooth crescendo obtainable from the swell box. This manner of playing was later to become an *idée fixe* with English builders and players: it works better on a Willis than on any other instrument until the 1900s. As a method it was taken so much for granted that it can be safely assumed that Willis's mixtures were not usually intended to be heard unless some reeds were already drawn, and in his instruments there is no provision for a chorus of principals and mixtures that can be used extensively on its own: this is quite different from the work of Hill and in complete contrast to German taste and the organs of Schulze. When they were added, the Willis Great Organ reeds were spectacular: on even a modest three-manual church organ the 178mm wind pressure often used produced an effect of astonishing boldness and impact.

The balance between bass and treble is also a characteristic feature of Willis organs. Individual stops, especially the softer ranks, are kept well up in power in the treble, providing a gentle melodic crescendo appropriate to romantic music. But in the diapasons Willis followed the pattern set by Samuel Green and apparent in many organs of the early nineteenth century: he provided a firm and large-scaled bass; further, where there were two Open Diapasons on the Great, one would be decidedly more powerful than the other. The Pedal Open Diapason, of wood, would be a large-scaled rank, blown hard, and developing a powerful, somewhat fluty tone. Pedal reeds, where provided, would be on a high pressure, and were commanding voices for use in full organ. These strong basses were balanced by the manual upperwork, kept bright in the treble, and by the manual reeds, where high pressures and weighted tongues in the bass ensured a strong treble line. Compared to French or German organs of the same period, it is the strong bass which immediately stands out, together with a smooth intensity in the tutti thanks to the unique style of reed voicing.

Willis's choice of softer stops was highly characteristic. He stuck to a simple but effective recipe which included narrow-scaled Lieblich Gedacts modelled on Schulze's example (at 16′, 8′ and 4′), wooden Claribel Flutes (8′) developed from the work of Bishop, and Harmonic Flutes (4′ and 2′) nominally derived from French practice but in fact much narrower in scale. Manual doubles were often of Gamba tone. Dulcianas, Salicionals and Gambas were cylindrical, the Gambas keener than those of his contemporaries in a deliberate attempt to imitate orchestral tone more closely. These families of stops appeared in various guises on all his instruments, to the point of being repetitive.

Very few Willis organs remain with the original fire and bravado undimmed by later alterations, and in any case organs built in the later years of his life are not as brilliant as the most characteristic organs of the 1870s and early 1880s. In these the brightness of the ensemble could be startling: later writers (admittedly commenting in a period when brightness of any kind was out of fashion) criticised the organ at the Royal Albert Hall, London (1871) for 'the excessive brightness of the chorus work and heavier reeds'[17] and that at Durham Cathedral (1876) for 'its extreme brilliance, particularly in the upperwork of the Great'.[18] However, in both these examples the comments echo certain opinions expressed at the time the instruments were built. The more conservative church musicians may have joined Dr Monk of York in deploring 'the Willisean monster; which (not to speak of the Horror in the Albert Hall) has found entrance into several of our Cathedrals – alack the day! This machine, with its heavy wind-pressures and obstreperous style of voicing, is totally unfit to accompany an average Choir; or, generally to do aught but stifle and drown it.'[19] Even a fan of Willis felt obliged to comment on 'the excessive brilliancy of the chorus work and reeds'.[20] When the Albert Hall organ was opened it is rumoured that W. T. Best sat in the auditorium and invited Willis to demonstrate the Diapason tone to him; after a few moments Willis was interrupted by Best roaring: 'I said your Diapasons, Willis, not your damned Gambas!'[21] Elsewhere, in characteristically caustic vein, Best wrote: 'That man does not know how to build an organ. Look at the organ in the Albert Hall. He put the Solo stops on such a high pressure of wind that it was necessary to chain them to the wind chest to keep them from blowing through the roof!'[22]

These criticisms are quoted here not in an attempt to lessen the status of Willis, but to balance the wholly uncritical accounts of his work that appeared in the early twentieth century and to explain why his instruments were so different from those of other builders. The atmosphere of vigorous debate also makes it clear that everything Willis did created a stir: whether his contemporaries entirely approved of him or not, he was becoming the most talked-about builder of his generation.

The main features of the Willis style were becoming apparent by the late 1860s, at a time when, after years of struggle against his more experienced competitors and several lean years in the turbulent economic climate of the years following a banking crisis in 1866, he at last hit a vein of spectacular grand projects that were to propel him into the bright light of success. The organs for the Royal Albert Hall and the Alexandra Palace, both in London, played a vital part in establishing his pre-eminence.

The enormous profits of the 1851 exhibition were directed towards a number of public projects, including the construction of the Albert Hall near the site of the exhibition in London. There is some evidence, awaiting further study, that Cavaillé-

[17] H. Snow, 'The Royal Albert Hall Organ, London', *The Organ*, 4 (1924–5), 129–37
[18] J. H. Grayson, 'The Organs of Durham Cathedral', *The Organ*, 13 (1933–4), 65–73
[19] Letter from Dr Monk (1879) quoted by B. B. Edmonds in 'A Sack of Shakings', *The Organ*, 37 (1957–8), 141
[20] *The Ecclesiologist*, 25 (1864), 135   [21] Traditional
[22] J. C. Hadden, 'W. T. Best and his "Humours"', *Musical Opinion*, 33 (1909–10), 484

Plate 62 The Albert Hall, London c 1907. The organ was built by Henry Willis and completed in 1871. This, and the instrument he built for the Alexandra Palace, London at about the same time, established Willis's credentials as a builder of successful large organs. The Albert Hall organ was especially lavish. The case emphasises the machine-like qualities of Willis's work, with three arches in the façade allowing the spectator a view of the interior pipework. The front pipes (the largest having a speaking length of 32' and a foot 8' long) are of 90 per cent tin. The organ was comprehensively rebuilt in the 1920s, but retaining almost all of the Willis pipework.

Coll was originally favoured to build the new organ.[23] In fact the contract, for a vast instrument of 111 stops, went to Willis, and the organ was completed in 1871. It has often been observed that the Great Organ at the Albert Hall followed closely, on paper at least, the scheme of Cavaillé-Coll's organ for St Sulpice (1861); this has encouraged some speculation on the extent of French influence on Willis. The truth may be rather that Willis adopted some elements of a scheme originally proposed by the French builder himself; in practice the work of Willis (narrow upperwork scales, ponderous diapason and pedal basses and smooth reeds with the basses controlled by the weighting of the tongues) is diametrically opposed to that of Cavaillé-Coll (broad-scaled Jeux de Fonds, mild fluework basses, blazingly free and brassy reeds with unweighted tongues).

The Albert Hall organ was spectacular in size and complexity, and built as a showpiece of Willis's technical skill. A façade of 32′ pipes of 90 per cent tin towered above the auditorium, through arches formed in the casework the audience could see the entire glittering array of pipes in the Great Organ in their natural order. This was the first time that the interior parts of an organ had been exposed to public view in this way.

The qualities of the Albert Hall organ may have been obscured by the famously difficult acoustics of the building. At the Alexandra Palace Willis was more fortunate. The organ shown at the International Exhibition of 1862 went first to the Agricultural Hall, Islington. It then became available to form the basis of an eighty-seven stop organ for the new Alexandra Palace, where it was opened in 1873. The appearance of the organ was similar to that at the Albert Hall, though with the front pipes made, more economically, of zinc. The scheme was as follows:[24]

Manuals C–a‴ (58 notes), Pedal C–f′ (30 notes)

Great	16. 16. 8. 8. 8. 8. 8. 5⅓. 4. 4. 2⅔. 2. 2. V. III. 16. 8. 8. 8. 4.
Swell	16. 16. 8. 8. 8. 8. 8. 4. 4. 4. 2⅔. 2. V. III. 16. 16. 8. 8. 8. 8. 4.
Choir	16. 8. 8. 8. 8. 8. 8. 4. 4. 4. 4. 2. III. 8. 8. 4.
Solo	8. 8. 8. 4. 4. 4. 2. 16. 8. 8. 8. 8. 8. 4.
Pedal	32. 32. 32. 16. 16. 16. 16. 8. 8. 4. III. II. 32. 16. 16. 8.

The organ was destroyed by fire almost immediately on completion: a near-identical replacement was opened on 1 May 1875 (at a speed which suggests the involvement of sub-contractors). This organ acquired a very special reputation despite long periods of neglect, and was well used in the 1930s when it was recognised by many players and listeners as an instrument of world status. The great hall of the Alexandra Palace was like a railway station: vast, aisled, and roofed in iron and glass. The organ stood behind the orchestra at the top of the raked choir seating; it occupied a hemispherical recess in the back wall. This last feature of its site almost certainly explains how it managed to speak with great presence and clarity in such a vast space: these qualities are plainly discernible in early recordings. Few organs

---

[23] C. and. E. Cavaillé-Coll, *Aristide Cavaillé-Coll, ses Origines, sa Vie, ses Oeuvres* (Paris 1929), 121
[24] Thistlethwaite, *The Making of the Victorian Organ*, 501–3

Plate 63   The console of Henry Willis's organ in the Alexandra Palace, London, completed in 1875. Willis had by now developed a number of features designed to make the organ easy to manage: the stop jambs at 45° to the keys, the radiating and concave pedalboard, and the introduction of pneumatic thumb pistons between each row of keys, allowing pre-selected combinations of stops to be brought into action at the touch of a button.

speak in such favourable conditions; few builders had an approach bold enough to take full advantage of the circumstances.

These two instruments established Willis in the secular arena and led to further commissions for concert organs. But Willis was also ready to occupy the high ground of church organ building. His organs in the cathedrals of Winchester, Carlisle and Wells were a start but, as discussed above, they were not universally welcomed. It may be that after the death of William Hill in 1870 more contracts were open to him, but the main feature of his new success was to be technical.

At St Paul's Cathedral, London in 1863 Willis was called in to add a Barker machine to the old Smith/Bishop organ, which had been moved from the screen to the north side of the chancel in 1860 (satisfying contemporary taste for the removal of choir screens and the discovery of uninterrupted vistas). Meanwhile the presence of a large modern organ in the cathedral was vindicated by the acquisition of the Hill organ from the Panopticon, which stood in the south transept 1860–73.[25] Willis was consulted about a more thorough rebuild of the organ; he boldly and confidently proposed to divide it into two parts, north and south, linked by a pneumatic movement.

The French had been experimenting with a key action in which the on/off message was transmitted as an impulse of air running through a small-diameter tube. Moitessier patented his *abrégé pneumatique* in 1835, and by 1850 had built a successful instrument on this system at Notre Dame de la Balade, Toulouse. In the 1850s pneumatic devices were the latest plaything: a notable incursion into everyday life was the Galy-Cazelat & Clarke patent letter-transporting device of 1854; experiments with atmospheric propulsion on the railways also date from this period, one example serving the rebuilt Crystal Palace at its new home in Sydenham. By 1866 the French builder Fermis had developed a simple and practical tubular pneumatic key action: Willis is thought to have seen it demonstrated at the Paris Exhibition of 1867[26] and took out a patent for his own version in 1868. According to a note in one of the firm's specification books an earlier version was in use at St Peter, Blackburn in 1865, and there is evidence of limited use simple tubular actions in Willis organs in the 1850s,[27] but the lodging of the 1868 patent suggests at least a period of development before the more extensive use of pneumatics at the Alexandra Palace and the Albert Hall.[28]

At St Paul's Cathedral, as completed by Willis in 1872, the console stood with the Great and Solo Organs on the north side of the chancel, with the Pedal in a pit behind the choir stalls immediately to the east. The Swell and Choir Organs stood opposite on the south side. Parts of the original mechanism remained until the rebuild of 1972–7. It is apparent that the link to the south side was, in effect, a split Barker Lever. Trackers ran from the keys to a trench under the chancel floor, operating on the inlet and exhaust valves of the pneumatic machine. From there tubes ran under the floor to pneumatic motors at floor level on the south side; these acted on trackers rising through rollerboards to the soundboards above. The Great and Solo had their own Barker machines; the couplers were mechanical but, according to the convention established by Cavaillé-Coll, were acted upon by the Great Organ Barker machine and thus did not add to the weight of touch.[29]

It is extremely unlikely that this action was a model of promptness and precision,

[25] Information kindly provided by A. Niland, currently working on a history of the organs in St Paul's Cathedral
[26] Letter from G. Bédart, 'Who Invented Tubular Pneumatic Action and When?', *Musical Opinion*, 31 (1907–8), 754   [27] Thistlethwaite, *The Making of the Victorian Organ*, 357–8
[28] Archive of H. Willis & Sons Ltd, list of patents taken out by the company in connection with the organ exhibited at the Inventions Exhibition of 1885, Specification Book 6, 151. Patent for tubular pneumatic movement no. 812 (1868)
[29] This attempt to describe the mechanism of the 1872 Willis organ is based on conversations with Ian Bell, in charge of design at N. P. Mander Ltd during the rebuild of 1972–7.

but it was reliable. The triumph of getting it to work at all quite overcame any questions of detail, and the political importance of the divided organ was immense. For ecclesiological reasons the screen was no longer the favoured position for a cathedral organ; in any case the new larger organs now demanded could scarcely be accommodated in the space occupied by a GG-compass instrument of only twenty-five stops or so. Flexibility in disposing the parts of the organ was an asset anywhere, perhaps even more so in the cramped chancel-sited organ-chambers now common in parish churches. Willis's solution was an immediate success and it helped win him the contracts for a pair of similar divided organs for Salisbury Cathedral[30] and Durham Cathedral,[31] both completed in 1877. At Salisbury Cathedral much of Willis's characteristically brilliant fluework tone can still be enjoyed (at a rebuild in 1934 the organist, Sir Walter Alcock, refused to allow the flue pipes to be removed from the building, almost certainly fearing that it would be altered by the less sympathetic hands of Willis's successors).[32] Sir Frederick Gore-Ouseley, who had been involved at first hand in promoting the German System in the 1850s and who had reacted with caution to Willis's work at Wells in 1857, wrote enthusiastically to Richardson, the organist at Salisbury: 'I honestly believe you have the finest church organ in the world – certainly, the best in England, and I heartily congratulate you on the same.'[33] The scheme was typical of Willis's larger organs (see plate 61, p. 258):[34]

Salisbury Cathedral: Henry Willis 1877

Manuals C–a''' (58 notes); Pedals C–f' (30 notes)

Great Organ		Swell Organ	
Double Open Diapason	16	Contra Gamba (stopped wood bass)	16
Open Diapason large	8	Open Diapason	8
Open Diapason small	8	Lieblich Gedackt (wood bass)	8
Claribel Flute (wood)	8	Viola da Gamba	8
Stopped Diapason (wood)	8	Vox Angelica	8
Principal	4	Octave	4
Flûte Harmonique	4	Flûte Harmonique	4
Twelfth	2⅔	Super Octave	2
Fifteenth	2	Mixture	III
Mixture	IV	Contra Fagotto	16
Double Trumpet	16	Cornopean	8
Trumpet	8	Hautboy	8
Clarion	4	Vox Humana	8
		Clarion	4

[30] B. Matthews, *The Organs and Organists of Salisbury Cathedral* (Salisbury 1972)
[31] R. Hird & J. Lancelot, *Durham Cathedral Organs* (Durham 1991)   [32] Traditional
[33] Matthews, *The Organs and Organists of Salisbury Cathedral*, 16
[34] Matthews, *The Organs and Organists of Salisbury Cathedral*, 16–17; E. J. Hopkins and E. F. Rimbault, *The Organ*, 3rd edn (London 1877), 534

Choir Organ

Lieblich Gedackt (wood bass)	16
Harmonic Flute	8
Lieblich Gedackt (wood bass)	8
Salicional	8
Gemshorn	4
Harmonic Flute	4
Lieblich Gedackt (wood bass)	4
Flageolet	2
Corno-di-Bassetto	8
Cor Anglais	8

Pedal Organ

Double Open Diapason	32
Open Diapason (wood)	16
Open Diapason (metal)	16
Violone	16
Bourdon (wood)	16
Octave	8
Flute (wood)	8
Mixture	IV
Contra Posaune (wood)	32
Ophicleide	16
Clarion	8

Wind pressures

Great Flues, 89mm & 97mm
Great Reeds, 203mm
Swell, 114mm throughout
Choir, 72mm throughout
Solo Flues and Orchestral Reeds, 102mm
Solo Tubas, Bass 391mm, Treble 470mm
Pedal Flues, 51mm, 64mm, 95mm, 102mm
Pedal Reeds, 229mm & 305mm

Solo Organ

Flûte Harmonique	8
Flûte Harmonique	4
Orchestral Oboe	8
Corno-di-Bassetto	8
Tuba	8

Couplers

Swell to Great
Swell Octave to Great
Swell sub-Octave to Great
Choir to Great
Solo to Great
Great to Pedal
Swell to Pedal
Choir to Pedal
Solo to Pedal

Accessories

4 thumb pistons to Great
4 thumb pistons to Swell
4 thumb pistons to Choir
4 thumb pistons to Solo
4 composition pedals to Pedal
Pedal acting on Great to Pedal
Tremulant to Swell

Willis's star was now in the ascendant. Before he died in 1901 he was to build organs for cathedrals at Hereford, Edinburgh, Glasgow, St David's, Gloucester, Oxford, Canterbury, Truro and Lincoln. Against his work the organs produced by his main rival, the Hill firm (now directed by William Hill's son, Thomas), would have seemed conservative and understated. Nevertheless, Hill remained in favour at Westminster Abbey (under Sir Frederick Bridge), at the cathedrals of Worcester, Chichester, Manchester and Peterborough, and in the three great Cambridge colleges, King's, Trinity and St John's. It is perhaps not unfair to present Hill's sphere of influence as gentlemanly and high-church; Willis's was commercial and popular.

Willis continued to work on the improvement of the technical side of his instruments, seeking an absolute perfection in voicing and mechanism. In this he was ably assisted by his sons Vincent and Henry, whom he took into partnership in 1878. Vincent was a brilliant voicer and inventor, as has already been seen in connection with the development of the Willis high-pressure reeds. In a host of patents issued from 1883 onwards Vincent repeatedly challenged and re-invented the status quo of organ actions. He had developed a reliable electro-pneumatic key action which was used on the organ at Canterbury Cathedral in 1885 (of which more later) but, in the short term, of far more importance was the compressed air movement, patent 15,182 of 1889. Although the tubular pneumatic mechanism had been in regular use since 1872, it still depended on an extensive array of mechanical connections: at the heart of the St Paul's, Durham or Salisbury organs was a four-manual mechanical-action console and coupling system, operating on the Barker or tubular actions as appropriate. This part of the organ required constant attention to keep it in good adjustment: in a large instrument action regulation would occupy much of the tuner's time before he could start attending to the pipes. The development of an all-pneumatic mechanism was, therefore, related to the need for reliability and easy maintenance. In the 1889 patent the key action was wholly replaced by tubes, with the coupling being achieved through pneumatic machines (only manual-to-pedal couplers remained mechanical). After twelve months with this mechanism Father Willis announced that the organ had reached 'finality'; 'nothing more was required'.[35]

From all this it would be easy to imagine that Willis swept all before him; he did not. One builder is purported to have said, 'if I thought Willis was right I would shut up shop tomorrow':[36] this was Thomas Lewis. T. C. Lewis started his business at about the time of the completion of the Schulze organ at Doncaster in 1862 and frankly admitted that it was his main source of inspiration: 'anything finer it is, I believe, impossible to imagine'; 'by far the grandest instrument I ever heard'.[37] Lewis's appreciation of Schulze is obvious enough from his own instruments and was clearly expressed: 'He is a great artist, and those who criticise his work are not worthy to lace his boots.'[38] He built important organs at St Mary's Roman Catholic Cathedral, Newcastle-upon-Tyne (1869), St Peter Eaton Square, London (1874), St Andrew's Hall, Glasgow (1877), Ripon Minster (1878), The People's Palace, Mile End Road, London (1884), the Anglican Cathedral, Newcastle-upon-Tyne (1890), and Southwark Cathedral, London (1897).

Despite his allegiance to Schulze, Lewis was no mere plagiarist. His instruments relied on a forthright, even austere, principal chorus in the German manner. Low pressures were the norm, even for chorus reeds. Lewis's trumpets added colour to the ensemble: he often used French domed shallots (probably imported from

[35] Willis, 'Recollections of my Father'
[36] G. Dixon, 'The Tonal Structure of the Organ', *The Organ*, 1 (1921–2), 133
[37] *Musical Standard*, 1 (1863), 354–5
[38] N. A. Bonavia-Hunt, 'The Organ of Christ Church Westminster Bridge Road', *The Organ*, 5 (1925–6), 150–5

Bertounèche) giving a free, splashy sound, but avoiding the devastating power characteristic of Cavaillé-Coll. On some organs a higher pressure was used for a reed chorus, notably at the People's Palace, Mile End, London, where it was intended that a reed and mixture chorus on 305mm pressure would be enclosed in the Swell box and made playable from either Great or Swell at will (only the reeds were ever installed). The Schulze-type Lieblich Gedackt featured in Lewis schemes, sometimes in a chorus at 16′, 8′, 4′ and 2′ pitches on the Choir organ. Strings and Harmonic Flutes leant slightly towards the French pattern, the Harmonic Flutes having a rôle in boosting the somewhat dry Open Diapasons as a foundation of the chorus. Lewis's view of fluework balance was exactly that familiar in France and Germany: basses were kept modest in power but clear in tone; the Pedal 16′ stops were little, if any, more powerful than their 8′ manual equivalents. The tonal recipe was backed up by very high standards of materials and finish: the Lewis organ was luxurious and expensive. Uncompromising, and less well adapted than some English organs to a dry acoustic, his instruments sounded at their best in a large building. However, he had a successful approach to concert organs too: at St Andrew's Hall, Glasgow three of the four manual divisions were enclosed in swell boxes, possibly in imitation of Cavaillé-Coll; the consultants were H. Smart and W. T. Best. Hans von Bülow was impressed: 'I never met with an organ so good in Germany, the instruments there not having the same amount of expression and flexibility.'[39] Lewis's last great work, at Southwark Cathedral (1897), was built at a time when everything he stood for had fallen out of fashion.[40] It stands restored today as a public rebuke to his contemporaries, and as a triumphant example of his dry and academic style. It lacks the roar of a German organ or the fire of a French organ, but the serene confidence of its magnificent choruses announce its elevated stature to all who hear it (p. 273).[41]

While the three great names, Hill, Willis and Lewis, expressed in three quite different ways their recipes for the English organ, there was still enough work to allow a host of other builders to develop their own patterns of tonal development and construction, both in London and the provinces. The remaining builder of the first rank in London was J. W. Walker & Sons: the unbreakable solidity, in tone and construction, of their organs gradually moved them from the second rank to the first. By the close of the century, under the leadership of James John Walker, they had developed a distinctive style which featured massive Great Diapasons (often three at 8′ pitch on a large instrument) on pressures as high as 127mm in some cases: these had some of the singing character of the eighteenth-century Diapason but with considerable power. On this basis a chorus of conservative character was built, except in a handful of organs in the 1880s and 1890s where the 4′ chorus reeds on Great and Swell were replaced by compound stops, called Clarion Mixtures. These

[39] *Musical Opinion*, 31 (1907–8), 266
[40] T. C. Lewis, *A Protest Against the Modern Development of Unmusical Tone* (London 1897)
[41] A. Freeman, 'The Organs of Southwark Cathedral', *The Organ*, 7 (1927–8), 193–201; G. Benham, 'Interesting London Organs XXXII', *The Organ*, 12 (1932–3), 90–7

London, Southwark Cathedral: Thomas C. Lewis 1897

Manuals C–c'''' (61 notes); Pedals C–f' (30 notes)

Great Organ

Contra Viola	16
Bourdon	16
Open Diapason I	8
Open Diapason II	8
Harmonic flute	8
Stopped Diapason	8
Octave	4
Harmonic flute	4
Octave quint	$2^2/_3$
Superoctave	2
Mixture	IV
Cornet	III–V
Trumpet	8

Swell Organ

Bourdon	16
Open Diapason	8
Rohr flöte	8
Viole de Gambe	8
Voix célestes	8
Geigen principal	4
Rohr flöte	4
Flautina	2
Mixture	IV
Contra fagotto	16
Horn	8
Oboe	8
Vox humana	8
Clarion	4
Tremulant	

Choir Organ (unenclosed)

Lieblich gedact	16
Geigen principal	8
Salicional	8
Dulciana	8
Lieblich gedact	8
Salicet	4
Lieblich gedact	4
Flauto traverso	4
Lieblich gedact	2
Mixture	III

Solo Organ (enclosed)

Harmonic flute	8
Vox angelica	8
Unda maris	8
Harmonic flute	4
Bombarde	16
Cor anglais (from c)	16
Tuba magna	8
Trompette harmonique	8
Clarinet	8
Orchestral oboe	8
Tremulant	

Pedal Organ

Great bass	32
Major violone	32
Great bass (ext. 16')	16
Violone (part ext. 32', part ext. Gt.)	16
Sub bass (Gt.)	16
Dulciana bass	16
Cello (Gt.)	8
Flute (ext. Sub bass)	8
Flute (ext. Sub bass)	4
Contra posaune	32
Posaune	16
Bombarde	16
Trompette	8

Accessories

3 interchangeable pedals for stops on LH side
3 interchangeable pedals for stops on RH side
6 knobs controlling the interchangeable pedals
10 key touches above each manual
Balanced crescendo pedal
Balanced pedal for Swell Organ
Lever pedal for Solo Organ

Wind pressures
Solo Tuba magna & Trompette harm. 305mm
Remainder entirely 89mm

Plate 64   The organ in Southwark Cathedral, built by Thomas C. Lewis and completed in 1897. Lewis's organ relied on a splendid flue chorus in the German manner for its grandeur, eschewing the high-pressure reeds used by Willis, and making a statement of determined opposition to the trends of the day. Despite the organ's awkward position in a chamber on the east wall of the south transept, this remains one of the finest essays in chorus building to have survived from the nineteenth century. The case is by Arthur Blomfield.

last were undoubtedly considered as a valid replacement for 4′ reeds, which suffered from unstable tuning and weak trebles unless Willis's methods were followed: twentieth-century commentators have discovered their additional value as Sharp Mixtures used in the classical manner.[42]

Other London builders of note included Gray & Davison (no longer taking the leading position they had occupied in the 1850s), Bishop, Bevington, Bryceson and Holdich. In the provinces substantial and well-equipped work-shops emerged to challenge the superiority of the London-made product. Both Charles Brindley of Sheffield (later to become Brindley and Foster)[43] and Forster & Andrews of Hull[44] claimed direct connections with Schulze, adopting to a greater or lesser extent a Germanic style that became a hallmark of organs built in the north-east of the country (although in practice copying of Schulze's tonalities rarely extended beyond the Open Diapason and the provision of familiar soft stops such as the Lieblich Gedackt). Other local builders flourished, and many operated on a scale that would have been the envy of a leading concern in any other country. For dozens of companies a staff of thirty to sixty people was the norm, and most were self-reliant, able to make their own metal pipework, keys and action parts and to voice both flues and reeds (even if the proliferation at this time of key-makers, part-makers, pipe-makers and specialist voicers suggests a wide use of sub-contractors where necessary). Most were able to rise to a great occasion. Whiteley Bros. of Chester built a notable organ for Chester Cathedral in 1876; Wilkinson of Kendal provided a 32′ front for his four-manual organ in Preston Public Hall in 1882. Other provincial builders (Norman & Beard of Norwich, Harrison & Harrison of Durham) will figure largely in the description of events after 1900 and can be introduced at the appropriate juncture.

While an examination of large and spectacular instruments gives a sure indica-tion of the artistic and technical progress of the great firms, it should not be for-gotten that the great majority of organ building was concentrated on the provision of new small organs, usually of two manuals, for almost every church in the country. Where the chamber organ of the eighteenth century had been an instrument in its own right, with a complete tonal structure provided at an appropriately reduced scale, the small Victorian organ was a different animal. It offered a group of stops selected to provide some of the basic tonal effects of its larger brethren, concen-trating on the Diapasons, the Swell with its enclosed reeds, and the softer stops. The Great chorus and independent Pedal were usually omitted or at least pruned, espe-cially later in the century. An example is the organ by Hill & Son at St George's Church Hanworth, Middlesex, built in 1888 (the nomenclature suggests a passing period of German influence on the Hill firm at this time and the organ is not

[42] C. Clutton, 'Two Important Walker Rebuilds', *The Organ*, 46 (1966–7), 1–11

[43] J. R. Knott, *Brindley & Foster, Organ Builders, Sheffield, 1854–1939* (Bognor Regis 1973)

[44] L. Elvin, *Forster & Andrews, Organ Builders 1843–1956* (Lincoln 1968); L. Elvin, *Forster & Andrews, their Barrel, Chamber and Small Church Organs* (Lincoln 1976)

entirely typical of the company; its inclusion here is justified by the fact that the instrument has been the subject of a recent scholarly article):[45]

Hanworth, St George: Hill & Son 1888

Manuals C–g''' (56 notes); Pedals C–f' (30 notes)

Great Organ		Swell Organ	
Open Diapason	8	Geigen Prin. (bass from Gamba)	8
Lieblich Gedackt (wood bass)	8	Viole di Gamba	8
Salicional (bass from Gedackt)	8	Voix Celeste (from c)	8
Octave	4	Rohr Flute (wood bass)	8
Harmonic Flute	4	Geigen Principal	4
		Mixture	II
Pedal Organ		Horn	8
Sub Bass	16	Oboe	8
Violoncello	8		

Swell to Great
Great to Pedal
Swell to Pedal
4 composition Pedals

The great success of the larger firms in creating an organ style appropriate for the second half of the century is clear; by the 1880s (and partly in the wake of Willis's famous successes of the 1870s) certain features were becoming established as part of the English tonal style. First and foremost, the Diapasons: the rich and solemn tonality of open 8' stops so cherished in the early nineteenth century was developed and expanded on a new and massive scale, appropriate to generally larger and more powerful instruments. Such stops needed prodigiously large scales (up to 200mm diameter at 8' C in organs by Walker) and lots of thick, heavy metal. The Victorian Diapason became something of a phenomenon, unmatched in other countries, and the power of the pedal flue basses had to be kept up in proportion. The grand, rolling tone produced is a national characteristic: 'toujours rosbif!', as Cavaillé-Coll is supposed to have described the English organ.[46] The Great chorus is increasingly regarded as a means of securing an even build-up from soft to loud, rather than as an end in its own right, and mixtures diminish in number and importance. The presence of the large Swell is vitally important. Both Hill and Willis introduced choruses of Swell reeds – 16', 8' and 4' – in the 1840s and 50s: with appropriate flue and mixture backing, these gradually became a staple part of any instrument of pretension, by the end of the century often being provided even where there was no 16' reed on the Great. The importance of the Swell in securing smooth gradations of power was finally championed by the organist Edwin Lemare in the organ

[45] C. Embleton, 'The Organ in St. George's Church, Hanworth – a Late-Nineteenth-Century Hill', *BIOS Journal*, 17 (1993), 80–91   [46] J. W. Hinton, *Musical Opinion*, 27 (1903–4), 217

he designed for St Margaret Westminster, London, built by J. W. Walker & Sons in 1897: here he specified that the Swell should actually be louder than the Great. The Choir Organ was a collection of softer stops, isolated for convenience of registration, and normally unenclosed. The Solo Organ offered, sure enough, solo stops, and was the home of the Tuba(s) if provided. The nature of these last departments illustrates that the orchestral sonorities introduced by Willis had moved decisively from the concert hall to the wider organ building arena. The Pedal Organ chorus had dwindled in favour of the provision of a number of bass stops of varying power and tonality. In many small organs a stopped wooden 16′ was the only pedal stop; even three-manual instruments might have a Pedal Organ consisting only of two 16′ flues, one open and one stopped.

Mechanically, the pattern established by Willis was followed by other leading builders. Until the 1880s mechanical action was the norm for small organs, with the addition of a Barker machine for some instruments with three or more manuals. Experiments with electro-pneumatic key action (of which more later) were made from the 1860s on, but lack of faith in the reliability of the system diverted attention to tubular pneumatic action in the 1880s and 90s. Each builder developed his own system: those by Willis, Hill and Walker (on the charge pneumatic system) were reasonably quick (provided the console was close to the organ) and reliable (but noisy in operation), with a crisp and comfortable touch at the keys. Norman & Beard organs worked on the exhaust system: quieter, quicker over long distances, and arguably more sophisticated, but with a rather indefinite feeling at the keys. Pneumatic actions by less competent builders could be uncomfortably sluggish and sometimes unreliable, but the potential flexibility of layout and their reliability gradually made pneumatics the action of choice for all but the smallest organs. It was only some generations later, when organ builders were confronted by hundreds of worn leather motors rendered inaccessible by intestinal masses of lead tubing, that the high reputation of English tubular actions became somewhat tarnished.

Certain details of construction gradually became common to the main builders: engraved solid ivory stop-knobs on jambs at 45° to the manuals, with the handles arranged in vertical columns department by department, foundations at the bottom, upperwork and reeds at the top (though there were exceptions, especially the organs of Lewis); radiating and concave pedalboards (pioneered by Willis, much argued about, and becoming more common by 1900), set well under the keyboards, encouraging the development of the English toe-and-heel legato technique; composition pedals, gradually being supplemented by the adoption of Willis's thumb pistons; finally, the appearance of the balanced Swell pedal, replacing the trigger type (which returned to the closed position when the foot was removed) towards the end of the century.

These mechanisms required high standards of materials and manufacture, and this was matched in every aspect of English organ building. The repeated siting of organs in awkward and cramped positions in the building prevented English builders from exhibiting much skill at design and layout, except in the largest and grandest instruments, but gradually the quality of bench work and the finish of individual components rose to an enviably high standard. The highly polished interiors of late Lewis organs, or many others of the period 1890–1914, are unequalled, as are the astonishingly luxurious consoles accepted as the norm in the British Isles. It is almost certain that only the Americans demanded or got such standards of technical finesse, even if the persistent allegiance to pneumatics made English organs less responsive (but less noisy) than the Barker-action instruments still being built by Cavaillé-Coll in France. The adoption of factory methods to make all this possible and to secure consistent standards can be traced back to the competitive atmosphere of the 1820s. The extent of standardisation in Willis organs is notable, but so successful is the basic recipe that one is never in much doubt as to the artistry of the conception, even in the smallest and least promising instrument. Small organs from lesser factories lack this inspiration, and it has to be admitted that many nineteenth-century English organs are workhorses first and finally.

As a summary of developments amongst the large firms before 1900, let us return to St Margaret Westminster, and the organ designed by Lemare and built by Walker in 1897.[47]

London, St Margaret Westminster: J. W. Walker & Sons 1897

Manuals C–c'''' (61 notes), Pedals C–g' (32 notes)

Great Organ		Swell Organ	
Double Open Diapason	16	Lieblich Bourdon	16
Open Diapason (large)	8	Open Diapason	8
Open Diapason (medium)	8	Lieblich Gedackt	8
Open Diapason (small)	8	Echo Gamba	8
Orchestral Flute	8	Voix Celestes	8
Wald Flöte	8	Principal	4
Principal	4	Flute	4
Harmonic Flute	4	Fifteenth	2
Twelfth	$2^2/_3$	Mixture (without tierce)	IV
Fifteenth	2	Double Trumpet	16
Mixture (with tierce)	III	Posaune	8
Contra Posaune	16	Oboe	8
Posaune	8	Vox Humana	8
Clarion	4	Clarion	4
		Tremulant	

[47] G. Benham, 'Interesting London Organs XIII, St. Margaret's Church Westminster', *The Organ*, 7 (1927–8), 202–8

Choir Organ (in a swell box)

Quintaton	16
Gamba	8
Dulciana	8
Vox Angelica	8
Lieblich Gedackt	8
Viola	4
Wald Flöte	4
Piccolo	2
Clarinet	8
Orchestral Oboe	8
Tremulant	

Pedal Organ

Double Open Diapason (wood)	32
Open Diapason (wood, ext. 32')	16
Open Diapason (metal)	16
Bourdon (wood)	16
Quint (wood)	$10\frac{2}{3}$
Octave (wood, ext. 16')	8
Principal (metal, ext. 16')	8
Flute (wood, ext. 16')	8
Bombarde (wood)	16
Trumpet (wood, ext. 16')	8

Couplers

Swell to Great
Swell to Choir
Choir to Great
Swell Octave
Swell Sub-octave
Swell Unison Off
Choir Octave
Choir Sub-octave
Choir Unison Off
Great to Pedal
Swell to Pedal
Choir to Pedal

Accessories

5 pistons to Great, + 1 adjustable piston
6 pistons to Swell, + 1 adjustable
3 pistons to Choir, + 1 adjustable
1 reversible piston to Great to Pedal
1 reversible piston to Choir to Great
5 combination pedals to Pedal
5 combination pedals to Swell
4 combination pedals to Choir
1 reverser pedal to Great to Pedal

Key action and stop action tubular pneumatic; pistons partly electro-pneumatic with current provided from dry batteries.

Wind pressures

Great Organ flues, 123mm; Great Organ large Open Diapason and reeds, 127mm; Swell Organ flues, Oboe & Vox Humana, 121mm; Swell Organ reeds, 178mm; Choir Organ, 102mm; Pedal flues, 102mm; Pedal reeds, 308mm

   Such an instrument is, by any standards, impressive enough, and the growing sophistication of tonal resources is evident. Lemare required an instrument of great flexibility, especially well able to cope with orchestral transcriptions. On this organ his performances of astonishingly difficult arrangements of music by Wagner became famous and were heard by large audiences: so large, in fact, as to incur the jealousy of the church authorities and to lead to Lemare resigning and starting his career as one of the first professional international recitalists.

   Looking back over the Victorian organ in as brief a description as this gives a kaleidoscopic impression of technical innovation, of companies struggling for supremacy, and of rapid and dauntless progress. On the other hand the finest of the surviving instruments show solidity and self-confidence, qualities which we can only envy today. Foremost among all these is the world's great surviving monument to English organ building, the instrument built by Hill & Son for the Town Hall at Sydney,

Plate 65   The organ in the Town Hall, Sydney, Australia, built by Hill & Sons and completed in 1890. This organ stands today without alteration as the greatest surviving monument to English organ building. It was the largest organ in the world at the time of its construction, and its stop list includes a full-length pedal reed of 64′ pitch (lowest speaking note CCCC, approximately 8 cycles per second). Apart from this one major innovation, the organ is otherwise conservative in design. The magnificent case, designed by William Hill's grandson Dr Arthur Hill, is derived from renaissance prototypes.

Australia and completed in 1890 (when it was the largest organ in the world). Of this organ it is necessary to say very little, regarded by all who know it well as a peerless work of art, it is successful in almost every detail – including the celebrated 64′ Pedal reed. The scheme is in many ways ultra-conservative, containing few of the orchestral effects demanded by Lemare, little of the flexibility of control advocated by contemporary writers such as G. A. Audsley, and relying on traditional flue choruses on light pressures for its grandeur of effect, backed up by reeds on pressures only slightly higher (completely eschewing the new voicing techniques used by Willis). William Hill's grandson Arthur described the organ to a meeting of the College of Organists and stated his by now old-fashioned rule concerning wind pressure: 'There is a limit to anything, and three inches [76mm] is the proper pressure for pure tone.'[48] The organ is preserved almost without alteration today.[49]

Sydney, Australia, the Town Hall: Hill & Son, 1890

Manuals C–c′′′′ (61 notes), Pedals C–f′ (30 notes)

Great Organ		Swell Organ	
Contra Bourdon [wood]	32	Double Open Diapason	16
Double Open Diapason	16	Bourdon [wood]	16
Open Diapason No. 1*	8	Open Diapason	8
Open Diapason No. 2	8	Hohl Flöte [wood]	8
Open Diapason No. 3	8	Viola di Gamba	8
Open Diapason No. 4	8	Salicional	8
Harmonic Flute*	8	Dulciana	8
Viola*	8	Vox Angelica	8
Spitz Flöte	8	Octave	4
Gamba	8	Rohr Flöte [wood bass]	4
Hohl Flöte [wood]	8	Harmonic Flute	4
Rohr Flöte [wood bass]	8	Gemshorn	4
Quint	5⅓	Twelfth	2⅔
Principal	4	Fifteenth	2
Octave	4	Piccolo	2
Gemshorn	4	Mixture	IV
Harmonic Flute*	4	Furniture	V
Twelfth	2⅔	Trombone	16
Fifteenth	2	Bassoon	16
Mixture	III	Trumpet	8
Sharp Mixture	IV	Cornopean	8
Furniture*	V	Horn	8
Cymbal*	IV	Oboe	8
Posaune	16	Clarion	4
Posaune	8	Tremulant [by foot lever]	
Trumpet	8		
Clarion	4		

[48] A. G. Hill's lecture to the College of Organists, 5 March 1890 in *The Musical Standard*, 40 (1890), 166
[49] D. Kinsela, 'The Restoration of the Organ in Sydney Town Hall', *BIOS Journal*, 2 (1978), 87–102

Choir Organ [reeds enclosed]

Contra Dulciana	16
Open Diapason	8
Hohl Flöte [wood]	8
Lieblich Gedackt [wood bass]	8
Flauto Traverso	8
Gamba	8
Dulciana	8
Octave	4
Violino	4
Celestino	4
Lieblich Flöte [wood bass]	4
Twelfth	2⅔
Fifteenth	2
Dulcet	2
Mixture	III
Bassoon	16
Oboe	8
Clarinet	8
Vox Humana	8
Octave Oboe	4

Solo [unenclosed]

Bourdon [wood]	16
Open Diapason	8
Violin Diapason [wood]	8
Flauto Traverso [wood]	8
Doppel Flöte [wood]	8
Stopped Diapason [wood]	8
Viola	8
Octave	4
Harmonic Flute	4
Flauto Traverso [wood]	4
Harmonic Piccolo	2
Contra Fagotto	16
Harmonic Trumpet	8
Corno di Bassetto	8
Orchestral Oboe	8
Cor Anglais	8
Octave Oboe	4
Tremulant	
Contra Tuba	16
Tuba	8
Tuba Clarion	4
Carillon Bells	2

Pedal Organ

Double Open Diapason	32
Double Open Diapason [wood]	32
Contra Bourdon	32
Open Diapason	16
Open Diapason [wood]	16
Violone [wood]	16
Gamba [wood]	16
Dulciana	16
Bourdon [wood]	16
Quint	10⅔
Octave	8
Prestant	8
Violoncello [wood]	8
Bass Flute [wood]	8
Twelfth	5⅓
Fifteenth	4
Mixture	IV
Mixture	III
Mixture	II
Contra Trombone [wood]	64
Contra Posaune	32
Posaune	16
Trombone [wood]	16
Bassoon	16
Trumpet	8
Clarion	4

Echo Organ (in a box without shutters)

Lieblich Gedackt [wood bass]	8
Viol d'Amour	8
Unda Maris [2 ranks]	8
Viol d'Amour	4
Flageolet	2
Glockenspiel	IV
Echo Dulciana Cornet	IV
Bassett Horn	8

Couplers

Great to Pedal
Swell to Pedal
Choir to Pedal
Solo to Pedal
Swell to Great*
Swell Super Octave to Great*
Swell Sub Octave to Great*
Choir to Great*
Solo to Great*
Solo Octave
Swell to Choir
Solo to Choir
Echo to Swell
Pedal Combinations to Great Pistons

Accessories

8 combination pistons to Great
8 combination pistons to Swell
7 combination pistons to Choir
7 combination pistons to Solo
3 combination pistons to Echo
6 combination pedals to Pedal

Wind pressures

Great flues (except *) 89mm, reeds and * 127mm
Swell flues and Bassoon 89mm, reeds 127mm
Choir 70mm
Solo flues 76mm, orchestral reeds 127mm, Tubas 254mm
Echo 57mm
Pedal flues 83mm, reeds 114mm

Action

Key action, mechanical from keys to mechanical coupling system with Barker Lever assistance to couplers marked *, thence charge pneumatic (but using vacuum not supply)
Stop and combination action tubular pneumatic (supply 'on', vacuum 'off')

CHAPTER FIFTEEN

PROGRESSIVE TRENDS
1880–1900

Towards the end of the century the established recipe may have appeared slightly restricting and conservative. At Willis & Sons, Father Willis rejected his sons' attempts to change the sound of his organs: 'Do what you like when I am gone'; he also argued with Vincent over the development of new actions, and Vincent left in 1895.[1] At Hill & Son, Thomas Hill diligently followed in the path laid down by his father towards the end of his life, clearly happy to allow the firm's instruments to offer a more restrained alternative to the brash organs of Willis, and only gradually allowing changes in fashion to affect his work. J. W. Walker & Son's devotion to the large Diapason ensured them a place amongst the traditionalists, and T. C. Lewis, though hardly guilty of providing an unvaried diet of roast beef, was nevertheless so opinionated as to resist any real suggestion of change: indeed at Southwark he was to step back into the near-forgotten classical tradition of chorus-building. A younger generation of players and builders was keen to explore further the possibilities offered by experiments in the voicing shop and by the exploration of new technologies. It is to a number of progressive builders that we must now turn.

That there was room in the market for adventurous new recipes gradually became clear during the 1880s. One of the first voices to be heard was that of Thomas Casson, a banker from Denbigh in Wales, who understood the mechanical flexibility offered by new pneumatic actions and developed an organ building method that centred round a complex console bristling with ingenious gadgets.[2] Over the years until his death in 1910[3] he promoted his method through pamphleteering and correspondence in the musical press, often accusing his rivals of plagiarism and little daunted by the mixed success enjoyed by the various organ building enterprises he set up after his retirement from banking in 1890. A major plank of the Casson method was the use of extension: from one conventional manual department he would, through the use of pneumatic octave derivation machines, provide a second semi-independent division an octave apart. Thus at the Church

---

[1] T. Willis, 'Recollections of my Father' (undated and unpublished biographical note on the subject of Vincent Willis)

[2] T. Casson, *The Modern Organ* (Denbigh 1883); T. Casson, *Reform in Organ Building* (London 1888); T. Casson, *The Pedal Organ* (London 1905)   [3] *Musical Opinion*, 34 (1910–11), 97

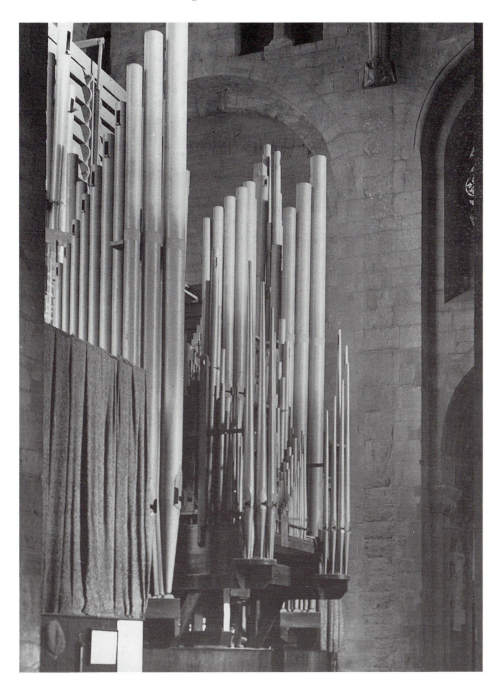

Plate 66   The Grove Organ in the north transept of Tewkesbury Abbey, built by Michell & Thynne for the Inventions Exhibition of 1885. This instrument challenged the conservative stance of the larger London builders, introducing a wide range of new voices in a completely original design. The entire pipework and mechanism of the organ were on display, and even after its move to Tewkesbury it still has no casework. The display of narrow-scaled tapered pipes hides the Choir Organ, mounted at the very front of the instrument in the manner of the ancient Chaire Organ – a feature carefully specified by Carlton Michell.

of the Sacred Heart, Omagh, Northern Ireland, the Swell and Echo divisions were derived from nine ranks:

Swell Organ			**Echo Organ**	
Rohr bordun	16	=	Rohr flöte	8
Contra viole	16	=	Viole	8
Open Diapason	8			
			Voix celeste	8
Hohl flöte	8	=	Hohl flöte	4
Harmonic flute	4	=	Harmonic Piccolo	2
Mixture	IV			
Fagotto	16	=	Hautboy	8
Cornopean	8			

Pneumatic console devices allowed the two departments to be played separately or together from the same row of keys, and gave a suitable pedal registration at the touch of a button.[4]

The technique was not actually new: we have seen how Renatus Harris used 'communication' (more properly called *duplexing*) to make stops available at the same pitch on two different manuals: the same technique was employed by Hill at Birmingham Town Hall in 1834 and by Schulze at Doncaster in 1862. At Doncaster Schulze also used *extension*: from each rank of Pedal pipes he derived two stops, one an octave apart from the other. Almost all builders occasionally used *borrowing*: economically providing only one set of bass pipes for two stops of the same pitch on the same manual. With a compact pneumatic action and switch gear these processes were potentially much easier, and by 1900 the possibility of extending the resources of the Pedal Organ through duplexing of basses from the manual divisions and extension to other pitches was much discussed.

The use of extension, duplexing and borrowing, combined with a bold statement of an alternative school of voicing, again came to the notice of the public with the arrival in 1884 of the new organ at the Italian Church Hatton Garden, London, built by Anneessens of Belgium. At an astonishingly low price Anneessens built a large organ at first sight redolent of the very highest artistic standards of the French tradition. Only later did it become apparent that the workmanship was of indifferent quality and that the number of stop-knobs at the console had been greatly swelled by the widespread use of extension and duplexing: for instance, much of the Choir Organ consisted of Great Organ stops appearing under different names.[5] The Anneessens organs (there were several more in the 1880s and 90s, many in Catholic churches) for ever linked extension with cheapness of the worst sort, and gave the established firms an opportunity to reject 'clever' mechanical devices out of hand.

[4] G. Dixon, 'Thomas Casson, an Appreciation', *The Organ*, 28 (1948–9), 49–58; *Musical Opinion*, 21 (1897–8), 815; *Musical Opinion*, 22 (1898–9), 23, 55
[5] *Musical Opinion*, 7 (1883–4), 349 and following issues; *Musical Standard*, 41 (1891), 79; author's examination of the similar instrument formerly standing in the old Catholic Cathedral, Middlesbrough

Meanwhile, attention focused on another of the large exhibitions that were so much a feature of Victorian life; the Inventions Exhibition of 1885 was the last at which organ builders exhibited on a grand scale. According to Father Willis's granddaughter 'It became known that a Gold Medal would be awarded for the most deserving invention, and it was soon rumoured that many works would depend on the awards in the coming Exhibition.'[6] Much was at stake.

Several builders provided instruments which showed one or other of the latest developments in mechanism, and the widespread use of tubular pneumatic action was significant. Some went further; for example August Gern (a foreman of Cavaillé-Coll who had settled in London in the 1860s) showed an organ with some extension.[7] The Bryceson, Walker and Willis exhibits demonstrated, amongst other features, the use of an electro-pneumatic key action (as did the instrument sent by Welte of Freiburg).[8]

The application of electricity to organ building had been under practical consideration for some time. It was not possible to open the pallet in the soundboard directly by electricity: the large magnet required would have been slow and noisy, and would have consumed a lot of current (far beyond the capacity of contemporary batteries). Thus the role of the electro-magnet was in moving the valves of the conventional pneumatic motor: the advantage was that a small flexible cable could replace the mechanical linkages of the Barker lever action or the bulky lead tubing of tubular pneumatic actions. In the 1860s Barker (of lever fame) and Péschard brought out patents covering electro-pneumatic actions of this sort. Barker-Péschard actions were made under licence in England by Bryceson, who built several from 1869 onwards.[9] The principles were perfectly sound, but in practice the extreme difficulties of providing sufficient current from batteries for prolonged and heavy use crippled most early electro-pneumatic actions. Pioneering work continued, and by the 1880s it was well known in England that Roosevelt had produced successful electro-pneumatic actions in America,[10] that Merklin was building electro-pneumatic actions in France[11] and that Anneessens was building new actions on the system patented by Schmoele and Mols of Antwerp.[12] Willis rebuilt his Inventions Exhibition organ at Canterbury Cathedral in 1886, using electro-pneumatic action which remained in working order until 1939 – it was the pneumatics which wore out.[13] None of this peaceful, if uncertain, development was to give any indication of the furore which was caused by the arguments for and against the use of electricity in the 1890s. Before discussing this however, we must return to the most remarkable of the exhibits at the 'Inventions' of 1885.

Carlton C. Michell and William Thynne, who had worked with Lewis, joined

[6] Willis, 'Recollections of my Father'   [7] *Musical Opinion*, 18 (1894–5), 154
[8] *Musical Opinion*, 8 (1884–5), 305, 408d (sic); 20 (1896–7), 549
[9] R. Whitworth, *The Electric Organ* (London 1930), 2nd edn (1940)
[10] *Hilborne L. Roosevelt, Manufacturer of Church, Chapel, Concert and Chamber Organs* (Catalogue) (New York c1883); reports of progress in American electric organ actions in *The Musical Standard*, 42 (1892) (several issues)
[11] *Musical Opinion*, 8 (1884–5), 135   [12] *Musical Opinion*, 10 (1886–7), 414
[13] H. Willis III, 'The Organ of Canterbury Cathedral', *The Organ*, 29 (1949–50), 1–11

forces to build an instrument representing 'an attempt to place in the hands of the player a grand and complete organ reduced to the smallest possible dimensions as regards the number of slides'.[14] The scheme was as shown (see plate 66, p. 285):[15]

London, the Inventions Exhibition (now at Tewkesbury Abbey, Gloucestershire): Carlton Michell and William Thynne 1885

Great Organ

Violone	16
Great open diapason	8
Small open diapason	8
Claribel (wood)	8
Octave	4
Flute octaviante	4
Quint mixture ($2^2/_3'$ + 2')	II
Great mixture	IV
Trombone	16
Trumpet	8

Choir Organ

Spitzflote	8
Viole sourdine	8
Gedact (wood bass)	8
Zauberflote (stopped harmonic)	4
Gemshorn	4
Flautino	2
Clarionet	8

Pedal Organ

Harmonic bass*	32
Great bass (wood)	16
Dolce (open wood)	16
Great flute (open wood)	8
Bombarde	16

Swell Organ

Open Diapason	8
Flauto traverso	8
Viole de gambe	8
Voix celestes	8
Geigen	4
Mixture	III
Contra posaune	16
Horn	8
Oboe	8

Solo Organ

Harmonic flute	8
Violoncello (2 ranks, one wood)	8
Voix humaine (enclosed)	8
Tuba	8

Couplers

Swell to Great
Solo to Great
Swell to Choir
Choir sub-octave to Great
Solo octave
Choir octave
Swell octave
Great to Pedal
Swell to Pedal
Choir to Pedal
Solo to Pedal

[14] *Musical Opinion*, 8 (1884–5) 391–2
[15] J. Budgen and C. Beswick, 'The Grove Organ, Tewkesbury Abbey', *BIOS Journal*, 6 (1982), 97–101

Ventils

Wind to Choir
Swell fluework & Oboe
Great to Quint mixture
Great mixture & reeds
Swell reeds
Solo fluework
Pedal – full minus Dolce 16′

Accessories

Tremulant Swell
Tremulant Solo
Four composition pedals to Great
Four composition pedals to Swell
Pedal to Great to Pedal coupler
Pistons acting on ventils & Bombarde 16′
Lever pedals to Swell & Solo

Wind pressures

Great flues (but not Great mixture IV): 89mm (bass), 102mm (treble)
Great reeds & Great mixture IV: 146mm
Swell flues & Oboe: 89mm
Swell Contra posaune 16′ & Horn 8′: 146mm
Choir: 89mm
Solo (except Tuba): 89mm
Tuba 8′: 305mm
Pedal flues: 89mm & 102mm
Bombarde 16′: 305mm

Key action: Choir mechanical; Great Barker Lever; Swell, Solo & Pedal tubular pneumatic;
stop action mechanical

*Pedal Harmonic Bass 32′: C–E two ranks 16′ + 10⅔′; F–B stopped 32′; c–f′ extended from
Great bass 16′

It is not known how the instrument was financed, but circumstantial evidence
suggests the involvement of J. Martin White, whose name is associated with several
of the progressive builders of the eighties and nineties. Whatever the situation,
Michell & Thynne invested the entire working capital of the newly formed
company in the organ,[16] only for disaster to strike. Despite their avowed attempt to
make this grand organ 'as small as possible', when they arrived at the exhibition
they found that there was a misunderstanding regarding its position and the site
chosen for it was not nearly big enough. They were obliged to alter it drastically at
the very last minute, and it finally appeared long after the other exhibits. The extra
work involved pushed the company into bankruptcy. Feelings were running high at
the time of the 'Inventions', and this incident caused a behind-the-scenes row, the
repercussions of which are still felt today; there is a long-standing rumour that
Michell & Thynne were deliberately 'spiked' by their well-established rivals. The
organ was sold off, finding its way to Tewkesbury Abbey, Gloucestershire, where it
stands little altered and is now known as the Grove Organ.

This instrument has an importance out of all proportion to the short-lived
company which built it. Its position in the development of the English organ has been
somewhat misrepresented in the past, hence it must be described here in more detail.
Most have accepted the easily grasped idea that it contains a 'Schulze-type diapason

---

[16] H. Stubington, 'The Organs of Tewkesbury Abbey', *The Organ*, 24 (1944–5), 97–108

chorus' coupled with 'Willis-type reeds':[17] this is not the case. The principals are indeed bold and bright, and the mixtures have no tierces; however, they are derived from the work of Lewis (and are thus already one remove from the work of Schulze) but are treated with a combination of breadth and boldness that has moved away from Lewis's dry and academic style. However, the choruses are backed up by an astonishing variety of soft and solo stops, quite unlike the simple families of gedacts, harmonic flutes and gentle strings known to Lewis (and, indeed, to Willis): the development of new imitative string tone and exotic innovations such as the Zauberflöte (a stopped pipe overblowing to the second harmonic, and therefore of three times the normal length) are characteristic. The chorus reeds (voiced by W. J. Northcott)[18] are also derived from Lewis's practice: despite his reputation for using low pressures, he also developed his own style of high-pressure reed voicing, which appeared at St Peter Eaton Square and in his concert organs. The Grove Organ reeds, with open shallots, large-scale tubes, no weights, no slots and no harmonic trebles, are the antithesis of the techniques developed by Vincent Willis. The quality of the result is outstanding: the organ is at once more colourful and more dynamic than anything before it, and the success of the overall result suggests a very confident hand.[19]

But which hand was it: Michell or Thynne? On this question argument raged for fifty years. The evidence is widely scattered, but there is good reason to believe that though the exquisite flue voicing was in the hands of Thynne, it was Michell, the musician and theorist, who was the architect of the scheme and had the clearest idea of just how such an instrument should sound. For example, in the Grove Organ the Choir Organ is at the front of the instrument, rather in the manner of the ancient Chaire organ, where its delicate strings and flutes can be heard to best advantage. Michell was to remark on the importance of this feature in subsequent writings.[20] The overall scheme of the organ was to reappear in other instruments where Michell had a hand, notably, after his emigration to America, at New York Avenue Methodist Church, Brooklyn (George S. Hutchings 1890), St Luke, Germantown, Pennsylvania (Cole, Woodberry & Michell 1892)[21] and elsewhere. Finally, the Michell-style scheme, with its colour, boldness, refinement and carefully differentiated departments, was to re-emerge in a different guise in the hands of Harrison & Harrison of Durham after 1904. Work by Thynne on his own never reached such a standard.

Whatever the importance of this organ (some of it, it must be admitted, potential never fully realised), its effect was soon to be entirely forgotten in the astonishing affray which marked the appearance on the scene of Robert Hope-Jones. So strong are the feelings aroused by the mention of his name that extreme care has to be taken in assessing his work. To one modern author he was 'a sort of *fin de siècle eminence grise*', whose instruments 'were incapable of playing any music ever written

[17] C. Clutton and A. Niland, *The British Organ* (London 1963), 105   [18] *Musical Opinion*, 44 (1920), 960–1
[19] Author's examination of the instrument
[20] C. C. Michell, 'The Organ of the Future, its Tone Colour', *Musical Opinion*, 12 (1888), 80
[21] O. Ochse, *The History of the Organ in the United States* (Indiana 1975), 235, 246–7, 258

for the organ';[22] another believes he was the builder of 'the worst organs ever made by a careful, professional builder'.[23] Given that Hope-Jones was admired by large numbers of otherwise sensible and well-educated musicians, that he was successful in landing a large number of contracts for new organs, and that his work was profoundly influential both in Britain and in America, these highly subjective statements clearly need to be treated with some circumspection.

Hope-Jones was a telephone engineer (he was chief electrician to the Lancashire & Cheshire Telephonic Exchange Co. Ltd and the National Telephone Co. Ltd, Liverpool District)[24] and organist and choirmaster at St John, Birkenhead. Here, from 1887, assisted by members of his choir and the organ builder Franklin Lloyd, he rebuilt the organ with an electro-pneumatic action of his own design and a detached console.[25] The instrument attracted interest, was visited, and before long was written up in the musical press.[26] Hope-Jones was flamboyant in character and a self-publicist: it is unlikely that he ever saw the humour in the photograph circulated of him playing the organ at St John's with the movable console situated in the churchyard.

By July 1892 his work had generated such interest that he was able to set up a company manufacturing parts for his actions and had issued licences for the use of his patents to twenty-one companies.[27] The new actions met with instant success: opening the rebuild of J. Martin White's house organ at Balruddery, Perthshire, the organist A. L. Peace of Glasgow Cathedral wrote: 'It's a wonderful thing; I've been trying my best to make it go wrong, but it won't.'[28] The London companies squirmed with displeasure, tried unsuccessfully to block his patent applications,[29] and then mounted a whispering campaign designed to put him out of business (there is strong evidence to suggest that some of the anonymous and highly mischievous letters that appeared in the *Musical Standard* and *Musical Opinion* in the 1890s were written by respected organ builders).

The reasons for this bitter opposition were obvious. Hope-Jones made many claims for his action, some of which may have been over-enthusiastic. But he had succeeded in making a series of design breakthroughs of critical importance: these have not always been fully understood or appreciated. First, he used an electro-magnet which incorporated an integral armature and pneumatic valve (pioneered by Schmoele & Mols of Antwerp, though Hope-Jones claimed not to have known this); secondly, he used self-cleaning round wire contacts mounted on the keyboards; thirdly, he used multi-contact electric switches to operate the couplers and any extensions or duplexing.[30] At a stroke he had removed most of the bulky and expensive machinery from the organ, replacing hundreds of hand-made parts with simple and potentially reli-

[22] Clutton and Niland, *The British Organ*, 106–7   [23] P. Williams, *A New History of the Organ* (London 1980), 182

[24] Hope-Jones pamphlet c1891, now in the British Organ Archive, Birmingham Central Library

[25] R. A. D. Pope, 'The Organs of St. John's Church, Birkenhead', *The Organ*, 16 (1936–7), 218–24

[26] *Musical Opinion*, 14 (1890–1), 294–5; *Musical Standard*, 40 (1890–1), 423

[27] Prospectus for the Hope-Jones Electric Organ Company Ltd, *Musical Standard*, 43 (1892–3), 29

[28] *Musical Standard*, 46(1894), 511

[29] V. Willis, Objections to claims in patent application 15461 of 1890, Henry Willis & Sons, Specification Book 8 (1890), 186   [30] R. Whitworth, *The Electric Organ* (London 1930); 2nd Edn (1940)

Plate 67 The console of the Hope-Jones organ of 1895 at St George Hanover Square, London. The Hope-Jones system offered a radical new alternative to the traditional organ. Everything was modernised: the pipes were of new kinds, the key action was electro-pneumatic and the console was entirely modernised with stop keys instead of stop knobs and an array of new gadgetry. Elements of this system later became the foundation of cinema organ design under Wurlitzer and others.

able devices that could be fully pre-manufactured in a specialist workshop. By using the combined armature/valve electro-magnet he was able to use low voltages and reduced the current consumption of the organ to manageable proportions, opening the way to a solution to the battery problem. Having disposed of so much mechanical encumbrance he moved to the console, replacing the traditional stop-knobs with a single row of teeth-like 'stop-keys' under the music desk, and reducing the console surround to a simple functional structure. Ingenious devices were provided to help the organist: pistons divided into three sections (called by Hope-Jones 'Compound Composition Keys' and by the world at large 'Liquorice Allsorts') giving a set combination, a suitable Pedal bass for it and appropriate couplers; a 'Stop Switch' allowing pre-set combinations to be brought into use; keyboards with 'Double Touch' – pressing the key beyond its normal limit operated a second set of contacts, allowing solo and accompaniment to be played on the same manual.

Hope-Jones did not rest at mere mechanical improvements. Having removed most of the traditional mechanism from the organ, he soon realised that the same radical approach could be applied to the pipework. With complete faith in the possibilities offered by experimental pipe-scales and voicing techniques, and in the use of hitherto undreamt-of pressures, he believed that the organ chorus was doomed, to be replaced by individual voices of great colour and variety, available at every level of power from the almost inaudible to the almost unbearable. To realise this vision he moved from part-making into organ building proper, and the first organ by the Hope-Jones Electric Organ Company of Birkenhead was inaugurated at Denton near Manchester on 7 October 1894.[31] Experiments with pipework continued. Open Diapasons of phenomenal power and ultra-smooth tone were developed by increasing the wind-pressure, raising the height of the mouth, and covering the upper lip with thin leather. Repeatedly cutting down a Stopped Diapason to increase the scale, he created the Tibia Clausa, and in a similar manner the Claribel became the Tibia Plena. Thynne's new string-voicing was imitated in pipes of emaciated scale: the new Viole d'Orchestre. Upper harmonics lost in the process of refinement were replaced by the new brilliant string tone and by the appearance of Quintadena and even Tiercina stops, sounding strong harmonics as well as their ground tone. Reeds were voiced for a 'smooth, French-Horn tone',[32] and the invention of the Diaphone (a reed pipe in which the tongue is replaced by a valve on a spring) extended this smooth horn tone to new levels of power.[33]

Almost as soon as he had started in organ building, Hope-Jones had the opportunity to demonstrate some of his experimental voices at Worcester Cathedral.[34] By November 1894 he had been awarded the contract to rebuild the two Hill organs there as a single instrument to his own design.[35] The organ was finished in 1896, to the scheme shown on p. 294–5.

[31] *Musical Standard*, 47 (1893–4), 311   [32] *Musical Opinion*, 18 (1894–5), 290

[33] The development of the Hope-Jones system was reported extensively in the *Musical Standard* and *Musical Opinion* from 1892 onwards.   [34] *Musical Opinion*, 18 (1894–5), 428   [35] *Musical Standard*, 48 (1894–5), 411

Worcester Cathedral: The Hope-Jones Electric Organ Company 1896

Manuals C–c''' (61 notes), Pedals C–f' (30 notes)

Great Organ
254mm pressure:

Diapason Phonon (wood & metal)	16
Diapason Phonon (metal)	8
Tibia Plena (wood)	8
Tuba Profunda (metal)	16
Tuba (metal)	8

127mm pressure:

Open Diapason (metal)	8
Hohl Flute (wood)	8
Viol d'Amour (metal)	8
Octave Diapason (metal)	4
Quintadena (tin)	4
Harmonic Piccolo	2

Choir Organ (unenclosed)
76mm pressure:

Double Open Diapason (wood & metal)	16
Open Diapason (metal)	8
Cone Lieblich Gedact (metal)	8
Viol d'Orchestre (tin)	8
Tiercina (tin)	8
Dulciana (metal)	8
Flute (metal)	4
Flautina (metal)	2
Clarinet (metal)	8
Cor Anglais (tin)	8

Pedal Organ
127mm pressure:

Gravissima (ext. 32', bass acoustic)	64
Double Open Diapason (wood)	32
Contra Violone (zinc)	32
Tibia Profunda (wood & iron)	16
Open Diapason (wood)	16
Violone (zinc, ext. 32')	16
Bourdon (wood)	16
Octave Violone (ext. 16')	8
Flute (wood, ext. Bourdon 16')	8

508mm pressure:

Diaphone (wood)	32
Diaphone (wood, ext. 32')	16
Tuba Profunda (metal)	16
Tuba (metal, ext. 16')	8

Swell Organ
254mm pressure:

Horn Diapason (metal)	8
Quintaton (tin)	8
Tibia Clausa (wood)	8
Harmonic Piccolo (metal)	2
Double English Horn (metal)	16
Cornopean	8
Clarion	4

127mm pressure:

Contra Viola (tin)	16
String Gamba (tin)	8
Violes Celestes II & III (tin)	8
Gambette (tin)	4
Harmonic Flute (metal)	4
Oboe (tin)	8
Vox Humana (metal)	8
Cor Anglais (free reed, tin)	8

Solo Organ

254mm pressure (enclosed)	8
Diaphonic Horn	8
Rohr Flute (metal)	4
Bombarde (metal)	16
Tuba Sonora (metal)	8
Orchestral Oboe (brass)	8

508mm pressure:

Tuba Mirabilis (metal)	8
(bass extended from Pedal Tuba)	

Compound Composition Keys
5 for Great, Pedal and Couplers
2 for Great Couplers
5 for Swell, Pedal and Couplers
2 for Swell Couplers
2 for   i Swell heavy reeds
ii Swell strings
iii both combined
3 for Choir, Pedal and Couplers
2 for Choir couplers
3 for Solo
2 for Solo couplers
Stop Switch

Composition Pedals
4 to Great & Couplers
4 to Swell & Couplers
Sforzando
Stop Switch

Couplers
Great superoctave (high pressure)
Great suboctave (low pressure)
Swell to Great sub
Swell to Great unison (double touch)
Swell to Great super
Choir to Great sub
Choir to Great unison
Solo to Great sub
Solo to Great unison (double touch)
Solo to Great super
Swell sub
Swell super
Solo to Swell (second touch)
Choir to Swell (second touch)
Choir sub
Choir super
Swell to Choir sub
Swell to Choir unison (double touch)
Swell to Choir super
Solo sub
Solo super
Great to Pedal
Swell to Pedal
Choir to Pedal
Solo to Pedal
Swell Tremulant

Some explanation of the features of this organ may be of interest. The division of the Great and Swell into 'heavy' and 'light' divisions is notable, as is the complete exclusion of any conventional upperwork or mixtures, now deemed unnecessary. The Swell was enclosed in a box formed from the walls of the building itself. The Swell Violes Celestes consisted of three ranks, sharp, unison and flat. The first two spoke when the stop was half drawn, the third rank was added when fully drawn. The Choir Viole d'Orchestre was only 27mm diameter at the 8′ pipe: the lowest notes were entirely encased in wooden supports. The Tubas had two tongues to each pipe. A proposal to mount a Tuba over the Canons' stalls on a pressure of 2,540mm was not carried out. Many of the more conventionally named stops survived from the two Hill organs.[36] Hope-Jones insisted that the many octave couplers were for soft effects only and were not a cheap attempt to amplify the power of the organ.[37]

Hope-Jones published testimonials that underlined the success of the instrument:[38]

[36] R. Clark, 'An Apparently Controversial Instrument', *BIOS Journal*, 17 (1992), 48–63
[37] *Musical Opinion*, 20 (1896–7), 95   [38] Clark, 'An Apparently Controversial Instrument'

In my opinion this organ is, from the power, dignity, and smoothness of the reeds, the grandeur of the diaphones, the delicacy of the softer stops, the beautiful touch of both manuals and pedals, and its ingenious mechanism, the finest I have ever heard or played upon.   (H. Keeton, Organist of Peterborough Cathedral)

One of the most remarkable exemplifications of organ building of the present day.
(A. L. Peace. Organist of Glasgow Cathedral)

An unqualified success. The new tone qualities introduced are excellent.
(C. W. Perkins, Organist of Birmingham Town Hall)

It reaches a standard of excellence far above anything I have seen before.
(H. Blair, Organist of Worcester Cathedral)

Flushed with triumph, Hope-Jones continued to build organs disregarding tradition, the bitter opposition of organ builders and conservative musicians, and any financial restraints suggested by the need to keep his business afloat (the company seems to have collapsed and reformed on more than one occasion). By 1897 (at the McEwan Hall, University of Edinburgh) he was exploring the possibilities offered by electro-pneumatic action in allowing the organ to be spread around the building: this instrument was divided into no less than seven sections. Before long Hope-Jones would be advocating wholesale duplexing, the abandonment of the traditional manual departments, and the division of the organ into sections based on the orchestra: string, brass, woodwind etc. After various ups and downs he was obliged suddenly to leave the country in 1903, to escape criminal prosecution[39] (allegedly for sexual misconduct).[40] In England the patents for his actions were acquired by Norman & Beard of Norwich (who had collaborated with him from time to time); they used Hope-Jones mechanisms successfully for some years after. In America Hope-Jones enjoyed a career as fast and confusing as that which he had just abandoned in Britain; his effect on American organ building was considerable. He eventually threw in his lot with Rudolph Wurlitzer, with whom he developed what was to become the cinema organ. He killed himself in 1914.[41]

   The sound of Hope-Jones's organs was novel and distinctive. Few commentators could separate themselves from the eulogists on the one hand or the vitriolic critics on the other. One such, however, visited the instrument Hope-Jones built at St George Hanover Square, London, and commented thoughtfully:[42]

. . . a full organ quite without brightness and vivacity – indeed, after listening to one or two full voluntaries, the dull cloying tone is rather wearying.

Mechanically, there was no reason why the Hope-Jones mechanism should not eventually have been as reliable as any other non-mechanical action of the period.

[39] C. I. G. Stobie, 'The Organ of the Anglican Cathedral of St. John the Baptist, Newfoundland', *The Organ*, 53 (1973–4), 56–65   [40] Traditional
[41] F. Webb, 'Robert Hope-Jones in the United States', *The Organ*, 13 (1933–4), 152–60; O. Ochse, *The History of the Organ in the United States*, 334–8   [42] Letter from L. K. Boseley, *Musical Opinion*, 18 (1894–5), 763

Indeed, it continued to be made to his designs after his departure for America (in some instruments surviving in working order for sixty years or more) and was the basis for most later actions. The fact that his instruments developed a reputation for chronic unreliability during his lifetime is probably due to malicious gossip generated by his rivals and incompetent maintenance, perhaps exacerbated by hurried or inexpert assembly when the company was under severe pressures of time and finance, as well as by a handful of design faults which could easily have been rectified. Such was the level of criticism that in 1899 several of his customers felt impelled (apparently spontaneously) to write to the musical press in defence. From Blackheath: 'we have never had any trouble with the electric part of the instrument';[43] from Warwick: 'our organ has never so far failed or given trouble';[44] from Worcester itself: 'the organ itself has given no trouble whatever; indeed it requires less care than large organs constructed in the usual manner'.[45] That these instruments did indeed fall into decay after Hope-Jones's departure is not surprising considering the absence of their designer and the profound antagonism of those who were now charged with their care.

If the conservative organ building establishment had been shaken to the core by the events of the 1890s, it was nevertheless only a foretaste of what was to come. The golden age of Victorian prosperity was over; before long the major firms were all to be in serious difficulties. Waves of progressive organ building from the 1880s onwards presaged further change. Against this pattern the death of Father Willis in 1901 marks the end of an era.

---

[43] *Musical Opinion*, 23 (1899–90), 113–14   [44] Ibid., 101
[45] Letter from the Dean of Worcester, *Musical Opinion*, 22 (1898–9), 812

CHAPTER SIXTEEN

THE IMPERIAL ORGAN
1900–1939

Father Willis died early in 1901; he had maintained complete control of his company and had been active in it right up to his death. His last major work was for Lincoln Cathedral (1898): it demonstrated the Willis tubular pneumatic action in its most advanced form. It was not an innovative instrument, rather consolidating all Willis's previous success; indeed some of the former brilliancy was gone. The tendency to draw on a relatively small tonal palette was beginning to show. There was little difference, for example, between full Great and full Swell; the characteristic Gedacts and Harmonic Flutes now looked repetitive; fine though the Willis high-pressure reeds were, the gradual taming of mixtures over the last years of his life left the tutti reed-dominated.[1] Mechanically, the Willis organ was efficient and reliable, but cautious as far as console accessories were concerned. Willis had provided adjustable pistons at Hereford Cathedral in 1893, but remarked: 'I only did them to please Sinclair [the Organist], but the complication was terrible and nearly drove me silly. I will never do it again.'[2]

The opening of the Lincoln organ was attended with keen interest by F. J. Livesey, the organist of St Bees Priory, Cumberland, together with his young friend George Dixon: Willis had just been commissioned to build a new three-manual organ for St Bees. The Lincoln organ was relevant, for 'St. Bees . . . on a considerably reduced scale . . . is a replica of it.'[3] Dixon was indeed a great fan of Willis's work: 'being on very friendly terms with Henry Willis, I visited the Rotunda Works frequently'.[4]

Dixon had shown a lively interest in tonal design as a teenager, contributing, from about 1889, to the extensive correspondence on organ matters conducted in the pages of the *Musical Standard* and *Musical Opinion*. His admiration for Willis was plain, as was his distaste for the organs of Hill. As an undergraduate at Cambridge he came to know well the Hill instruments at Trinity, St John's and King's Colleges, and he made his contempt for them clear in the clearest terms.[5] When the Hope-Jones rebuild at Worcester Cathedral was in the offing, he again stated his dislike of

---

[1] G. Dixon, 'The Tonal Structure of The Organ', *The Organ*, 1 (1921–2), 129–39, 215–26; L. Elvin, 'The Organ in Lincoln Cathedral', *The Organ*, 23 (1943–4), 49–59   [2] Letter from G. Dixon, *The Organ*, 10 (1930–1), 190
[3] Note contributed by G. Dixon in Elvin, 'The Organ in Lincoln Cathedral', 49–59   [4] Ibid., 49–59
[5] Letters from G. Dixon, *Musical Opinion*, 16 (1892–3) 457, 525

Plate 68 The organ in St Mary Redcliffe, Bristol, built by Harrison & Harrison in 1911. The use of electro-pneumatic action has now freed the organ builder to dispose the different parts of the organ exactly as he wishes. In this view of 1933, taken from the south side of the crossing looking north east into the chancel, the console can be seen adjacent to the choir stalls. On the north side of the chancel stands the Great Organ, with a large Swell division housed behind in a chamber formed between the north transept and the north choir aisle. On the south side of the chancel stand the Choir and Solo divisions and the Tuba. The Pedal stops are divided between all three sections. There is now no attempt to provide casework or indeed to find an architecturally satisfactory place for the organ: it is designed to flood the church with sound from an unidentifiable source. The organ was damaged during the Second World War but remains today in a state close to the original.

the Hill sound: 'I never had the pleasure of hearing the Worcester organs [both by Hill], but I have heard a great many instruments by the same builders. My experience has been that, however excellent the softer flue-work was, the louder combinations were spoilt by the poor and uneven quality of the reeds and the rather harsh tone of the mutation and mixture work. Moreover, the reeds were too coarsely toned to be used alone.'[6] Such outspoken criticism is remarkable (especially today, when the work of Hill is particularly admired), and perhaps illustrates the vein of antagonism towards the more conservative builders that allowed their progressive competitors a foothold in the 1890s. For Dixon was by no means alone in his views: that *doyen* of English musicology, J. S. Bumpus, wrote of the Hill in Westminster Abbey that it was 'coarse and unsatisfactory beyond expression'.[7] It is interesting to

[6] Letter from G. Dixon, *Musical Opinion*, 20 (1896–7), 94   [7] *Musical Standard*, 40 (1890), 33

see how Willis, from his beginnings as an impudent young upstart, had risen to become the *ne plus ultra* of cathedral organ builders, quite overtaking Hill's position.

Dixon took an active interest in the design of the St Bees organ, and was also involved in the alterations made in 1901 to the Hill organ at St John's College, Cambridge by Norman & Beard of Norwich.[8] He became involved in further schemes for new organs and rebuilds. Though he was not alone in providing comment on the progress and future of organ building – G. A. Audsley and N. A. Bonavia-Hunt were far more prolific as writers – circumstances conspired to make him the most influential organ consultant of his generation. His schemes were practical and realistic. Audsley's perfectionism led him down a path of organ design that was eccentric and had no imitators, despite his extensive writings;[9] Bonavia-Hunt spent much of his life in search of the ideal Open Diapason, and one cannot help feeling a little uneasy at his attempts to tackle wider issues of tonal architecture, ensemble and blend. His own opinion of his skill as a voicer is poorly supported by the instruments that passed through his hands. Both these authors were perhaps more influential in America than they were at home.

The first new instrument with which Dixon was involved was to be of enormous significance, launching the most successful phase of activity of the company who built it. Dixon had approached Willis in 1901, asking for a quotation for a new organ for St Nicholas, Whitehaven. The specification already shows some unusual features. In a three-manual organ, the third manual is a combined Choir and Solo Organ. There are no great reeds, their place being taken by the high-pressure reeds 8 and 4 on the Solo. The Pedal Organ consists of only three independent ranks, an Open Wood, a Bourdon and a Trombone, extended to various pitches, and backed up by the duplexing of the Great Double Open Diapason 16. The Great and Swell mixtures are different from each other, that on the Great containing a tierce, that on the Swell having only unisons and quints.[10] However, the contract for the Whitehaven organ went not to Willis, but to the less well-known firm of Harrison & Harrison, based in Durham, who completed it in 1904 (p. 301).[11] Dixon's scheme, of remarkable originality, was to set the tone for organ building for the next forty years. Executed with assiduous care and finesse by Harry and Arthur Harrison, it was to make their organs the instruments of choice for a whole generation of organists.

Dixon wrote extensively about his views on tonal design,[12] and it is not difficult to detect the influences on his thinking. First, the assumption that the Willis recipe is the essential foundation of the organ, both in distribution of resources and in such details as the use of high pressures for the chorus reeds. Secondly, the assumption that this recipe can be improved, especially in variety, by the adoption of a much wider range

[8] R. Whitworth, 'Lt. Col. George Dixon, T.D., M.A.', *The Organ*, 31 (1951–2), 67–74
[9] R. Huby, 'The Versatility of George Ashdown Audsley Ll.D. (1838–1925)', *BIOS Journal*, 10 (1986), 112–13
[10] H. Willis & Sons Ltd, Specification Book 10, 643
[11] F. J. Arnold, 'The Organ in St. Nicholas' Church Whitehaven', *The Organ*, 12 (1932–3), 25–8, 128; R. Whitworth, 'The Organ in St. Nicholas' Church Whitehaven', *The Organ*, 21 (1941–2), 149–56; leaflet issued by Harrison & Harrison c1905
[12] Dixon, 'The Tonal Structure of The Organ'; C. Clutton and G. Dixon, *The Organ, Its Tonal Structure and Registration* (London 1950)

Whitehaven, St Nicholas: Harrison & Harrison 1904

Manual I: Great & Choir Organ		Manual II: Swell Organ	
Quintatön (from c)	32	Lieblich Bordun (wood bass)	16
Contra Geigen	16	Open Diapason	8
Double Claribel (wood)	16	Gedeckt (wood bass)	8
Large Open Diapason	8	Echo Gamba	8
Small Open Diapason	8	Vox Angelica (tuned flat)	8
Geigen	8	Octave Gamba	4
Wald flöte (wood)	8	Lieblich flöte	4
Rohr flöte (wood bass)	8	Gemshorn	2
Stopped Quint	5⅓	Mixture	III
Octave	4	Double Trumpet	16
Geigen Principal	4	Cornopean	8
Hohl flöte (wood, triangular)	4	Oboe	8
Octave quint	2⅔	Cor Anglais	8
Superoctave	2	Clarion	4
Harmonic piccolo	2	Tremulant	
Harmonics (with tierce & septième)	IV		

Swell to Great
Solo to Great

Manual III: Solo & Bombarde Organ
(enclosed)

Pedal Organ			
Major Bass (wood, C–E harmonic)	32	Contra Viola	16
Open Wood (ext. 32′)	16	Flûte harmonique (wood bass)	8
Violone (Great Organ)	16	Viole d'Orchestre	8
Subbass (wood)	16	Violes célestes	8
Octave (ext. Open Wood)	8	Concert flute	4
Violoncello	8	Corno di Bassetto	8
Flute (ext. Subbass)	8	Tremulant	
Ophicleide	16	Solo Octave	
Tromba (ext. Ophicleide)	8	Swell to Solo	

Great to Pedal
Swell to Pedal
Solo to Pedal

Tuba harmonic (unenclosed)   8
Octave Tuba (unenclosed)   4
Tubas to Great

Accessories

6 thumb pistons to Great Organ
5 thumb pistons to Swell Organ
4 thumb pistons to Solo Organ
6 combination pedals to Pedal Organ
1 reversible thumb piston Great to Pedal
1 stop knob Pedal and Accompaniment to Solo Pistons
1 stop knob Great & Pedal Pistons coupled
1 stop knob Pedal and accompaniment to Swell pistons
Balanced swell pedals to Swell and Solo

Wind Pressures

Action & Pedal reeds: 279mm; Tubas: 254mm; Swell trumpets 16′, 8′ & 4′: 178mm, remainder 102mm; Solo Organ & Pedal Violoncello: 140mm (146mm according to Whitworth); Great Organ and rest of Pedal Organ: 76mm (89mm according to Whitworth) & 95mm of tone colours in the flue and reed-work (derived eclectically from Lewis, Hope-Jones, Michell & Thynne, Casson and others) and by giving each department a specific tonal characteristic. Thirdly, and again 'improving' on the Willis bench-mark, re-establishing the primacy of the flue-work in the ensemble by ensuring a very complete Great chorus and restoring some mutations and upperwork. Fourthly, providing some of the flexibility of console control suggested by the work of Casson or Hope-Jones, but relying on simple-to-use devices and the provision of an adequate number of pistons in a convenient and comfortable layout. Fifthly, making the maximum economical use of the resources available, avoiding any duplications of tone and allowing some extension and borrowing on the Pedal Organ. Dixon was quite open about the debts he owed to various pioneers: to Schulze, for the extended Great chorus built on a 32′ foundation; to Lewis, for the idea of a 'floating' reed division; to Casson for the introduction of 'scientific' mixtures (including not just the tierce, but also the next harmonic in the series, the septième), to Hope-Jones for the adoption of certain ultra-smooth diapasons and reeds, to Thynne and Hope-Jones's voicer J. W. Whiteley for the new keen orchestral string tone; to Casson again for certain ideas about stop control, and the idea of manual departments with more than one function.

Harrison & Harrison had built an organ that fulfilled many of the hopes and expectations of the progressive builders of the 1880s and 1890s. They were by no means alone in their success. In 1907 Dixon became involved with a scheme for another new organ in Whitehaven, that at St James's Church. This was completed by Norman & Beard of Norwich in 1909. A smaller organ than that at St Nicholas, it showed the *multum-in-parvo* thinking that Dixon had surely derived from Carlton Michell, together with a modern approach to tone-production and balance.[13] At Norman & Beard the guiding hand at this time was Herbert Norman, who presided over one of the finest organ factories in the world at Norwich. Like Harrisons', this provincial firm had grown from simple beginnings, in this case to become a giant amongst its contemporaries. Norman & Beard boasted 300 employees, their own railway siding, and a telephone. In 1899 they had landed the contract for the new organ at Norwich Cathedral; they were extensively involved with the various enterprises of Robert Hope-Jones, and wished to continue the remarkable growth that had marked the firm since its start in 1868.[14] Herbert Norman's tonal style was similar to Dixon's, and perhaps influenced by it. The same concerns with variety and colour are evident, together with many of the same individual debts to the progressive builders of the previous generation. The Norman & Beard organ of 1908 for Winchester College Chapel (p. 303) had an especially up-to-date feel, not least because of its electro-pneumatic action (on the Hope-Jones system, to which Norman & Beard held the rights, but here using pneumatics for the couplers, derivations and combination action).[15]

---

[13] G. Dixon, 'Modern Organ Design', *The Organ*, 9 (1929–30), 69–71; R. Whitworth, 'The Organ in St. James Whitehaven', *The Organ*, 21 (1941–2), 102–8
[14] H. Norman, 'The Normans 1860–1920', *BIOS Journal*, 10 (1986), 53–61
[15] E. T. Sweeting, 'The Organs of Winchester College Chapel', *The Organ*, 4 (1924–5), 211–20

Winchester College Chapel: Norman Bros. & Beard Ltd 1908

Great Organ

Double Diapason (wood)	16
Open Diapason	8
Geigen Diapason	8
Stopped Diapason (wood)	8
Corno Flute	8
Octave	4
Spitzflöte (harmonic)	4
Twelfth	$2^{2}/_{3}$
Fifteenth	2
Mixture	IV
Harmonic Tromba	8
Harmonic Clarion	4
Swell to Great	
Choir to Great	
Choir suboctave to Great	

Choir Organ (enclosed)

Section I:

Echo Diapason	8
Aeoline	8
Viole d'orchestre	8
Viole céleste	8

Section II:

Hohl flöte	8
Harmonic claribel	4
Lieblich piccolo	2
Corno di Bassetto	8
Orchestral Oboe	8
Tremulant	
Octave	
Sub octave I	
Sub octave II	
Unison of	
Swell to Choir	

Swell Organ

Violone	16
Open Diapason	8
Violoncello	8
Lieblich Gedeckt (wood bass)	8
Echo Salicional	8
Vox Angelica	8
Geigen Principal	4
Nason flute (wood)	4
Harmonic Gemshorn	2
Viole Mixture	III
Contra Hautboy	16
Horn	8
Oboe	8
Tremulant	
Octave	
Suboctave	
Unison Off	

Pedal Organ

Sub bourdon (wood)	32
Open Diapason (wood)	16
Open Diapason (metal)	16
Bourdon (ext. 32')	16
Violone (from Swell)	16
Flute (ext. Bourdon 16')	8
Trombone	16
Tromba	8
Great to Pedal	
Swell to Pedal	
Choir to Pedal	

Accessories

5 pistons to Great Organ
5 pistons to Swell Organ
5 pistons to Choir Organ
Piston acting on Great to Pedal
Piston acting on Swell to Great
5 composition pedals to Pedal (which could be
    connected to Great or Swell pistons)
Pedal acting on Great to Pedal
Balanced swell pedals to Swell and Choir

► *Plate 69*   The organ in the chapel of Winchester College, built by Norman & Beard of Norwich in 1908–10. This view of c1920 is taken from the organ console, situated on a gallery at the other end of the building. The detached console is one of the new possibilities offered at this time by the widespread introduction of electro-pneumatic action. The organ stands on a reinforced concrete platform across the west end of the mediaeval chapel, with wind supplied by an electric rotary fan blower housed in a shed on the roof of the adjacent chantry. The exceptionally good case is by W. D. Caroë. The organ was rebuilt on several occasions and was replaced by a new organ in the old case in 1983.

The organ stood on the west gallery of the chapel, with the console (of conventional drawstop type) on a gallery over the choir stalls about 28 metres away. The Great Organ Trombas, on 203mm pressure, were enclosed in the Choir box and were playable independently from that manual by means of duplicate stop-knobs. They were also carried down an extra octave for use with the choir suboctave coupler. The Pedal Trombone and Tromba were also enclosed in the Choir box. Several stops were of unusual construction unique to Norman & Beard, notably the Corno Flute, harmonic Spitzflöte and Harmonic Claribel. There was also wide use of diapasons with inverted languids and leathered lips, both Hope-Jones innovations adopted by Herbert Norman.[16]

Harrison & Harrison and Norman & Beard enjoyed their success in the early years of the century and built on it; it gradually became clear that they were doing so at the expense of the established firms: Hill, Lewis and especially Willis. The fame of the Willis firm was such that it might well have been expected to continue with almost as much success as before, despite the death of the founder. Surely a Willis organ was still the benchmark of English cathedral sound?

In fact the prestigious new contracts escaped to other firms. At Peterborough Cathedral in 1894 the organist, Haydn Keeton, was keen on Hope-Jones, but the donor specified Hill.[17] At Southwark Cathedral in 1897 the organ was built by Lewis: the donors, the Courage family, had a controlling interest in the firm.[18] At Norwich Cathedral in 1899 the new organ was by Norman & Beard, the local firm.[19] The Willis organ at Lincoln opened in 1898, to a mixed reception, as has been seen. It was followed by a massive new organ for St Patrick's Cathedral, Dublin, completed by Henry Willis II in 1902.

Contemporary opinions of the Dublin organ are few, but the instrument itself survives. It is of towering stature and quality, but one can certainly see that it might have been seen to miss the opportunities offered by modern developments in tone. It relies for its power on extensive batteries of reeds on very high pressures: 16', 8', 8' and 4' on the Great; 16', 8', 8', and 4' on the Swell, Tubas 16', 8' and 4' on the Solo, and Ophicleides 32', 16' and 8' on the Pedal. Against this formidable array

[16] Author's examination of the organ before dismantling in 1983
[17] W. A Roberts, 'Peterborough Cathedral and its Organs', *The Organ*, 10 (1930–1), 1–10
[18] G. Benham, 'Interesting London Organs XXXII', *The Organ*, 12 (1932–3), 90–7
[19] G. Paget, 'The Organs of Norwich Cathedral', *The Organ*, 14 (1934–5), 67

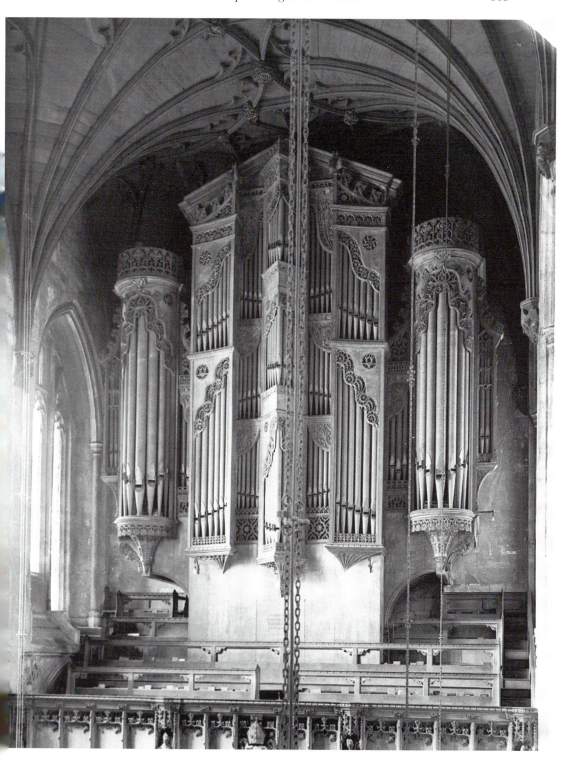

the flue-work has little chance to make its presence felt (particularly as the mixtures are by now rather tame) and, as all the reeds are of bright tuba-like tone, the charge of repetition is difficult to contest.[20]

In fact the Willis company was only to build two further landmark organs after Dublin, those at Liverpool Anglican Cathedral (opened in 1926 after protracted delays) and Westminster Roman Catholic Cathedral (installed in 1922, but not completed until 1932). As the century progressed J. W. Walker & Sons carried out major rebuilds at York Minster (1903), Bristol Cathedral (1907) and Rochester Cathedral (1905): they found themselves regarded, at last, as builders of the first rank. However, the self-appointed spokesmen of the new organ criticism felt they had not gone far enough. Of York Minster, James Wedgwood wrote: 'the whole instrument is very smooth and refined . . . but a little lacking in boldness and brilliancy'.[21] Dixon typically expressed his misgivings in even clearer terms: the organ was, admittedly 'vastly superior to the old one' (by Hill), but he found that it 'rather lacks brilliancy . . . I should have preferred the flue chorus work on Lewis lines, as I think the *ensemble* too flutey'. Walker pursued their own style of reed voicing at this time, using moderate pressures and less loading of the tongues than Willis, combined with rather eccentric-looking 'pepper pot' resonators capped with a wooden disc, below which was a row of circular holes to let the sound out. Dixon was unconvinced: 'the chorus reeds at York are ineffective, compared of course with the best modern standards'; they were also 'rather thin in tone, especially in the treble'. Dixon's final sally was against the stop-list of the organ: 'The instrument . . . literally teems with "vain repetition".'[22]

It was left to Harrison & Harrison to fulfil the Dixon ideals. They were invited to rebuild the Willis at Durham Cathedral; they completed the first phase of this work in 1905. Then, in quick succession, came a new organ for Belfast Cathedral, a rebuild at Carlisle Cathedral, a major rebuild at Ely Cathedral, a rebuild at Wells Cathedral, a number of important new instruments in London, and a large new organ for St Mary Redcliffe, Bristol. Their success was to continue unabated after the First World War.

Before looking at the style evolved by Harrison and Dixon in greater detail, it has to be asked how the Willis firm fell from grace: the death of Father Willis in 1901 cannot alone explain why potential customers (including Willis fans, such as Dixon himself) turned to less well-known companies for important new contracts. Indeed there were other reasons: at the opening of the twentieth century the Willis company was in serious difficulties. Father Willis died leaving personal debts estimated at £15,000 – a colossal sum at the time.[23] The estranged older son Vincent was appointed executor and trustee, and he and his younger brother Henry could

---

[20] R. A. D. Pope, 'The Organs of St. Patrick's Cathedral, Dublin', *The Organ*, 15 (1935–6), 201–8; Author's examination of the instrument
[21] J. I. Wedgwood, 'The New Organ in York Minster', *Musical Opinion*, 26 (1902–3), 693
[22] G. Dixon, 'The York Minster Organ', *Musical Opinion*, 27 (1903–4), 531
[23] Archive of Henry Willis & Sons Ltd., Letter from Henry Willis II to Kate Willis, 16 October 1913

not agree on how to proceed. It seems likely that Vincent wanted the firm wound up to clear the debts, and Henry II wanted to carry on. It took six years before the matter was settled.[24] It is certain that this unfortunate state of affairs became known to the public. Dixon was not the only organ enthusiast who was a friend of the family: it seems likely that Vincent Willis's circle of friends included Carlton Michell and Thomas Casson.[25] Furthermore, while the will was being contested no provision was made for Father Willis's widow, and a public fund had to be launched for her support.[26] We know that Dixon knew both Michell and Casson; it is quite possible that these three influential figures all had Vincent Willis's side of the story and were not inclined to be sympathetic to Henry Willis II, now running the family firm. Moreover, with the heavy burden of debt to be paid off, it was impossible for Willis to offer competitive prices, and he was substantially undercut by Hill, Harrison & Harrison and others. This problem is referred to in correspondence.[27] The Willis firm might well have recovered in due course, but for further difficulties. Henry Willis II began to crumble under the strain of events, and by 1910 or so it seems that he was prone to repeated breakdowns. He took his young son Henry III into partnership with him. Before long they were at loggerheads: a long and bitter war ensued, resulting in Henry II retiring on health grounds, and again their dispute almost certainly became public knowledge.[28] In 1908 and 1909 a series of warnings was published in *Musical Opinion*, almost certainly at the insistence of Henry Willis II, hinting darkly at comments being made in public and threatening legal action against any slanderous statements regarding the administration of the Willis firm or the quality of its product.

Dixon had become the country's leading commentator on organ matters and, as a man of independent means he was able to devote plenty of time to his hobby. The reasons why he might not be disposed to consult with the Willis company are now clearer. It remains to be asked why he favoured Harrison & Harrison so much, for there is every reason to suppose that, at the time of the two Whitehaven organs, Norman & Beard of Norwich were just as well able to build excellent organs in the new style. The reasons were partly to do with the rapport between the two north-country gentlemen, George Dixon and Arthur Harrison. Arthur Harrison was in charge of the tonal side of the firm's work, his brother Harry dealt with the mechanical side. Arthur was polite and deferential, and worked to extraordinarily high standards, especially obvious in his on-site finishing of new organs. It was not unknown for Arthur Harrison to stand at a vantage point in the church, individually adjusting the speech of pipes which were handed out of the organ to him by a relay of men forbidden to talk, cough, sneeze or be excused in any way for hours on end, and who had to wear cloth bags on their feet to muffle their

[24] T. Willis, 'Recollections of my Father' (undated and unpublished biographical note on the subject of Vincent Willis)   [25] Information kindly given by B. Q. S. F. Buchanan and J. A. McKenzie

[26] *Musical Opinion*, 26 (1902–3), 910; *Musical Opinion*, 27 (1903–4), 156

[27] Archive of Henry Willis & Sons Ltd, Letter from Henry Willis III to G. R. Sinclair 31 May 1916

[28] Information kindly provided by Henry Willis IV and from the archive of Henry Willis & Sons Ltd

foot-falls.[29] This spectacular (and expensive) perfectionism was fascinating to the customer, and may have made an interesting contrast with the more factory-like methods practiced at Norwich (Norman & Beard organs might be finished on site by any one of a number of local representatives).[30] In due course there came a further reason for Dixon to turn to Harrison rather than to Norman & Beard: at the start of the First World War it became impossible for Norman & Beard to run their factory in Norwich as the mostly young staff had gone to the front. They amalgamated with William Hill & Son of London, and the Norwich works closed. To Dixon, whose antagonism to Hill was well known, the idea of purchasing an organ from a factory run by Dr Arthur Hill was anathema.

This amalgamation is an indication not just of difficulties experienced in war time, but of the beginning of more serious decline. The reasons for Britain's failure to maintain its industrial leadership in the twentieth century are outside the scope of this book, but this author is not alone in tracing the seeds of change back to the time of the Great Exhibition in 1851: the rise and fall of Willis is perhaps an intriguing analogy of the process. The savage nature of the Depression became evident in the 1920s and 30s, but in organ building it may have been apparent by 1910 that the outlook was less rosy than it had been for many years. Was this one reason why Hope-Jones so frightened the established builders? By building thousands of organs of sterling quality the Victorian builders had flooded the market. The great period of new church building was over: indeed it is possible that many of the new churches so optimistically erected and so munificently endowed between 1850 and 1900 were never able to encourage congregations large enough to do more than keep them afloat. All the old cathedral and college organs had been replaced with modern examples; every public school speech-room and town hall had a recently erected instrument; the majority of parish churches contained an organ less than fifty years old. In a country with, perhaps, more organs per head of population than anywhere else in the world, was there actually any space for yet more instruments?

The amalgamation of up-to-date Norman & Beard with conservative Hill & Son may have been an unlikely match; it was shortly followed by another surprising marriage forced on the respective partners by unforeseen circumstances. The company run by T. C. Lewis was supported by the Courage family, of brewing fame, but by 1901 Lewis's extravagant manner of building organs had tested the Courage financial resources to the limit and the firm reformed as Lewis & Company, without the involvement of Lewis himself. Despite some successes, Lewis & Co. quickly became short of orders – their style could hardly be less fashionable in the early 1900s – and their magnificent factory in Brixton, designed by Bentley, the architect of Westminster Cathedral, was under-used. Meanwhile, in 1908 Willis had been ejected (by compulsory purchase by the London County Council) from the Rotunda Works in Camden Town, and had been forced to move to a small factory in lowly Homerton. In these cramped conditions it was scarcely possible to

---

[29] Information kindly provided by M. Venning and P. Hopps   [30] Information kindly provided by H. Norman

build an instrument on the scale of Liverpool Anglican Cathedral (discussions had started as early as 1905), and, like Norman & Beard, during the 1914–18 war Willis was short of staff. Negotiations between the two firms were under way by 1917, and by 1919 Willis had moved to Brixton (the company was known briefly as Henry Willis & Sons and Lewis & Company to satisfy a legal point, before becoming Henry Willis & Sons again).[31] Thus the two rivals finally combined in circumstances that neither Father Willis nor Thomas Lewis could possibly have envisaged.

While Walker smarted at Dixon's criticisms and Willis, Lewis, Hill and Norman & Beard moved towards amalgamation, Dixon and Harrison & Harrison established their bridgehead. At Ely Cathedral in 1908 a fully fledged version of their combined efforts, building on the success of Whitehaven, emerged to wide acclaim. The scheme (including some pipework from the previous Hill organ, but rearranged and re-voiced) was as shown below.[32]

Ely Cathedral: Harrison & Harrison 1908

Great Organ

Sub Bordun	32
Contra Clarabella (wood)	16
(bass from Pedal Subbass 16)	
Gross Geigen	16
Open Diapason I	8
Open Diapason II	8
(bass from Ped. Open Diap. 16′)	
Open Diapason III	8
Geigen	8
Hohl Flöte (wood)	8
Quint	5⅓
Octave	4
Geigen Principal	4
Wald Flöte (wood)	4
Octave Quint	2⅔
Super Octave	2
Harmonics (with tierce & septième)	V
Mixture	V
Trombone	16
Tromba	8
Octave Tromba	4
Reeds on Solo	
Swell to Great	
Choir to Great	
Solo to Great	

Swell Organ

Lieblich Bordun (wood)	16
Open Diapason	8
Lieblich Gedeckt (wood bass)	8
Echo Gamba	8
Vox Angelica (from c)	8
Principal	4
Lieblich Flöte (wood)	4
Fifteenth	2
Sesquialtera (with tierce)	V
Oboe	8
Vox Humana	8
Tremulant	
Double Trumpet	16
Trumpet	8
Horn	8
Horn Quint	5⅓
Clarion	4
Octave	

[31] Information kindly provided by Henry Willis IV from the archive of Henry Willis & Sons
[32] Leaflet issued by Harrison & Harrison c1908

Choir Organ (unenclosed)

Double Salicional	16
Open Diapason	8
Gedeckt (wood)	8
Salicional	8
Dulciana	8
Flauto Traverso	4
Salicet	4
Dulcet	2
Dulciana Mixture	III
Swell to Choir	
Solo to Choir	

Pedal Organ

Double Open Wood	32
Double Stopped Diapason (from Great)	32
Open Wood (bass from 32')	16
Open Diapason	16
Stopped Diapason (from Great 32')	16
Sub Bass	16
Violone (from Solo 16')	16
Salicional (from Choir 16')	16
Octave Wood (bass from 16')	8
Violoncello (from Solo 16')	8
Flute (from Sub Bass 16')	8
Bombardon	32
Ophicleide (from Bombardon 32')	16
Posaune (from Ophicleide 16')	8
Great to Pedal	
Swell to Pedal	
Choir to Pedal	
Solo to Pedal	

Solo Organ (enclosed)

Contra Viola	16
Viole d'Orchestre	8
Viole Céleste	8
Viole Octaviante	4
Cornet de Violes (with tierce)	III
Harmonic Flute	8
Concert Flute	4
Harmonic Piccolo	2
Clarinet	16
Orchestral Hautboy	8
Tremulant	
Tuba (unenclosed)	8
Octave	
Sub Octave	
Unison Off	
Swell to Solo	

Accessories

6 thumb pistons to Great Organ
1 adjustable thumb piston to Great Organ
5 thumb pistons to Swell Organ
1 adjustable thumb piston to Swell Organ
5 thumb pistons to Choir Organ
1 adjustable thumb piston to Choir Organ
6 thumb pistons to Solo Organ
1 adjustable thumb piston to Solo Organ
1 piston Clarinet 8', drawing Solo
    Clarinet 16', octave, unison off
7 combination pedals to Pedal Organ
1 adjustable combination pedal to Pedal
    Organ
1 reverser pedal Great to Pedal
1 reverser thumb piston Great to Pedal
1 reverser thumb piston Swell to Great
1 stop knob Great and Pedal
    Combinations Coupled
1 stop knob Pedal to Swell Pistons

Wind pressures

Pedal flues 64mm–152mm; reeds 508mm; Great flues 114mm; reeds 305mm; Swell flues 114mm; reeds 254mm; Choir 64mm; Solo flues and orchestral reeds 152mm; Tubas 508mm; Action 305mm

Key action tubular pneumatic (Great, Swell and part Pedal) and electro pneumatic (remainder)

The debts owed by Dixon to his predecessors are as plainly apparent as they were at Whitehaven, and he admitted these influences with good grace. In addition this scheme, the prototype for all Harrison organs up to the Second World War, and imitated by many other builders, shows the distinct character of each of the divisions of the organ.

The Great Organ comprises a massive Principal chorus, modelled in scope on Schulze's work at Doncaster, but made more foundational by the inclusion of the very latest in Diapason tone: the Open Diapason I, of prodigious scale and with leathered upper lips, was directly descended from the Hope-Jones Diapason Phonon. Dixon was concerned to restore to the organ the brilliant flue chorus that had declined under Father Willis and been omitted altogether by Hope-Jones. The Harmonics V was an attempt to provide a scientific solution to the 'problem' of mixtures: it included the tierce and the septième, giving it a reedy, even acid tone, and was continued for three and a half octaves before the first break. It was, in effect, a kind of Cornet, bridging the gap between the fluework and the arrival of the reeds. The Mixture V, on the other hand, contained only unisons and quints, and was inspired by the work of Schulze: indeed Dixon and Arthur Harrison (accompanied, interestingly enough, by Carlton Michell) made the pilgrimage to the Schulze at St Bartholomew, Armley, Leeds, during the planning stages.[33] The Trombas, of ultra-smooth tone and derived from the reeds of Hope-Jones, added further foundational weight to the tutti.

The Swell Organ was more than a foil to the Great, as its contrasting tones were a vital part of securing a smooth build-up to the power of full organ, and it can be assumed that in use the Swell-to-Great coupler was drawn much of the time. The Principal chorus is of a minor nature, the Swell relying for much of its effect on the brilliant Mixture and the chorus of reeds, which included the rare Horn Quint $5\frac{1}{3}$. The Swell reeds were considerably thinner and more fiery than the Great Trombas.

The Choir Organ was developed as a miniature Great Organ, following perhaps from Lewis at Southwark, but also owing something to the schemes of Carlton Michell. All the expressive and orchestral colour was moved to the enclosed Solo Organ, where the new Violes d'Orchestre were provided in a complete chorus, including a string-toned Mixture, and where the imitative flutes and woodwind found a natural home. The Tuba was now a commanding voice, no longer extending the tonality of the Great and Swell reeds as in the organs of Willis and Hill, but providing smooth and opaque tone at a level of power that made it audible in single notes through full organ.

On the Pedal Organ there were only four independent ranks: Open Wood, Open Diapason, Sub Bass, and Ophicleide. These were extended to various pitches and supplemented by basses borrowed from other divisions. The Open Wood and Ophicleide ranks were characterised by great weight and smoothness, under-

---

[33] L. Elvin, *The Harrison Story* (Lincoln 1973), 113

pinning the massive Diapasons and Trombas of the Great Organ. Sufficiently flexible and expressive basses for lighter combinations were provided by the duplexing of manual stops. By now there was no desire to provide the Pedal division with an independent chorus of metal principals.

Dixon and Harrison had established a particularly comfortable and easily understood console layout at Whitehaven, and this became standard. Traditional stopknobs were used (rather than the Hope-Jones stop-keys), mounted on angled jambs. Each department was arranged in a double column, with the foundation at the bottom and the reeds at the top, an arrangement common to many English builders. Acting on a suggestion first made by Casson, the couplers were grouped respectively with the stops of the department they augmented, rather than being massed together in one place. The stop-knobs themselves were of solid ivory, mounted on ebonised panels, and the key coverings were of thick ivory with no surface joints. This was a Rolls-Royce amongst organs.

The Harrison and Dixon collaboration was highly influential. A new instrument at St Mary Redcliffe, Bristol (1911), consolidated their position, and introduced a number of Pedal stops enclosed in the Swell box (similar to Norman & Beard's Winchester College organ of 1908) (see plate 68, p. 299). Henry Willis III wrote wistfully to W. J. Ridley, the author of the scheme for Liverpool Anglican Cathedral, stating frankly his admiration of the Redcliffe organ and hoping that they could provide some enclosed Pedal stops in the Liverpool scheme.[34] At about the same time Dixon became involved in the scheme for a still larger organ at St Paul, Toronto, Canada, to be built by the local firm of Casavant. He specified which voicers should be involved, and the names are a kind of roll-call of the influences on Dixon's thinking. The big reeds on the Pedal, Swell and Solo were to be voiced by Frank Wesson, who had trained with Vincent Willis. The Trombas and Tubas were the work of W. C. Jones, the Hope-Jones reed voicer who had introduced the smooth reed to Harrisons. The Great chorus was in the hands of Carlton Michell, descended from the Lewis tradition. One of the Casavants spent some time in Europe and studied English methods. The finished organ was visited by the blind organist Alfred Hollins, and it greatly influenced his scheme for the large Norman & Beard organ of 1916 at Johannesburg Town Hall, South Africa (the last organ to be built at the Norwich works).[35]

The First World War marked the end of this supremely confident period, and in the years that followed organ builders faced practical and economic difficulties of a new kind. Henry Willis and Sons, already in the midst of turmoil, were struggling with the Leviathan instrument for Liverpool Anglican Cathedral.

The Liverpool organ was the gift of Mrs James Barrow; the stop-list originated with her nephew W. J. Ridley, a banker and organ enthusiast. The decision to give the contract to Willis reflects the fact that planning of the stupendous new building

---

[34] Archive of Henry Willis & Sons, letter from Henry Willis III to W. J. Ridley 11 July 1912
[35] Letter from C. Clutton, *The Organ*, 30 (1950–1), 53

had started before 1900, and illustrates the money-no-object atmosphere that permeated the whole project. The Willis firm was consulted at least as early as 1905;[36] a contract was signed in June 1912 and work began. The planning and construction of this vast organ, originally intended to have 168 speaking stops, took place at exactly the period when Henry Willis II and Henry Willis III were struggling for control of the firm; as a result it is scarcely possible to tell how much credit should be given to which Willis, or indeed to Ridley. Henry II was initially sceptical about aspects of Ridley's scheme,[37] but in the end Henry III and Ridley seem to have reached agreement on many points. To Henry III we probably owe the greater development of the flue choruses and especially the Mixtures. Isolated from the Michell-Casson-Dixon sphere of influence, the Willis company struggled to adapt to emerging new thinking. Henry III gradually assumed control of tonal matters, and by 1915 he had started work on voicing. Ridley was clearly coming forward with suggestions for techniques of which Willis had no experience: Mixtures with carefully graduated breaks[38] (Father Willis's mixtures usually broke by a whole octave at each break); wide mouths for some of the Open Diapasons (Father Willis used narrow mouths throughout). On this last point the enthusiast Noel Bonavia-Hunt was consulted: there were originally to be no less than six Open Diapasons on the Great Organ, and making them sufficiently different from each other would be something of a test.[39] Henry III was well aware of the strides being made by Harrison & Harrison, as noted above; indeed his unexecuted scheme for Johannesburg Town Hall included many Harrison-like features.[40] As work proceeded, further changes were made. A Stentor Diapason had been proposed for the Solo Organ: experiments led Henry III to the conclusion that it was impossible to produce true diapason tone of great power – the results were too fluty.[41] This stop was replaced by a Grand Chorus of ten ranks – a complete organ available on one stop-knob. The organ gradually emerged to its final scheme (p. 315).[42]

[36] Archive of Henry Willis & Sons, Specification book 11, 228–34
[37] Archive of Henry Willis & Sons, Specification book 12, 172 and following
[38] Archive of Henry Willis & Sons, correspondence between Henry Willis III and W. J. Ridley, 19 December 1916
[39] Archive of Henry Willis & Sons, correspondence between Henry Willis III and W. J. Ridley, 15 December 1915, 1 March 1916   [40] Archive of Henry Willis & Sons, Specification book 12, 371
[41] Archive of Henry Willis & Sons, letter from Henry Willis III to W. J. Ridley 29 November 1916
[42] *Liverpool Cathedral, The Organ* (London 1926; reprinted 1937)

Plate 70   The Anglican Cathedral, Liverpool, seen at about the time of the installation of the organ by Henry Willis & Sons Ltd in the 1920s (note that the case on the south side of the chancel is still without any front pipes). The cases are by Giles Gilbert Scott, the architect of the cathedral. The organ is housed in two large chambers on either side of the chancel with cases facing inwards and into the transepts; the console is visible in the gallery on the north side. There was originally preparation for a remote Echo Organ, and in 1940 plans existed for further sections in the tower (Corona Organ), at the west end and in the central space under the crossing. The Corona Organ and west end section were under construction in 1939 but were destroyed with Willis's London factory in 1941. None of these additional sections has been installed.

Liverpool Anglican Cathedral: Henry Willis & Sons Ltd 1912–26

Compass: Manuals C–c'''' (61 notes), Pedals C–g' (32 notes)

Great Organ		**Swell Organ**	
Contra Violone	32	Contra Geigen	16
Double Open Diapason	16	Contra Salicional	16
Contra Tibia (wood)	16	Lieblich Bordun (wood bass)	16
Bourdon (wood)	16	Open Diapason	8
Double Quint (wood)	$10^{2}/_{3}$	Geigen	8
Open Diapason No. 1	8	Tibia (wood)	8
Open Diapason No. 2	8	Flauto Traverso	8
Open Diapason No. 3	8	Wald Flöte (wood)	8
Open Diapason No. 4	8	Lieblich Gedackt	8
Open Diapason No. 5	8	Echo Viola	8
Tibia (wood)	8	Salicional	8
Doppel Flöte (wood)	8	Vox Angelica (from F)	8
Stopped Diapason (wood)	8	Octave	4
Quint	$5^{1}/_{3}$	Octave Geigen	4
Octave No. 1	4	Salicet	4
Octave No. 2	4	Lieblich Flöte	4
Principal	4	Nazard	$2^{2}/_{3}$
Flûte Harmonique	4	Fifteenth	2
Flûte Couverte	4	Seventeenth	$1^{3}/_{5}$
Tenth	$3^{1}/_{5}$	Sesquialtera (with tierce)	V
Twelfth	$2^{2}/_{3}$	Mixture	V
Super Octave	2	Double Trumpet	16
Fifteenth	2	Waldhorn	16
Mixture (with tierce & septième)	V	Contra Hautboy	16
Fourniture (with tierce)	V	Trompette Harmonique	8
Double Trumpet	16	Trumpet	8
Trompette Harmonique	8	Cornopean	8
Trumpet	8	Hautboy	8
Clarion	4	Krummhorn	8
		Octave Trumpet	4
		Clarion	4

Choir Organ		**Solo Organ**	
Unenclosed:		Unenclosed:	
Contra Dulciana	16	Contra Hohl Flöte (wood)	16
Open Diapason	8	Hohl Flöte (wood)	8
Rohr Flöte	8	Octave Hohl Flöte	4
Dulciana	8	Enclosed:	
Flûte Ouverte	4	Contra Viole	16
Dulcet	4	Viole de Gambe	8
Dulcina	2	Viole d'Orchestre	8
Enclosed:		Violes Célestes (from F)	8
Contra Viola	16	Flûte Harmonique	8
Violin Diapason	8	Octave Viole	4
Viola	8	Concert Flute	4
Claribel Flute (wood)	8	Violette	2
Unda Maris (wood, from F)	8	Piccolo Harmonique	2
Octave Viola	4	Cornet de Violes (with tierce)	III
Suabe Flöte (wood)	4	Contra Tromba	16
Lieblich Piccolo	2	Cor Anglais	16
Dulciana Mixture (with tierce)	V	Tromba Réal	8
Bass Clarinet	16	Tromba	8
Baryton	16	French Horn	8
Trumpet	8	Clarinet (orchestral)	8
Corno di Bassetto	8	Oboe (orchestral)	8
Cor Anglais	8	Bassoon (orchestral)	8
Vox Humana	8	Tromba Clarion	4
Clarion	4		

Pedal Organ

Unenclosed:

Resultant Bass	64
(bass harmonic, rest from Op. Bass 32′)	
Double Open Bass (wood)	32
Double Open Diapason	32
Contra Violone (from Great)	32
Double Quint (wood)	21⅓
Open Bass No. 1 (bass from 32′)	16
Open Bass No. 2 (wood)	16
Tibia (from Great)	16
Open Diapason	16
Contra Basso	16
Dolce	16
Bourdon (wood)	16
Quint (bass from 21⅓′)	10⅔
Octave (bass from Op. Bass I)	8
Principal (bass from Op. Diap.)	8
Stopped Flute (bass from Bourd.)	8
Twelfth (bass from Quint)	5⅓
Fifteenth (bass from Principal)	4
Mixture (with tierce)	III
Fourniture	V
Contre Bombarde	32
Bombarde (from Ctre. Bomb.)	16
Ophicleide	16
Bombarde (from 16′)	8
Clarion	8
Bombarde (from 8′)	4

Enclosed:

Geigen	16
Violon	16
Violoncello	8
Open Flute (wood)	8
Flûte Triangulaire (wood)	4
Contra Trombone	32
Trombone	16
Fagotto	16
Octave Bassoon	8

Bombarde Organ

Grand Chorus	X
Contra Tuba	16
Tuba Magna	8
Tuba	8
Tuba Clarion	4

Echo Organ (enclosed) (never installed)

Quintaton	16
Echo Diapason	8
Cor de Nuit	8
Flauto Amabile (wood)	8
Muted Viole	8
Aeoline Céleste (from F)	8
Célestina (wood)	4
Fern Flöte	4
Rohr Nasat	2⅔
Flautina	2
Harmonica Aetheria (with tierce)	III
Chalumeau	16
Trompette	8
Cor Harmonique	8
Musette	8
Hautbois d'Amour	8
Voix Humaine	8
Hautbois Octaviante	4
Carillon (gongs, from c)	8

Echo Pedal (enclosed in Echo box)

Salicional (wood)	16
Echo Bass (wood)	16
Fugara	8
Dulzian	16

(The Bombarde & Echo organs were to be playable from the fifth manual)

Couplers etc.

Swell to Great

Choir to Great

Solo to Great

Bombarde to Great

Echo to Great

Solo Trombas on Great

Grand Chorus on Great

Choir Octave

Choir suboctave

Choir unison off

Swell to Choir

Solo to Choir

Echo to Choir

Tremulant to Choir

Great to Pedal

Swell to Pedal

Choir to Pedal

Solo to Pedal

Solo, tenor solo to Pedal

Bombarde and Echo to Pedal

Great pistons to Pedal pistons

Pedal box on Swell pedal

Pedal box on Solo pedal

Pedal box on Choir pedal

Swell octave

Swell suboctave

Swell unison off

Solo to Swell

Echo to Swell

Tremulant to Swell (127mm wind)

Tremulant to Swell (178mm wind)

Solo octave

Solo suboctave

Solo unison off

Echo to Solo

Tremulant to Solo

Bombarde 'on'

Echo 'on'

Echo octave

Echo suboctave

Echo unison off

Tremulant to Echo

Great adjustable piston lock

Swell adjustable piston lock

Choir adjustable piston lock

Solo adjustable piston lock

Echo adjustable piston lock

Pedal adjustable piston lock

Accessories

Great (in keyslip):

9 pistons to Great Organ, adjustable at switchboard

1 instantly adjustable piston (with locking knob), operating on the stops of the Great Organ, the Solo Trombas, Solo Trombas on Great, the Bombarde Grand Chorus, and Grand Chorus on Great

6 reversible pistons to Great to Pedal, Swell to Great, Choir to Great, Solo to Great, Bombarde to Great and Solo Trombas on Great

Swell (in keyslip):

9 pistons to Swell Organ, adjustable at switchboard

1 instantly adjustable piston (with locking knob)

3 reversible pistons to Swell to Pedal, Echo to Swell, Solo to Swell

Choir (in keyslip):

9 pistons to Choir Organ, adjustable at switchboard

1 instantly adjustable piston (with locking knob)

5 reversible pistons to Choir to Pedal, Bombarde to Choir, Echo to Choir, Solo to Choir and Swell to Choir

Solo (in keyslip):
9 pistons to Solo Organ, adjustable at switchboard
1 instantly adjustable piston (with locking knob)
2 reversible pistons to Solo to Pedal and Echo to Solo

Bombarde and Echo (in keyslip):
4 pistons to Bombarde Organ
9 pistons to Echo Organ, adjustable at switchboard
1 instantly adjustable piston to Echo (with locking knob)
1 reversible piston to Bombarde and Echo to Pedal

9 pistons (3 each in tops of Choir, Great and Swell bass key-frames) giving Great and Pedal combinations 1–9, duplicated in the treble frames
5 adjustable pistons in fronts of bass key-frames giving special combinations on manuals, pedals and couplers, duplicated in the treble frames

Pedal pistons etc.:
9 pedal pistons to Pedal Organ, adjustable at switchboard
1 instantly adjustable pedal piston (with locking knob)
3 reversible pedals duplicating reversible pistons to Great to Pedal, Bombarde to Pedal and Bombarde to Great
10 pedal pistons duplicating Swell pistons, actuating in addition suitable pedal combinations separately adjustable at a special switchboard, and independent of the normal Pedal combinations
4 reversible pedals to Swell, Choir, Solo and Echo Tremulants
1 reversible pedal to Great & Pedal Combinations Coupled
2 pedals (crescendo and diminuendo respectively) acting on the stops of the Great & Pedal Organs simultaneously
Balanced swell pedals to Swell, Choir, Solo, Echo and Pedal boxes

Wind pressures
Great flues: mostly 127mm; 32′: 152mm; heavy Diapasons 16′, 8′, 4′ & 2′: 254mm.
Great reeds: 381mm
Swell flues: 127mm
Swell Tibia, Hautboys, Krummhorn: 178mm
Swell Waldhorn, Cornopean, Clarion: 254mm
Swell Trumpets 16′, 8′, 8′ & 4′: 381mm
Choir mostly 102mm; Trumpet & Clarion 178mm
Solo mostly 254mm; Trombas 508mm
Bombarde Grand Chorus: 254mm; Tubas: 762mm; Tuba Magna: 1270mm (sic)
Echo mostly 89mm; Chalumeau, Trompette, Cor Harmonique & Pedal Dulzian: 178mm

Extensive delays in the building of the cathedral meant that this organ, conceived before the First World War and mostly finished and in storage by 1916, was not heard until 1926. Meanwhile Henry Willis III had no *chef-d'œuvre* to show the public. On taking over the Lewis company he inherited another vast organ, that for Westminster Roman Catholic Cathedral. With John Courage providing money and Bentley as the architect of the new Cathedral, Lewis & Company had been the obvious choice for the initial Apse organ in 1908. It is almost certain that Lewis was intended to build the large organ: T. C. Lewis himself had been discussing schemes for it with, of all people, Arthur Harrison, as early as 1902 or 1903.[43] By the time the building was ready, Willis was occupying the Lewis works in Brixton and it was he who built the organ. The contract was signed in 1920 and part of the organ was installed in 1922, however, it could not be heard in its entirety until 1932. John Courage's influence (he was friendly with players such as Guy Weitz, Louis Vierne, Marcel Dupré and Lynwood Farnham) accounts for the west end position and for certain aspects of the scheme that were seen as 'continental' at the time. Once these two great organs were ready, it was clear that Henry Willis III was offering a bold tonal outlook, yet more forceful than Harrison, and perhaps less refined. The Liverpool and Westminster organs are astonishing for their sheer power, and in the huge acoustic of the two vast buildings their dynamic range, their huge palette of colour and their sheer impact on the listener is unforgettable, even if the louder effects have to be used with great discretion if they are to be bearable.

By the time Liverpool and Westminster were finished, Harrison and Harrison had stolen Willis's position as the premier builder in the country, taking on a thorough rebuild and tonal alterations to Father Willis's organ in the Royal Albert Hall, working at York Minster, Gloucester Cathedral, and Worcester Cathedral, at many of the Oxford and Cambridge colleges, including Trinity and King's Colleges in Cambridge, and had built dozens of organs for churches and schools up and down the country. The King's College organ (1934) was particularly influential, setting an ideal for organ tone in choral accompaniment that is still highly regarded today. As a final triumph, they were asked to build a new organ for Westminster Abbey in time for the Coronation of King George VI in 1937. Sadly, Arthur Harrison died before it was finished.

Economic circumstances had by now made life very difficult for all organ builders. The First World War disrupted manufacture and caused a serious interruption in continuity of training and administration. It also introduced serious inflation: Willis was obliged to re-negotiate the contract at Liverpool and introduce extension in the Pedal Organ to cover his costs over the long period of the project. By the late twenties and early thirties the Depression was biting hard, and there was room for other builders to move in if they could offer lower prices. One example was Rushworth & Dreaper of Liverpool, a company established since the nineteenth century, who now took the advantage to offer well-made organs of the modern type at prices lower than the London firms. At Christ's Hospital School, Sussex in 1930 a new organ was needed. Willis quoted £8,540; Harrison & Harrison £8,500; Hill, Norman & Beard £7,280. Rushworth & Dreaper clinched the deal at £6,975, throwing an additional fifth manual into the scheme. Such contracts were few and far between in the 1930s: there were new organs for some concert halls and school or college chapels, but commissions in the Anglican church had suddenly become a rarity.

[43] Elvin, *The Harrison Story*, 130

At the same time a newcomer amongst the London builders was offering a quite different kind of instrument: John Compton emerged as the main proponent of the extension organ. The ideas of duplexing, extension and borrowing, described in the last chapter, were not new. For most builders they were used, as in the organs of Harrison, solely as a means of amplifying the resources of the Pedal Organ without the expense of many large bass pipes and their mechanism. Others used the system more widely: Brindley & Foster of Sheffield, perhaps in the wake of the Anneessens organs and experiments by Gern,[44] built many instruments on the 'Metechotic' system after 1890.[45] The use of sliderless soundboards, in which each pipe had its own valve, allowed flexible derivation of the pipework through pneumatic switch gear. Ranks could be duplexed on different manuals, or could appear twice over, at pitches an octave apart. Hope-Jones suggested much wider use of duplexing, with nearly all of the stops available on all of the manuals,[46] but it was not until after he left for America in 1903 that he began to put these ideas into practice.[47] Compton, who started his own company immediately after Hope-Jones's departure and inherited many of his ideals (he was supported, at least from 1912, by the wealthy J. Martin White, who seems also to have sponsored Michell & Thynne, Casson and Hope-Jones),[48] experimented further.[49] Lewis & Company tried extension on a much more thorough scale at St Matthias Richmond in 1911: from twenty-two ranks they extended an organ of no less than fifty-one speaking stops. As the key action was pneumatic, the switch gear required took up a prodigious amount of space and required 5 tonnes of pneumatic tubing.[50] The company never recovered from the experience.

Compton made little headway before the First World War, suffering perhaps from being associated with Hope-Jones's ideals and from the destruction by fire of his early magnum opus at Selby Abbey in 1906[51] and of his works in Nottingham in 1907.[52] After the First World War he took over the business and premises of August Gern, and from a base in West London he began to flex his muscles.

The first area of success was in his ability to understand electro-pneumatic key action with unusual clarity and to build it with great technical accomplishment. The established firms, perhaps still wary after the Hope-Jones *débâcle*, used no method that had not already been tested. Hill, Norman & Beard continued to use the Hope-Jones patents in a simplified form, and when they introduced an action with elec-

[44] *Musical Opinion*, 18 (1894–5), 154

[45] Announcements of new organs by Brindley & Foster in the 1890s in *The Musical Standard*, 39 (1889) and following

[46] Paper read by Hope-Jones to the College of Organists, 5 May 1891 in *The Musical Standard*, 40 (1890–1) 381, 400   [47] F. Webb, 'Robert Hope-Jones in the United States', *The Organ*, Vol. 13 (1933–4), 152–60

[48] L. Elvin, *Pipes and Actions* (Lincoln 1995), 49; G. L. Miller, *The Recent Revolution in Organ Building* (New York 1909); 2nd edn (1913), 52. I am grateful to R. Clark for this information.

[49] R. Illing, 'John Compton', *The Organ*, 37 (1957–8), 70–1; Extensive correspondence from John Compton in the pages of *Musical Opinion* from 1903 onwards; Reports of new Compton organs in the 'New Organs' Column of *Musical Opinion*, 1903 onwards

[50] J. Burns, 'The Organ at St. Matthias Richmond, Surrey', *The Organ*, 26 (1946–7), 114–21

[51] F. Stubbs, 'Selby Abbey and its Organs', *The Organ*, 14 (1934–5), 75–82   [52] Illing, 'John Compton'

tric switch gear in 1926 they used a system acquired from Farrand & Votey of Chicago.[53] Henry Willis III, perhaps lacking the technical inventiveness of his grandfather or his uncle Vincent, consulted with E. M. Skinner of Boston, and introduced the Skinner electro-pneumatic action and console design to England, together with Pitman-type sliderless soundboards (a Skinner invention) and certain Skinner tonalities (especially the French Horn, and the Erzähler, which Willis modified to produce his Sylvestrina). Compton was much more adventurous. Committed to the widespread use of extension, he used sliderless soundboards and an electro-pneumatic action of his own design, far more sophisticated than any made by his rivals.

Compton's use of extension was daring. From a core group of ranks he would extend stops at many pitches. For example, a soft Great Organ Diapason might be extended to provide various ranks of upperwork and a Pedal 16', as well as being duplexed for use on the Choir Organ. A Trumpet rank might appear as a chorus at 16', 8' and 4' pitches. The wholesale use of extension is open to serious criticism: the organ can be short of colour and in large chords there is a problem of 'missing notes': one or several notes can fall silent because the pipe or pipes in question are already sounding as part of the chorus sounded by another key. Compton tried to avoid this by selective use of the parent ranks, and in his larger instruments by the use of clever dodges. For example, in 1929 at St Luke Chelsea, where a three-manual organ of ninety-eight speaking stops was derived from 28 parent ranks, Compton made the following use of six of them:[54]

Rank	Great Organ					Choir Organ						
Open Diapason I		8'										
Open Diapason II	16'		4'				8'					
Open Diapason III		8'			2'			4'				
Violone	16'	8'					8'					
Salicional I		8'		2⅔'	2'	16'		4'			1⅓'	1'
Salicional II			4'				8'		2⅔'	2'		

The initial appeal of such a system was in situations where space and money were limited; small extension organs were the cheapest real pipe organs available, and between 1925 and 1970 thousands were made. Willis and Harrison & Harrison were amongst the few who would not allow their artistic integrity to be sullied by the indiscriminate use of extension. For Compton, the provision of organs in multi-purpose halls was also a source of work, leading in the later twenties and thirties to the building of cinema organs. An early large example stood in the Pavilion Theatre, Shepherd's Bush, London (1923)[55] and led to a contract for a new organ in the Liberal Jewish Synagogue, St John's Wood, London.[56] This latter instrument,

---

[53] Norman, 'The Normans 1860–1920'
[54] F. Burgess, 'The Organ in St. Luke's Church, Chelsea', *The Organ*, 14 (1934–5), 129–34; J. Compton, 'The Extension Organ', *The Organ*, 1 (1921–2), 89–95   [55] Elvin, *Pipes and Actions*, 61
[56] Elvin, *Pipes and Actions*, 56

though an extension organ, was executed on 'church' rather than 'theatre' lines, and Compton immediately became established as a serious player in the organ building world. His specialty remained instruments for secular use, and his cinema organs (a field in which he competed with Wurlitzer of America and with Hill, Norman & Beard, building under the Christie label) were especially successful, re-introducing many of the fearsome tonalities originally developed by Hope-Jones in a more successful form and, arguably, dedicated to more appropriate use.

However, the importance of Compton was far-reaching. He was the only builder whose style of manufacture was completely adapted to the use of electro-pneumatic action, and the mechanisms he invented and used show a quality of design and manufacture unmatched by his contemporaries. He introduced a characteristic 'luminous' console, in which stop-knobs were replaced by touch-sensitive discs which lit up when on (first used by Estey in America c1923).[57] This was useful in the organ for the BBC studios at Maida Vale, London (1936), where the noise of moving parts might be picked up by the microphones. In addition he provided pistons which were all instantly adjustable at the console: the entirely electro-mechanical system used is a model of ingenuity and engineering skill.[58] He was also prepared to explore the possibilities of organ tone more fully than any of his rivals in England (perhaps with an eye to certain developments in America). He perfected Hope-Jones's Diaphone, mainly for use in the cinema, developed the use of very high pressures to get round the problem of organs sited in awkward chambers (cinemas again) and used polyphonic bass pipes: some gave two notes from one pipe; the still more remarkable polyphonic cubes produced six notes in the $16'$ octave from an object the size and shape of a tea-chest.

In addition Compton developed his upperwork on a scale never seen in Britain before. The use of extension had plenty of critics, and much of their argument revolved around the inartistic use of extension for deriving a chorus with few pipes of its own. They also pointed out that, thanks to the vagaries of temperament, a quint-sounding stop could not be derived from a normal unison rank without being badly out of tune. Correspondence flared on this subject in the pages of *The Organ* in 1938–9;[59] Compton was elusive about how he achieved his effects, as well he might be. He had, from 1896 onwards, explored thoroughly the use of remote off-unison harmonics to generate synthetic tones or to give the illusion of bass pipes from what was, in effect, a Cornet; the harmonics used now included not just the tierce and septième, but the ninth, eleventh and thirteenth partials. An instrument at the Compton factory contained, by 1932, diapasons at the following pitches: $6\,^2\!/_5{}'$, $4\,^4\!/_7{}'$, $3\,^5\!/_9{}'$, $2\,^{10}\!/_{11}{}'$, $2\,^6\!/_{13}{}'$, and $2\,^2\!/_{15}{}'$.[60] Compton habitually covered up the true contents of his Mixture stops. It was daring enough to present the customer, so soon

---

[57] O. Ochse, *The History of the Organ in the United States* (Indiana 1975), 347
[58] Author's examination of the organ
[59] F. Burgess, 'The Organ at Southampton Guildhall', *The Organ*, 17 (1937–8), 1–10; correspondence in *The Organ*, 17 (1937–8), 125–6, 187–8, 254–5; 18 (1938–9), 60–1
[60] J. Compton, 'Towards a More Complete Diapason Chorus', *The Organ*, 29 (1949–50), 60–6

after the Hope-Jones period, with multi-rank stops labelled Plein Jeu VIII, Acuta III or Grand Cornet de Bombardes XII–XIV (Downside Abbey 1931);[61] patrons might have been still more surprised to learn that, during the site finishing, additional derived ranks were added to the chorus by altering the wiring in the electric switch stack. Some of the Compton mixtures had, in fact, yet more ranks than were advertised at the console.[62]

The organ at Downside Abbey (where, intriguingly, Casson had proposed an organ on his own semi-extension system as early as 1901) was Compton's masterpiece.[63] It was completed in 1931 to the synoptic scheme shown below, derived from thirty ranks.[64]

Downside Abbey: The John Compton Organ Company 1931

Parent ranks:

Great & Choir Organs (Chamber A)	Swell & Solo Organs (Chamber B)
Diapason I	Diapason
Diapason II	Violone
Diapason III	Geigen
Diapason IV	Strings
Salicional	Gamba
Dulciana	Harmonics
Tierce	Harmonic Flute
Gemshorn	Stopped Flute
Vox Angelica	Tuba
Celeste	Trumpet
Flauto Traverso	Horn
Hohl Flute	Hautboy
Gedeckt	Oboe
Diaphone	
Posaune	
Tromba	
Clarinet	

Pedal   32. 32. 16. 16. 16. 16. 16. 16. 16. 16. $10^2/_3$. 8. 8. 8. 8. 8. 8. $5^1/_3$. 4. 4. VI. 32. 16. 16. 16. 16. 16. 16. 8. 4.

Great   16. 16. 16. 8. 8. 8. 8. 8. 8. 8. $5^1/_3$. 4. 4. 4. 4. $2^2/_3$. 2. 2. IX–XIII. VII–IX. 16. 8. 8. 4.

Swell   16. 8. 8. 8. 8. 8. 8. 8. 4. 4. 4. $2^2/_3$. 2. $1^1/_3$. 1. V–X. 16. 16. 8. 8. 8. 4. 4.

Choir   16. 16. 8. 8. 8. 8. 8. 8. 8. 8. 8. 4. 4. 4. 4. 4. 4. $2^2/_3$. $2^2/_3$. 2. 2. 2. $1^3/_5$. III. IV–V. 16. 8. 8. 8.

Solo   16. 16. 16. 8. 8. 8. 8. 4. 4. 4. $2^2/_3$. 2. II. 16. 16. 8. 8. 8. 8. 8. 4.

Bombarde   16. 8. 8. 4. VII. XII–XIV. 16. 8. 8. 4. 4. Echo 8. 8. 8.

---

[61] Elvin, *Pipes and Actions*, 83–6
[62] I am grateful to Ian Bell for this description of Compton practice regarding upperwork.
[63] G. Dixon, 'Thomas Casson, an Appreciation', *The Organ*, 28 (1948–9), 49–58
[64] Elvin, *Pipes and Actions*, 83–6

John Compton's mission was to introduce modern technology in its most advanced form to the art of organ-building. Given that this was the case, it is no surprise to find that by the 1930s Leslie Bourn of the Compton firm had begun to develop an electronic organ without pipes. Hope-Jones had predicted this development as early as 1891,[65] and the period between the wars was littered with various experiments in electronic musical instruments: the *Ondes Martenot* and the *Theremin* have the most distinguished reputations. Here we see the start of a development that illustrates a challenge facing all organ builders in the mid twentieth century. Could the organ, an instrument whose technology owes much to the craftsmen of the late middle ages, be brought up to date? Or, in fact, is the logical conclusion of adopting such a path an organ with no pipes at all?

This may be only one of the fundamental challenges facing the continuing life of the organ in a technologically advanced society. At this stage we should simply observe that while Compton was pushing the frontiers of the craft forward according to the most modern principles, in other countries a new movement was afoot which sought to recapture the glories of the past – in America and France a classical revival; in Germany an *Orgelbewegung* or organ reform movement. The full effect of these new movements was not to filter into the British Isles until after the Second World War.

[65] Report of Hope-Jones lecture at the College of Organists 5 May 1891, *Musical Standard*, 40 (1890–1), 400

CHAPTER SEVENTEEN

THE CLASSICAL REVIVAL
1939–1980

However great the appeal of late nineteenth- and early twentieth-century organs – their dynamic range, their vast palette of colours, their technical sophistication and ease of control – that appeal would not last for ever. To a small group of musicians and commentators it had become clear that the gap between contemporary instruments and the music and organs of the past had become unbridgeable: was the modern organ, with its giant quasi-orchestral structure and its kaleidoscopic changes of colour, really an appropriate vehicle for the works of Bach and his contemporaries?

The history of the classical revival in European and American organ building and playing is beyond this work, but some key names and events will hint at the wide extent of the movement. Around 1900 in France Alexandre Guilmant and Joseph Bonnet revived and played recitals of early music. In Germany, Karl Straube was engaged in similar work. Interest in a forgotten repertoire grew. Cavaillé-Coll was encouraged to restore to his organs some of the mixtures and mutations deleted in deference to romantic taste. Albert Schweitzer used the whole question of how the music of Bach should sound to launch an attack on the contemporary organ and an appeal to rediscover the beauty of tone found in old instruments.[1] After the First World War the movement gathered pace: the glories of the organs of Arp Schnitger and Gottfried Silbermann were inspirational; organ builders began to attempt to copy the sounds they heard, and in a seminal conference on German Organ-Art at Freiburg in 1926 some important principles of a classical revival were established.

Arnold Dolmetsch described how this new historical awareness was in conflict with the instruments of the day:[2]

The makers of 1815 worked on much the same principles as those of 1615 . . . The church organs in addition had that power based on sweetness which constitutes majesty. The change came on, and for the sake of louder tone, pressure of wind was doubled and trebled. The same pressure acting on the valves which let the wind into the pipes made them too

---

[1] A. Schweitzer, *J. S. Bach, le musicien-poète* (Leipzig 1905); A. Schweitzer, *Deutsche und französische Orgelbaukunst*, Leipzig 1906
[2] A. Dolmetsch, *The Interpretation of the Music of the XVII and XVIII Centuries* (London 1915), 436–7

Plate 71　The organ in the Royal Festival Hall, London, designed by Ralph Downes and built by Harrison & Harrison and completed in 1954. The use of an exposed display of pipework is derived from American organs of the period, especially those by Walter Holtkamp. This uncompromisingly 'new' look was reflected in the revolutionary (to English ears, at least) neo-classical sound of the instrument.

heavy for the fingers to move through the keys. A machine was then invented which did the work at second hand . . . So the music of the organ dragged on after the player's fingers as best it could. Personal touch, which did so much for phrasing and expression, was destroyed . . . Modern compositions are intended for this machine, and all is well with them; but it is a revelation to hear Handel's or Bach's music on a well-preserved old organ.

By the 1930s attempts were being made in Germany and France to lower wind-pressures, to reintroduce mechanical action, and to remove many 'romantic' aspects of voicing – heavy nicking of the languids, tuning and regulating slots at the top of the pipe, beards on the mouth to encourage orchestral string tone and so on. With this movement there was inevitably a rejection of all that the previous generation stood for, and within a generation nineteenth-century organs would be widely and disparagingly referred to as 'romantic'. Very few people in Britain were informed of what was going on across the English Channel, and those who happened to encounter the organ reform movement seem to have regarded it as something of a joke. However, the Belgian organist Guy Weitz encouraged Henry Willis III to add mutations to the Choir Organ at the Jesuit Church, Farm Street, London in 1926: with these stops, two Mixtures on the Great Organ, a Piccolo 1 on the Swell and independent Pedal upperwork this instrument took on something of a continental feeling, probably owing much to its origins as an Anneessens organ of 1887.[3] Softly voiced mutations appeared on many larger Choir organs of the 1930s, but they were normally seen as a way of providing new synthetic semi-orchestral effects, rather than in relation to the needs of the early repertoire. Despite his claims to have introduced elements of new thinking to Britain, Willis was quite content, at the Masonic Peace Memorial in 1933, to build a three-manual organ with an alarmingly foundational Great Organ of 16. 16. 8. 8. 8. 8. 4. 4. 2. 8. – of which three were Open Diapasons.[4] Later in life Willis was to become bitterly opposed to 'this "Baroque" business', and through his domination of the Federation of Master Organ Builders and the Incorporated Society of Organ Builders influenced many of his less able contemporaries to agree with him.[5]

In an atmosphere where the work of Harrison & Harrison, with its indebtedness to Hope-Jones and the progressive organ builders of the 1890s, was regarded as something of a benchmark, moves towards a classical revival could make little headway. The Austrian organist Susi Jeans, wife of the astronomer and musician Sir James Jeans, had a small organ built for their home at Cleveland Lodge, Dorking, Surrey in 1936. The structure of the organ, with its mechanical key action in the traditional manner, was by Hill, Norman & Beard. The scheme, however, was designed in consultation with the neo-classical composer Johann Nepomuk David and the pipework and voicing were by the firm of Eule from

[3] J. A. G. Beaumont, 'The Organ in Farm Street Church, Mayfair', *The Organ*, 6 (1926–7), 26–9
[4] H. Willis, 'The Organ in the Grand Temple of the Masonic Peace Memorial', *The Rotunda*, 5/3, 51–4
[5] Letter from Henry Willis III in *The Organ*, 22 (1942–3), 183–5; Letters from Henry Willis III in C. Callahan, *The American Classic Organ* (Richmond, Virginia 1990); Letter from Henry Willis III in the *Journal of the Incorporated Society of Organ Builders*, 1/3 (1951), 11–12

Bautzen in Germany.[6] The elder Herbert Norman was delighted at the seemingly infinite way that all stops could combine – the English organ had by now become an instrument of loud and soft stops where blend depended on the use of certain conventions of registration – but he was baffled by the irregular 'chiffing' attack of the un-nicked pipes.[7] Interesting though this organ was, it made no impression whatever on the English organ builders' belief in the quality and authority of their own way of doing things; such an instrument was fine as the domestic plaything of a country lady, but surely had no relevance to the needs of worship in the Anglican Church.

Meanwhile in America the classical revival followed a slightly different path; one of its leaders was English by birth and training: G. Donald Harrison (unconnected with Harrison & Harrison of Durham). To turn back for a moment: it is now clear that between the Inventions Exhibition of 1885 and the appearance of the Dixon and Harrison style around 1910 there was considerable and varied debate about the future of the organ. T. C. Lewis had contributed largely to this debate in a practical way – especially through his late cathedral organs at Newcastle upon Tyne and Southwark – and in his *A Protest against the Modern Development of Unmusical Tone*.[8] At least one of the progressive builders of the late nineteenth century, Michell & Thynne, had followed a Lewis-inspired path. However, in England there were no further champions and the Lewis style finally expired with the amalgamation of Lewis & Co. with Henry Willis & Sons in 1919.

G. Donald Harrison kept a candle burning for Lewis's principles in these dark days. Born in 1889, brought up on Lewis organs, and hoping to pursue a career in organ building, he was turned away by Lewis himself – 'there is no money in it'. He was eventually to enter the Lewis factory at Brixton as an employee in 1919, but by then it was through the friendship and influence of Henry Willis III, now in charge of the amalgamated companies. Made a director in 1921, he became friendly with the organist Marcel Dupré and frequently visited France.[9] In 1924 Willis was visited by the American builder Ernest Skinner, and there began a fruitful exchange of ideas between the two companies. The idea was that Willis would benefit from Skinner's advanced electric consoles and mechanism, and that Skinner – an ultra-romantic steeped in orchestral ideals and influenced by Hope-Jones – would learn something of the Willis reed and mixture *ensemble*.[10] Willis found it difficult to encourage Skinner to follow what he regarded as a more wholesome tonal recipe, and before long suggested that Harrison could be spared to join the Skinner company in America.[11]

It was not unusual at this time for English-trained builders to find useful employment in the United States. Carlton Michell and Robert Hope-Jones were amongst those who made the journey before the First World War. In the 1920s and 1930s

[6] C. Clutton, 'Lady Jeans' Baroque Chamber Organ', *The Organ*, 19 (1939–40), 39–42
[7] H. Norman, 'The Normans 1860–1920', *BIOS Journal*, 10 (1986), 53–61
[8] T. C. Lewis, *A Protest Against the Modern Development of Unmusical Tone* (London 1897)
[9] Callahan, *The American Classic Organ*, xx–xxii.   [10] Ibid., 1–14   [11] Ibid., 15–16

English organ building continued to decline; meanwhile American organ building was in a period of rich expansion in which the crash of 1929 was only an incident. The Willis-trained Richard Whitelegg worked in turn for Aeolian, Welte and Möller.[12] Vincent Willis's son Henry Vincent ('Harry') Willis worked for Welte, before being hired by Midmer-Losh where he made a considerable contribution to the voicing of the mammoth instrument at Atlantic City Auditorium – the largest organ ever made (under construction 1929–32).[13] English ideals were still cherished by the English-born Austin brothers (who were later to employ the Englishman Richard Piper) and were emulated at Estey by James B. Jamison.[14] In Canada, the Casavant firm was moving towards a more English style under the English-born Stephen Stoot.[15]

At the Skinner Company, Harrison worked slowly and diplomatically at first. However, he had the ear of the firm's owner, Arthur Hudson Marks, and was in sympathy with a younger generation of organists and enthusiasts who had travelled in Europe. By the mid 1930s Harrison's organs had moved away from the Skinner house style – they had become fresh, bright, lean and avowedly continental in inspiration. Skinner himself retired to sulk. At the Church of the Advent, Boston in 1936 Harrison built an organ combining fully developed Germanic choruses with light-pressure reeds fitted with French shallots. Both in reading the specification of this instrument and hearing it in the flesh one is left in no doubt that the spirit of Thomas Lewis has informed Harrison's work: this is not, of course, a Lewis organ, but so many of the fundamental assumptions about chorus building, balance, and provision of colour are similar as to leave little doubt as to where Harrison's first love lay.[16]

Harrison turned American organ building round to his ideals and enjoyed a career of almost unbroken success. With other builders such as Walter Holtkamp he introduced what has become known as the American Classic Organ, meeting perfectly the needs of the younger generation of organists and delighting visitors from mainland Europe, including Schweitzer. As Harrison took in more and varied influences, so the organs became more continental rather than English, although he never abandoned E. M. Skinner's preferred Pitman chests and electro-pneumatic action.

Perceptive readers of *The Organ* might have noticed that the mood was different abroad. Henry Willis III wrote about the old organ in Roskilde Cathedral, Denmark,[17] and about the work of the German firm Steinmeyer.[18] The distinguished Dutch historian M. A. Vente introduced readers to the great historic instruments of the Netherlands.[19] William Leslie Sumner wrote about Schnitger

[12] Ibid., 21n   [13] Ibid., 39n   [14] Ibid., 68n

[15] Letter from C. Clutton, *The Organ*, 30 (1950–1), 53; Callahan, *The American Classic Organ*, 22n

[16] Callahan, *The American Classic Organ*, 453–4; author's examination of the Boston instrument

[17] H. Willis, 'The Organ of Roskilde Cathedral, Denmark', *The Organ*, 9 (1929–30), 144–8

[18] H. Willis, 'The Organ at Trondhjem Cathedral', *The Organ*, 11 (1931–2), 88–92

[19] M. A. Vente, 'The Schnitger Organ in the Groote or St. Laurentskerk at Alkmaar', *The Organ*, 17 (1937–8), 100–6; M. A. Vente, 'The Organ in the Great (or St. Eusebius) Church at Arnhem', *The Organ*, 18 (1938–9), 26–31

and the Silbermanns.[20] Cecil Clutton described the new Gonzalez organ at Rheims Cathedral in France, with its mechanical action and low wind pressures (76 and 89mm throughout).[21]

Events in America were also quite well reported in the English musical press, but Harrison's work for the Skinner Company (later Aeolian-Skinner) was not well understood. Henry Willis III became anxious about the kind of work his *protégé* was undertaking: 'Don is not doing what he went to Skinners for, and that was to give Skinner organs a Willis ensemble . . . [he] is striking out on what might be termed an individual line.'[22] As Harrison moved increasingly towards neo-classicism he became aware that things at home were standing still: 'I may be underrating the intelligence of some of those boys, but from reading the British periodicals I see very little change from the old days, and in fact the schemes they suggest and the arguments they put forward are mere repetition of what has been going on for twenty or thirty years.'[23] Cecil Clutton seemed to agree in his analysis of the organ at Rheims, and openly doubted the usual views prevalent in England at the time: 'In studying a foreign organ it is more profitable to see where one can learn from it, rather than to think in what ways the English organ is superior' . . . 'The English organ is a fine and beautiful thing . . . but at the moment it is in danger of becoming badly out of date' . . . 'The Rheims organ is something altogether magnificent; but it represents the Church Militant rather than the Church Dormant. Which shall we choose?'[24]

By the end of the 1930s English organ building was indeed stagnant. Economic decline in the industry had begun as early as 1900. The First World War slowed progress to a crawl: the Depression of the 1930s stopped it altogether. Few new organs were built, and most of them were for concert halls and public auditoria or public school chapels: there were few in Anglican churches. Conservatism represented safety, and secured contracts for the hard-pressed builders. There was no real challenge to the tonal designs of Dixon and the organs of Harrison & Harrison of Durham. In such a situation the Second World War was a further devastating blow. Work on new organs halted; the factories of Willis and Hill, Norman & Beard were destroyed by bombs. When peace came in 1945 Britain was on its knees, and for a further decade or more new organs were a rare luxury.

By this time, although the directors of the larger companies and their voicers were still able to maintain tonal standards, the lack of new organ contracts and the upheavals of war and depression had ruined English organ builders' ability to plan and lay out a new organ from scratch. The grand engineering of the Victorians was a thing of the past: only the electrical work of Compton struck a really modern

---

[20] W. L. Sumner, 'Arp Schnitger and his Organs', *The Organ*, 17 (1937–8), 139–147, 193–204; W. L. Sumner, 'The Silbermanns and their Organs', *The Organ*, 18 (1938–9), 129–39, 221–30

[21] C. Clutton, 'The Great Organ at Rheims Cathedral', *The Organ*, 18 (1938–9), 193–201

[22] Letter from Henry Willis III to Senator Emerson L. Richards, 8 July 1935, quoted in Callahan, *The American Classic Organ*, 132

[23] Letter from G. Donald Harrison to William King Covell, 8 February 1944, quoted in Callahan, *The American Classic Organ*, 195–6   [24] Clutton, 'The Great Organ at Rheims Cathedral'

note. Even for a leading firm like Harrison & Harrison much prestigious work came in the form of rebuilds: organs by Hill, Willis and others would receive a new console and electro-pneumatic key action as well as tonal alterations, but much of the structure and pipework remained to serve again. The old spirit of invention seemed to have faded; it has already been seen how Henry Willis III came to rely on American influence to keep his organs up to date: when it came to adding a special Trompette Militaire to his flagship instrument at St Paul's Cathedral, London he simply ordered the stop from Midmer-Losh in America. Midmer-Losh were snowed under with the organ for Atlantic City and subcontracted in turn. The stop that arrived in London and can still be heard today is in fact a standard Wurlitzer Brass Trumpet as used in their cinema organs.[25] The over-ambitious rebuild of the two organs in Tewkesbury Abbey, started by Walker in 1947 but never completed, incorporated a certain amount of second-hand material from other sources, including old soundboards and pipes put together in a makeshift way. The new five-manual console was impressive enough to satisfy the customer, but the interior of the organ simply did not reach the same standard.[26]

The amount of new work declined. When Cecil Clutton reviewed the 1950 Walker in St Mary the Virgin, Oxford, he was truthfully able to describe it as 'probably the only completely new British organ of consequence to be completed since the war'.[27] The decline was due partly to post-war shortage of materials, partly to high taxation designed to discourage expenditure on luxuries, and partly to the dwindling market for organ building in general. Many less healthy companies did not long survive the end of the war.

From what has been said already it will be obvious that the economic pressures on organ builders had become severe to say the least, and quality suffered. The habit of rebuilding existing organs was a long-established one, but in the past a builder would take care to leave the instrument as near in style to his own product as possible. When George Pike England rebuilt the organ at Chichester Cathedral in 1806, he provided new soundboards and a great deal of new pipework.[28] When GG-compass organs were rebuilt on the German System, they emerged as truly Victorian instruments. Father Willis, in particular, would always modify old material in such a way as to leave the organ as an unmistakable example of his own ideals, and would ensure that pipework, soundboards and mechanism were new or largely so. In the twentieth century there was still good workmanship in rebuilt organs: consoles especially, and indeed any new parts, showed excellent bench work and quality of materials. However, with the practice of electrifying existing

---

[25] Information given to Noel Mander by the former Willis employee Aubrey Thompson-Allen.; Author's examination of the instrument
[26] H. Stubington, 'The Rebuilt Organ in Tewkesbury Abbey', *The Organ*, 36 (1956–7), 1–17; Author's examination of the instrument
[27] C. Clutton, 'The New Organ in the University Church of St. Mary the Virgin Oxford', *The Organ*, 31 (1951–2), 60–7
[28] A. Thurlow and N. M. Plumley, 'The Organ in Chichester Cathedral', *BIOS Journal*, 10 (1986), 118–25; Author's examination of the instrument

mechanical or pneumatic actions and the need to economise on larger components came a reluctance to replace soundboards or to re-dispose them in the organ. The results were three-fold: first, organs rebuilt in the twentieth century were no longer fully representative of modern ideals; secondly, they became confused in layout; and thirdly they were often left with components of differing ages and life expectancy, hastening the need for further rebuilds in the near future.

After the war it also became customary to describe as 'new' instruments that included large quantities of old material. Willis's 'new' Dome Diapason Chorus at St Paul's (1949) was in fact largely the Lewis Great Organ from Christ Church, Westminster Bridge Road.[29] The 'new' Walker organ at Brompton Oratory (1954) also had Lewis soundboards.[30] The organ for Guildford Cathedral, installed by Rushworth & Dreaper in 1961, had a previous life as a Harrison of 1880.[31] Even as late as 1966 the 'new' organ by N. P. Mander Ltd at Sheffield Cathedral included the soundboards and pipework of a three-manual instrument originally by Father Willis,[32] and the Hill, Norman & Beard instrument of 1967 for the Royal College of Organists included the soundboards and some pipework from the former Norman & Beard organ of 1903.[33]

In such an atmosphere it was still more difficult for new tonal ideas to make themselves felt, all the more so because the economic difficulties facing organ builders were tacitly encouraged by a general conservatism amongst the majority of organists. The Harrison & Harrison recipe of c1910 was still cherished as an ideal. A few voices were raised in doubt. The enthusiast Cecil Clutton had never quite agreed with his older friend George Dixon: Clutton had a taste for Victorian organs by Hill and others, and was able to travel extensively abroad (a luxury beyond the means of the average Englishman). His catholic taste incorporated a knowledge of a wide range of organ types and an increasing interest in the vast repertoire of early music now coming to light. He was soon committed to the provision of balanced flue choruses as the backbone of any organ scheme, together with the provision of mutations and some independent pedal upperwork, and admired the possibilities offered by low-pressure reeds. He was by nature opposed to the typical organ of the period 1900–30: 'Its forced unblending unison diapasons; thick adenoidal reeds; insipid secondary choruses and rumbling overweighted pedal were the utter negation of chorus building of singing, musical tone.'[34] These trenchant views became widely known through Clutton's many written descriptions of old and new organs both at home and abroad.

In 1952 W. L. Sumner published *The Organ*, clearly intended to be a replacement for the similar heavyweight volume written by Hopkins and Rimbault and first published in 1855. In its pages one could certainly find an interest in organ history and a wide range of appreciation of different organ types. Sumner even went as far

[29] W. L. Sumner, 'The New Diapason Chorus in St. Paul's Cathedral, London', *The Organ*, 30 (1950–1), 172–6
[30] R. Downes, *Baroque Tricks* (Oxford 1983), 158
[31] J. Norman, *The Organs of Britain* (Newton Abbot 1984), 284–5
[32] C. Clutton, 'The Organ at Sheffield Cathedral', *The Organ*, 47 (1967–8), 151–5
[33] Norman, *The Organs of Britain*, 215
[34] C. Clutton, 'The Rebuilt Organ in St. Mark's Milverton', *The Organ*, 33 (1953–4), 64–70

as to sound a note of caution concerning the performance of Bach and other early repertoire on the typical English instrument. Generally, however, the book was eclectic, and though it reported the emerging organ reform movement in Europe and the appearance of the American Classic, it drew no decisive conclusions from these phenomena.

Meanwhile Clutton and others were becoming aware of new work of particularly high quality being carried out in Scandinavia and the Netherlands. The Danes and the Dutch had taken the classical revival to heart, and a handful of builders combined a return to first principles with superlative design and workmanship. Most notable were Frobenius and Marcussen in Denmark and Flentrop in Holland. For all three firms mechanical action and low pressures had become the norm, as they had been before the romantic influences of the nineteenth century. They identified certain principles of design that they felt were the foundation of the success of the great organs of the seventeenth and eighteenth centuries, and a philosophy emerged under the loose heading of *Werkprinzip*, related especially to the work of Arp Schnitger and the Hamburg school of the period 1660–1730. Low pressures were combined with large footholes in the pipes and virtually no nicking on the languid, encouraging an articulate 'chiffing' speech that could, in theory, be manipulated by the touch of a sensitive player (provided the action was mechanical). Flue choruses were vigorous with brilliant mixtures, reeds adding colour not power. Each manual department was an entity in its own right, with its own complete principal chorus and a balanced provision of flutes, mutations and reeds. 'Decadent' romantic string stops were eschewed, and all means of expression (swell boxes, crescendo pedals, combination actions) were deleted in favour of terraced dynamics played in dialogue and registered by hand: indeed to some experts all romantic music was foreign to the true nature of the organ and could be ignored. The various departments of the organ were distinguished from each other not by power or by colour but by pitch emphasis and position: a Great Organ based on an 8′ principal would be supported by a Pedal based on 16′ pitch and balanced by a 4′ Positive. The departments would be arranged vertically, with no section standing behind another, the usual manual divisions (in Dutch) being Hoofdwerk (Great), Rugwerk (Positive behind the player) and Boorstwerk (lit: 'Breast-work', a small, usually 2′-based, department above the console). Finally the organ would speak in one direction only, being housed in a carefully designed case with sides, back and roof, in which the status of the various departments was visually expressed.

For Clutton these organs were a revelation, and the Flentrop of 1952 at Doetinchem left him especially enthusiastic,[35] but articles praising it and other similar instruments left the majority of readers baffled and even angry, especially in so far as they implied criticism of the home-built product.

Meanwhile a widely travelled musician who had been strongly influenced by his contact with the classical revival was ready to make a still greater impact through his

[35] C. Clutton, 'The New Organ at Deotinchem, Holland', *The Organ*, 34 (1954–5), 92–7

work as a consultant. Ralph Downes had, like G. Donald Harrison, been inspired by contact with a Lewis organ in his youth; his admiration was made concrete by his appointment as assistant organist at Southwark Cathedral in 1923. In 1928 he crossed the Atlantic to be the first organist and director of music in the new gothic chapel at Princeton University: here the organ, by the Skinner Company, was one of the first in which G. Donald Harrison had had a hand. Contact with Harrison followed, and Downes also met many of the young organists and musicians in America who were aware of the organ reform movement and the possibilities of the early repertoire. Unlike many enthusiasts and consultants, Downes was keen to get his hands dirty: with professional help he began to experiment with the pipework of the Princeton instrument, which he found less satisfactory than its paper specification suggested. Pressures were lowered, pipes re-scaled and revoiced, and the main choruses of the organ re-balanced. Downes just had time to appreciate the first neo-classical organs of Harrison when he returned to England in 1938 to become the organist of Brompton Oratory, London. Further travel and experiment followed. France was visited, and the organs at the Oratory and at Buckfast Abbey were re-balanced.[36]

During the war Downes had begun to reach some firm conclusions, and his opinions appeared in print. The organist and composer Percy Whitlock had dared publish an appreciative account of the classical revival in the pages of *The Organ*, only to be put down firmly by Henry Willis III in subsequent correspondence.[37] Downes joined the fray with a carefully argued critique of the contemporary British organ:[38]

Generally, even in moderate sized instruments (no matter who the builder) the great organ is voiced to give the maximum power from the smallest number of stops 'commercially possible', beauty of tone being set aside, especially in the upper work. The swell is sometimes even worse in its main structure, and its powerful reeds may well engulf the great flue work. The choir organ (on lower pressure and with smaller scales) will be a quiet 'accompanimental' section, and the solo and pedal departments will be quite extraneous and will stand away from the rest. In organs conceived on the idea of separate 'choruses', – diapason, geigen, flute, string, &c.: an idea germane to the orchestra, not the organ – the above defects are usually even more pronounced.

With his remarks couched in such terms it was not surprising that Downes should be challenged at once by George Dixon, whose principles of design had received a direct hit.[39]

Would musicians desire that we should revert to the intractable, coarse-toned woodwind and brass of (say) Mozart's time in the present-day performances of his symphonies because he wrote for these and was unacquainted with the beautiful tone of our modern instruments?

Of course this was exactly the logical conclusion of the path that Downes had begun to pursue, and in recent times the event that Dixon believed impossible has not just happened but has been a source of new inspiration to a whole generation

[36] Downes, *Baroque Tricks*
[37] Letter from H. Willis III, *The Organ*, 22 (1942–3), 183–5 and correspondence in following issues
[38] R. Downes, 'Tonal Balance', *The Organ*, 23 (1943–4), 47–8
[39] Letter from G. Dixon, *The Organ*, 23 (1943–4), 92–3

of musicians and listeners. We now know the problem under the broad title of 'authenticity', but in the 1940s the philosophical struggle was at a more basic level.

During all this it became clear to a few that Downes's understanding of the tonal resources of the organ offered a rare combination of musical analysis and practical experience. Early in 1948 he was asked to be the consultant for the organ to be erected in a large new concert hall on London's South Bank. Downes's scheme evolved over a longish period and his inspiration was eclectic: D. A. Flentrop and G. Donald Harrison were influential, as were the old organs of the Netherlands, the instruments of Cavaillé-Coll and the recent work of Marcussen. Downes had by now a lively interest in the science of pipe scaling and the art of voicing, and in the final scheme combined all these new found areas of interest together with reed stops to be voiced by Rochésson of Paris. Harrison & Harrison of Durham were chosen as builders on the grounds of quality and because Cuthbert Harrison, who now unexpectedly found himself at the head of the family firm, was less antagonistic to the scheme than the other builders approached.

'Antagonistic' is perhaps an under-statement. From the publication of the scheme in 1949 until the completion of the instrument in 1953 the new organ in the Royal Festival Hall was openly ridiculed by critics on all sides. To advance neo-classical ideas around 1950 was considered eccentric; to combine this with out-spoken criticism of typical English organs was no less than treason. The level of argument was not very distinguished: Ralph Vaughan Williams's contribution, in a letter to the *Times*, contained the following hasty remarks:[40]

I admit that we have some bad organs in England, but at their worst they cannot surely make so nasty a noise as most of those on the Continent. As to the so-called 'Baroque' organ, which, I presume, I have heard at its best at the hands of the most distinguished performers. I can only compare it to a barrel organ in the street. This type of instrument is said to be right for playing Bach. For myself I want nothing better than Bach as played by Dr. Harold Darke on his typically English organ at St. Michael's Cornhill.

Sir George Dyson, the president of the Royal College of Organists, offered the following illuminating remark:[41]

even the harpsichord cannot bear the weight of the modern pianist's repertory.

Meanwhile the voicing of the Festival Hall organ continued: the work was carried out largely on site, using completely new methods of which English voicers had no experience whatever, and battling against the frankly abysmal acoustics of the 3,000-seat hall. It was a tremendous struggle: Downes fearful, the voicers working in the dark, and the critics baying at the leash. The result horrified those who were so disposed, delighted many more, and astonished almost everyone. The organ received slight modifications soon after its completion and in 1969 and 1973 (all under Downes's guidance); it is difficult to analyse, not least because the acoustics

[40] R. Vaughan Williams, Letter to the Editor, *The Times* 14 January 1951
[41] Sir G. Dyson, Presidential Address to the Royal College of Organists (1953), quoted in J. P. Rowntree, 'Organ Reform in England – Some Influences', *BIOS Journal*, 3 (1979), 5–16

of the hall are so profoundly unfriendly to organ tone of any kind. The wide-spread layout at the back of the stage with no casework and the electro-pneumatic action make the organ diffuse and somewhat unfocused, but this is compensated for by the forthright neo-classical voicing, with wide foot-holes and virtually no nicking. The harshness of the choruses is not as apparent now as it was to listeners in the 1950s, who were used to an altogether more refined manner of voicing. It has never really been clear just how good a reed-voicer Rochésson was, and much criticism has been centred round the reeds. Some have supposed that it was a mistake to try and marry Germanic choruses with French reeds, others have suggested that the reeds were simply not very good ones. One could perhaps also point out that Downes's habit of drawing generally on a wide range of sources – Dutch, American, German, French – made inevitably for problems of blend, perhaps exacerbated by his free use of 'fixed-variable scaling', in which the pipe-diameters seem studiously to *avoid* any regular mathematical progression or relationship to one another. Despite all this the instrument was a revelation to many: traditionally educated musicians included. For Sir Thomas Beecham it was 'a magnificent instrument . . . people who have written to the contrary are jackasses; it is one of the best organs in the world. It only requires someone to play it who knows the instrument.'[42] The final specification was as shown on p. 338–9.[43]

At the same time Downes was working on a new organ along similar lines for Brompton Oratory with J. W. Walker & Sons, introducing to another workshop the problems of carefully planned classical balances and open-foot voicing with no nicking. The technique was characterised by:[44]

cohesive synthesis of all the divisions on an 'equality' basis to give a genuine additive effect; and well-developed wide and narrow choruses on all divisions, with bold but not *loud* voicing of individual pipes: and 'characterisation' of each division in accordance with its particular function, both by specification, scaling and voicing.

This statement clearly leaves a lot to the interpretation, and Downes's intentions are perhaps better expressed in a similar statement about the Festival Hall, again containing implicit criticism of standard English methods:[45]

The tonal divisions, great, swell, positive, etc., are not differentiated on a colouristic basis, nor on the basis of power, but as complete and independent organs, each with a characteristic accent, but all mutually complementary. Each contains a complete diapason or principal chorus, a wide chorus (however rudimentary), and a reed chorus. The most important stop of the principal family is in every case put at the front of the division, and these principals stand in octave relationship, pedal 32ft., great 16ft., positive and solo 8ft., swell 4ft. and choir 2ft. To a great extent the presence of these stops and their location have the effect of determining the particular character of the division they inhabit.

---

[42] L. Elvin, *The Harrison Story* (Lincoln 1973), 183
[43] Downes, *Baroque Tricks*, 233–5; Leaflets issued by Harrison & Harrison 1951 and 1980
[44] R. Downes, 'Notes on the New Organ in Brompton Oratory', *The Organ*, 33 (1953–4), 118–21
[45] R. Downes, 'Notes on the Organ in the Royal Festival Hall', *The Organ*, 33 (1953–4), 153–60

London, The Royal Festival Hall: Harrison & Harrison 1954

Manuals C–c'''' (61 notes), Pedals C–g (32 notes)
All pipes 50 per cent tin, 50 per cent lead unless otherwise stated

Great (manual II)

Unenclosed:

Principal	16
Gedacktpommer	16
Principal (tin)	8
Diapason	8
Harmonic Flute (12 wood)	8
Rohrgedackt	8
Quintflute (stopped)	5⅓
Octave (I–II ranks)	4
Gemshorn (conical)	4
Quintadena	4
Quint	2⅔
Superoctave	2
Blockflute	2
Tierce	1⅗
Mixture	V
Sharp Mixture	IV
Cornet (from c')	V
Bombarde	16
Trumpet	8
Clarion	4

Positive (manual I, transferable to II)

Unenclosed:

Principal	8
Gedackt (30 per cent tin)	8
Quintadena	8
Octave	4
Rohrflute	4
Rohrnazard	2⅔
Spitzflute (conical)	2
Tierce	1⅗
Larigot	1⅓
Mixture	V
Sharp Mixture	V
Carillon	II–III

Enclosed in Choir box:

Trumpet	8
Dulzian	8

Tremulant

Swell (Manual IV)

Enclosed:

Quintadena	16
Diapason	8
Gemshorn (conical)	8
Quintadena	8
Viola	8
Celeste	8
Principal	4
Koppelflute	4
Nazard (conical)	2⅔
Octave	2
Openflute	2
Tierce (from f)	1⅗
Flageolet	1
Mixture	IV–VI
Cymbel (tin)	III
Bombarde (12 half length)	16
Trumpet	8
Hautboy	8
Vox Humana	8
Clarion	4

Tremulant

Choir (Manual I, transferable to IV)

Enclosed:

Salicional	16
Open Wood (oak)	8
Stopped Wood (oak)	8
Salicional (conical)	8
Unda Maris (conical)	8
Spitzoctave (conical)	4
Openflute (30 per cent tin)	4
Principal	2
Quint	1⅓
Octave	1
Sesquialtera	II
Mixture	IV
Cromorne	8
Schalmei	4

Tremulant

Solo (Manual IV)

Enclosed:

Diapason	8
Rohrflute	8
Octave	4
Waldflute (conical, 30 per cent tin)	2
Raschquint	II
Tertian	II
Mixture	VI
Basset Horn	16
Harmonic Trumpet	8
Harmonic Clarion	4
Tremulant	

Pedal

Principal (12 zinc, 4 haskelled) (ext. Great Principal 16)	32
Majorbass (pine)	16
Principal	16
Subbass (stopped, pine)	16
Salicional (Choir 16')	16
Quintadena (Swell 16')	16
Quintflute (stopped, 30 per cent tin)	$10^2/_3$
Octavebass	8
Gedackt (stopped, 30 per cent tin)	8
Quintadena (ext. 16')	8
Nazard (conical, 30 per cent tin)	$5^1/_3$
Superoctave	4
Spitzflute (conical, 30 per cent tin)	4
Openflute (30 per cent tin)	2
Septerz (30 per cent tin)	II
Rauschquint	II
Mixture	V
Bombarde (12 zinc, ext 16')	32
Bombarde	16
Dulzian (ext. Positive 8')	16
Trumpet	8
Cromorne (Choir)	8
Clarion	4
Schalmei (Choir)	4
Cornett	2

Normal unison couplers
Transfers as indicated
Swell Octave (16', 8' & 4' stops only)
Great Suboctave

Accessories

Eight foot pistons and cancel to Pedal organ
Eight pistons and cancel to each manual department – including a series each for Positive and Choir, in pairs
Eight general pistons
(all above instantly adjustable by setter piston)
General cancel
Reversible pistons to all unison couplers
Reversible foot pistons to Pedal couplers
Reversible foot piston to full organ, with indicator
General crescendo pedal, with indicator, adjustable at switchboard
Eight foot pistons duplicating either Swell pistons or general pistons, controlled by a rocking switch

Wind pressures

Great: 92mm, upperwork & reeds 76mm
Swell: 92mm
Positive: 70mm
Choir: 81mm
Solo: 115mm
Pedal: Principal 32' 90mm, foundation 100mm, main and Bombardes 92mm, mixtures and other reeds 76mm

The Festival Hall organ blew a gaping hole in assumptions about style and tonal appointment, and ushered in the classical revival in Britain, albeit twenty years later than in the rest of Europe and the United States. As new organ contracts revived during the 1950s, so some of the major builders responded to Downes's challenge at least some of the time. Amongst these were, of course, Harrison & Harrison and J. W. Walker & Sons, both of whom had direct experience of the new methods. Hill, Norman & Beard were not far behind, especially in the 1960s under the enthusiastic direction of the young John Norman. Henry Willis III had finally driven himself into isolation, and had developed a habit of walking out of recitals on new organs, a public statement of his opposition to everything classical.

For continental builders old organs were a source of inspiration. In Britain this was not usually appropriate, as the few surviving eighteenth century instruments belonged to an insular school: with GG compass and no pedals they were not suitable for a wide repertoire, ancient or modern. One organ builder had a slightly different approach. Noel Mander viewed old organs in a manner that anticipated later attitudes towards conservation. As well as carrying on a modest organ building business in London, he collected old chamber organs and restored larger instruments. At the end of the 1950s he tackled two important restoration projects which brought the old English organ into the limelight. The 1765 Byfield at St Mary Rotherhithe was thoroughly overhauled in 1959, preserving its state as conservatively rebuilt by Gray & Davison in 1886, but restoring the Mounted Cornet V and Clarion 4 to the Great.[46] At the same time, at Adlington Hall in Cheshire, the unique seventeenth-century organ in the great hall had been silent for generations, its pipework collapsed or trampled underfoot. Mander returned it to working order in 1958–9. The extent to which he was prepared to keep old material and restore the wreckage of the pipework was unusual even by European standards of the period: almost all the pipes were salvaged, most of the tongues of the reeds were kept, the very low pitch was retained (though not the unequal temperament), the key action was restored with only a little new bushing, and the original wind system was retained with the addition of an electric blower supplying one of the diagonal bellows.[47] It should be noted that the techniques employed in this project compare very favourably with the much more invasive methods employed by Flentrop, Marcussen and Beckerath at about the same time.

These restorations and Mander's other sympathetic work came to the attention of Cecil Clutton and his friend Austin Niland (the organist at Rotherhithe) at about the time they were writing *The British Organ*, first published in 1963.[48] This was a

[46] A. Niland, *The Organ at St. Mary's Rotherhithe* (Oxford 1983)
[47] J. P. Mander, 'Some Notes on the Organ in Adlington Hall', *BIOS Journal*, 10 (1986), 62–75
[48] C. Clutton and A. Niland, *The British Organ* (London 1963)

particularly interesting publication. Niland's contribution was a detailed history of the English organ case, following from the work of Andrew Freeman and as yet unsurpassed. Clutton contributed three remarkable elements: first, an amazingly succinct general history of the organ, including a description of the various national types and hinting at the repertoire associated with them; secondly, a history of the organ in Britain, couched in trenchant terms and leaving no doubt as to Clutton's dislike of the organs of 1900–50 and his admiration for all things neo-classical; thirdly, a useful guide on musical use – basically how to make the best of a bad job when playing general repertoire on an English romantic instrument designed to accompany a cathedral choir with semi-orchestral effects.

By the late 1950s the question of key action was being raised; the link between the 'classical' organ and its mechanical key action was clear enough to anyone who had seen a new Flentrop, Marcussen or Frobenius on the continent. It had always been realised by those with sensitive fingers that mechanical action was ideal. Even Edwin Lemare, the doyen of romantic recitalists, transcriber of music by Wagner, and designer of the 1897 Walker at St Margaret Westminster, London, had appreciated its virtues. For him mechanical action gave the best touch (when uncoupled); Barker Lever actions were second best; good charge pneumatic was sometimes acceptable; exhaust pneumatic was unsatisfactory and electro-pneumatic action the worst.[49] The building of large organs with high pressures, where the tonal schemes led to the extensive use of couplers in normal playing, rendered mechanical action completely impracticable. Returning to low pressures and classical tonal ideals made mechanical action suitable again, and a new understanding of the engineering of soundboard pallets and key action components led builders on the continent of Europe to believe that it was desirable for all organs, even large ones. Amongst some a theory grew that mechanical action gave a touch that was not only instantaneous, but also sensitive: it was possible to modify the articulation or 'chiff' of the pipes depending on whether the key was pressed quickly or slowly. Another influential argument was longevity: the many organs surviving from the seventeenth and eighteenth centuries proved the long-term durability of a simple mechanical action. Any mechanism incorporating pneumatics needed complete and thorough renewal every thirty to fifty years.

The first English response was to retain mechanical action (often known as tracker action) as part of a rebuild, for instance by J. W. Walker & Sons at St Helen York in 1959,[50] or by N. P. Mander Ltd at St Vedast Foster Lane in the City of London in 1961.[51] Mander's approach was conservative: he was making new charge pneumatic actions as late as 1947, wary even then of electro-pneumatics, and his use of mechanical action was closely related to his admiration of old instruments.

---

[49] E. H. Lemare, 'Modern Organ Touch', *Musical Opinion*, 35 (1912), 321–3
[50] Rowntree, *Organ Reform in England*
[51] N. P. Mander, 'A Short Account of the Organs of St. Vedast Foster Lane', *The Organ*, 43 (1963–4), 1–12

But he was not afraid to investigate new materials: in the 1960s his actions used squares and backfalls made of perspex, and he was well aware of developments abroad, becoming friendly with D. A. Flentrop in the Netherlands and sending his voicers on foreign study tours: 'English organ-builders will cease being progressive and artistic if they think they have nothing to learn from any other country.'[52]

Gradually the true nature of the continental classical revival became apparent in Britain through a handful of imports. Those in Swedish, Dutch, Finnish and Danish churches in London (Mårtensson 1953,[53] Van Leeuwen 1954,[54] Marcussen 1958,[55] Frobenius 1959[56]) were barely noticed, but when in 1965 Frobenius installed a new organ at Queen's College, Oxford the arrival of the newcomer could hardly be more significant.[57]

Oxford, Queen's College Chapel: Frobenius 1965

Manuals C–g''' (56 notes), Pedals C–f' (30 notes)

Great		**Brustpositive** (enclosed):	
Gedeckt	16	Gedeckt	8
Principal	8	Principal	4
Rohrflute	8	Rohrflute	4
Octave	4	Gemshorn	2
Octave	2	Quint	$1^1/_3$
Sesquialtera $2^2/_3 + 1^3/_5$	II	Scharff	III
Mixture	IV	Cromorne	8
Trumpet	8	Tremulant	
Pedal		**Couplers**	
Subbass	16	Great to Pedal	
Principal	8	Brustpositive to Pedal	
Gedeckt	8	Brustpositive to Great	
Octave	4		
Mixture	III		
Fagot	16		
Schalmei	4		

Mechanical key action
Mechanical stop action

The Queen's organ is of unforgettably high quality: beautiful to look at, to listen to and to play. Its arrival caused a shock; to many an organ of this kind was (and remains) incomprehensible, its tonal appointment (and complete lack of gadgetry) seeming to have no relation to the accompaniment of the choral service – often

[52] N. P. Mander, letter to the editor, *The Organ*, 39 (1959–60), 106
[53] T. M. N. Whitehall, 'The Organ of the Swedish Seamen's Church Rotherhithe', *The Organ*, 44 (1964–5), 90–4
[54] Norman, *The Organs of Britain*
[55] J. P. Rowntree and J. F. Brennan, *The Classical Organ in Britain*, vol. I: *1955–1974* (Oxford 1975), 46
[56] Ibid., 34   [57] Ibid., 16, 77

Plate 72   The organ in Queen's College, Oxford, built by Frobenius of Denmark in 1965. The first organ in
England that offered a chance to see the fully fledged classical revival in action. The two manual divisions (Great
Organ in the centre above a grille hiding the Swell Organ) are clearly visible in the façade, with the pedal organ
in free-standing towers on either side, following northern European tradition. The quality of this organ,
beautifully designed and made, immediately set a standard that English builders found difficult to equal.

stated to be the prime function of an English organ. To the majority of English organ builders at this period it represented a style of manufacture so complex, precise and luxurious (the case probably costing a quarter of the total price of the instrument) that there was no real hope of emulation. Frobenius had already been working at this recipe for the best part of forty years, and was steeped in the traditions of the historic north European organ. If the English chose to follow this path, would it take them forty years to achieve something similar?

With the cathedrals and collegiate churches dominating the church music establishment there was, perhaps, little encouragement to follow the classical path. The Queen's College organ could be put down to the eccentricity of an Oxford don (James Dalton). Mechanical action could be provided on occasion, especially in smaller organs and at a price – the competition at the bottom end of the market was the universally cheap small extension organ and anything else was a 'special'. However, for a handful of younger builders who knew the European organ reform movement, mechanical action was only the start: they wished to incorporate the integrated structure of casework and organ together with tonal schemes of an advanced kind. For Peter Walker of R. H. Walker (a splinter from the J. W. Walker factory) the classical organ came like a conversion on the road to Damascus, and he became an evangelist for the Scandinavian type. The young Peter Collins, after working for a time with Rieger of Austria, produced an important true classical organ at Shellingford, Oxfordshire in 1968.[58] But the most spectacular and accomplished early British effort came from a wealthy amateur. Maurice Forsyth-Grant, an electronics wizard rapidly rising to the top of his profession, had been interested in the organ since his youth. In 1960 he had encouraged a group of ex-Compton employees to start up on their own (Degens & Rippin). In a remarkably short time, through personal conviction and repeated foreign travel, he steered the company firmly towards classical revival. As a model they took the most advanced work of German builders, whose approach, using new technology, owed much to the Modern Movement in architecture and product design; it was a style much less traditional than that practised by the Dutch and the Danes. Forsyth-Grant put much of his own money into the increasingly confident and stylish new instruments. When Peter Hurford, then organist of St Alban's Abbey, mounted the first International Organ Festival there in 1967, he invited English builders to show small mechanical-action organs. Forsyth-Grant's company (by now Grant, Degens & Bradbeer) exhibited a remarkably accomplished two-manual organ of eight stops, incorporating a steel frame and modern materials, and ingeniously crammed into a tiny case. Forsyth-Grant's very confident understanding of the neo-classical organ quickly led to larger contracts, and in 1969 Grant, Degens & Bradbeer built a truly astounding new instrument for New College, Oxford, in consultation with the organist David Lumsden.[59]

[58] Ibid., 73   [59] M. Forsyth-Grant, *Twenty-one Years of Organ-Building* (Oxford 1987)

Oxford, New College Chapel: Grant, Degens & Bradbeer 1969

Manuals C–g′′′ (56 notes), Pedals C–f′ (30 notes)

Great		**Swell** (enclosed)	
Quintade	16	Flûte à cheminée	8
Prinzipal	8	Salicional	8
Spitzflöte	8	Céleste	8
Oktave	4	Prinzipal	4
Spitzgedackt	4	Flûte conique	4
Terz	$3\frac{1}{5}$	Nazard	$2\frac{2}{3}$
Quint	$2\frac{2}{3}$	Quarte	2
Oktave	2	Tierce	$1\frac{3}{5}$
Mixtur	IV–VI	Larigot	$1\frac{1}{3}$
Cornet (from c)	V	Teint $1\frac{1}{7}$ + $\frac{16}{19}$	II
Messingregal	16	Fourniture	V
Trompete	8	Trompette	16
Tremulant		Hautbois	8
		Trompeta real	8
		(horizontal, unenclosed)	
		Tremulant	

Ruckpositive		**Pedal**	
Holzgedackt	8	Prinzipal	16
Quintadena	8	Subbass	16
Praestant	4	Oktave	8
Rohrflöte	4	Rohrflöte	8
Prinzipal	2	Oktave	4
Quintatön	2	Nachthorn	2
Oktave	1	Mixtur	IV
None	$\frac{8}{9}$	Fagot (ext. 16′)	32
Scharfzimbel	III	Fagot	16
Holzregal	16	Kupfer-trompete	8
Schalmei-Krummhorn	8	Rohrschalmei	4
Tremulant		Tremulant	

Couplers

Great to Pedal
Swell to Pedal
Ruckpositive to Pedal
Ruckpositive to Great
Swell to Great

Mechanical key action
Electric stop and combination action

► *Plate 73*   The organ in New College, Oxford, built by Grant, Degens and Bradbeer in 1969 with casework by
Frank Bradbeer and George Pace. Maurice Forsyth-Grant was prepared to take up the challenge of the classical
revival, and in this instrument presented the English organ world with an uncompromising modern-movement
vision, brashly extolling the virtues of contemporary German thinking. The use of tin, copper and brass in the
visible pipework, together with brushed aluminium, painted steelwork and glass swell shutters combine to make
an unforgettable visual impact, matched by the sound of the organ.

The organ establishment regarded this instrument as a horrible freak, giving
Grant, Degens & Bradbeer much the same treatment as had been given to Hope-
Jones in the 1890s. Paradoxically there are many similarities. The New College
organ was intended to be revolutionary, presenting a package of modern materials,
tonal ideas and construction that departed completely from existing commercial
practice. Where Hope-Jones had suppressed every trace of upperwork, Grant,
Degens & Bradbeer provided it in profusion, reducing the foundation to the most
slender support possible. Just as in the Hope-Jones organ, strange nomenclature and
unusual materials and scales were a feature of the specification. To those who had
ears to hear, the instrument was stimulating and successful, albeit something of a
one-off; it has been particularly interesting to watch the rising careers of those who
were organ scholars there in the 1970s.

By the 1970s the classical organ had become a force in Britain; in 1975 a book
(*The Classical Organ in Britain 1955–1974*) was devoted to the trend, and there have
been further volumes since.[60] But to concentrate on these instruments would gloss
over the fact that the overall production of organs in Britain in the period 1960–80
covered a very wide range of styles.

The British organ building industry had become centred round the tuning and
maintenance of existing instruments, most of them Victorian. This generated
repair and refurbishment work on a regular basis, continuing to support the activities of firms whose names had been familiar for generations. Against this background the practice of rebuilding old organs in a revised form remained, often
including tonal alterations in keeping with the latest trends (the addition of a neo-
classical Positive section to an otherwise Victorian organ was typical of the 1960s
and 70s), and invariably with electro-pneumatic action. Where such work was
carried out in cathedrals, or churches with a strong musical tradition, the instruments were often enlarged to cope with a wider solo repertoire and more complex
liturgical demands. The N. P. Mander Ltd rebuild of the organ at St Paul's
Cathedral, London (1972–7, in consultation with Cecil Clutton) struck a new note
in several ways. First, the structure and mechanism of the organ were completely
replaced with new material. Secondly, there was a deliberate intention to respect
the Willis pipework of 1872 and to leave it intact without further alteration (though
in practice the various Willis rebuilds since 1872 have probably left the instrument
a long way from Father Willis's original intentions). Thirdly, the organ grew consid-

---

[60]   Rowntree and Brennan, *The Classical Organ in Britain*, vol. I; J. P. Rowntree and J. F. Brennan, *The Classical Organ
in Britain*, vol. II: *1975–197*, (Oxford 1979); J. P. Rowntree and J. Brennan, *The Classical Organ in Britain*, vol. III:
1979–1990 (Oxford 1993)

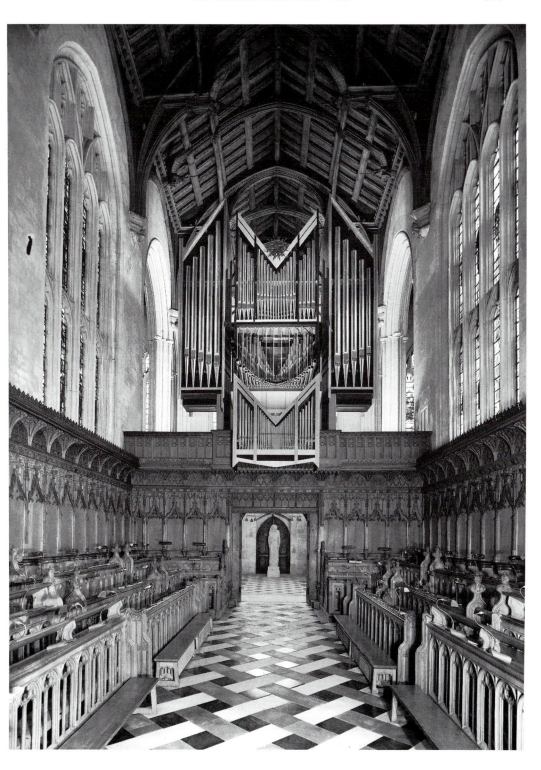

erably, acquiring a new Positive section (in addition to the existing Choir Organ) and substantial new sections in the dome and at the west end of the building, providing synchronised support for massed congregational singing in most parts of the building, as well as offering certain special effects (a chorus of Trumpets on 635mm and 889mm wind pressure are mounted horizontally above the west door). This work secured the reputation of Mander as a major player, and similar thorough rebuilds followed at Canterbury Cathedral (1979) and elsewhere.[61]

Such work represented the taste of the organ establishment in Britain: these instruments, sometimes of considerable complexity, were designed as machines to accompany choir and congregation on a daily basis. Questions of unity of technical and tonal design were rendered subsidiary to the perceived view of the practical tasks in hand. In order to make concessions to the needs of a solo repertoire much wider than that envisaged or enjoyed by the Victorians, new material was grafted on: this often displayed continental or other outside influences. Frequently the results were unconvincing: Cecil Clutton led the rebuilding by Harrison & Harrison in 1975 of their own organ at Ely Cathedral (the instrument that pioneered George Dixon's new thinking in 1908). The lowering of pressures, brightening of the fluework, revoicing of the reeds and addition of a Positive section resulted in a curious hybrid, lacking either the pedigree or musical conviction of the Harrison masterpiece on the one hand or of a good neo-classical organ on the other. Many distinguished Victorian and Edwardian instruments were altered in this way; not one emerged with its original character intact, and in only a very few instances has the result been a coherent statement of a new style.

As far as new organs are concerned, the financial stringencies of the post-war period and the debilitating effects of repeated war and depression slowed reform in style or quality. At the bottom end of the market a substantial number of cheap extension organs were built (between four and eight ranks extended to provide a two-manual organ of 25–30 stops). The paper advantage of these schemes was that they offered a large number of stops fairly cheaply, using only a few pipes. By the 1980s the arrival of 'acceptable' electronic organs with yet more stops and no pipes at all had begun to eat into this market. It seems likely that further attempts to make ultra-cheap pipe organs are doomed: for those who imagine that numbers of stops are more important than numbers of pipes, the electronic is the only sensible answer.

Further up the scale, larger new organs were of conventional 'straight' (i.e. non-unit) design. Neo-classicism might influence the specification, but electro-pneumatic action was the norm. Typical showpiece instruments seemed to owe at least something to the American Classic Organ of the 1930s and 40s. In the Mormon Hyde Park Chapel, South Kensington, London (1961), Hill, Norman & Beard built an instrument strongly reminiscent of Walter Holtkamp.[62] That at Coventry

---

[61] Information gained by the author as an employee of N. P. Mander Ltd
[62] Norman, *The Organs of Britain*, 213–14

Cathedral by Harrison & Harrison (1962) retained some continuity with the firm's earlier traditions, but also showed influence from the Festival Hall and other instruments built in consultation with Ralph Downes.[63] J. W. Walker & Sons Ltd offered a slightly more neo-classical recipe; their large new instrument for the Roman Catholic Liverpool Metropolitan Cathedral (1967) is typical of several built at this time.[64] N. P. Mander Ltd built a new organ for Corpus Christi College, Cambridge in 1968, in consultation with Michael Gillingham and others. This owed much more to historical themes, with elements of traditional English and French designs woven into a neo-classical framework and built behind a splendid classical case by Stephen Dykes-Bower. However, the action was still electro-pneumatic and the internal layout unreformed.

The tonal design of these instruments was highly eclectic, stirring ingredients from many different periods and styles into a somewhat lumpy sauce. The intention was to render possible the performance of music of all styles and periods. In practice the result was often chaotic: a stop-list that was littered with stop names chosen seemingly at random from half a dozen different countries rarely conjured up any impression of assured stylistic unity. It is unlikely that any organ at this time did actually include an Italian Principal, a Cor Anglais and a Spanische Trompete all playable from the same console, but such a combination would have raised few eyebrows.

In contrast, Ralph Downes's personal convictions helped make the instruments he worked on remarkably cohesive, despite the varied sources of inspiration. He continued to act as consultant on new organs and rebuilds, building on experience gained at the Festival Hall and Brompton Oratory, and invariably with electro-pneumatic action. He continued to work with Harrison & Harrison and with J. W. Walker & Sons Ltd, but also joined forces with Hill, Norman & Beard on the rebuild of the Willis/Harrison organ at Gloucester Cathedral in 1971. Here, with typical thoroughness (and causing some controversy), Downes removed all trace of the previous romantic instrument, rather using the surviving seventeenth-century pipes (reputedly Thomas Harris 1666) and the old case as the basis for a neo-classical scheme. This, the Downes/Harrison rebuild at St Albans Abbey (1962), and organs such as Coventry Cathedral and Liverpool Metropolitan Cathedral brought a more coherent classical sound to the centres of the established churches, and showed that classicism was not necessarily an enemy of choral accompaniment.

Downes, however, had always found working with England's larger companies a trying business (a feeling that was warmly reciprocated); they would simply not move as fast or as far as he would have liked. It is quite probable that he would have liked to encourage mechanical actions, but for the time being he dared not push for a further technical revolution. Mechanical actions were being built, even by some of the establishment firms, but usually as premium-price rarities constructed for

[63] D. Lepine, 'The Organs in the Parish Church and Cathedral Church of St. Michael in Coventry', *The Organ*, 42 (1962–3), 1–10

[64] N. Sterrett, 'The Organ in Liverpool Metropolitan Cathedral', *The Organ*, 49 (1969–70), 49–60

prominent clients only. Downes had long wondered whether the organ building establishment was capable of radical change: 'If there is ever to be a tonal renaissance in our organ-building, I venture to suggest . . . that it will be at the hands of the "small man" – the "artist-craftsman" – if he still exists.'[65] The work of Grant, Degens & Bradbeer and Peter Collins in the 1970s certainly suggested that this was the case: they proved able, at their best, to grasp the questions of design and tone on a level that would have been familiar and acceptable to any continental builder.

The larger companies worked on mechanical-action organs with less consistent success, and very little notice was taken of the engineering advances made by organ builders on the continent. In the 1970s British industry in general was characterised by problems with design quality and component manufacture; organs were no exception, and the seventies and eighties saw the building of a number of poor mechanical-action instruments. Some merely lacked finesse, others were embarrassing and expensive failures.

Against such lack of conviction either in design or execution it was inevitable that organs should continue to arrive from abroad, to satisfy the taste of those organists who had caught the classical 'bug'. The best of these, like the Frobenius at Queen's College, Oxford, were instruments of astonishing quality and beauty. It is easy to single out a handful of them: Eton College School Hall (Flentrop, Netherlands, 1973); St Mary the Virgin, Nottingham (Marcussen, Denmark 1973); Clifton Roman Catholic Cathedral, Bristol (Rieger, Austria 1973); Hexham Abbey, Northumberland (Phelps, USA, 1974), Trinity College, Cambridge (Metzler, Switzerland 1976), Reid School of Music, University of Edinburgh (Ahrend, Germany, 1978).[66] All of these are challenging instruments, all of them controversial to a greater or lesser degree, but all displaying many excellencies of tone, design and manufacture (though the organ at Hexham can be marked down on account of its unattractive case).

Other imports have been less successful. The organ by von Beckerath (Germany, 1971) at Clare College, Cambridge is ugly in appearance and was originally too loud: a rare miscalculation from this builder. In the intimate chapel at Gonville and Caius College, Cambridge the organ by Klais (1981) was a bizarre choice: the fame of this firm rests on large instruments in big resonant buildings. The organ at Christ Church Cathedral, Oxford was originally intended to be by Phelps, but the company collapsed before the organ could be delivered. A second contract was let to Rieger of Austria. The organ (1979) is a fine one, but involved unsympathetic alteration to a Father Smith case and has a tone too sharp and spiky to blend with voices – far removed from the suave elegance of the Metzler at Cambridge.[67] Amongst some advisers to the Catholic Church there has been a policy of building

[65] Letter from R. Downes, *The Organ*, 23 (1943–4), 188
[66] Rowntree and Brennan, *The Classical Organ in Britain* vol. I; Rowntree and Brennan, *The Classical Organ in Britain*, vol. II
[67] Rowntree and Brennan, *The Classical Organ in Britain*; Rowntree and Brennan, *The Classical Organ in Britain*; vol. II; Rowntree and Brennan, *The Classical Organ in Britain*, vol. III

small, cheap classical organs by lesser-known builders, some English and many foreign. This is somewhat reminiscent of the wave of Anneessens instruments in Catholic churches in the 1880s: organs that appear to have all the credentials of new continental thinking at a greatly reduced price. The best of these have been good workhorses, though none is really distinguished. The worst, especially one or two of the instruments by the now defunct firm of Tamburini (Italy), join the Anneessens organs in a spectacular display of cost-cutting and have surely made a negative contribution to the debate.

From the above it will be seen that the image of the classical organ has become very mixed, with instruments varying widely in style and quality. The purchase of such organs has been in the hands of a minority of intellectual organists and consultants, many of whom are perceived as having devoted part or whole of their interest to problems of solo repertoire, rather than to problems of music in worship and choral accompaniment. To the majority of organists, executing humble tasks in parish churches, the classical organ is a brash, unpleasant and irrelevant intruder. These musicians continue to write to the musical press in large numbers, doubting the virtues of mechanical action (too heavy), classical voicing (too spiky), and particularly of foreign organs (too, well, *foreign*). The truth is that the organ reform movement, like Modern Movement architecture and avant-garde music, has only received grudging and limited acceptance in Britain. However much one may appreciate the virtues of the best classical organs, right up to the most extreme works of Grant, Degens & Bradbeer, it must be admitted that, outside a circle of *cognoscenti*, they are simply not much liked.

CHAPTER EIGHTEEN

EPILOGUE
1980 ONWARDS

It may not have escaped the reader's attention that the events surrounding the classical revival of 1939–80 are remarkably similar to those that led to the German System instruments of 1840–65. In both periods a new organist-led movement, inspired by the music of Bach and extensive foreign travel, introduced a number of controversial foreign instruments and forced English builders to effect a complete change of style.

Indeed, this indicates a strong cyclical element permeating the history of the instrument in the British Isles. A crisis (religious turmoil, war, economic decline) is followed by foreign influence and radical change. A period of consolidation and confidence in the next generation is ultimately followed by insularity and complacency. Amongst the major crises we recognise the English Reformation, the Civil War, the Napoleonic Wars (and stagnation in the church in the early nineteenth century), the two World Wars in the twentieth century and the Depression in the 1930s. Amongst the foreigners or foreign-influenced craftsmen are the itinerant Flemings whose existence was postulated in Chapters 3 and 4, Bernard Smith and Renatus Harris in the late seventeenth century, Schulze and Cavaillé-Coll in the nineteenth, and the continental builders associated with the modern classical revival. The confident triumphs of English style belong to the Dallams; to Jordan, Byfield, Bridge and the Englands; to William Hill and Father Willis. The insular phases are represented by Samuel Green and his early nineteenth-century successors, and perhaps by Hope-Jones and Arthur Harrison.

There is every sign that since 1980 English organ-building has blossomed, despite decline in church attendance and continuing uncertainty in the economy at large. Even if we are right in assuming that the classical organ has been fully understood and enjoyed only by a minority of organists, it is nevertheless true that the classicists have had all the best arguments and have been highly influential. In new work mechanical action is now the norm (as it has been on the continent since the 1950s or earlier); well-designed casework is taken for granted; 'reformed' tonal ideas are widely accepted, even if they have not yet settled into a definite (or completely successful) new style. There are still companies, some of them well-known, offering to build new organs with electro-pneumatic action and even to build extension

Plate 74   The organ in St Ignatius Loyola, New York City, USA, built by N. P. Mander Ltd and completed in 1992. The casework was designed by Didier Grassin and Stephen Bicknell. This organ is in many ways one of the grandest statements to be made by an English builder since the Second World War, and is claimed to be the largest mechanical-action organ ever built in Britain. The opulent case is matched in the details of interior construction and layout, suggesting a revival in English builders' confidence and competence.

organs, but these are now in decline and are unlikely to be entrusted with important contracts. The market for cheap pipe organs is being rapidly eroded by the
marketing of electronic substitutes; customers who have decided that they want
pipes, not circuitry, are likely to understand that an organ with mechanical action
and a case is an important investment in an ancient craft: they have already decided
that they do not want a factory product, reliant on modern technology and gadgets.

With the return to an atmosphere of artistic, craft-based production a situation
has arisen (as predicted by Ralph Downes during the Second World War) where
young artisan builders are controlling a significant portion of the market for new
organs. Grant, Degens & Bradbeer did not long survive the retirement of Maurice
Forsyth-Grant, closing in 1989; as yet no one has taken up their futuristic stance.
Peter Collins (originally at Redbourn, Hertfordshire, now at Melton Mowbray,
Leicestershire) has built successfully on early promise, maintaining a fairly strict
classical philosophy – mechanical action, good modern-movement case designs,
continentally influenced tonal schemes. His successes include exports to Australia,
Norway and Germany. Many feel that his best and most characteristic organ is that
at St Peter Mancroft, Norwich (1984), a three-manual *Werkprinzip* instrument on the
west gallery of a fine mediaeval church.

Great	16. 8. 8. 4. 4. 2²/₃. 2. 2. 1³/₅. IV–V. II. 8.
Rückpositiv	8. 8. 4. 4. 2. 1¹/₃. II. IV–V. 16. 8.
Echo (enclosed)	8. 8. 8. 4. 2. 1. II. 8.
Pedal	16. 16. 8. 8. 4. IV. 16. 8.

Nigel Church operated on a smaller scale, achieving particular success and
acknowledgement for an organ at Wallsend-on-Tyne, built in consultation with and
to the drawings of Georges Lhôte of Geneva in 1979. This fruitful collaboration
introduced excellently responsive mechanical action of the suspended variety (the
key pivoted at the tail, the tracker rising directly from the key) together with a
warmer, more restrained version of the classical tonal recipe. After building a series
of attractive small organs Church retired in 1989.

These two companies, and one or two others smaller still, have managed to
survive entirely on the building of new mechanical-action organs, a path that most
of the larger well-established firms considered commercially impossible. One man
was not convinced that there was any real problem in such a route. Robert Pennells
took a controlling interest in J. W. Walker & Sons in the late 1970s. By 1978 he had
moved the company to Brandon in Suffolk, where he was already running the manufacture of organ parts for sale to other builders. The Walker company was now
re-established with new plant, new management, mostly new staff and new ideals.

► *Plate 75*   The organ in St Peter Mancroft, Norwich, built by Peter Collins in 1984. The English version of the
European neo-classical organ. The casework, broadly of modern-movement inspiration, is divided into sections
to allow a clear understanding of the positions of the different parts of the organ, as in organs in northern
Europe from 1650–1750. This *Werkprinzip* tradition is here used as the peg on which to hang a twentieth-century
philosophy of form following function.

Considerable investment was made in equipment, including a pioneering system of computer-assisted design and manufacture. This effort was devoted at once to the building of new organs with mechanical action. Like Maurice Forsyth-Grant, Pennells was happy to acknowledge the importance of good design and foreign influence. The architect David Graebe joined the company to produce some of the best English case designs of the twentieth century, some design work was carried out by Michael Tramnitz (a freelance designer associated with Klais of Germany), and Pennell's son Andrew trained with Klais and at the German organ builders' school at Ludwigsburg. In 1985 the organ world and J. W. Walker's competitors sat up and took notice when the firm built a technical *tour de force* for the church of Our Lady of the Angels, Worcester, Massachusetts, USA. Divided in three cases on the west gallery of the church, with the Great and Swell on soundboards trapezoid in plan and with a detached console, this instrument nevertheless stuck to the company policy in having mechanical key action throughout.[1]

Great	16. 8. 8. 4. 4. 2. II. IV. III. 8
Swell	8. 8. 8. 4. 4. 2⅔. 2. 1⅗. V. 16. 8. 4.
Positive	8. 4. 4. 2. 2. 1⅓. IV. 8.; 8 (horizontal).
Pedal	16. 16. 8 (ext. 16). 8. 4. IV. 32. 16. 8.

Since 1980 Britain has also been introduced to instruments by Kenneth Jones, an Irish builder based in Dublin and hovering between the British scene and a wider international market (including some major work in America). Trained as an engineer, Jones exhibits great confidence in tackling complex problems of layout and design in a completely original manner. Large organs in Dublin illustrate his skill, as does the sixty-stop four-manual organ at St Peter Eaton Square, London.

Meanwhile the international organ reform movement has entered a new phase. Despite the intentions of the *Orgelbewegung* to pursue the ideals of a supposed 'Golden Age' in organ building, specifically represented by the *Werkprinzip* instruments of Arp Schnitger and his contemporaries, it has become obvious that the results often owe more to the twentieth-century Modern Movement than they do to historical prototypes. As the move towards authentic performance and interest in early instruments has grown, so too has a degree of dissatisfaction with the average organ reform instrument. An alternative philosophy, resulting in organs that are more historically 'pure', that relies more on traditional techniques and materials, and that produces instruments that are considerably less brash and shrill, could be observed first in the work of Ahrend & Brunzema (later Ahrend *solo*) in Germany and, by the mid seventies, in organs by Metzler of Switzerland. Pioneering work was also being done by Noack, Fisk, Brombaugh and others in the United States. At the same time it has been realised that the neo-classical organ tends to exclude, as a matter of principle, any romantic influence, and equally excludes much of the still popular romantic repertoire. Interest in nineteenth-

---

[1] J. Norman, 'British Organbuilding in 1985', *The Organbuilder*, 4 (1986), 37

century organs has revived, especially in the works of the great French builder Cavaillé-Coll.

N. P. Mander Ltd has been well placed to take advantage of this new thinking. Having maintained an interest in organ restoration and being noted for relatively conservative rebuilds of nineteenth century organs, the company attracted the interest of Cecil Clutton, Michael Gillingham and others. Gradually the contact with old instruments began to influence the firm more and more, leading to a new organ in the Father Smith style at Pembroke College, Cambridge, built in consultation with Clutton in 1980. This instrument was designed and voiced by Noel Mander's son John, who had trained with von Beckerath in Germany and was alive to the possibilities offered by attempting to recreate an historic tradition.

Nevertheless, in the 1970s the state of Britain's own organ heritage was causing widespread anxiety. Valuable old organs in Britain received (and still receive) no state protection or listing, and though reasonably sympathetic restorations were being carried out here and there, the general picture was one of decay and indifference. Victorian and Edwardian organs suffered throughout the post-war period from cheap rebuilding and tonal alterations, sometimes in dubious late-romantic taste, and sometimes in dubious neo-classical taste. Even an outwardly sympathetic firm like N. P. Mander Ltd was occasionally guilty of over-zealous 'improvement': the 1862 Hill at the Ulster Hall, Belfast was considerably enlarged in 1978, not entirely to its benefit.[2] Other companies treated old organs in a frankly cavalier manner; in addition, thanks to the decline in church attendance and the closure of many places of worship, many more were being broken up for scrap.

In 1976 a group of concerned individuals (among them Michael Gillingham and Nicholas Thistlethwaite) met in Cambridge, and founded the British Institute of Organ Studies (BIOS).[3] This educational charity aims to promote research into the organ in Britain, to conserve related source materials, to work for the careful conservation and restoration of old organs, and to encourage the exchange of ideas with other bodies at home and abroad. Through regular meetings and high quality publications it has proved to be an important and influential forum for new ideas.

The activities of BIOS have been a sure sign of renewed activity and interest in the organ; so have the series of books by J. P. Rowntree and J. F. Brennan on the classical organ in Britain. To these we should add many organ-related monographs, and the annual appearance of *The Organbuilder*, a magazine devoted to the latest trends, and confidently recording each year the growing production of encased mechanical-action organs. The activities of organisations representing the 'old guard' of anti-classical organ building firms (the Incorporated Society of Organ Builders, the Federation of Master Organ Builders) have gone into steep and potentially terminal decline. Peter Hurford's bi-annual International Organ Festival at St Albans has taken root and has been a decisive influence: its informal exhibition of

[2] N. J. Thistlethwaite, *The Making of the Victorian Organ* (Cambridge 1990), 534
[3] D. Wright, 'BIOS, The First Ten Years', *BIOS Journal*, 10 (1986), 4–6

small mechanical-action instruments by various builders has been of great importance in making the classical organ seem more accessible and friendly.

The pattern of training for organists has changed. Several English players have been able to carve out careers as international recitalists, and many (but not all) of the teaching institutions have begun to reform their syllabuses. Today's student is no longer articled as an apprentice-assistant to a cathedral organist, but learns in the more academic environment offered by an Oxford or Cambridge organ scholarship or a degree course at a music college. There is a small but significant (and influential) number of organists who have trained and even worked abroad. The availability of good recordings has opened the wider spectrum of organ sound from round the world to those who cannot afford to travel.

With so much new and renewed activity there is every reason to suggest that, after a period in the doldrums, organs and organ playing are once again regarded seriously by the wider musical world.

Even if it is clear that all the significant British organ builders have adopted the neo-classical philosophy to a greater or lesser extent, this nevertheless leaves room for a wide variety of activity. Many of the larger companies engaged in rebuilds and restorations have been stung by criticism into a reformed approach. For N. P. Mander Ltd the rebuild at the Ulster Hall, Belfast was the last such project to be tackled in a head-on, invasive manner. By the 1980s their rebuilds were becoming more sympathetic to the original material, and for the first time since the 1950s included retention and restoration of good pneumatic actions rather than their automatic electrification (the 1987 rebuild of the four-manual Hill at Eton College Chapel is a notable example).[4] Harrison & Harrison have also learnt from some of the slightly uncomfortable rebuilds of the 1960s and 70s: recent major work has been notable for the carefully judged respect for the tonal and technical qualities of old material. This approach, in turn, has reached the upper levels of the Anglican musical world: rebuilds during the 1980s at the cathedrals at Chichester (Mander)[5] and Peterborough (Harrison),[6] both carried out in consultation with Michael Gillingham, were conservationist in spirit. More remarkable still are first, the Mander restoration of the 1907 Walker at Bristol Cathedral, retaining its charge pneumatic action (but, less happily, with the addition of a new Mixture stop and the electrification of the stop and combination action), and secondly the 1986/1991 Harrison restoration of the 1897 Lewis at Southwark Cathedral, reversing most of the unfortunate tonal alterations made by Henry Willis III in 1952 (though retaining the Willis console and modern pitch).

With some older or less altered organs the problems of restoration are fewer, and a more 'pure' result is easier to achieve. There are nevertheless many potential areas of controversy. Lack of interest and funding has prevented the kind of large-scale restoration of historic instruments familiar on the continent, and a number of

[4] N. J. Thistlethwaite, *Organs at Eton*, (Eton, 1987)
[5] A. Thurlow and N. M. Plumley, 'The Organ in Chichester Cathedral', *BIOS Journal*, 10 (1986), 118–25
[6] N. J. Thistlethwaite, 'The Rebuilt Organ in Peterborough Cathedral', *BIOS Journal*, 7 (1983), 108–11

important old organs in the British Isles remain in a parlous or derelict state at the time of writing: the 1730 Bridge at Christ Church Spitalfields is unplayable; the 1826 Lincoln at Thaxted, Essex is barely working; the 1848 Hill from St Mary-at-Hill, City of London is dismantled and stored after serious fire damage, with no immediate prospect of restoration; the 1851 Gray & Davison at St Anne Limehouse, London has received only minor repairs since it was built and is in poor condition; the 1882 Wilkinson from Preston Public Hall (resplendent with 32′ front) is in storage in a temporary home.

Nevertheless there have been some successes: amongst older organs the work of Goetze & Gwynn on chamber organs is notable, and the 1991 William Drake restoration of the 1786 Seede organ at Lulworth Castle Chapel, Dorset, has set a new standard.[7] N. P. Mander Ltd upholds its existing reputation in this field with work at Wollaton Hall, Nottingham (Anon c1690, Henry Holland 1799), the Holywell Music Room, Oxford (John Donaldson 1790) and the Catholic chapel at Everingham, Yorkshire (Charles Allen 1839). Larger, later organs are also being restored to a high standard: the Mander restoration of the 1906 Lewis & Co. organ at the Kelvingrove Art Gallery, Glasgow and the 1993 Harrison & Harrison restoration of the 1909 Binns at the Albert Hall, Nottingham have retained tubular pneumatic action, the original tonal schemes, and the original consoles and combination actions. It is now possible to envisage the removal of inappropriate neo-classical additions from good romantic organs. One awaits with interest the application of similar techniques of conservation to surviving early electro-pneumatic-action organs.

The revival of interest in Britain's organ heritage has had a conspicuous influence on the design of some new organs. In 1988 Goetze & Gwynn, a small firm leading the field in careful historical research and its application to new organs, built a two-manual instrument for the Anglican Church in The Hague, Holland, inspired by the work of Richard Bridge (see plate 76, p. 360).[8] This extremely interesting reversal of the usual trend of imports from the continent is backed up in the Netherlands by the appearance of a large number of restored Victorian organs rescued from redundant churches in the British Isles. The most notable appearance to date of English eighteenth-century techniques in a new organ is in the 1991 William Drake organ at the Grosvenor Chapel, Mayfair, London, housed in a case of 1732 by Jordan (specification p. 361; see also plate 77, p. 362).[9]

[7] W. Drake, 'Lulworth Castle Chapel Organ, The Reconstruction of the Organ', *BIOS Journal*, 16 (1992), 60–6; J. P. Rowntree, 'Lulworth Castle Chapel Organ; Some Reflections', *BIOS Journal*, 16 (1992), 67–9

[8] G. Verloop, 'The Organ in the Anglican Church of St. John & St. Philip in the Hague', *BIOS Journal*, 13 (1989), 107–13

[9] M. Lindley and W. Drake, 'Grosvenor Chapel and the 18th Century English Organ', *BIOS Journal*, 15 (1991), 90–119; N. Thistlethwaite, 'The New Organ in the Grosvenor Chapel, South Audley Street, London W1', *BIOS Journal*, 16 (1992), 112–15

Plate 76   The organ in the Anglican church of St John and St Philip, The Hague, The Netherlands, built by Martin Goetze and Dominic Gwynn in 1988. This organ illustrates two recent trends: first, the renewed interest in old English organs (allowing this instrument to be designed and constructed in the manner of the eighteenth-century builder Richard Bridge); secondly, an emerging new interest in English organ culture.

London, The Grosvenor Chapel, Mayfair: William Drake 1991

Great GG,AA–f''' (58 notes)		**Swell** C–f''' (54 notes)	
Open Diapason	8	Open Diapason	8
Stopt Diapason	8	Stopt Diapason	8
Principal	4	Principal	4
Flute	4	Fifteenth	2
Twelfth	2⅔	Cornet bass/treble	III
Fifteenth	2	Mixture	III
Sesquialtera	III–IV	Trumpet	8
Furniture	III	Hautboy	8
Trumpet bass/treble	8	Tremulant	
Cornet (from c')	V		

Pedal C–f' (30 notes)	
Stopt Diapason	16
Principal	8
Trumpet	16

Swell to Great
Swell to Pedal
Great to Pedal
(four levers allow the lowest notes of the Great to be played through the Great to Pedal
coupler)

Restoration and reproduction of these early instruments has led, as in other countries, to lively debate: on the appropriateness of modern materials in organ building, on the provision of period wind systems, and, especially, on the option of tuning a new organ to an unequal temperament.[10] It has also led to a gradual revision of opinions about the nature of 'classical' voicing: it is now clear that open-foot voicing was an over-simplified attempt to emulate past traditions. There were as many variations of wind pressure, tip size, mouth height and voicing treatment in the seventeenth and eighteenth centuries as there are today, and most of the possibilities were thoroughly explored in one local tradition or another. Equally, nicking of pipe-languids is not the *faux-pas* it appeared to the organ reformers: nicking can now be shown to have existed in the seventeenth century, and in England is present, for example, at Adlington Hall. There are many ways of nicking a pipe, each appropriate to a particular style of manufacture.

A new and much clearer sense of style is the obvious hallmark of historically inspired work. With a parallel revival of interest in romantic organs and music it is not surprising that some new instruments have begun to draw inspiration from the Victorian tradition. The most notable of these is the 1989 N. P. Mander Ltd

[10] C. A. Padgham, *The Well-Tempered Organ* (Oxford 1986)

Plate 77   The organ in the Grosvenor Chapel, Mayfair, London, built by William Drake in 1991 and housed in the case of the original Abraham Jordan instrument of c1730. A further example of a new organ consciously and successfully adopting some of the stylistic parameters of an earlier English tradition, here drawing inspiration from a number of eighteenth-century sources. This and other similar instruments have been received with the warmth and enthusiasm that escaped the less subtle neo-classical organs of the post-war period.

instrument at St Andrew Holborn, housed in an eighteenth-century case from the Foundling Hospital, London. Here is an organ that seems to have sprung from the pages of Hopkins and Rimbault's great Victorian treatise.[11]

London, St Andrew Holborn: N. P. Mander Ltd 1989

Great C–a''' (58 notes)		**Swell** C–a''' (58 notes)	
Double Diapason (wood)	16	Open Diapason	8
Open Diapason	8	Clarionet Flute (wood)	8
Stopped Diapason (wood)	8	Salicional	8
Gamba	8	Principal	4
Principal	4	Fifteenth	2
Suabe Flute (wood)	4	Echo Cornet (with tierce)	III
Twelfth	$2^2/_3$	Mixture	II
Fifteenth	2	Cornopean	8
Flageolet (wood)	2	Hautboy	8
Sesquialtera (with tierce)	III	Clarion	4
Mixture	III	Tremulant	
Posaune	8	Undulant (operating Open Diapason with	
Corno di Bassetto	8	restricted wind, to give a celeste effect	
Clarion	4	with the Salicional)	

Pedal C–f' (30 notes)	
Open Diapason (wood)	16
Bourdon (wood)	16
Quint (wood)	$10^2/_3$
Principal	8
Fifteenth	4
Bombarde (wood)	16

Swell to Great
Great to Pedal
Swell to Pedal

2 composition pedals to Great
2 composition pedals to Swell
2 composition pedals to Pedal
Wind pressures: Manuals 76mm; Pedal 89mm

The organs at the Grosvenor Chapel and St Andrew Holborn are both widely admired, and one can at once understand the kind of general acclaim for these instruments which completely escaped the more severe neo-classical organ of the 1960s and 1970s, not least because both are sweet and elegant, and impeccably finished, avoiding the brash choruses and uncertain voicing quality of some classical organs. Inevitably they have offended those experts who hold the Germanic influences and

---

[11] M. Gillingham, 'Victorian Values', *BIOS Journal*, 14 (1990), 81–6; N. J. Thistlethwaite, 'St Andrew's Holborn', *BIOS Journal*, 14 (1990), 86–9

technical principles of the *Orgelbewegung* to be inviolable truths. The situation is exactly parallel to the debate about the future of architecture, with the modernists in retreat from varied waves of post-modernism, vernacularism and neo-classicism.

Meanwhile Harrison & Harrison have begun, later than most, to build new mechanical-action instruments on a regular basis. This, and the quality of their restoration work, keeps them amongst Britain's leading firms. The only other 'old' firm making a significant contribution to the picture is J. W. Walker & Sons Ltd, whose output of new organs from their plant in Suffolk has been remarkable, especially in the 1980s. Always ambitious, in 1986 they tackled a new organ for Lancing College Chapel in Sussex, incorporating parts of the former Walker instrument of 1911–14. With four manuals, two 32′ stops and a magnificent case by David Graebe this is an instrument full of promise, but its uneasy tonal compromises, eccentric layout (the Great and Swell treble pipes are situated behind the basses), and peculiar mix of actions suggest an uncertain sense of style (the key action is basically mechanical, but with pneumatic assistance in the basses; some individual bass pipes are operated by tubular pneumatic action; part of the Pedal Organ is electro-pneumatic; the couplers are operated electro-mechanically).[12] The greater part of their output has been eclectic, perhaps ultimately bearing some similarity to the work of Klais, though thinner and lighter in sound. Recently they have tried their hand at other styles: Old English (Oriel College Oxford, in consultation with John Harper and with design and pipe scales by the present author), Franco-American Eclectic (St Martin-in-the-Fields, London, in consultation with Gillian Weir and with pipe scales by the retired American builder Phelps) and French Romantic (Exeter College, Oxford).

Meanwhile the organs of Peter Collins have begun to move away from their strict neo-classical roots, incorporating more romantic possibilities (larger Swell organs) and traditional rather than modern casework. New builders making a positive contribution include Kenneth Tickell in Northampton and Neil Richerby (Lammermuir Pipe Organs) near Edinburgh, both building in the neo-classical manner.

Recent organs in England by N. P. Mander Ltd have tended to follow the Victorian pattern started at St Andrew Holborn, notably those at St John's College, Cambridge (1993) and Chelmsford Cathedral (Nave Organ 1994), both built in consultation with Nicholas Thistlethwaite. While attractive, these instruments deny access to parts of the repertoire and are on that score alone unlikely to attract the admiration of the recitalist-consultant. At St John's, Cambridge there are some surprisingly insular features, such as the provision of two Open Diapasons and both Principal 4 and Gemshorn 4 on the Great Organ; the presence of both Tuba 8 and Cornet V suggests further uncertainties about style. Much of the scheme is arranged according to inherited conventions regarding choral accompaniment, but Mander's work at St Ignatius Loyola, New York City (1992) shows that an organ of

---

[12] J. Norman, 'Lancing College Chapel, The New Organs', *The Organbuilder*, 5 (1987), 2–9; M. Butler, 'West Organ, the New Reeds', *The Organbuilder*, 5 (1987), 2–9; D. Graebe, 'The Design of the Organ Cases', *The Organbuilder*, 5 (1987), 2–9; author's examination of the instrument

Plate 78 The west end organ in the chapel of Lancing College, Sussex, built by J. W. Walker & Sons Ltd in 1986, and housed in a case designed by David Graebe. The case announces a magnificent attempt to restore English organ building and design to the stature it occupied in the nineteenth century. The organ includes a substantial amount of old Walker pipework from a previous instrument in the chapel. The use of mixed key actions and an unorthodox internal layout suggests a vision somewhat tempered by compromise.

similar size can still be near-ideal in accompaniment while offering a far better pro-vision for the wider repertoire, in an overall design which still carries all the weight of stylistic confidence (see plate 74, p. 353).

New York City, USA, St Ignatius Loyola: N. P. Mander Ltd 1992
Compass: Manuals C–c'''' (61 notes); Pedal C–g' (32 notes)

Grand Orgue

Montre	16
Montre	8
Flûte harmonique	8
Violoncelle	8
Bourdon (wood)	8
Prestant	4
Flûte à fuseau	4
Quinte	2²⁄₃
Doublette	2
Tierce	1³⁄₅
Fourniture	V
Cymbale	IV
Bombarde	16
Trompette	8
Clairon	4
Cornet (from g')	V
Tremblant	
Récit – Grand Orgue	
Positif – Grand Orgue	
IVe Clavier – Grand Orgue	

Récit Expressif

Bourdon	16
Diapason	8
Salicional	8
Unda Maris	8
Cor de nuit	8
Octave	4
Flûte ouverte (wood)	4
Doublette	2
Plein jeu	IV
Cornet	III
Basson	16
Trompette harmonique	8
Clarinette	8
Clairon harmonique	4
Tremblant	
IVe Clavier–Récit	

IVe Clavier – Petit Récit (enclosed)

Flûte traversière	8
Viole de gambe	8
Voix céleste	8
Bourdon	8
Flûte octaviante	4
Octavin	2
Cor anglais	16
Trompette	8
Basson-hautbois	8
Voix humaine	8
Tremblant	

Positif

Montre	8
Flûte à cheminée	8
Prestant	4
Flûte douce	4
Nazard	2²⁄₃
Doublette	2
Quarte de nazard	2
Tierce	1³⁄₅
Larigot	1¹⁄₃
Plein jeu	V
Trompette	8
Cromorne	8
Tremblant	
Récit – Positif	
IVe Clavier – Positif	

IVe Clavier – Chamades

Bombarde	16
Trompette en chamade	8
Clairon en chamade	4

Pédale

Soubasse (wood)	32
Montre	16
Contrebasse (wood)	16
Soubasse (bass from 32′, wood)	16
Principal	8
Flûte bouchée (wood)	8
Octave	4
Mixture (with tierce)	V
Bombarde	32
Bombarde (bass from 32′)	16
Basson	16
Trompette	8
Clairon	4
Grand Orgue – Pédale	
Récit – Pédale	
Positif – Pédale	
IVe Clavier – Pédale	

Accessories

Orage (storm effect)
Etoile (zimbelstern)
12 general thumb pistons
8 thumb pistons to each manual
1 thumb piston to each coupler
1 thumb piston to full organ
1 toe piston to full organ
8 toe pistons to Pédale
12 toe pistons duplicating gen. pistons
1 toe piston to each Pédale coupler
1 toe piston Récit – Grand Orgue
General Cancel piston
Setter piston

Key action: mechanical (pneumatics for some basses and chamades); stop action: electric

Wind pressures

Grand Orgue 85mm; Récit Expressif 85mm; Positif 75mm; Petit Récit 85mm; Chamades 140mm; Pédale main 95mm; Pédale Soubasse 32 & Contrebasse 16: 110mm; Pédale Bombardes 32 & 16: 140mm

The technical (but not tonal) design of this organ was in the hands of the author while employed at N. P. Mander Ltd, therefore this account is not impartial. I believe that it is an instrument that rises above many of the problems that have been experienced since the Second World War. First, it maintains grandeur of concept and execution at every stage, from the solid oak case through to the oak staircases provided for access to the various levels. Secondly, it has the sense of style lacking in many eclectic neo-classical instruments. (The stop-list is fashionably reminiscent of Cavaillé-Coll; in practice the organ owes much to the Mander firm's experience with English organs of various periods.) Thirdly, it is technically confident, with a good mechanical action. Fourthly and finally, it is a good musical instrument.

The great variety of recipes available to English builders underlines the difficulty they face in finding a stylistic niche in which they feel comfortable and which will support them commercially. Never completely confident with the international organ reform style, they still find that important contracts in the British Isles are landed by continental builders. Large new organs by Flentrop, Frobenius, Marcussen, Rieger and Klais continue to appear, mostly at the behest of consultants or organists who were brought up in the heyday of the organ reform movement and are still not clear how to move forward into a new style for the twenty-first century. It can be argued that the continental firms mentioned above reached their artistic peak in the 1960s; only Rieger has begun to change to adapt to the different musical taste of the 1990s. There is much to suggest that in purchasing these organs Britain remains some decades behind the times. The arrival of an instrument by van den Heuvel at the Royal Academy of Music strikes a more contemporary note: this Dutch company is known for instruments that owe a great deal to the work of Cavaillé-Coll, and the Academy organ is French romantic in inspiration.

The arrival of organs from abroad continues to cause great anguish to those who feel the pangs of patriotism, especially, of course, the organ builders. On the day that this paragraph was being written several leading organ builders were in conference with their opposite numbers among the players and consultants, addressing a potentially damaging rift between them. With the prospect of further large new organs in this country by Klais and Marcussen, the organ builders are bewildered and affronted by being turned down in favour of continental builders, or even being excluded from invitations to tender. Their argument is that if English organ building is to flourish then it must be adequately encouraged and patronised. The consultants have a ready-made reply: there is no doubt that through the entire post-war period English organ building has been late and reluctant in assimilating new ideas, and has had to make major efforts to build organs to acceptable standards of design and finish. There have been successful new organs, but there have also been conspicuous failures. Is the evidence really there that an English builder can build, for example, a really first-class modern concert-hall organ suited to a wide international repertoire?

Both consultants and builders need to recognise their own limitations if they are to unite and progress. Among the consultants there is a lack of the kind of practical and stylistic knowledge that made Ralph Downes's work so influential; some of the better known of today's advisers are hiding the fact that their basic knowledge of the organ and its mechanism is extremely patchy. The author has seen a scheme for a large new organ in a well-known school, prepared in consultation with a famous recitalist, so ill-considered and so riddled with fundamental misunderstandings as to cause serious concern. The apparent habit of relying on a handful of continental builders who made their name in the 1950s and 1960s is stifling to creative progress, and suggests an inability to perceive the nature of new trends and any possible path of change in the future. The clear impression given by many advisers that idiomatic English elements are not worth exploring is overly dismissive and confrontational, and quite at odds with the warm appreciation of English organs and organ building shown in Europe and America. Until the consultants as a body can show that they have a real grasp of organ architecture and a better awareness of current trends they will not be taken seriously.

The organ builders also have much to learn. Reluctance to explore was a terrifying obstacle to reform after the Second World War, and it was this problem that Ralph Downes tackled head-on. Such attitudes, endemic in the fifties, sixties and seventies, are still to be found today, and there are plenty of organ builders who feel they have nothing to learn from the work of others. The author has had the experience of arranging for the directors and voicers of a well-known English company to visit a new continental organ described by one player as 'a quite exceptional instrument': the inability of the visitors to appreciate what they heard and saw was shown by the fact that they admired only those (few) elements that they felt conformed to their own way of doing things, and condemned the rest out of hand. This is all too reminiscent of the English organ builders who saw Cavaillé-Coll's organ at La Madeleine, Paris in the 1850s, mentioned in Chapter 13, who found this seminal early work of one of the world's greatest builders to be: 'altogether beastly . . . a big brass band and nothing more'.[13] Noel Mander's remark that 'English organ-builders will cease being progressive and artistic if they think they have nothing to learn from any other country'[14] has been quoted already, and is no less relevant to the current generation of builders. Reluctance to learn has left glaring lacunae: fundamental re-engineering of mechanical actions came late to England and some builders have yet to make their first good new mechanical-action organ; concepts of blend and balance common internationally are still poorly understood in Britain and there are few builders in 1995 who can make a flue chorus as noble and convincing as the best by William Hill or Thomas Lewis; the significance of the movement towards 'authentic' performance practice has not received full enough attention and some builders regard an historical approach to new instruments as an irrelevancy or, at best, a sales pitch.

In the organ builders' favour is the argument that times are still difficult. The churches of England – Anglican or otherwise – are poorly funded; only some of the more historic buildings receive any kind of state support. Congregations have dwindled in town and country alike, leading to extensive church closures. Choirs, choirmasters and professional liturgical music have disappeared from all but the wealthiest parishes, the collegiate foundations and the cathedrals. The modernising of the liturgy has left many church musicians feeling isolated and rejected; disputes with clergy seem to be legion. The availability of cheap electronic instruments (offering elaborate consoles and pleasing organ-like effects for less than the price of all but the smallest pipe organ) has eroded the bottom end of the market. Even for the builder who can produce new organs with some success, the profit margins, usually in the order of 3 to 5 per cent, are dangerously small. Employees' pay is accordingly low, and talent accordingly difficult to encourage. To the customer, in a world where any hand-made product seems outrageously expensive compared to its mass-produced equivalent, the capital sum required to purchase a new organ is, to say the least, daunting.

In such a climate one cannot help but rejoice, not just at the presence of several English builders doing consistently good work, but at the numbers of instruments of world class, only some of which have been mentioned here. No one instrument can represent a peak of progress or some unmatched pinnacle of the art. Its success may be due to many factors, but especially to willingness on the part of builder, advisers, clients and players to look forward, to explore, to learn and, where necessary, to change. The careful tending of the nursery of learning will ensure that the English organ has a rich future.

---

[13] *Musical World*, 31 (1853), 594   [14] N. P. Mander, letter to the editor, *The Organ*, 39 (1959–60), 106

GUIDE TO SURVIVING
ENGLISH ORGANS

In reading this book it will have become obvious that there are relatively few examples of old English organs that have been left as they were originally built: the consequences of religious and liturgical upheavals and of changes in musical taste have been that many of the landmark instruments of the past have either been destroyed or have, at least, been altered out of all recognition. Thus, though it is in theory possible to draw up a long list of historic material surviving in the British Isles and elsewhere, much of this would be of only academic interest, consisting only of casework or of instruments that are no longer representative of the style of the original builder. At the time of writing the British Institute of Organ Studies is engaged on an ambitious project to list as many of Britain's organs as it can, and in due course a large database of information will become available to the public. In the meantime it makes more sense to offer a short guide to those instruments that from which interested visitors can learn substantially. Such a list is a personal matter: thus this guide consists mostly of the author's favourite instruments, plus a few more that have been highly recommended by others or that have a distinguished reputation. The instruments are described as they stand in June 1995: further instruments may be restored as time goes by.

Of very early material only a handful of cases and some battered pipework survive, thus our guide starts with the instruments built by members of the Dallam family during their sojourn in France in the middle of the seventeenth century. Here one notable organ by Robert Dallam survives, that at Lanvellec in Brittany, built in 1653. However, its restoration by Bartolomeo Formentelli has not fully convinced most English visitors and, in any case, it seems that it may have been partly rebuilt by Robert Dallam's son Thomas Dallam de la Tour at the end of the seventeenth century. Perhaps more interesting is the instrument at Guimiliau, built by Thomas Dallam de la Tour sometime after the return of his father and brothers to England in 1661. This has been restored in recent years by Gérard Guillemin, and is highly thought of.

Of the organs built immediately after the Restoration of the monarchy little survives. The organ at Framlingham in Suffolk, formerly in Pembroke College, Cambridge, is usually attributed to Thomas Thamar and dated 1678. My own examination suggests that much of the Great Organ may be eighteenth-century in date, perhaps with one or two part ranks of older pipes. The Swell and Pedal organs are modern, incorporating nineteenth-century material. Nor is there anything coherent surviving of the work of Bernard Smith, still less of the work of Renatus Harris.

The first organ that merits real attention is that at Adlington Hall, now thought to date from 1693, by an unknown builder working broadly in the style of Bernard Smith. This is a full-sized two-manual instrument, though with various quirky features, and retains almost all its original pipes and mechanism. It is one of Europe's most important early domestic instruments. The reed stops, Trumpet, Bassoon and Vox Humana are very rare survivals.

The work of Smith's and Harris's immediate successors has fared no better. The best survivor is the organ at Finedon in Northamptonshire, usually attributed to Christopher Shrider and dated 1717. It retains most of the original pipework, but at a rebuild in the nineteenth century by Holdich it received new soundboards and most of the pipework was revoiced. Much about its sound is reminiscent more of Holdich than of any earlier builder's work.

There is nothing to tell us exactly what an organ by the younger Harris, the elder John Byfield, Richard Bridge or the Jordans might have sounded like, though the restoration of the 1735 Bridge at Christ Church Spitalfields, London (silent since 1955) may eventually redress the balance. With John Byfield II we are more fortunate. The three-manual organ at St Mary Rotherhithe, London survives with only some alterations and in its original position. Though later changes have made this instrument less than wholly authentic, it is in many ways a convincing representative of the mid-eighteenth-century ideal. It is backed up by the survival of a fine chamber organ by Byfield in the collection of keyboard instruments at Finchcocks, near Goudhurst, Sussex. This organ was built in 1766.

The work of George England is represented by the large chamber organ of 1760 now at Hall Place, Bexleyheath, Kent; the work of John England by the slightly smaller instrument at Wardour Castle, near Tisbury, Wiltshire, dated 1767. Much George England material of 1764 survives at St George, Gravesend, Kent, but the instrument is at present unplayable.

Of Snetzler's larger organs only revoiced pipework survives, though in some quantity. However, the janglingly brilliant choruses which I believe to have been characteristic of his work survive in a number of chamber organs, such as that now at St Andrew by the Wardrobe in the City of London, originally built for Teddesley Hall, Staffordshire in 1769. My own favourite is the two-manual chamber organ now in the parish church at Hillington in Norfolk, built in 1756.

At Blandford Forum in Dorset stands the three-manual organ built by George Pike England in 1794. Much of the original pipework survives. The organ is now very mild in tone; one cannot help suspecting that after many years of creeping in the soft plain metal pipework, combined with the damage caused by tuning, the feet of the pipes may have become smaller, the languids may have sunk a little, and the mouths of the smaller pipes may have become distorted. Nevertheless, standing on the west gallery of a fine eighteenth-century church, this organ offers an informative lesson in eighteenth-century manners, second only to the Byfield at Rotherhithe.

Samuel Green's larger organs have also suffered badly, despite the survival of quantities of material at the Royal Hospital Chapel, Greenwich, London (1789) and at St Katherine Regent's Park, London (1778, formerly at St Katherine by the Tower, London). At Armitage in Staffordshire stands the remains of the organ Green built in 1790 for Lichfield Cathedral. This is altogether more interesting, despite later alterations: it tells the listener a good deal about Green's individual approach to tone and balance, though it must be borne in mind that it was designed and voiced for a different and much larger building.

Two smaller eighteenth-century organs deserve special mention, both having been restored in recent years. The organ at Lulworth Castle Chapel in Dorset was installed (and built?) by Richard Seede of Bristol c1785. It is a large one-manual organ with several unusual features, most notable of which is its reversed console. It illustrates the best of the west-country school and seems indebted to the traditions passed down by Renatus and John Harris. In style, quality and the extent of its preservation it stands close comparison with the organ at Rotherhithe. Another instrument, built by John Donaldson of Newcastle in 1790 for Belvedere House in Dublin, now stands in the Holywell Music Room, Oxford. Donaldson's work seems to owe something to Snetzler, but the overall effect of this instrument, which is very delicately voiced, is perhaps even more reminiscent of the taste of Samuel Green.

The early nineteenth century is represented by several instruments by Elliot. That at Crick in Northamptonshire is the former instrument from the Chapel Royal, St James's, London, built in 1819. Organs at Scone Palace, Perthshire (1813) and at Ashridge, Hertfordshire (1818) add to the picture.

From the same period there is the three-manual H. C. Lincoln organ of 1821 at Thaxted parish church in Essex, built for St John's Chapel, Bedford Row, London. It is now in poor condition. The three-manual Gray of 1820 built for St Mary, Bathwick, Somerset is now, after an eventful life, in a museum in Berlin, and is one of the only examples surviving of an old English instrument with a Choir Organ in a separate case, in the manner of the old Chaire Organ. However, pride of place goes to the organ built by Charles Allen of London in 1839 for the Roman Catholic chapel at Everingham in Yorkshire: this is one of the very few instruments on which one can enjoy the peculiar grandeur offered by a long-compass Great Organ backed up by the then fashionable unison pedal pipes; it also retains its four original reed stops: two Trumpets, an Hautboy and a Cremona.

Of the experimental organs of the insular period of the 1830s and 40s there is now virtually nothing surviving, except the 1829 J. C. Bishop at St James Bermondsey, London. However, at the time of writing only the Great Organ is playable and no restoration is planned. Another Bishop organ survives at St Giles Camberwell, London. As late as 1844 this large instrument was built under the direction of Samuel Sebastian Wesley retaining many archaic features, although at least with German System C-compass manual and pedal keyboards. There have been only minor alterations. Bishop was not at his best in large instruments, and this organ illustrates the extreme difficulty faced by English builders in the 1840s in trying to grasp what a large organ was really about. It is, in some ways, quite difficult for the player to make good musical sense out of the material that Wesley and Bishop have jointly provided.

The first fully developed German System organs have fared no better, the vitally important work of William Hill being especially poorly represented. His organ of 1848 from St Mary at Hill in the City of London is now dismantled and in storage after being badly damaged in a fire. There is no immediate prospect of restoration. The pioneering organ of 1841 at Great George Street Chapel, Liverpool, survived until modern times only to be comprehensively vandalised and then broken up. One of the last survivors is the organ at Kidderminster Town Hall, West Midlands, built in 1855. Of work turned out towards the end of William Hill's life the organ of 1862 in the Ulster Hall, Belfast is perhaps the best example, but this was considerably enlarged at a rebuild in 1978, not in my opinion to its advantage.

Gray & Davison are represented by the splendid instrument of 1851 at St Anne Limehouse, London, exhibited in the Great Exhibition of that year. It is now in very poor condition and restoration is eagerly awaited. The instrument built by the same firm in 1861 for Llandaff Cathedral is now in the parish church of Usk in Monmouthshire. It is a very fine example of the continental influence prevalent in the 1860s and remains in good voice.

The J. W. Walker organ of 1858 at Romsey Abbey is of great interest and beauty, despite some enlargement at later dates. Walker is also represented by the organ of 1861 at St Audoen, Dublin. Like the ex-Llandaff organ by Gray & Davison, this latter instrument shows some continental influence.

Examples survive of the work of Edmund Schulze in Britain, of which the best is that at St Bartholomew, Armley, Yorkshire, built in 1869 and added to in 1879. The much larger organ at Doncaster parish church, completed in 1862, survives but there has been some revoicing. It is now the most significant survival of Edmund Schulze's work in either Britain or Germany, and deserves to be fully restored reinstating the original Barker Lever key action. Cavaillé-Coll is represented by the organ now in the Parr Hall, Warrington, built for Ketton Hall, Rutland, the home of John Hopwood, in 1870. Unfortunately the original Barker Lever key action was wantonly destroyed in the 1970s, to be replaced by an inappropriate electro-pneumatic action. A small, late example of the work of the Cavaillé-Coll firm stands at Farnborough Abbey in Hampshire. I believe that it was provided new in 1905 when the firm was under the management of Charles Mutin, but it still represents the best traditions of the *maître*.

Lesser builders of the mid nineteenth century are better represented. The reputation of the Schulze-inspired Charles Brindley rests partly on his instrument of 1861 at the remote Town Hall of Launceston, Tasmania. Schulze influence also permeated the work of Forster & Andrews: their organ at West Bromwich Town Hall (1878 and 1888) survives. The large instrument built by Wilkinson of Kendal for Preston Public Hall in 1882, with four manuals and a 32′ front, is presently in storage awaiting a new home. It is still possible to find good examples of the work of Holdich, Bevington, Bryceson and others.

Quite a large number of instruments survive from the workshops of Henry Willis, but few have escaped alteration of some kind. Though his organs were much admired by later generations, the great brilliancy he provided was often tamed when the instruments were overhauled in the early twentieth century. Amongst those that have escaped any tinkering, the organ at Reading Town Hall, started in 1864 and completed in 1882, is an excellent example of his work. From Willis's mature period the organ in Salisbury Cathedral (1877) still has original character in the main choruses, and it shows how he eventually managed to occupy the high ground of cathedral organ building, despite the reservations of conservative players. My own favourite Willis organ is that at St Dominic's Priory, Haverstock Hill, London; this was installed in 1867 and completed in 1883. It retains its original sharp pitch, its original pipework, and its Barker Lever action. Standing in a marvellous acoustic, it is an instrument of unforgettable impact and quality.

The organs of T. C. Lewis have mostly been swept away, but a recent restoration of his late masterpiece at Southwark Cathedral, London (1897) has revealed its superlative quality. His organ at St George Cullercoats, Tyne and Wear of 1885 is very highly spoken of, and another recent restoration has been of the 1890 Lewis at St Paul's Anglican Cathedral, Melbourne, Australia.

The later work of the Walker company has suffered various blows, not least being the unfortunate rebuilding of Edwin Lemare's organ of 1897 at St Margaret Westminster in the 1970s. The 1891 organ at St Mary Portsea survives with its pipework largely intact, but it is not in a very good position and to my ears it is not wholly convincing. It may be that a further restoration will reveal some lost glory. The best of the Walker organs from this period is now that in Bristol Cathedral (1907), containing much old pipework from the 1860s and earlier: this is an unusually grand and persuasive instrument.

Of the work of the progressive builders of the late nineteenth century there is not much left, much of it having fallen prey to mechanical unreliability. However, the seminal Michell & Thynne organ built for the Inventions Exhibition of 1885 is intact in the north transept of Tewkesbury Abbey in Gloucestershire. Hope-Jones's work was systematically removed by later generations, and it is now very difficult to judge what his instruments may have sounded like.

By some miracle the leviathan instrument built by William Hill and Sons for Sydney Town Hall in 1888–90 survives with very few alterations. At this time the Hill firm was conservative in many ways, and this instrument sums up the progress of the nineteenth century rather than looking forward to the future. It is generally acknowledged to be one of the world's organ masterpieces, offering astonishing breadth of vision within an aesthetic of restraint and academic good taste. In England a fine late Hill of 1904 survives unaltered at All Saints, Hove, Sussex.

Of the 1,000 organs that left the works of Norman & Beard in Norwich there were a number of masterpieces. The last and largest, built for Johannesburg Town Hall, South Africa, in 1914, has been altered beyond rescue. A similar smaller instrument at the Usher Hall, Edinburgh (1914) awaits restoration, and for the time being the student of their work must go to the Town Hall in Wellington, New Zealand to hear, restored, an example from 1906.

The later work of the Willis company is well covered. An important organ finished under Henry Willis II survives at St Patrick's Cathedral, Dublin, Ireland, completed in 1902. The mammoth Henry Willis III organs at Liverpool Anglican Cathedral (1912–26) and Westminster Cathedral, London (1922–32) survive in good condition; they rank amongst the most spectacular organs ever built in the British Isles.

Of the important early instruments by Harrison & Harrison one of the more interesting is at All Saints Tooting Graveney, London, built in 1904. The reeds were voiced by the ex-Hope-Jones voicer W. C. Jones, and the Choir Organ, following the principles of Carlton Michell, is located away from the rest of the organ behind the choir stalls. The 1911 Harrison at St Mary Redcliffe, Bristol, was damaged by fire in the 1940s, but restored along the original lines, and remains a significant major example of the firm's best work before the First World War. Other important Harrisons survive at the Caird Hall, Dundee (1923, recently restored) and at the City Hall, Newcastle-upon-Tyne (1927, not at present in good order).

Other early twentieth-century builders of note include J. J. Binns (represented by his organ of 1906 in the Albert Hall, Nottingham, now restored) and Rushworth & Dreaper (the five-manual organ of 1931 at Christ's Hospital School, Horsham, Sussex and the four-manual of 1940 at the church of the Holy Rood, Stirling survive relatively unscathed.) Several John Compton organs survive, including a fine example of an organ designed for broadcasting at the BBC studios in Maida Vale, London (1936), and his magnum opus of 1937 at Downside Abbey.

From the period after the Second World War many important instruments remain, understandably enough. The best of the Ralph Downes organs is probably that built for him by J. W. Walker & Sons at the Brompton Oratory, London in 1954, though the examples at the Royal Festival Hall, London (Harrison & Harrison 1954), St Albans Abbey, Hertfordshire (Harrison & Harrison 1963), Paisley Abbey, Renfrewshire (J. W. Walker & Sons Ltd. 1968) and Gloucester Cathedral (Hill, Norman & Beard 1971) are notable.

Neo-classical organs from the same period survive in some quantity: there are many large instruments of which those by J. W. Walker, Harrison & Harrison and Hill, Norman & Beard are probably the best. The foreign imports of 1965 onwards are also well represented. These instruments are still so recent in date as to resist classification or categorisation, and thus a guide of this kind should eschew any attempt to judge them. The interested reader is referred to the three volumes of *The*

Classical Organ in Britain, by John Rowntree and John Brennan, published in Oxford
in 1975, 1979 and 1993, and to recent issues of the annual *Organbuilder* magazine
and the *Journal* of the British Institute of Organ Studies.

Apart from the instruments mentioned here and in the text, there are many
others that will reward the keen explorer in varied and sometimes unexpected ways.
I apologise if some important instruments or notable builders have been left out of
this list.

Finally, the visitor is asked to approach all old organs with a sense of discrimina-
tion. It is not easy to build a really good organ, and the great majority of instruments all over the world fall far short of being masterpieces, though almost all are
cherished by those who play them and care for them. Care is also needed: no organ
should be played without the permission of those in charge of it, and on no account
should a visitor go inside an organ.

Glossary

Action   Key action – the mechanism linking the keys to the pallets in the soundboard. Stop action – the mechanism linking the stop knobs at the console to the slides in the soundboard (or providing a similar on/off mechanism to stops mounted on a sliderless chest).

Backfall   A lever in a mechanical key action.

Balanced action   A mechanical key action in which the key is pivoted near the centre.

Barker Lever   A pneumatic device named after Charles Spackman Barker (its reputed inventor). Mechanical linkages from the key open a valve admitting air to a pneumatic motor; the motor inflates, doing the work of opening the pallets in the soundboard. This was the first device developed to significantly lighten the key action in large nineteenth-century organs.

Barrel organ   An organ played automatically by means of a rotating pinned barrel.

Blockwerk   The term borrowed from German describing a mediaeval organ with no stop action: each key plays a number of pipes and there is no possibility of making the sound louder or softer or of varying the tone.

Borrowing   The practice of making one stop available independently on two different manuals, or of using the bass pipes of one stop to serve the bottom notes of another.

Brustwerk   The German term for a division of pipes mounted immediately above the console of the organ.

Building frame   The frame on which an organ is constructed, separate from the case-work (usual in England from c1800).

Bureau organ   A chamber organ in the shape of a desk or bureau, a speciality of John Snetzler.

C fa ut   The C two octaves below middle C (C in Helmholtz notation) according to the Guidonian scale (used by English organ builders before 1750).

Chaire Organ   The English term for a division of pipes mounted in a separate small case behind the player's back.

Chamber organ   A small organ intended for domestic use.

Charge pneumatic action   A tubular pneumatic action in which the on/off message is sent by air under pressure from the key, to pneumatic motors in the soundboard or chest.

Chest   In England, the term often used to indicate a sliderless soundboard, but also applied colloquially to soundboards of all types.

Chiff   An onomatopoeic word used to describe the audible starting transients of a flue pipe, especially noticeable where there is little or no nicking.

Choir Organ   Probably a corruption of Chaire Organ; the division of pipes played by the lowest manual in a three-manual instrument.

Choir pitch   In the period before c1670, English organs were built to a pitch a fifth lower than that used by choirs; hence the terms 'choir pitch' and 'organ pitch'.

Chorus   A group of stops intended to sound together as a family; especially the chorus of principal-toned stops that form the backbone of organ tone.

Cipher   A fault causing a note to play unbidden.

Claviorganum   An instrument combining a harpsichord with a small organ.

Closed shallot   A shallot with a small opening in the face, reputedly invented by J. C. Bishop and a hallmark of English high-pressure reed voicing as developed by the Willis firm c1870 and used also by other builders in the early twentieth century.

Combination action   Any mechanism allowing groups or combinations of stops to be brought on or off by means of a single pedal or piston.

Combination pedal   A pedal bringing on or off a group or combination of stops (usually non-mechanical, as opposed to the mechanical 'shifting movement' or 'composition pedal').

Common Bass   The use of one set of pipes to provide the bottom notes for two different stops standing on the same soundboard.

Communication   Renatus Harris's term for the practice of duplexing or borrowing: making one stop available to be played independently on two manuals.

Compass   The term describing the number of keys in a keyboard or pedalboard.

Composition pedal   A mechanical pedal bringing on or off a fixed combination of stops.

Compound stop   A stop with more than one rank, i.e. in which two or more pipes sound when each key is pressed.

Concussion bellows   A small sprung bellows fitted to a wind-trunk or soundboard designed to damp the shock waves caused by sudden demands made by the player, and therefore to make the wind supply audibly more steady.

Cone tuning   The practice of tuning small- and medium-sized open flue pipes by hitting them with brass cones, flaring the top of the pipe outwards to sharpen, and closing it to flatten.

Console   The keyboards and their surround, including the stop knobs, music desk and so on.

Conveyance   A tube leading air from a soundboard to a remotely positioned pipe, e.g. a pipe on display in the case.

Cornet   A compound stop, usually with five ranks of flue pipes and including a tierce rank, with a bold, reedy sound.

Cornet Décomposé   The French term for a Cornet available as five separate ranks each with its own stop-knob.

Cornet Séparé   The French term for a Cornet made available for solo use, sometimes from it own (separate) keyboard.

Coupler   A device allowing the keys of one manual or the pedals to pull down the keys of another manual.

Cut-up   The height of the mouth of a flue pipe, often expressed as a fraction of its width.

Derivation   The practice of borrowing the pipes of one stop to be played from another manual, possibly at a different pitch.

Diagonal bellows   A bellows hinged at one end.

Diapason   The English term indicating (1) in the Tudor organ a stop playing an octave below the Principal; (2) in the eighteenth century (by which time the Open Diapason was regarded as sounding at unison pitch) used in the term 'Diapasons' to describe the use of an Open Diapason and Stopped Diapason together as the foundation of the chorus; (3) in the late nineteenth and early twentieth centuries expanded in the term 'Diapason chorus' to cover the entire family of Principal-toned stops.

Diaper, diapering   The practice of decorating the front pipes of an organ with patterns in gold and/or colour, common in England in the seventeenth century and again in the nineteenth.

Division   A group of pipes regarded as an entity, usually located together, and played from one keyboard of the organ.

Double   As a prefix to a stop name, the English term for a rank speaking an octave lower than unison pitch.

Double organ   The term used in the seventeenth century for a two-manual organ with separate cases for the Great Organ and Chaire Organ.

Duplexing   The practice of making one stop available independently on two different manuals.

Duplication   The term usually used to describe the English practice, especially in the early nineteenth century, of providing two or more stops of identical pitch and tone in order to thicken the overall effect (if not actually succeeding in making it more powerful).

Ears   Small tabs of metal soldered on either side of the mouth of a flue pipe.

Echo Organ   Before 1712, the third manual division in a three-manual organ, consisting of pipes concealed in the base of the organ or placed in a sealed wooden box. In the nineteenth century and later, a division (usually relegated to the fifth manual in a five-manual instrument) which through voicing or placement suggests an impression of great distance.

Electric action   A loose term often used to describe both electro-pneumatic and electro-mechanical actions.

Electro-mechanical action   A key action in which the work of opening the pallet in the soundboard is performed by an electro-magnet.

Electronic organ   A twentieth-century substitute for an organ in which the pipes have been replaced by an electro-mechanical or electronic tone generation system, the sound of which is amplified and transmitted through loudspeakers.

Electro-pneumatic action   A key action in which the on/off message is sent from the key through an electric cable to a pneumatic motor (or relay of motors) opening the pallet in the soundboard.

Emboss, embossing   The practice of applying decoration to front pipes by scoring the back of the metal or pressing it into a mould, used in England before c1650.

Equal temperament   The system of tuning an organ in which all intervals are of equal size and music in all keys may be performed. Equal temperament was not widely adopted in English organ-building until c1850. It should be noted that in equal temperament the major thirds are considerably out of tune, causing severe dissonances when tierce (third-sounding) ranks are used in the chorus.

Exhaust pneumatic action   A tubular pneumatic key action in which the on/off message is transmitted by opening a valve at the end of a tube; the tube is exhausted, operating a pneumatic motor or relay of motors at the soundboard or chest.

Extension   The practice of deriving one or more stops at different pitches from one rank of pipes.

Extension organ   – or unit organ: an organ in which extension is used to provide an instrument apparently having many stops from only a few ranks of pipes, as in the Cinema organ developed by Rudolph Wurlitzer from the ideas of Robert Hope-Jones.

Feeder   A bellows whose movement supplies a larger reservoir with a supply of wind.

Flat   In casework, the term given to a group of façade pipes arranged in a straight (or gently curved) line.

Finish, finishing   To finish an organ is to effect the final balancing of tone and power of each pipe on site.

Floating action   A mechanism developed in the twentieth century to allow a mechanical key action to remain in constant adjustment regardless of changes in temperature and humidity.

Flue   The windway in the mouth of a flue pipe.

Flue pipe   A pipe, either open or stopped, functioning on the same principle as a flute or whistle (i.e. with no moving parts).

Flute   The term usually used to describe flue pipes of wide scale and fluty tone.

Foot hole   The hole at the tip of an organ pipe through which air passes from the sound-board or chest.

Front pipes   Pipes used to form the decorative façade of an organ.

Gamut   The term, derived from the Guidonian scale, used to refer to the G one octave and a half below middle C (G in modern Helmholtz notation).

Gamut in D sol re   The term apparently used in the seventeenth century to describe a transposing organ in which the Gamut key on the organ (G in organ pitch) sounded the same note as D sol re sung by the choir (d in choir pitch, a fifth higher).

G compass or GG compass   An organ in which the keyboards go down to a note a fourth lower than C (the lowest note usually found on a modern organ), referred to in English notation and modern Helmholtz notation as GG.

General swell   A swell box enclosing all the pipes in an organ, especially found in late eighteenth-century and early nineteenth-century chamber organs.

Grand Jeu   The French term for a registration employing the massed sounds of reed stops (especially those of the Trumpet family) with a Cornet.

Great Organ   The main manual division of an English organ, corresponding to the German Hauptwerk or French Grand Orgue, usually played by the middle keyboard in a three-manual organ.

Grid   The frame of wooden bars and wind channels forming the core of a slider sound-board.

Groove   A wind channel formed in a piece of timber; the wind channels in the grid of a slider soundboard.

Harmonic   The naturally sounding overtones of any musical note; the first harmonic is the octave above, the second is the octave quint, the third is the superoctave, the fourth is the tierce and so on. As a prefix, the term harmonic is applied to a stop-name to indicate that the pipes (for some of the treble notes at least) are of harmonic construction, i.e. of twice the normal length.

Hauptwerk   The German term for the main manual division of an organ.

Horizontal bellows   A type of bellows developed in England towards the end of the eighteenth century in which the top frame rises horizontally.

Jeu de tierce   The French term for a registration employing stops sounding at unison, octave, octave quint, superoctave and tierce pitches.

Key action   The term given to the mechanism linking the keys to the pallets in the sound-board or chest.

Languid   The circular plate of metal dividing a flue pipe into foot and body, leaving a small slot or gap at the lower lip of the mouth for the air to pass through.

Lip   The bottom lip and top lip are the upper and lower edges of the mouth of a flue pipe.

Long compass   The term used to describe keyboards descending below the C normally found as the bottom note on modern organs.

Long octave   In a GG-compass organ, the term used to indicate that all the lowest notes (except perhaps GG♯) are present, as opposed to 'short octave', where some (usually GG♯, AA♯, BB and C♯) are left out on the grounds of space or economy.

Mandrel   The cylindrical or cone shaped former on which flat plates of metal are beaten into shape during the manufacture of organ pipes.

Meantone temperament   The system of keyboard instrument tuning, prevalent in England until c1850, in which the thirds in the keys with three accidentals or less are kept pure or relatively so, at the expense of serious dissonances in the more remote keys, and an unplayable 'wolf' interval between E♭ and G♯.

Mixture   A compound stop of principal-toned pipes. At the low end of the keyboard a mixture will sound a group of high harmonics; as the stop ascends each rank will break back in turn to a lower harmonic, perhaps more than once. Thus a Mixture stop adds point, clarity and definition in the bass, and fullness and solidity in the treble.

Motor   The term usually given to a small pneumatic bellows which, when it is inflated, moves the key action or stop action.

Mounted Cornet   A Cornet stop mounted in an elevated position, above the other pipes of the department to which it belongs, so that it may be more clearly heard.

Murmur   A fault where a pipe or pipes sound faintly without the key being pressed, or when another pipe is sounding.

Musick   In the sixteenth and seventeenth centuries the term 'keys and musicks' corresponded to the modern naturals and accidentals of the keyboard.

Mutation   A stop sounding at a pitch other than the unison or octave; e.g. a quint (fifth sounding) or tierce (third-sounding) stop.

Nag's head swell   The early form of swell box, in which the front consists of one large shutter rising and falling in a frame, rather like a sash window.

Nick, nicking   The practice of forming small nicks or indentations with a knife on either side of the flue of a flue pipe, in order to steady the tone and control to a greater or lesser degree the tendency of the pipe to chiff. In England nicking on the languids is evident by c1700 and universal soon after. Nicking on the lower lip appears in the middle of the nineteenth century, increasing in depth in later years to allow the smooth, chiffless speech characteristic of high-pressure voicing in the early twentieth century.

None   A rare ninth-sounding mutation stop.

Oberwerk   The German term for a division of pipes mounted at the top of the organ case, above the Hauptwerk.

Open shallot   A shallot with a wide opening in the face, in contrast to the closed shallots preferred, for example, by the house of Willis.

Organ pitch   In the period before c1670, English organs were built to a pitch a fifth lower than that used by choirs; hence the terms 'choir pitch' and 'organ pitch'.

Organ reform movement   The English name given to the neo-classical movement in organ design, first apparent on a large scale at the Royal Festival Hall in 1953, and followed in more recent years by the revival of mechanical action and casework in new organs.

Orgelbewegung   The German term for the organ reform movement.

Pair of organs   The archaic English term for an organ (singular): similar to usages such as 'a pair of trousers' or 'a pair of scissors'. The term does not necessarily denote an organ with two manuals.

Pallet   The valve in a soundboard or chest which admits air into the pipes.

Pallet Box   The part of the soundboard in which the pallets are housed, mounted immediately below the grid, and supplied with air under pressure ready to allow the pipes to speak when the pallet is opened.

Partial   Another term for the harmonics of a note, but strictly speaking numbered differently: the first partial is the unison, the second partial is the octave, the third partial is the octave quint, the fourth partial is the superoctave, the fifth partial is the tierce and so on (compare Harmonic).

Pedalboard   The pedal keyboard to be played with the feet.

Pedal Organ   The division of pipes in the organ operated by the pedal keys.

Plain metal   The English term (equivalent to the French *étoffe*) for a pipe metal consisting mostly of lead (usually from 5 per cent to 30 per cent lead, the bulk of the remainder being tin).

Plant, planting   The arrangement of the pipes on a soundboard or chest is the 'planting'; the designer will 'plant' the pipes on a template when he is laying out the soundboard plan.

Plein Jeu   The French term for a registration consisting of the principal chorus only, hence in English an alternative name for the principal chorus itself; sometimes used as a name for a mixture stop.

Pneumatic action   Any key action operated through the agency of pneumatic motors, whether Barker lever or tubular pneumatic.

Pneumatic lever   A pneumatic device often called the Barker Lever (named after Charles Spackman Barker, its reputed inventor). Mechanical linkages from the key open a valve admitting air to a pneumatic motor; the motor inflates, doing the work of opening the pallets in the soundboard. This was the first device developed to significantly lighten the key action in large nineteenth-century organs.

Pneumatic motor   The term usually given to a small pneumatic bellows which, when it is inflated, moves the key action or stop action.

Pipe shade   Decorative carving surmounting the façade pipes in an organ case.

Piston   A small button situated between the keyboards controlling pre-set combinations of stops.

Portative   A small organ that can be carried around easily; in mediaeval representations often played with one hand and blown with the other.

Positif   The French term (properly *Positif de dos*) for a division of pipes placed behind the player's back.

Positive   The modern English term (usually used instead of the archaic Chair Organ) for a division of pipes placed behind the player's back; also in mediaeval times any modest-sized organ that was fixed in position, i.e. too large to be a *portative*.

Principal   In the English organ this is the name usually given to the main octave-sounding flue stop on the organ (Principal 4′); however it properly refers to all pipes of medium scale, open cylindrical construction and 'normal' organ tone – as opposed to wide-scaled flutes, narrow-scaled strings and all reed pipes. Hence the term 'principal chorus' used to describe the several stops of different pitches that make up the backbone of organ sound.

Quarter tones   The term used by Bernard Smith in the seventeenth century to describe additional notes provided so that D♯ and E♭, and G♯ and A♭ could be played from different keys (making fourteen keys in the octave). This system was used by Smith at the Temple Church and at Durham Cathedral.

Quint   Any fifth-sounding rank of pipes.

Rank   A row of pipes, one for each pitch on the keyboard. A stop will sometimes have one rank, sometimes more than one (compound stops, including the Mixtures and Cornet). In an *extension organ* each rank will serve for two or more stops.

Récit   The French term for a manual division, usually of short compass (treble only) on which solos could be played.

Récit Expressif   The nineteenth-century French term for the English Swell Organ: a division of pipes enclosed in a swell box.

Reed pipe   A pipe in which a brass tongue vibrates against an opening in the face of a metal tube or *shallot*; the tone is amplified and the pitch steadied by a *resonator*.

Regal   A reed stop with very short resonators; a small organ based on regal pipes.

Registration   The art of combining stops to good effect; any combination of stops, especially with reference to musical use.

Regulator   A term widely used, but most often encountered in referring to small wind-pressure regulating devices mounted in soundboards, intended to replace, in some modern organs, traditional bellows.

Reservoir   A bellows used for storing a quantity of wind (in contrast to a *feeder*, which supplies the wind).

Resonator   The tube of a reed pipe, amplifying the tone and steadying the pitch of the note created by the tongue.

Ripieno   The Italian term for the principal chorus, especially referring to the Italian practice of providing high-pitched stops of one rank only in place of mixtures.

Rollerboard   A part of a mechanical key action consisting of a board with rollers mounted on it. Each roller has two arms, one connected to the key, one to the pallet. By this means the bass-to-treble order and narrow spacing of the action at the keyboard can be converted to the symmetrical order and wide spacing of the action at the soundboard.

Rückpositiv   The German term for a division of pipes placed behind the player's back.

Running   A fault where wind, destined for the playing of one note, escapes through a crack and causes other notes to murmur or sound.

Scale, scaling   The scale of a pipe is a measurement of its diameter in relation to its pitch, varied by the organ builder to secure different kinds of tone colour from the pipes. Hence the art of scaling is the process of determining all aspects of the size, shape and manufacturing details of the pipes before the organ is built.

Schwimmer   A small wind-pressure-regulating device mounted in soundboards, intended to replace, in some modern organs, traditional bellows.

Septième   A seventh-sounding mutation rank.

Shaking stop   The archaic English term for the Tremulant.

Shallot   The small brass tube fitted into the block of a reed pipe with an opening against which the tongue is fitted and vibrates when the note is sounded.

Shifting movement   A variety of combination pedal found especially in eighteenth-century English organs. Its effect is to silence any louder stops that have been drawn without moving the stop-knobs.

Short compass   A keyboard which does not extend as far down as C (two octaves below middle C), the normal bottom note on modern organs. Especially used with reference to the English Swell Organ of the eighteenth century and early nineteenth century, which usually started at g (though examples are recorded descending to E).

Short octave   In a GG-compass organ, the term used to indicate that some of the lowest notes (usually GG♯, AA♯, BB and C♯) are left out on the grounds of space or economy, as opposed to 'long octave', where all (except perhaps GG♯) are present.

Shutter   The flaps in the front of a swell box which, when opened or closed, cause the effect of crescendo and diminuendo.

Slide, slider   The perforated wooden strip in a slider soundboard linked to the stop-knob at the console. When the holes in the slider line up with the holes in the table below and the upperboard above, the stop is on. When the slide is moved, the holes no longer line up, and the stop is off.

Slider soundboard   A soundboard of traditional construction in which all stops in a given division stand over common wind channels, controlled by slides linked to the stop-knobs at the console.

Sliderless chest; sliderless soundboard   A soundboard where each pipe is provided with its own valve or pallet, the stop action consisting of ventils, admitting wind to each rank as required, or by pneumatic or electro-mechanical switchgear cutting out the action to one or other row of pallet motors.

Solo Organ   A division of pipes played from the top manual of a four-manual organ of the late nineteenth or twentieth centuries.

Soundboard   In organ building, the word soundboard has a meaning different from that understood in connection with other musical instruments. Rather than being a tensioned wooden plate as in a harpsichord or piano, it is the mechanical component on which all the pipes of one division stand, fed with wind from a trunk and containing the pallets (linked to the key action) and slides or other mechanism (linked to the stop action). See Plate 2 (Introduction, p. 4) for further details.

Specification   The stop list of an organ.

Spotted metal   A pipe alloy popular in England consisting of approximately 50 per cent lead and 50 per cent tin, with a characteristic mottled appearance on the surface.

Spring chest   A variety of soundboard not known in England, of which some examples survive on the Continent, in which the slides are replaced by many additional small pallets, one to each pipe, connected together in rows (one row of pallets for each rank of pipes) and thence to the stop-knob at the console.

Square   In a mechanical key action a square transmits the movement through a right angle.

Sticker   Part of a mechanical key action transmitting movement from one place to another by a pushing motion.

Stop   Any rank or ranks of pipes controlled by a single stop-knob at the console.

Stop action   The mechanism linking the stop-knobs at the console to the sliders of a slider chest (or to other on/off mechanism in the case of sliderless chests).

String   A stop of flue pipes of narrow scale, with a keen sound faintly reminiscent (and sometimes deliberately imitating) orchestral string tone.

Suspended action   A mechanical key action in which the key is pivoted at the tail and the tracker rises from near the centre of the key.

Swell, swell box   A box enclosing one division of pipes, fitted with shutters linked to a pedal at the console, allowing some degree of crescendo and diminuendo.

Swell Organ   The primary division of pipes enclosed in a swell box; in an English organ from 1712 until the present day the division played by the top manual in a three-manual organ.

Sympathy   Organ pipes standing close together may put each other out of tune when sounded, an effect known as 'sympathy'.

Table   In a slider soundboard the table is the thin layer of wood glued on to the upper surface of the grid on which the sliders run.

Temperament   If a keyboard instrument is to be used in the performance of music in more than one key, compromises must be made in the tuning so that at least some intervals are no longer pure. The system of tuning chosen is known as the temperament.

Thumb piston   A small button situated between the keyboards controlling pre-set combinations of stops.

Tierce   A third-sounding mutation rank.

Tin   As used in organ pipes the term 'tin' usually means an alloy rich in tin, usually 70 per cent to 90 per cent tin, the remainder mostly lead.

Toe piston   A button situated near the pedalboard controlling pre-set combinations of stops.

Tongue   The brass reed in a reed pipe.

Tower   In casework, the term used to describe a group of pipes arranged in a group, usually of five, three or seven pipes, either flat, semicircular or pointed.

Tracker   Part of a mechanical key action transmitting movement from one place to another by a pulling motion.

Tracker action   A common term for any mechanical action.

Transposing organ   The term used to describe an organ in which the C key on the organ (C in organ pitch) sounded the same note as F sung by the choir (F in choir pitch, a fifth higher).

Tremulant   A device, usually operated by a stop-knob, causing a vibrato effect.

Trompe   The term given to free-standing towers of bass pipes in large mediaeval organs

Tubular pneumatic action   A key action in which the on/off message is transmitted from the keys to the interior of the organ by means of charges of air passing through small-bore tubing in association with a relay of pneumatic motors.

Tuning cone   Small and medium-sized open flue pipes may be tuned by hitting them with brass cones, flaring the top of the pipe outwards to sharpen, and closing it to flatten.

Tuning slide   A small cylinder, usually made of tinned steel, fitted to the top of a cylindrical flue pipe as a means of tuning it, almost universal in England from the second quarter of the twentieth century.

Tutti   Full organ: i.e. either the use of all the stops at once, or at least those that contribute to the full power of the instrument.

Undulating stop   A stop tuned either slightly sharp or slightly flat which, in use, will 'beat' with other stops, giving a pleasant slow tremolo.

Unequal temperament   A temperament which favours intervals used in some keys at the expense of others.

Unit organ   (or extension organ): an organ in which extension is used to provide an instrument apparently having many stops from only a few ranks of pipes, as in the Cinema organ developed by Rudolph Wurlitzer from the ideas of Robert Hope-Jones.

Upperwork   All higher pitched stops, usually understood to mean principal-toned stops of 2′ pitch and higher, all principal-toned mutations, and the mixtures.

Venetian swell   The type of swell mechanism, adapted by Samuel Green from harpsichords by Shudi, in which a row of horizontally mounted shutters, similar to those of a venetian blind, are connected to the swell pedal.

Ventil   A device for interrupting the wind supply to a stop or group of stops, either used as the stop action in a sliderless chest, or (as it can effect a whole division at a time) as a means of pre-selecting a new registration which can be brought into use during performance by opening the ventil.

Voice, voicing   To voice an organ pipe is to make it speak and to set its characteristic tone and speech characteristics.

Voicing machine   A small skeletal organ on which pipes can be voiced in the factory.

Werkprinzip   The German term, applied in the twentieth century, to a style of organ building practised in parts of northern Europe, especially in the seventeenth and eighteenth centuries. In the *Werkprinzip* organ each division stands towards the front of the instrument in its own case, and each division is given a pitch emphasis an octave apart from the others.

Wolf   The howlingly dissonant interval, usually found between E♭ and G♯, in a keyboard instrument tuned to meantone temperament.

Select bibliography

The American Organist (formerly *Music*), New York 1979–

Armstrong, W. H. *Organs for America: the Life and Work of David Tannenberg*, Philadelphia 1967

H. Arnaut de Zwolle, MS treatise. Paris, Bibliothèque Nationale lat. 7295

Audsley, G. A. *Organ Stops and their Artistic Registration*, New York 1921

    The Art of Organ-building, 2 vols., New York 1905

    The Organ of the Twentieth Century, New York 1919

Barnes, A. and M. Renshaw. *The Life and Work of John Snetzler*, Aldershot 1994

Barnes, W. H. *The Contemporary American Organ*, New York 1925; 4th edn 1950

Baron, J. *Scudamore Organs, or Practical Hints Respecting Organs for Village Churches and Small Chancels, on Improved Principles*, London 1858; 2nd edn 1862

Bédos de Celles, F. *L'Art du Facteur d'Orgues*, 4 vols., Paris 1766–78

Bedwell, G. G. *The Evolution of the Organ*, London 1907

Brisay, A. D. C. de. *The Organ and its Music*, London 1934.

Belcher, J. *The Organs of Chester Cathedral*, Chester 1970

Bertalot, J. *The Organs of Blackburn Cathedral*, Blackburn 1970

Beswick, C. *The Organs of Worcester Cathedral*, Worcester 1967

BIOS (British Institute of Organ Studies) *Journal*, Oxford 1977–

BIOS (British Institute of Organ Studies) *Reporter*, Oxford 1976–

Bishop, C. K. K. *Notes on Church Organs, their Position and the Materials Used in their Construction*, London 1873

Blew, W. C. A. *Organs and Organists in Parish Churches*, London 1878

Blewett, P. R. W. and H. C. Thompson. *The Duddyngton Manuscripts at All Hallows by the Tower*, London 1977

Blewitt, J. *A Complete Treatise on the Organ to which is added a Set of Explanatory Voluntaries etc.*, London c1795

Bonavia-Hunt, N. *Modern Organ Stops*, London 1923

    Modern Studies in Organ Tone, London 1933

    The Church Organ: an Introduction to the Study of Modern Organ-building, London 1920

    The Modern British Organ, London 1948

    The Organ Reed, New York 1950

Bowers, R., L. S. Colchester and A. Crossland. *The Organs and Organists of Wells Cathedral* (Wells) 1979

British Organ Archive, Birmingham Central Library (collections of archival material related to organs and organ building in the British Isles)

Brooksbank, J. *The Holy Harmony*, London 1643
  The Organ's Echo, London 1641
  The Organ's Funeral, London 1642
  The Well-Tuned Organ, London 1660
Buckingham, A. MS Journals (private collection)
Bunker Clark, J. *Transposition in Seventeenth Century English Organ Accompaniments and the Transposing Organ*, Detroit 1974
Burney, C. *Account of the Musical Performances in Westminster Abbey & The Pantheon on May 26, 27, 29 and June 3, 5, 1784 in Commemoration of Handel*, London 1785
  A General History of Music, London 1789
  The Present State of Music in France and Italy, London 1771; 2nd edn London 1773
  The Present State of Music in Germany, the Netherlands and the United Provinces, London 1773
Callahan, C. *The American Classic Organ*, Richmond, Virginia 1990
Casson, T. *Reform in Organ Building*, London 1888
  The Modern Organ, Denbigh 1883
  The Pedal Organ, London 1905
Cavaillé-Coll, C. & E. *Aristide Cavaillé-Coll, ses Origines, sa Vie, ses Oeuvres*, Paris 1929
The Christian Remembrancer London 1819–65
Clarke, W. H. *An Outline of the Structure of the Pipe Organ*, Boston 1877
  Concerning Organ Mixtures, Boston 1899
  Standard Organ Building, Boston 1913
Clutton, C. and G. Dixon. *The Organ: Its Tonal Structure and Registration*, London 1950
Clutton, C. and A. Niland. *British Organ:*, London 1963; 2nd edn 1982
Cobb, G. *English Cathedrals, the Forgotten Centuries*, London 1980
Cobb, G. F. *A Brief History of the Organ in the Chapel of Trinity College Cambridge*, Cambridge 1895; 2nd edn (ed. A. Gray) 1913
Cumming, A. *A Sketch of the Properties of the Machine Organ Invented for the Earl of Bute*, London 1812
Davidson, C. H. *Sir John Sutton, A study in True Principles*, Oxford 1992
Dolmetsch, A. *The Interpretation of the Music of the XVII and XVIII Centuries*, London 1915
The Diapason, Chicago 1909–
Dickson, W. E. *Practical Organ-building* London 1881; 2nd edn 1882
Done, J. *A Complete Treatise on the Organ*, London 1839
Douglass, F. *Cavaillé-Coll and the Musicians*, 2 vols., Sunbury 1980
Downes, R. *Baroque Tricks*, Oxford 1983
Dufourcq, N. *Livre de l'Orgue Français*, 4 vols., Paris 1935–
Early Music, Oxford 1973–
Edwards, C. A. *Organs and Organ Building*, London 1881
Ellis, A. J. *The History of Musical Pitch*, London 1881
Elliston, T. *Organs and Tuning*, London 1898
Elvin, L. *Bishop & Sons, Organ Builders*, Lincoln 1984
  Family Enterprise: the Story of some North Country Organ Builders, Lincoln 1986
  Forster & Andrews, Organ Builders 1843–1956, Lincoln 1968
  Forster & Andrews: their Barrel, Chamber and Small Church Organs, Lincoln 1976
  Organ Blowing, its History and Development, Lincoln 1971
  Pipes & Actions, Lincoln 1995
  The Harrison Story, Lincoln 1973

England, G. P. (traditional attribution), MS transcript of notebook (private collection)

Essex, W. H. MS booklet *S. Mary Woolnough – The Organ – by Robert Dallams & Father Smith* London 1881 (private collection)

Fischer, H. *100 Jahre Bund Deutscher Orgelbaumeister*, Munich 1991

Flight, B. *Practical Theory and Instruction to Tune the Organ or Pianoforte*, London 1818

Förner, C. *Vollkommener Bericht, wie eine Orgel aus wahrem Grunde der Natur in allen ihren Stücken nach Anweisung der mathematischen Wissenschaften soll gemacht, probiert und gebraucht werden, und wie man Glocken nach dem Monochordo mensurieren und giessen soll*, Berlin 1684

Forster, L. W. *Janus Gruter's English Years*, London 1967

Forsyth-Grant, M. *Twenty-one Years of Organ-Building*, Oxford 1987

Freeman, A. *Church Organs and Cases*, London 1946

   English Organ Cases, London 1921

   Father Smith, London 1926

   MS *Notes on Organs*, British Organ Archive

   'Records of British Organ Builders' (First Series), in *The Dictionary of Organs and Organists*, London 1921

   'Records of British Organ Builders' (Second Series), in *Musical Opinion*, 1922–5

   MS *Small Scrap Book*, British Organ Archive

Freeman, A. and J. Rowntree. *Father Smith*, Oxford 1976

Gauntlett, H. J. *A Description of the New Organ Erected in the Church of St Olave, London Bridge, Southwark*, London 1846

Gillingham, M., R. Downes, H. and J. Norman and B. Frith. *Gloucester Cathedral Organ*, Gloucester 1971

Goetze, M. *Walton on Thames: Remains of the 1673 Father Smith Organ*, Harley Foundation Technical Report, 1992

Gray, A. *The Modern Organ*, London 1913

Greening, R. *The Organs of Lichfield Cathedral*, Lichfield 1974

Gwynn, D. *St Leonard Shoreditch*, Harley Foundation Technical Report 1990

Gwynn, D. and D. C. Wickens. *St George Gravesend*, Harley Foundation Technical Report 1990

Haine, M. *Les Facteurs d'instruments de musique à Paris au XIXème siècle, des artisans face à l'industrialisation*, Brussels, 1985

Hamilton, D. *Remarks on Organ Building and the Causes of Defective Instruments*, Edinburgh 1851

   Remarks on the State of Organ Building Past and Present, London 1863

Hamilton, J. A. *Catechism of the Organ*, London 1838; 2nd edn 1842; and subsequent editions

Hale, P. *The Organs of Rochester Cathedral*, Rochester 1989

Hamel, P. J. *Nouveau Manuel Complet du Facteur d'Orgues*, Paris 1849

Hawkins, J. *A General History of the Science and Practice of Music*, 5 vols., London 1776

Hayne, L. G. *Hints on the Purchase of an Organ*, London 1867

Hiles, J. *Catechism of the Organ*, London 1876

Hill, A. G. *The Organs and Organ Cases of the Middle Ages and Renaissance*, 2 vols., London 1883, 1891

Hill, D. G. *Henry Smart*, Schagen 1988

Hinton, J. W. *Facts about Organs*, London 1882

   Organ Construction, London 1900

Story of the Electric Organ, London 1909

Hird, R. and J. Lancelot, *Durham Cathedral Organs*, Durham 1991

Hope-Jones, R. *Recent Developments in Organ Building*, New York 1904

Hopkins, E. J. *The English Mediaeval Church Organ*, Exeter 1888

Hopkins, E. J. and E. F. Rimbault, *The Organ, its History and Construction*, London 1855; 2nd edn 1870; 3rd edn 1877

Huray, P. le. *Music and the Reformation in England 1549–1660*, London 1967

Johnstone, K. I. *The Armley Schulze Organ*, Leeds 1978

Klotz, H. *Über die Orgelkunst der Gotik, der Renaissance und des Barock*, Kassel 1975

Knott, J. R. *Brindley & Foster, Organ Builders, Sheffield, 1854–1939*, Bognor Regis 1973

Langwill, L. G. and N. N. T. Boston. *Church and chamber Barrel Organs*, 2nd edn, Edinburgh 1970

Leffler, H. MS notebooks (private collection)

Lewis, T. C. *A Protest Against the Modern Development of Unmusical Tone*, London 1897
  Organ Building and Bell Founding, London 1871; 6th edn 1883

Lewis, W. & T. *Modern Organ Building*, London 1911

Liverpool Cathedral, The Organ, London 1926 (reprinted 1937)

Mace, T. *Musick's Monument*, London and Cambridge 1676

Macrory, E. *Notes on the Temple Organ*, London 1861; 3rd edn 1911

McSweeney, P. The Organ and Harpsichord in Ireland before 1870, MA Thesis, University of Cork, 1979

Marr, P. *The Organ in Reading Town Hall: a Symposium*, Reading 1982

Marsh, J. *Eighteen Voluntaries for the Organ . . . To which is prefix'd an Explanation of the . . . Stops etc.*, London 1791

Matthews, B. *The Organs and Organists of Exeter Cathedral*, Exeter 1974
  The Organs and Organists of Salisbury Cathedral, Salisbury 1972
  The Organs and Organists of Winchester Cathedral, Winchester 1970

Matthews, J. *A Handbook of the Organ*, London 1897
  The Restoration of Organs, London 1918

Mayes, S. *An Organ for the Sultan*, London 1954

le Men. *Monographie de la Cathédrale de Quimper*, Paris 1877

Mercurius Rusticus. *The Country's Complaint recounting the Sad Events of this Unparalleld Warr*, London 1647

Mersenne, M. *L'Harmonie Universelle*, vol. II, Paris 1635 (Latin), 1636 (French)

Miller, G. L. *The Recent Revolution in Organ Building*, New York 1909; 2nd edn 1913

Milner, H. F. *How to Build a Small Two-Manual Chamber Pipe Organ; a Practical Guide for Amateurs*, London 1925

Morgan, R. T. *St Mary Redcliffe Bristol, a Short Account of its Organs*, Bristol 1912

Musical Opinion London 1878–

The Musical Standard London 1862–1933

The Musical Times London 1844–

The Musical World London 1836–91

Nicholson, S. H. *Carlisle Cathedral, its Organs and Organists*, Carlisle 1907

Niland, A. *An Introduction to the Organ*, London 1968
  The Organ at St Mary's, Rotherhithe, Oxford 1983

Norbury, J. *The Box of Whistles*, London 1877

Norman, H. and J. Norman, *The Organ Today*, London 1967

Norman, J. *The Organs of Britain*, Newton Abbot 1984

Ochse, O. *The History of the Organ in the United States*, Bloomington 1975

OHTA (Organs Historical Trust of Australia) *News*, Camberwell (Vic.) 1977–

Ord-Hume, A. W. J. G. *Barrel Organ*, London 1978

   Harmonium: the History of the Reed Organ and its Makers, London 1986

The Organ, London 1921–

The Organbuilder, Oxford 1983–

The Organ Yearbook, Amsterdam 1970–

The Organists Review, Bromyard 1919–

Pacey, R. *The Organs of Oxford*, Oxford 1980

Padgham, C. A. *The Organ of St Botolph's Church Aldgate, London, E.C.3*, London 1975

   The Well-Tempered Organ, Oxford 1986

Pearce, C. W. *Notes on English Organs of the Period 1800–1810, Taken Chiefly from the Ms. of Henry Leffler*, London 1912

   Old London City Churches, their Organs, Organists & Musical Associations, London 1909

   The Life and Works of Edward John Hopkins, London, 1910

   The Evolution of the Pedal Organ, London 1927

Peeters, F. & M. A. Vente. *De Orgelkonst in de Nederlanden van de 16de tot de 18e Eeuw*, Antwerp 1971; English translation by P. Williams, Antwerp 1971

Perrot, J. *l'Orgue de ses origines hellenistiques à la fin du XIII siècle: étude historique et archéologique*, Paris 1965; English translation London 1971

Phelps, L. I. *A Short History of the Organ Revival*, St Louis 1967

Plumley, N. M. *The Christ's Hospital Papers I: The Organs and Music Masters*, Christ's Hospital 1981

Plumley, N. M. and J. Lees, *The Organs and Organists of Chichester Cathedral*, Chichester 1988

Pole, W. *Musical Instruments in the Great Industrial Exhibition of 1851*, London 1851

Praetorius, M. *Syntagma Musicum, II. De Organographia*, Wolfenbüttel 1619

Rees, A., ed. *The Cyclopaedia, or Universal Dictionary of Arts, Sciences, and Literature*, 45 vols., London 1802–20

Robertson, F. E. *A Practical Treatise on Organ Building*, London 1897

Roosevelt, H. L. Manufacturer of Church, Chapel, Concert and Chamber Organs (Catalogue), New York c1883

The Rotunda, London 1926–34

Routh, F. *Early English Organ Music from the Middle Ages to 1837*, London 1973

Rowntree, J. P. and J. F. Brennan, *The Classical Organ in Britain*. Vol I: *1955–1974*, Oxford 1975; vol. II: *1975–1978*, Oxford 1979; vol. III: *1979–1990*, Oxford 1993

Sayer, M. *Samuel Renn, English Organ Builder*, London 1974

Schlick, A. *Spiegel der Orgelmacher und Organisten*, Speyer 1511

Schweitzer, A. *Deutsche und französische Orgelbaukunst*, Leipzig 1906

   J. S. Bach, le musicien-poète, Leipzig 1905

Seidel, J. J. *The Organ and its Construction: a Systematic Handbook for Organists, Organ Builders, etc.*, London 1852

Servières, G. *La Décoration Artistique des Buffets d'Orgues*, Paris and Brussels 1928

Shaw, W. *The Organists and Organs of Hereford Cathedral*, Hereford 1976

Shepherdson, W. *The Organ, Hints on its Construction, Purchase, and Preservation*, London 1873

Skinner, E. M. *The Modern Organ*, New York 1917

Spark, W. *Life of Henry Smart*, London 1881
  Musical Reminiscences, Past and Present, London 1892
  Musical Memories, London 1888

Sperling, J. H. MS notebooks, 3 vols., Royal College of Organists, London

Stanley, J. *Thirty Voluntaries*. Op. 5, London 1748; Op. 6, 1752; Op. 7, 1754

Statham, H. H. *The Organ and its Position in Musical Art*, London 1909

Steele, J. English Organs and Organ Music from 1500 to 1650, Ph.D. dissertation,
  University of Cambridge 1958

Sumner, W. L. *Father Henry Willis, Organ Builder, and his successors*, London 1955
  The Organ, Its Evolution, Principles of Construction and Use, London 1952; 2nd edn 1955;
    3rd edn 1962; 4th edn 1973
  The Organs of St Paul's Cathedral, London 1931
  The Parish Church Organ, London 1961

Sutton, F. H. *Church Organs*, London 1872
  Some Account of the Mediaeval Organ Case Still Standing at Old Radnor, South Wales, London
    1866; 2nd edn 1872; 3rd edn 1883

Sutton, J. (attributed). *A Short Account of Organs Built in England from the Reign of King Charles
  the Second to the Present Time*, London 1847

Talbot, J. (attributed). MS treatise, Christ Church Oxford, Mus MS 1187

Temperley, N. *The Music of the English Parish Church*, 2 vols., Cambridge 1979
  Birmingham Town Hall Organ, Birmingham 1984
  Organs at Eton, Eton 1987
  The Making of the Victorian Organ: Cambridge 1990
  The Organs of Cambridge, Cambridge 1983

Thornsby, F. W., ed. *Dictionary of Organs and Organists*, Bournemouth 1912; 2nd edn 1922

Thurley, S. *The Royal Palaces of Tudor England*, New Haven and London, 1993

Töpfer, *Die Orgelbaukunst*, Weimar 1833
  Lehrbuch der Orgelbaukunst, Weimar 1855

The Tracker, Wilmington, Ohio 1956–

Vente, M. A. *Die Brabanter Orgel*, Amsterdam 1963

Warman, J. W. *The Organ: Its Compass, Tablature, and Short and Incomplete Octaves*, London
  1884
  The Organ: Writings and other Utterances on its Structure, History, Procural, Capabilities, etc.
    (incomplete) London 1901–4

Warren, J. *Hamilton's Catechism of the Organ*, London 1838; 2nd edn 1842

Wedgwood, J. I. *A Comprehensive Dictionary of Organ Stops, English and Foreign, Ancient and
  Modern*, London 1905
  Continental Organs and their Makers, London 1910

Whitworth, R. *The Cinema and Theatre Organ*, London 1934
  The Electric Organ, London 1930; 2nd edn 1940; 3rd edn 1948

Wickens, D. C. Unpublished paper, A Comparison of the Scaling Practice of Father
  Smith, at the End of the 17th Century, with that of G. P. England, at the End of the
  18th Century; with Some Comments about Scaling in the Intervening Years, 1992
  The Instruments of Samuel Green, London 1987

Wicks, M. *Organ Building for Amateurs*, London 1887

Williams, C. F. A. *The Story of the Organ*, London 1903

Williams, P. F. *A New History of the Organ*, London 1980

    English Organ Music and the English Organ under the First Four Georges, unpublished Ph.D. dissertation, University of Cambridge 1962

    The European Organ 1450–1850, London 1966

    The Organ in Western Culture 750–1250, Cambridge 1993

Williams, P. F. and B. Owen, *The Organ*, London 1988

Willis, T. Unpublished MS, Recollections of my Father, undated

Wilson, M. *The English Chamber Organ*, Oxford 1968

Index

Page numbers in bold type refer to plates and their captions;
page numbers in italic type refer to organ specifications